The Queen's
Anniversary Prizes
1996

The Queen's Anniversary Prizes for Higher and Further Education recognise the contribution of universities and colleges to the social, economic, cultural and intellectual life of the nation.

In 1994, the inaugural year of the competition, The Queen's University of Belfast was awarded a prize for the work of Servicing the Legal System.

The prize citation for SLS in 1994 read:

> *"This is an outstanding service to overcome the special problems of distributing knowledge about new law inside a small jurisdiction. It is an international exemplar."*

The Servicing The Legal System Programme

This programme was inaugurated in August 1980 in the Faculty of Law at Queen's University, Belfast to promote the publication of commentaries on various aspects of the law and legal system of Northern Ireland. Generous financial and other support for the programme has been provided by the Northern Ireland Court Service, the Inn of Court of Northern Ireland, the Bar Council of Northern Ireland, the Law Society of Northern Ireland and Queen's University. Details of other SLS publications may be obtained from the SLS Office, School of Law, The Queen's University of Belfast, Belfast BT7 1NN.

Residential Property Law in Northern Ireland

A practitioner's guide to conveyancing

Sarah Witchell, LL.B.
Solicitor

Consultant Editor: Ruth Craig, LL.B, Solicitor

SLS Legal Publications (NI)
2000

© Sarah Witchell

All rights reserved.
No part of this publication may be reproduced, stored in a retrieval system, or transmitted in any form or by any means, including photocopying and recording, without the prior written permission of the publisher.

The reproduction of Crown Copyright material is in accordance with the requirements of Her Majesty's Stationery Office; all sources are indicated in the text.

The author has expressly asserted her moral right of paternity in this work.

First published 2000 by SLS Legal Publications (NI),
School of Law, Queen's University, Belfast BT7 1NN.

ISBN 0 85389 761 1

Typeset by SLS Legal Publications (NI)
Printed by MPG Books Ltd., Cornwall

FOREWORD

It is with considerable pleasure, and, I must confess, some relief, that I provide this foreword to Sarah Witchell's text on residential property law in Northern Ireland. My pleasure stems from the view that the text should prove to be a very valuable addition to practitioners' libraries. My relief derives from the thought that its appearance to some extent gets me "off the hook"! Perhaps I should explain, if only for the benefit of the younger practitioners.

When I wrote the original version of my text *Irish Conveyancing Law* (which first appeared in 1978), it purported to cover the law and practice in both parts of Ireland. This approach had already been adopted in the earlier text *Irish Land Law* (which first appeared in 1975), but it proved to be a very problematic task with the conveyancing text. It is one thing to cover the general principles of the land law which are largely derived from the same sources and have the same historical foundations shared by the two jurisdictions, but quite another thing to deal with an intensely practical subject like conveyancing in two jurisdictions. Conveyancing depends so much on current practice and procedures in the particular jurisdiction that it is extremely difficult to cover more than one jurisdiction in the same text. Notwithstanding my efforts back in the mid 1970s, the original version of my conveyancing text was regarded by some, including myself, as somewhat unsatisfactory. For that reason the publishers of the new edition which appeared in 1996 decided that it should be confined to the law and practice of the Republic of Ireland. This was a decision taken with much reluctance and I am fully aware that it caused disappointment amongst practitioners in Northern Ireland. The demands on my time these days are such that it was unlikely that I could do anything about this matter in the foreseeable future, hence my relief at Sarah Witchell stepping in the breach.

It is important to emphasise that her text is very much a practical guide or handbook. It is split into two parts. The first part deals with the conveyancing process and takes the reader through all aspects of the procedures governing the sale and purchase of residential property. The discussion here is a very clear illustration of the point I made earlier, about how on such practical matters procedures will vary from jurisdiction to jurisdiction. Much of the discussion is based upon the admirable Home Charter Scheme introduced a few years ago by the Law Society of Northern Ireland, which has no equivalent in the Republic. Much also depends upon the General Conditions of Sale which differ in many respects from those operating in the Republic. This part of the text is very clearly written and full of useful information for both the experienced and inexperienced practitioner.

The other part of the book contains a summary of land law as it currently applies in Northern Ireland. It is not intended to provide a comprehensive text, but rather concentrates on the basic features which underpin conveyancing law and practice. As such it provides much useful background information for the first part of the book. It is particularly opportune to include this part because of some of the matters it covers, such as areas of the law where the courts have been particularly active in recent times - the area of mortgages is a good example. Of especial significance is, of course, the Property (NI) Order 1997, much of which has now come into force. This has also caused some difficulties for the author because the ground rent redemption provisions have not come into force and, indeed, are expected to be subject to substantial amending legislation before they do. The impact on conveyancing practice will be considerable, but the author and publishers no doubt will console themselves with the thought that this may create the opportunity for a new edition.

In the meantime I unreservedly commend this text to the legal profession in Northern Ireland.

Professor J C W Wylie
March 2000

PREFACE

As a practising conveyancer I felt that there was a need for a text specifically relevant to the conveyancing process in Northern Ireland. It was not my intention to write an academic work but I hoped to be able to provide a book that would be of assistance to practitioners in a day to day conveyancing. I also thought that it would be beneficial if all the relevant material could be assimilated into one book.

I am aware that the path of commercial conveyancing has diverged to some extent from that of residential conveyancing and that different factors assume importance according to the nature of the property involved. For that reason I have concentrated solely on domestic property and have not attempted a more comprehensive guide. Of course there are some aspects of the conveyancing process, such as investigation of title, which are common to both sectors and I hope that this book may have some relevance to the two together in that respect.

I would like to emphasise that this is a handbook which is intended as a practical text to assist practitioners when queries arise in the conveyancing process. I have endeavoured to set out the basic principles first of the law of conveyancing where appropriate and secondly of the elements of land law which I feel are most useful to practitioners. I have stated the aspects of law which I have considered to be the most important and relevant in practice without examining them in great detail because this book is not intended to be either an academic or a definitive work. Instead it should be used as a guide and a first point of reference.

Conveyancing is essentially a practical process and I have tried to present the issues in the order in which they will normally arise in the sale or purchase of residential property. The result is not entirely perfect and to some extent may appear somewhat cumbersome but I hope that readers will understand the reasoning behind it. The first part of the book deals with the actual process of an ordinary conveyance within the framework of the law of conveyancing whereas the second part describes the background context of land law. I have provided greater detail in areas where there have been more recent developments in case law and have tried to illustrate the principles, where possible, with up-to-date examples.

During the time that I have been writing this book there has been an element of uncertainty surrounding the proposals for substantial land law reform. This has caused me some difficulty in finalising the text. However, at the time of going to print much of the Property Order (NI) 1997 has come into force. Important provisions regarding the prohibition of the creation of long leases for dwelling-houses and the prohibition of the creation of any new fee farm grants came into effect on 10 January 2000 but insufficient time has elapsed to be able to assess the full impact and consequences.

As yet, the provisions for a fast-track scheme of ground rent redemption have not been enacted but a proposed Ground Rents Bill has been published in draft. It remains to be seen how and when this will be enacted but it is largely dependant upon political factors both as to the time and the means of introduction.

I have benefited greatly from much help and assistance in writing this book, although I alone must remain responsible for any errors and omissions. I would like to express particular thanks to Mrs Ruth Craig of the Institute of Professional Legal Studies for her contribution to this book as consultant editor. She has been of enormous help to me in commenting on and correcting various versions of the text. I am also indebted to her for making available to me her materials and the notes that she uses in teaching the conveyancing course at the Institute. I would also wish to thank the Law Society of Northern Ireland for its kind permission to reproduce the Home Charter Scheme forms.

I am extremely grateful to Professor John Wylie for taking the trouble to read the manuscript and more especially for his very kind remarks in the foreword. My thanks also go to Neil Faris of Cleaver Fulton Rankin and Alan Hewitt of L'Estrange and Brett for reading the draft text and making suggestions as to improvements. Master Kennedy of the High Court provided me with valuable assistance by reading and commenting on the chapter dealing with matrimonial and other interests.

I would like to express additional thanks to SLS Legal Publications and in particular to Mrs Sara Gamble for her help throughout the long gestation period of this book, as well as her professional editing of the text. Further thanks are extended to all those solicitors who provided me with the encouragement and support which has helped me to bring this project to fruition. Above all I must record my appreciation of the forbearance and unfailing enthusiasm of my husband John and my children Harriet, Michael and Rose.

Sarah Witchell
April 2000

CONTENTS

Foreword	iv
Preface	vi
Table of Cases	xiii
Table of Legislation and Rules	xix
INTRODUCTION	3

PART ONE - CONVEYANCING

CHAPTER 1	**MODEL PROCEDURE**	5
CHAPTER 2	**DUTIES OF THE PARTIES**	13
	PURCHASER: *CAVEAT EMPTOR*	13
	VENDOR: DEDUCTION OF TITLE	16
CHAPTER 3	**CONTRACT**	25
	FORMATION OF THE CONTRACT	25
	TYPES OF CONTRACT	28
	CONTENTS OF THE CONTRACT	31
	THE DEPOSIT	33
CHAPTER 4	**MISDESCRIPTION, MISREPRESENTATION AND MISTAKE**	35
	MISDESCRIPTION	35
	MISREPRESENTATION	36
	MISTAKE	40
CHAPTER 5	**SEARCHES AND PROPERTY CERTIFICATES**	43
	SEARCHES	44
	PROPERTY CERTIFICATES	46
CHAPTER 6	**TITLE: (1) REGISTRY OF DEEDS**	53
	UNREGISTERED LAND	53
	CHAIN OF TITLE	55
CHAPTER 7	**TITLE: (2) LAND REGISTRY**	65
	REGISTERS	66
	FIRST REGISTRATION	67
	CLASSES OF TITLE	71
	PROOF OF TITLE ON FIRST REGISTRATION	72
	CHARGES	74
	REGISTRATION OF OWNERSHIP	75
	LIMITATIONS OF THE LAND REGISTRY SYSTEM	76
	CHANGES OF OWNERSHIP	79
CHAPTER 8	**TITLE: (3) FLATS AND APARTMENTS**	89
	MANAGEMENT COMPANY	89
	THE LEASE	90
CHAPTER 9	**TITLE: (4) BUILDING AND DEVELOPMENT PROPERTY**	97
CHAPTER 10	**FINANCING THE PURCHASE**	101

	FACTORS TO BE TAKEN INTO ACCOUNT	101
	MORTGAGE SCHEMES	103
CHAPTER 11	**PLANNING PERMISSION**	107
	DEVELOPMENT	107
	ACTIVITIES WHICH ARE NOT DEVELOPMENT	109
	MAKING AN APPLICATION FOR PLANNING PERMISSION	117
CHAPTER 12	**BUILDING CONTROL**	125
	WORK REQUIRING APPROVAL	125
	PROCEDURE FOR MAKING A BUILDING REGULATION APPLICATION	129
	COMPLETION CERTIFICATES	132
	COMFORT LETTERS	132
	REGULARISATION CERTIFICATES	132
	MISCELLANEOUS MATTERS	133
CHAPTER 13	**NATIONAL HOUSE-BUILDING COUNCIL**	135
CHAPTER 14	**FIXTURES, FITTINGS AND CHATTELS**	143
	GENERAL RULE	143
	DEGREE OF ANNEXATION	144
	PURPOSE OF ANNEXATION	145
	LEGAL RELEVANCE OF DISTINCTION	146
	RIGHT TO REMOVE CHATTELS	146
	RIGHT TO REMOVE FIXTURES	147
CHAPTER 15	**POST-CONTRACT**	151
	VENDOR	151
	PURCHASER	152
	REQUISITIONS ON TITLE	154
	BREACH OF CONTRACT	155
	REMEDIES FOR ENFORCEMENT OF THE CONTRACT	157
	TAKING POSSESSION BEFORE COMPLETION	163
CHAPTER 16	**STAMP DUTY**	165
	PRINCIPLES OF STAMP DUTY	165
	AD VALOREM DUTY	169
	FIXED DUTY	174
	NO DUTY	176
	STAMP DUTY ON NEW PROPERTY	178
CHAPTER 17	**POST-COMPLETION REMEDIES**	181
	MERGER	181
	COVENANTS FOR TITLE	181
	OTHER REMEDIES	185

PART TWO - LAND LAW

CHAPTER 18	**ESTATES AND INTERESTS IN LAND**	189
	FREEHOLD ESTATES	189
	LEASEHOLD ESTATES	195
	FUTURE INTERESTS	198
	JOINT INTERESTS	201

CHAPTER 19	**LEASEHOLD LAW**	207
	CREATION OF THE RELATIONSHIP	207
	ASSIGNMENT AND SUBLETTING	208
	DETERMINATION OF THE RELATIONSHIP	210
CHAPTER 20	**COVENANTS AND AGREEMENTS**	217
	LEASEHOLD COVENANTS	218
	FREEHOLD COVENANTS	225
	REMEDIES FOR BREACH OF COVENANT	228
	MODIFICATION AND REMOVAL OF COVENANTS	229
CHAPTER 21	**INCORPOREAL HEREDITAMENTS**	231
	EASEMENTS	231
	PROFITS À PRENDRE	233
	ACQUISITION OF EASEMENTS AND PROFITS	234
	EXTINGUISHMENT OF EASEMENTS AND PROFITS	239
	SIMILAR CONCEPTS	240
CHAPTER 22	**OTHER RIGHTS IN LAND**	243
	LICENCES	243
	CARETAKERS' AGREEMENTS	245
	TIED ACCOMMODATION	245
	LODGER AND GUESTS	245
	RIGHTS OF RESIDENCE	245
	AGRICULTURAL ARRANGEMENTS	246
	PROPRIETARY ESTOPPEL	247
CHAPTER 23	**EXTINGUISHMENT OF INTERESTS**	251
	ADVERSE POSSESSION	251
	MERGER	256
CHAPTER 24	**SETTLEMENTS**	259
	STRICT SETTLEMENT	259
	POWERS OF THE TENANT FOR LIFE	261
	TRUSTEES OF THE SETTLEMENT	262
CHAPTER 25	**TRUSTS AND POWERS**	265
	TRUSTS	265
	CREATION OF TRUSTS	265
	COMMON TYPES OF TRUST	269
	ADMINISTRATION OF TRUSTS	271
	BREACH OF TRUST	274
	POWERS	277
CHAPTER 26	**MORTGAGES**	283
	REGISTERED LAND	283
	UNREGISTERED LAND	284
	FEATURES OF A MORTGAGE	285
	REMEDIES AGAINST THE LAND	286
	RIGHTS OF THE MORTGAGOR	293
	RIGHTS COMMON TO BOTH PARTIES	296
	SECOND MORTGAGES	296
CHAPTER 27	**BANKRUPTCY AND VOLUNTARY CONVEYANCES**	299
	BANKRUPTCY PROCEEDINGS	299
	BANKRUPT'S HOME	302

	EFFECT OF BANKRUPTCY ON	
	CONVEYANCING TRANSACTIONS	303
	TRANSACTIONS AT UNDERVALUE	305
	PREFERENCES	306
	TRANSACTIONS DEFRAUDING	
	CREDITORS	307
	ORDERS	307
	GIFT ON TITLE	307
CHAPTER 28	**MATRIMONIAL AND OTHER INTERESTS**	311
	GENERAL PROPERTY RIGHTS	311
	RIGHTS OF OCCUPATION	314
	CONSENT	322
	UNDUE INFLUENCE	323
	CHARGING ORDERS AFFECTING	
	INTERESTS IN LAND	333
	MATRIMONIAL HOME RIGHTS	335
CHAPTER 29	**PROPERTY (NI) ORDER 1997**	339
	COMMENCEMENT	340
	PROHIBITION OF CREATION OF GROUND	
	RENTS	340
	FREEHOLD COVENANTS	342
	GROUND RENT REDEMPTION	348
APPENDIX A	**HOME CHARTER SCHEME FORMS**	353
APPENDIX B	**HOME IMPROVEMENT GRANTS**	373

Index   379

TABLE OF CASES

Abbey National Building Society v Cann [1990] 1All ER 1085 (HL) .... 28.13, ... 28.14, 28.29
Allied Irish Banks Ltd v McAllister [1993] 5 NIJB 82 .... 26.11
Allied Irish Banks Ltd v McWilliams and another [1982] NI 156 .... 28.08
Anns v London Borough of Merton [1978] AC 728 .... 12.23
Ards Borough Council v Franklin and another, (Cty Ct) (Judge Hart QC)
  1 July 1996 .... 21.40
Armstrong and Holmes Ltd v Holmes and another [1994] 1 All ER 826 .... 3.12
Attorney General for Hong Kong v Reid [1994] 1 All ER 1 .... 25.28
Bain v Fothergill (1874) LR 7 HL 158 .... 15.40
Baker v Baker [1993] EGCS 35; (1993) 25 HLR 408 .... 22.18, 28.29
Banco Exterior International v Mann and others [1995] 1 All ER 936 .... 28.26
Bank Melli Iran v Samadi-Rad [1995] NPC 76. .... 28.28
Bank of Credit and Commerce International v Aboody [1982] 4 All ER 955 .... 28.23
Barclays Bank plc v O'Brien [1992] 3 WLR 593 (CA) 28.28
  [1993] 4 All ER 417 (HL) 28.24, 28.25, 28.26, 28.27, 28.31
Barclays Bank plc v Thomson [1997] 4 All ER 816 .... 28.26
Barvis v Secretary of State for the Environment (1971) 22 P&C 710 .... 11.03
Belfast City Council v Donohue and others [1993] 5 BNIL 83 .... 23.01
Benn v Hardinge (1993) 66 P&CR 246 .... 21.36
Billson and others v Residential Apartments Ltd [1992] 01 EG 91 (HC) 19.22
Bishopsgate Investment Management Ltd (in liquidation) v Maxwell No 2
  [1994] 1 All ER 261 .... 25.28
Boardman v Phipps [1967] 2 AC 67. .... 25.28
Boosey v Davis (1988) 55 P&CR 83. .... 23.10
Borokat v Ealing LBC [1996] EGCS 67 .... 19.13
Boyd v Dickson (1867) 1R 10 Eq 239 .... 2.15
Bristol & West Building Society v Ellis [1996] EGCS 74 .... 26.11
Britannia Building Society v Johnston [1994] NIJB 21 .... 28.03, 28.08
Brown v Wilson (1949) 156 EG 45 .... 19.23
Bruce v Brophy [1906] 1 IR 611 .... 26.19
Buckinghamshire County Council v Moran [1989] 2 All ER 225 .... 23.01
Burdle v Secretary of State for the Environment [1972] 3 All ER 240 .... 11.06
Cambridge CC v Secretary of State for the Environment [1992] 21 EG 108 .... 11.03
Carrel v London Underground Ltd [1996] 12 EG 129 .... 11.33
Central London Commercial Estates Ltd v Kato Kaguka Ltd (AXA Equity and
  Law Life Assurance Society plc, third party) [1998] 4 All ER 948 .... 23.04, 23.09
Chartered Trust plc v Davies [1997] 49 EG 135 .... 20.08
Cheese v Thomas [1994] 1 All ER 35 .... 28.29
Cheltenham & Gloucester Building Society plc v Norgan [1996] 1 All ER 449 .... 26.11
CIBC Mortgages v Pitt [1993] 4 All ER 433 (HL) 28.25, 28.27
CIT v Pemsel [1891] AC 531 35 .... 25.15
City of London Building Society v Flegg [1987] 3 All ER 435 (HL) 28.12
Cohen and Moore v IRC [1933] 2 KB 126. .... 16.02

Coldunell Ltd v Gallon [1986] 2 WLR 466 (CA)..28.28
Coleshill and District Investment Co Ltd v Minister of Housing and Local
    Government [1969] 2 All ER 525..11.03
Commission for the New Towns v Cooper (GB) Ltd [1995] 2 All ER 929 .... 4.23
Co-Operative Insurance Society Ltd v Argyll Stores (Holdings) Ltd
    [1997] 3 All ER 297 ....20.30
Costain Property Developments Ltd v Finlay & Co Ltd [1989] 1 EGLR 237 ....20.29
Courtney, Re [1981] NI 59 ....18.09
Cowcher v Cowcher [1972] 1 WLR 425 ....28.03
Credit Lyonnais Bank Nederland NV v Burch [1997] 1 All ER 144..............................28.26
Crofter Properties Ltd v Genport Ltd, unreported, 15 March 1996 (HC,RoI)...................20.17
Day and another v McCrum and another [1996] NI 607..15.25
Dent v Dent [1996] 1 All ER 659..22.14
D'Eyncourt v Gregory (1866) LR 3 Eq 382 ....14.04
Dillwyn v Llewelyn (1862) 4 De GF&J 517..22.18
Dodd v Crown Estate Commissioners [1995] EGCS 35 ....4.11, 4.12
Dolphin's Conveyance, Re [1970] Ch 654...20.29
Doyle v Hort (1880) 4 LR Ir 455..20.22
Doyle v O'Neill, Irish Current Law Digest 106, February 1996 ....23.01
Dunbar Bank plc v Nadeem and another [1998] 3 All ER 876 ....28.27
Duncan v Makin [1985] 2 NIJB 1..20.17
Durant v Heritage [1994] EGCS 134 ....22.18
Dyce v Lady James Hay (1852) 1 Macq 305..21.02
Elitestone Ltd v Morris and another [1997] 2 All ER 513 ....14.03
Elliston v Reacher [1908] 2 Ch 374..8.15, 20.29
Emanuel (Rundle Mall) Pty Ltd v Commissioner for Stamps (1986)
    39 SASR 582...14.02
Emile Elias & Co Ltd v Pine Groves Ltd (1993) 66 P&CR 1 ....20.29
Enfield Borough Council v Castle Estate Agents Ltd [1996] EGCS 30............................. 4.14
Erlanger v New Sombrero Phosphate (1878) 3 App Cas 1218......................................28.27
Expert Clothing Service v Hillgate House [1986] 1 Ch 340 ....19.21
Fairweather v Marylebone Property Co Ltd [1963] AC 510 ....23.04
Falconer v Falconer [1970] 1 WLR 1333..28.03
Filering Ltd v Taylor Commercial Ltd [1996] EGCS 95..19.13
First National Securities Ltd v Hegerty [1985] QB 850...28.31
Folio 35420 Co Tyrone, In the matter of [1991] NI 273 ....28.30
Foott v Benn (1884) 18 LRT 90 ....20.17
Forkhurst v Secretary of State for the Environment (1982) 46 P&CR 255..........................11.12
Gafford v Graham and anor TLR 1 May 1998 ....20 30
Gibson v Hammersmith & City Railway Co (1863) 32 LJ Ch 337 ....14.10
Gissing v Gissing [1971] AC 886 (HL) 28.03, 28.04
Goodchild v Goodchild [1996] 1 All ER 670 ....25.09
G Percy Trentham Ltd v Gloucestershire CC [1966] 1 All ER 701..................................11.06
Gran Gelato v Richcliff (Group) Ltd [1992] 1 All ER 865 .... 4.13
Griffiths v Evans (1977) 248 EG 947 ....22.18
GS Fashions Ltd v B&Q plc [1995] EGCS 68 ....19.19
Halifax Mortgage Services v Stepsky [1995] 4 All ER 656 ....28.28
Hallett's Estate, Re (1880) 13 Ch D 696..25.29
Halsall v Brizell [1957] Ch 169..8.12, 20.28
Harvey v Secretary of State for Wales 1990 JPL 420 ....11.35

Table of Cases

Hazell v Hazell [1972] 1 WLR 301 .... 28.03
Hedley Byrne & Co Ltd v Heller [1964] AC 465 .... 4.13
Hellawell v Eastwood (1851) 6 Exch 295 .... 14.04
Hobley deceased, *In re, The Times*, 10 June 1997 .... 25.09
Holland v Hodgson (1872) LR 7CP 328 .... 14.02, 14.03
Hughes v Cork [1994] EGCS 109 .... 23.01
Hughes v Hughes [1995] NI 119 .... 28.31
Hunt v Luck [1902] 1 Ch 428 .... 28.08
Huntley v Russell (1849) 13 QB 572 .... 14.03
Jaggard v Sawyer [1995] 1 All ER 189 .... 20.30
James Wills, bankrupt, *In the matter of*, unreported, 30 November 1992 .... 28.03
Jervis v Harris [1996] 1 All ER 303 .... 20.16
John Lewis Properties plc v Viscount Chelsea [1993] 46 EG 184 .... 20.17
Johnston v Secretary of State for the Environment (1974) 28 P&CR 424 ..... 11.06
JR, a Ward of Court, *Matter of* [1993] ILRM 657 .... 22.18
Keech v Sandford (1726) Sel Cas Ch 61 .... 25.28
Kingsnorth Finance Co Ltd v Tizard [1986] 2 All ER 54 .... 28.14
Kingsnorth Trust Ltd v Bell [1986] 1 All ER 423 (CA) 28.18
LCC v Wilkins [1957] AC 362 .... 14.02
Leigh v Taylor [1902] AC 157 .... 14.04
Leschallas v Woolf [1908] 1 Ch 641 .... 14.08
Lister v Stubbs [1890] 45 Ch D 1 .... 25.28
Lloyd v Byrne (1888) 22 LR Ir 269 .... 8.14
Lloyds Bank plc v Rosset [1988] 3 All ER 915 (CA); [1990] 2 WLR 867 (HL)
.... 28.03, 28.14
Long v Gowlett [1923] 2 Ch 177 .... 21.24
Mansetter Development Ltd v Garmanson Ltd [1986] 2 WLR 871 .... 14.08
Mannai Investment Co Ltd v Eagle Star Life Assurance Co Ltd
  [1997] 2 WLR 945 (HL) 19.07
Marshall v Nottingham City Corpn [1960] 1 All ER 659 .... 11.04
Marylebone Property Co Ltd v Fairweather [1963] AC 510 (HL) 23.09
Massey v Midland Bank [1995] 1 All ER 929 .... 28.28
Mathuru v Matharu [1994] EGCS 87 .... 22.18
McCullough v Lane Fox & Partners [1996] 18 EG 104 .... 4.13
McDonough v Shrewbridge (1814) 2 Ba & B 555 .... 26.19
McFarlane v McFarlane [1972] NI 59 .... 28.03, 28.04
Midland Bank plc v Cooke [1995] 2 FLR 915 .... 28.03
Midland Bank plc v Dobson (1985) 135 NLJ 751 .... 28.03
Midland Bank plc v Massey [1994] 2 FLR 342 .... 28.26
Midland Bank plc v McGrath [1996] EGCS 61 .... 26.11
Midland Bank plc v Wyatt [1995] 1 FLR 696 .... 27.21
Minshall v Lloyd (1837) 2 M&W 450 .... 14.02
Moritt v Wonham [1993] NPC 2 .... 3.05
Mulholland v Corporation of Belfast [1859] Dru temp Nap 539 .... 2.15
Mulligan v Carroll, unreported, 28 July 1995, High Court (ROI) 20.08
Murphy v Brentwood District Council [1990] 2 All ER 908 .... 12.23
National and Provincial Building Society v Lynd and another [1996] NI 47 .... 26.11
National and Provincial Building Society v Williamson and another [1995] NI 366 .... 26.11
National Carriers Ltd v Panalpina [1981] 1 All ER 161 (HL) 19.31
National Westminster Bank plc v Morgan [1985] 1 AC 686 (HL) 28.19

Nelson v Rye [1996] 2 All ER 186 ....25.28
Nestle v National Westminster Bank [1994] 1 All ER 118..25.28
New Zealand Government Property Corpn v HM & S [1982] QB 1145 (CA)...................14.02
Newbury District Council v Secretary of State for the Environment
   (1993) 67 P&CR 68..11.35
NH Dunn Pty Ltd v LM Ericsson Pty Ltd (1979) 2 BPR 9241..14.04
North Shore Gas Co Ltd v Commissioner of Stamp Duties (NSW)
   (1940) 63 CLR 52...14.02
Northern Bank Ltd v Adams, unreported, 1 February 1996..18.42
Northern Bank Ltd v Haggerty [1995] NI 211... 18.41, 28.31, 29.16
Northern Bank Ltd v McCarron [1995] NI 259 ....28.26, 28.28
Onyx (UK) Ltd v Beard [1996] EGCS 55...22.04
Palmer deceased, Re [1994] 3 All ER 835...18.41
Parker-Tweedale v Dunbar Bank plc [1990] 2 All ER 577..26.15
Parkes v Secretary of State for the Environment [1979] 1 All ER 211..............................11.02
Patman v Harland (1881) 17 Ch D 353 ....2.23
Pennell v Payne [1995] 2 All ER 592...19.23
Perry v Woodfarm Homes Ltd [1975] IR 104..23.04
Pettitt v Pettitt [1970] AC 777..25.07, 28.04
Pollard v Jackson (1994) 67 P&CR 327 ....23.07
Poole's Case (1703) 1 Salk 368 ....14.09
Poster v Slough Estates Ltd [1968] 1 WLR 1515...14.14
Powell v McFarlane (1979) 38 P&CR 452 ....23.01
Proctor v Dale [1993] 4 All ER 134...25.09
Proudreed Ltd v Microgen Holdings plc [1996] 12 EG 127..19.13
Provincial Bill Posting Co v Low Moor Iron Co [1909] 2 KB 344...................................14.03
Prudential Assurance Co Ltd v IRC [1993] 1 WLR 211...16.37
Redhouse Farms (Thorndon) Ltd v Catchpole (1976) 244 EG 295....................................23.01
Rhone v Stephens [1994] 2 All ER 65..20.29
Richards, Re (1869) 4 Ch App 630...14.03
Royal Bank of Scotland v Etridge (No 1) [1997] 3 All ER 628...28.26
Royal Bank of Scotland v Etridge (No 2) and other Conjoined Appeals
   [1998] 4 All ER 705 ....28.26
Saunders v Vautier (1841) Cr & Ph 240...25.26
Savva v Hussein [1996] NPC 64 ....19.21
Scala House & District Property Co Ltd v Forbes [1974] 1 QB 575. ....19.21
Sindall v Cambridgeshire County Council [1994] 3 All ER 932..............................4.11, 4.12
Sledmore v Dalby [1996] NPC 16 ....22.18
Smith v Bush and Harris v Wyre Forest District Council [1989] 17 EG 68 (HL)............... 2.05
Solle v Butcher [1950] 1 KB 671 .... 4.22
Spiro v Glencrown Properties Ltd [1991] Ch 537 .... 3.12
Street v Mountford [1985] AC 809 ....19.01, 22.04
Target Holdings Ltd v Redferns (a firm) and another
   [1995] 3 All ER 785 (HL)...25.27, 25.28
Target Holdings Ltd v Redferns (a firm) [1994] 1 All ER 118 (CA)..................................25.28
Target Home Loans Ltd v Clothier and another [1994] 1 All ER 439 ....26.11
Tecbild Ltd v Chamberlain (1969) 20 P&CR 633..23.01
Thomson's Mortgage Trusts [1920] 1 Ch 508 ....26.31
Tichborne v Weir (1892) 67 LT 735...23.04
Tickner v Buzzacott [1965] Ch 426 ....23.04

Table of Cases

Tinsley v Milligan [1993] 3 All ER 65 .... 25.07
Todd v Unwin and others [1994] NIJB 230 .... 19.03
Transworld Land Co Ltd v J Sainsbury plc [1990] 2 EGLR;
   (1997) 23 EG 141(HL) 20.29
Tribe v Tribe [1995] 4 All ER 236 .... 25.07
Tubman v Johnston [1981] NI 53 .... 28.31
Tulk v Moxhay (1848) 2 Ph 774 .... 20.24, 20.28
Ulster Bank Ltd v Carter [1998] NI 93 .... 18.42, 28.31, 29.17, 29.19
Ulster Bank Ltd v Shanks [1982] NI 143 .... 28.08
Ungurial v Lesnoff [1990] Ch 206 .... 22.18
Union Eagle Ltd v Golden Achievement Ltd, *The Times*, 7 February 1997 ...... 15.20
Venus Investments Ltd v Stocktop Ltd [1996] EGCS 173 .... 22.04
Viscount Hill v Bullock [1897] 2 Ch 482 .... 14.04
Wake v Hall (1883) 8 App Cas 195 .... 14.04
Wandsworth Borough Council v Attwell [1995] EGCS 68 .... 19.11
Wayling v Jones (1993) 69 P&CR 170 (CA) 22.18
Webber v Minister of Housing and Local Government [1967] 3 All ER 981 ...... 11.08
Wheeldon v Burrows (1879) 12 Ch D 31 .... 21.23
Whitby v Mitchell (1890) 44 Ch D 85 .... 18.27
William A Lees (Concrete) Ltd and others v Lees and others
   [1992] 11 NIJB 44 .... 22.18
Williams & Glyn's Bank v Boland [1980] 2 All ER 408 (HL) 28.06, 28.07-28.09,
   .... 28.11, 28.12, 28.13, 28.17, 28.34
Wilson v Martin's Executors [1993] 24 EG 119 (CA) 23.01
Wood v Secretary of State for the Environment [1973] 2 All ER 404 .... 11.06
Woolwich Building Society v Dickman and Todd [1996] 3 All ER 204;
   [1996] NPC 22 .... 7.43, 28.07
Workers Trust and Merchant Bank Ltd v Dojap Investments
   [1993] 2 All ER 370 .... 15.41

TABLE OF STATUTES, RULES AND OTHER ENACTMENTS

Access to the Countryside (NI) Order 1983 .... 5.28
   art 3 .... 21.40
Administration of Estates Act (NI) 1955 .... 6.18, 18.29
   s 2(3) 25.02
   s 34 .... 16.32
   s 34(4) 6.18
   s 34(5) 17.08
   s 34(8) 16.32, 16.36
   s 40(5) 24.11
Administration of Justice Act 1970 ....26.11, 26.14
   s 36 .... 26.11
Administration of Justice Act 1973 ....26.11, 26.14
   s 8 .... 26.11
Agricultural Holdings Act 1986
   s 10 .... 14.09
Arbitration Act 1996 .... 13.12
Betting, Gaming, Lotteries and Amusements (NI) Order 1985 .... 5.28
Building Regulations (NI) Order 1972 .... 12.01
Building Regulations Order (NI) 1979 .... 12.17
   art 18 .... 12.17
Building Societies Act 1986 .... 10.04
Building Societies Act 1997 .... 10.04
Building Societies Act (NI) 1967
   s 37 .... 26.25
Business Tenancies (NI) Order 1996 .... 18.15, 19.06, 19.09, 19.23, 20.13
   art 26 .... 20.11
Caravans Act (NI) 1963 .... 5.28
   Sch 11.18
Charities Act (NI) 1964
   s 22 .... 25.16
   s 24 .... 25.17
Cinemas (NI) Order 1991 .... 5.28
Church Temporalities Act 1833 .... 18.07
Commission on Sales of Land Act 1972
   s 1(1) 2.25
Companies (European Communities) Order (NI) 1972
   art 3 .... 6.21
Companies (NI) Order 1986
   art 45 .... 6.21
   art 402 .... 5.10
Companies (NI) Order 1990
   art 46 .... 6.21
Companies (No 2) (NI) Order 1990
   art 44 .... 6.21

art 65 .... 6.21
Compulsory Registration of Title Order (NI) 1995 .... 7.01, 7.07
Compulsory Registration of Title Order (NI) 1999 .... 7.07
Consumer Credit Act 1974 .... 10.01, 26.14
   s 126 .... 26.11
Consumer Arbitration Agreements Act 1988 .... 13.12
Conveyancing Act 1881 .... 2.18, 7.48, 20.01, 20.21,
.... 26.05, 26.15, 26.18, 28.31
   s 2 .... 14.02
   s 3(1) 2.22
   s 3(3) 2.19
   s 5(1) 26.23
   s 5(2) 26.23
   s 6 .... 14.10, 21.24, 21.34
   s 6(1) 25.34
   s 7 .... 7.48, 17.03, 17.05, 17.09, 17.14, 20.25
   s 10 .... 20.21
   s 11 .... 20.21
   s 13(1) 2.23
   s 14 .... 18.06, 19.21
   s 14(6) 19.21
   s 16(1) 26.22
   s 18 .... 26.26
   s 19 .... 26.15
   s 19(1) 26.18
   s 20 .... 26.15
   s 21 .... 25.15
   s 21(1) 26.15
   s 21(3) 25.11, 26.15
   s 21(7) 26.15
   s 22 .... 26.15
   s 51 .... 18.02
   s 52(1) 25.34
   s 58 .... 20.28
   s 62(1) 21.19
   s 65 .... 19.30
Conveyancing Act 1892 .... 7.48, 18.06, 28.31, 29.31
   s 3 .... 26.26
   s 3(1) 2.09
   s 4 .... 19.23
Conveyancing Act 1911 .... 7.48, 28.31
   s 5(1) 26.15
Deasy's Act *see* Landlord and Tenant Law Amendment Act (Ir) 1860
Defective Premises (NI) Order 1975 .... 13.01
   art 3 .... 13.01
Dogs (NI) Order 1983 .... 5.28
Enduring Powers of Attorney (NI) Order 1987 .... 25.39
   art 11 .... 7.69
Evidence Act (NI) 1939
   s 4 .... 6.09

Table of Legislation and Rules

Family Homes and Domestic Violence (NI) Order 1998 .... 6.03, 27.11, ...28.03, 28.32, 28.34
Family Law (Miscellaneous Provisions) (NI) Order 1984 ....27.11, 28.32
   art 5(7)..28.33
Finance Act 1891
   s 57...16.20
Finance Act 1910
   s 74(1)..16.28
Finance Act 1930
   s 42...16.33
Finance Act 1965
   s 90(1)..16.04
Finance Act 1973
   s 50...16.01
Finance Act 1974
   s 49...16.34
Finance Act 1981
   s 107...16.19
Finance Act 1982 ....10.20
   s 129...16.34
Finance Act 1985 ....16.30
   s 83(1)..16.30
   s 84(1)..16.30
   s 84(4)..16.30
   s 84(5)..16.30
   s 84(7)..16.30
Finance Act 1994
   s 224...16.10
   s 226...16.23
   s 227...16.19
   s 228...16.24
   s 244...16.07
   s 245...16.07
Finance Act (NI) 1954
   s 11...16.33
Finance Act (NI) 1962
   s 3(1)..16.36
Finance Act (NI) 1970
   Sch 2 Pt 1 ....16.36
Finance Act (NI) 1971
   s 5(1)..16.36
Fines and Recoveries (Ir) Act 1834
   s 2...18.10
   s 12...18.10
Game Preservation Act (NI) 1928..21.16
Health & Safety at Work (NI) Order 1978 ....5.28
Housing (NI) Order 1981 ....5.29
Housing (NI) Order 1992 ....Appendix B
Incumbered Estates (Ir) Act 1855 ....24.02
Inheritance (Provision for Family and Dependants) Act 1975
   s 2...25.09

Insolvency (NI) Order 1989	6.03, 6.22, 27.01, 27.22, 27.23, 27.24
art 257	15.08, 15.14, 27.14, 27.17
arts 295-305	27.08
art 309	29.33
art 309(2)(a)	29.33
art 312	27.19, 27.23
art 313	27.20
art 315	27.23
art 315(2)	27.19, 27.20, 27.23, 27.24
art 328	25.12
art 367	25.12, 27.21
art 368	27.21
art 369	27.21
art 369(2)	27.21
Sch 4	27.08
Sch 10	28.33
Insolvency (No 2) Act 1994	6.22, 27.19, 27.20, 27.24
Irish Church Act 1869	18.07
Judgments Enforcement Act (NI) 1969	28.30
Judgments Enforcement (NI) Order 1981	5.08, 28.30, 28.31
art 13	26.11
art 45	28.30
art 46	28.31, 29.17
art 47	5.08
art 49	18.41
art 51	26.15
art 52	28.31
Judicature (Ir) Act 1877	15.23, 23.16
Judicature (NI) Act 1978	23.16
s 86(3)	26.14
s 91	26.18
s 92	20.30
Land Registration Act 1925	
s 70	28.07
s 70(1)(f)	23.04
s 75(1)	23.04
Land Registration Act (NI) 1970	7.01, 7.27, 7.30, 7.57, 23.04, 26.04, 29.01
s 10	7.03
s 11(1)	7.42, 27.23
s 25(1)	7.07
s 34(4)	7.38, 27.23
s 34(5)	7.38
s 36	7.50
s 40	28.30
s 43	26.30
s 47	22.14, 24.04
s 53	7.41, 7.53, 23.08
s 53(2)	23.08
s 53(4)	7.41, 23.08
s 59(5)	7.51
s 66	7.57

s 67A	27.23
s 69	7.70
Sch 1 Pt para 5(2)	26.14, 26.17
Sch 2	7.07, 7.36
Sch 2 Pt 1	7.07
Sch 2 para 30A	11.35
Sch 3 para 1	7.26
Sch 3 para 2	7.26
Sch 5	7.16, 7.39, 23.08, 23.09, 28.07, 28.10
Sch 5 Pt 1 para 15	22.18, 28.07, 28.24, 28.31
Sch 6	7.28, 7.39, 24.04, 28.07, 28.10
Sch 7	26.12, 26.15
Sch 7 Pt 1	7.52
Sch 7 Pt 1 para 1(2)	28.31
Sch 7 Pt 1 para 5(2)	26.17
Sch 13	7.26, 7.37
Landlord and Tenant Act 1851	14.09
Landlord and Tenant Law Amendment Act (Ir) 1860 (Deasy's Act)	18.05, 20.01, 20.21
s 3	18.09, 18.13, 19.01, 19.03
s 4	19.02, 19.05
s 5	18.15, 18.17
s 7	19.13
s 9	18.16, 19.04
s 10	19.04, 20.13
s 11	19.04
s 12	19.04, 20.21
s 13	19.04, 20.21
s 14	19.04, 20.22
s 15	19.04
s 16	19.04, 20.22, 29.11
s 17	14.09
s 18	19.04, 19.05, 20.13, 20.17
s 22	20.17
s 26	20.09
s 40	19.13, 19.31
s 41	17.09, 17.16, 20.08
s 42(1)	20.09
s 42(2)	20.09
s 43	20.17
ss 52-58	19.28
Law of Property Act 1925	
s 49(2)	15.41
Law of Property Amendment Act 1859	
s 24	2.08
s 25	2.08
Leasehold (Enlargement and Extension) Act (NI) 1971	19.30, 29.20
Leases Acts 1849 and 1850	25.33
Limitation (NI) Order 1989	1.19, 7.41, 23.01, 23.03, 26.25
art 12	25.28
arts 20-27	23.09

art 21	23.01
art 42(1)	25.28
art 43	25.28
art 43(1)(b)	23.07
art 44	23.07
Local Government Act (NI) 1972	21.35
Local Government (Misc Provs) (NI) Order 1985	5.28
Local Registration of Title (Ir) Act 1891	7.01, 7.04, 7.26, 7.37
Married Women's Property Act 1882	18.29
s 17	28.03, 28.04
Matrimonial Causes (NI) Order 1978	16.28, 28.04, 28.05
art 26	25.26, 28.05
Matrimonial Homes Acts 1967 and 1983	28.32
Minerals Development Act (NI) 1969	7.43, 21.14
Misrepresentation Act 1967	
s 2	4.13
Misrepresentation Act (NI) 1967	4.11, 28.15
s 1	4.11
s 2(1)	4.10, 4.11
s 2(2)	4.11
s 3	4.11
Partition Act 1868	18.42, 27.11, 28.31, 28.33, 29.17
s 4	28.31
Partition Act 1876	18.42, 28.31, 29.17
Perpetuities Act (NI) 1966	18.28
Petroleum (Consolidation) Act (NI) 1929	5.28
Petroleum (Production) Act (NI) 1964	7.43
Planning (General Development) (Amendment No 2) Order 1995	11.20
Planning (General Development) Order (NI) 1993	11.13-11.20, 11.21
Planning (NI) Order 1972	11.36
Planning (NI) Order 1991	5.20, 5.21, 11.02
art 2(2)	11.03
art 3(3)	11.12
art 11(1)	11.02
art 11(2)	11.09
art 11(3)	11.04
art 12	11.02
art 20(1)	11.21
art 41	11.02
art 43	11.36
art 64	11.37
art 65	11.37
art 68(4)(b)	11.31, 11.35
art 94(1)(a)	11.34
Planning (Use Classes) Order (NI) 1989	11.09, 11.10
art 3(5)	11.10
Planning and Building Regulations (Amendment) (NI) Order 1990	12.01, 12.17
Planning and Compensation Act 1991	
s 171B	11.35
Planning and Land Compensation Act (NI) 1971	5.21
Planning Applications (Exemption from Publication) Order (NI) 1999	11.27

Table of Legislation and Rules

Planning Blight (Compensation) (NI) Order 1981 .... 5.21, 11.33
    art 4(1) 11.33
    art 4(2) 11.33
Powers of Attorney Act (NI) 1971 .... 25.35, 25.38
    s 4 .... 7.69
    s 9 .... 25.35
Prescription Act (Ir) 1858 .... 21.28-21.33
    s 7 .... 21.32
    s 8 .... 21.32
Private Streets (NI) Order 1980
    art 24 .... 5.14
    art 32 .... 5.14, 9.07
Property (Discharge of Mortgage by Receipt) (NI) Order 1983 .... 26.25
Property (NI) Order 1978 .... 20.33, 29.01
    art 3 .... 20.33
    art 5(2) 20.33
    art 5(5) 20.33
    art 13 .... 18.40
Property (NI) Order 1997 .... 6.24, 7.01, 8.01, 9.02, 18.03, 18.14, 19.01,
    .... 20.19, 20.21, 20.23, 20.26, 20.33, 29.01-29.20
    arts 5-27 .... 29.02
    art 7(7) 29.19
    art 7(8) 29.19
    art 24 .... 26.05
    art 25 .... 20.03, 29.10
    art 28 .... 7.08, 9.02, 18.03, 18.05, 20.19, 29.04, 29.19
    art 29 .... 20.23, 29.05, 29.19
    art 29(3) 6.24, 20.23, 29.05
    art 29(3)(c) 6.24
    art 30 .... 6.24, 9.02, 18.03, 18.14, 24.08, 26.26, 29.06, 29.19
    art 30(5)(c) 26.05
    art 31 .... 29.02, 29.07, 29.19
    art 34 .... 18.03, 20.01, 20.26, 20.30, 20.31,
    .... 29.10, 29.11, 29.14, 29.19, 29.20
    art 34(4) 29.12
    art 34(6) 29.13
    art 34(7) 29.13
    art 36 .... 18.08, 18.12, 29.08, 29.19
    art 37 .... 29.09, 29.19
    art 38 .... 29.19
    art 39 .... 29.02, 29.15, 29.19
    art 39(3) 24.08, 26.26
    art 40 .... 29.15, 29.19
    art 41 .... 29.15, 29.19
    art 42 .... 29.15, 29.19
    art 43 .... 29.15, 29.19
    art 44 .... 29.15, 29.19
    art 45 .... 20.30, 20 31, 29.15, 29.19
    art 45(1) 29.14
    art 46 .... 29.15
    art 47 .... 29.15, 29.19

art 48	18.42, 28.31, 29.02, 29.17, 29.19
art 49	28.31, 29.02, 29.19
art 50	18.41, 28.31, 29.02, 29.18, 29.19
art 52(1)	29.20
art 53(1)	29.30
Sch 2	29.08, 29.19
Sch 3	29.09, 29.19
Sch 4	29.20
Sch 5	29.20
Property Misdescriptions Act 1991	4.14
Protection of Animals Acts (NI) 1952 and 1961	21.16
Public Health (Ir) Act 1878	12.22
Quia Emptores 1290	18.26

Real Property Act 1845

s 3	18.42, 19.02
s 5	8.14
Registration (Land and Deeds) (NI) Order 1992	6.03, 7.01
art 6	7.03
art 7	7.24
art 40	6.32

Registration of Deeds Act (NI) 1967

s 1	6.08
Registration of Deeds Act (NI) 1970	6.03, 29.20
s 2(1)	6.32
s 3A	27.15
s 3B	27.15
s 4	20.28
Registry of Deeds (Ir) Act 1707	6.32
Renewable Leasehold Conversion Act 1849	18.08, 19.30
Rent Act 1977	7.43
Rent (NI) Order 1978	7.43, 15.42, 18.15, 18.18, 19.06, 19.09, 19.10
Rights to Light Act (NI) 1961	21.33
Roads (NI) Order 1980	21.40

Roads (NI) Order 1993

art 68	21.36, 21.40
Satisfied Terms Act 1845	26.25
Settled Land Act 1882	7.33, 18.11, 18.26, 22.14, 22.18, 24.02, 24.03, 24.04, 24.05, 24.11, 25.01, 25.13, 25.30
s 2(8)	24.11
s 3	24.07
s 6	24.08
s 18	24.09
s 20	24.07
s 25	24.10
s 26	24.10
s 39	24.11
s 40	24.11
s 58	24.05
Settled Land Act 1884	7.33, 18.11, 18.26, 22.14, 22.18, 24.02, 24.03, 24.04, 24.05, 24.11, 25.01, 25.13, 25.30

Table of Legislation and Rules

Settled Land Act 1890	7.33, 18.11, 18.26, 22.14, 22.18, 24.02, 24.03, 24.04, 24.05, 24.11, 25.01, 25.13, 25.30
s 15	24.10
s 16(i)	24.11
s 16(ii)	24.11
Solicitors (Amendment) (NI) Order 1989	
art 71(b)(i)	2.25
Solicitors (NI) Order 1976	
art 70	2.25
Stamp Act 1891	16.01
s 1	16.35
s 5	16.19
s 15(2)(a)	16.10
s 54	16.17
s 57	16.30
s 117	2.25
s 122	16.10
Sch 1	16.01, 16.35
Stamp Duties Management Act 1891	16.01
Stamp Duty (Temporary Provisions) Act 1992	16.17
Statute of Frauds (Ir) 1695	3.03, 3.05, 3.12, 3.14, 3.15, 3.20, 15.27, 19.02, 22.03, 22.16
s 2	3.03-3.05, 3.10
s 4	25.03
Statutory Charges Register Act (NI) 1951	5.07
Town and Country Planning Act 1990	11.35
Trustee Act (NI) 1958	6.15, 24.11, 25.18, 25.30
s 12-34	25.23
s 16	25.23
s 24	25.25
s 26	25.25, 25.35
s 35	25.20, 25.22
s 38	25.21
s 39	25.20
s 43	25.20
s 56	25.26
s 57	25.26
s 62	25.27
Trustee (Amendment) Act (NI) 1962	25.18
Unfair Contract Terms Act 1977	2.05
Vendor and Purchaser Act 1874	2.18, 15.24
s 1	2.17, 6.09
s 2	2.21
s 2(2)	6.09
Water Act (NI) 1972	
s 7	5.18, 9.11, 11.39
s 8	5.18, 9.11, 11.39
s 9(3)	5.18
Water and Sewerage Services (Amendment) (NI) Order 1993	9.10
Water and Sewerage Services (NI) Order 1973	11.39
art 17	9.10

art 22 .... 5.19, 11.39
Wildlife (NI) Order 1985 .... 21.16
Wills Act 1837 .... 25.04
   s 28 .... 18.11
Wills and Administration Proceedings (NI) Order 1994 .... 25.04, 29.01
Works Regulations Act 1906 .... 11.11

STATUTORY RULES

Building (Amendment) Regulations (NI) 1995 .... 12.01, 12.11, 12.12
Building (Amendment) Regulations (NI) 1997 .... 12.01, 12.13, 12.20
Building Regulations (NI) 1994 .... 12.01
   Sch 1 .... 12.03
   Sch 1 para 2 .... 12.09, 12.10
Registration of Deeds Regulations (NI) 1997 .... 6.03
Stamp Duty (Exempt Instruments) Regulations 1987 .... 16.20, 16.28, 16.30
Stamp Duty (Production of Documents) (NI) Regulations 1996 .... 16.07

Insolvency Rules (NI) 1991 .... 27.01
Land Registration Rules (NI) 1994 .... 7.05
   r 31 .... 16.15
   r 53 .... 7.26
   r 54 .... 7.26
   r 128(1) 7.27, 7.63
   Sch 2 .... 7.48

PART ONE

CONVEYANCING

INTRODUCTION

The land law and conveyancing law of Northern Ireland are unique. Each derives partly from English common law and statue law; partly from Irish statue and common law. Although the law in this jurisdiction shares some characteristics with those of England and others with those of the Republic of Ireland it is nevertheless quite distinct from both.

English common law was introduced into Ireland with the feudal system, following the Norman invasion in 1172. From that time many English statutes relating to land were also applied to Ireland. It was only in the nineteenth century, when major land law reform took place in Ireland to alleviate the great social and economic problems existing at that time, that Irish land law began to diverge significantly from that of England.

New legislation gave agricultural tenants in Ireland security of tenure and eventually the land purchase schemes enabled them to acquire the freehold of their property. Ultimately the tenants became owner occupiers and ownership of most rural land in Ireland is now freehold. There was no similar reform in England where many tenant farmers continue to occupy land with limited security on a leasehold basis. Even within Ireland there was not the same necessity to extend the reforms to the ownership of urban property. As a result title to property in a town or city is seldom a freehold in possession and is far more likely to be a very long leasehold.

Although a single common law system continued to exist throughout Ireland until partition in 1922 there has been considerable divergence since the two separate jurisdictions emerged. Subsequently, land law in Northern Ireland and the Republic of Ireland has evolved from its common foundations along different lines.

In England property law diverged further from that of Ireland following the introduction of comprehensive reforms there in 1925. Although parts of that legislation have been extended to Northern Ireland much of the remainder cannot suitably be imposed on our existing structure and it is unlikely that the two systems will converge again.

Land law and the law of conveyancing are closely connected to such an extent that it is sometimes difficult to see where the distinction lies between them. The difference is that land law generally concerns the definition of the various estates and interests which make up the ownership of land; while conveyancing is primarily the acquisition and transfer of estates and interests in land. Conveyancing is more concerned with the procedures whereby the owners of those estates and interests may dispose of them. In practice much of the time involved in a conveyancing transaction concerns ancillary matters such as finance and preliminary enquiries rather than questions of law.

A basic knowledge of land law is essential in understanding conveyancing practice because it places the procedures in context and explains the historical background from which they have evolved. Ownership of land in Northern Ireland is extremely complex. Any particular property may be fragmented into numerous interests and sub-interests. Fragmentation of ownership is especially common in urban areas where the title may be split up amongst a number of different people. For this reason the disposition of the land and the conveyancing may also be complicated.

There has been much debate in recent years about substantive land law reform. It has been generally recognised that traditional systems of tenure are unnecessarily complex for modern requirements.

The Land Law Working Group which was established to review all aspects of land law and the conveyancing system in Northern Ireland published its final report in 1990. Although the report contained draft legislation which was designed to implement its many recommendations, the comprehensive reforms proposed have not yet been introduced. The Property (NI) Order 1997 is one of the measures which is based on proposals in the report. It is preparing the ground for major reform by simplifying land tenure and removing the complexities of pyramid titles.

There has also been a quite separate debate about the shortcomings in conveyancing practice and procedure. Public concerns have been expressed about unjustifiable delays in the conveyancing process and about the expense. The attention focused on solicitor's costs has reduced the fees charged for conveyancing and made pricing more competitive.

The Law Society of NI introduced the Home Charter Scheme on a voluntary basis in 1994 to address the allied issue of maintaining proper standards and setting out correct procedures. The Law Society General Conditions of Sale (3rd edition) were issued simultaneously and incorporated in a new printed form of contract, which has since been revised. At the time of writing it is envisaged that the Home Charter Scheme will become compulsory.

CHAPTER ONE

MODEL PROCEDURE

Introduction

1.01 This section is intended to provide a framework to place conveyancing law and land law into context. It sets out the various steps in a common conveyancing transaction relating to residential property and lists the sequence of events from the beginning when instructions are taken to the end when registration of the transfer of ownership to the purchaser is complete.

1.02 Although ideally a solicitor likes to have instructions to act in the sale or purchase of a property at an early stage, this does not always happen and sometimes the solicitor will only be told about the sale when he receives a letter from the estate agent with details of the terms agreed. It is particularly helpful for a solicitor to receive instructions from a vendor when the property is placed on the market for sale, so that he can begin the preliminary work and find out as much as possible about the property before a purchaser is obtained. Preferably a purchaser's solicitor should also be given instructions by his client in good time before he receives any documents from the vendor's solicitor but again that does not always happen.

1.03 The Home Charter Scheme was introduced by the Law Society of Northern Ireland to promote, improve and monitor a standard of service to the public. It was launched in conjunction with the General Conditions of Sale (3rd edition, later revised, referred to throughout as 'GCS'). Both were initiated with the intention of imposing a greater obligation of disclosure on the vendor and departing to an extent from the principle of *caveat emptor* (let the buyer beware) which was thought not to be a relevant or responsible approach to conveyancing in today's environment.

1.04 The Home Charter Scheme relates only to *domestic* properties. That means property primarily used for residential purposes and not acquired or disposed of by a client in the course of a commercial business activity.

The Scheme sets out:

- the rights of clients
- the responsibilities of the firm
- bye-laws
- rules.

The Scheme lays down standards requiring solicitors:

- to observe the procedures recommended
- to properly record all information
- to keep the client informed at each stage of the transaction

- to make specified checks
- to give appropriate undertakings
- to use the suggested forms provided or similar ones.

1.05 Full details of the Home Charter Scheme and the recommended forms are set out in Appendix A.

The Home Charter Scheme forms are as follows:

    Form 1A – sale instructions sheet
    Form 1B – purchase instructions sheet
    Form 2 – terms of business
    Form 3A}
    Form 3B} forms of undertaking
    Form 3C}
    Form 3D}
    Form 4A – notice of potential conflict of interest
    Form 4 B – notice of actual conflict of interest
    Form 5 – mortgage letter
    Form 6 - funds letter
    Domestic conveyancing charges.

Vendor

1.06 The sequence of events in a conveyancing transaction is as follows:

At the outset, a solicitor acting in the sale of a residential property

- takes full instructions from the vendor (Form 1A) and confirms vendor's identity
- gives a written estimate of his costs and terms of business (Form 2 and estimate)
- obtains the title deeds to the property from the vendor or his lender if there is a mortgage
- drafts a contract
- makes sure that the property is properly insured
- obtains information from the vendor to draft replies to enquires before contract
- applies for property certificates
- applies for searches

Conveyancing 7

1.07 The vendor's solicitor will forward the following when available to the purchaser's solicitor:
- title deeds
- draft contract
- replies to enquiries before contract
- searches
- property certificates

Title[1]
1.08 In relation to the title, the vendor has an obligation to show good title. When the vendor's solicitor has obtained the deeds, either from his client or from the mortgagee, he should check the title to ensure that it is in order before sending it to the purchaser's solicitor.

Contract[2]
1.09 The vendor's solicitor has to draft the contract to send to the purchaser's solicitor. This will include a description, both legal and physical, of the property to be sold. It will also contain the essential terms such as the price, the deposit and the completion date, if these have been agreed.

Replies to enquiries before contract[3]
1.10 The vendor's solicitor takes instructions from his client to enable him to draft the replies to the enquiries which cover a range of topics. The enquiries are in a standard form although a purchaser may add further questions if he has particular concerns that are not covered by the standard enquiries.

Searches[4]
1.11 The vendor should apply for:
- a bankruptcy search against the vendor
- an Enforcement of Judgments Office search against the vendor
- a Registry of Deeds search against the vendor from the date he acquired the property to date or a Land Registry folio search of the folio on which the title is registered
- a Statutory Charges search

to ensure that no acts have been registered which might affect a purchaser.

---

[1] Cf paras 2.10-2.26.
[2] Cf paras 3.01-3.20.
[3] Cf paras 4.12-4.13.
[4] Cf paras 5.02-5.11.

Property certificates[5]

1.12 The vendor should apply for property certificates from:

- the Department of the Environment on matters relating to planning, roads, water and sewerage
- the local district council on questions of building control approval, smoke control and other statutory issues dealt with by the council

to verify that all necessary permissions have been obtained and there are no outstanding breaches of any relevant legislation.

Purchaser

1.13 Meanwhile, a solicitor acting in the purchase of a property:

- takes full instructions from the purchaser (Form 1B)
- gives a written estimate of his costs and terms of business (Form 2 and estimate)
- finds out how the purchaser intends to finance the purchase and checks that the money will be available in time, as well as finding out if any financial advice is required
- ascertains whether any undertakings will be required in relation to the finance
- enquires as to the most suitable date for completion (i.e. the date when the purchaser will pay over the money and take possession of the house).

1.14 If the purchaser is obtaining a mortgage, the lender will require the purchaser's solicitor to obtain bankruptcy and Enforcement of Judgments Office searches against the purchaser.

The traditional position of the purchaser when buying property is *caveat emptor* (let the purchaser beware). This means that the purchaser takes the property at his own risk. He has to raise questions and make the necessary enquiries to satisfy himself both as to the physical state of the property and the title.

1.15 When the title deeds, draft contract and other documents arrive from the vendor's solicitor the purchaser's solicitor should examine them carefully. He should raise any queries about any of the documentation furnished. In particular he should ensure that replies to enquiries before contract have been properly answered.

After perusing the title and all other documents furnished the purchaser's solicitor should arrange an appointment with his client and take the client

---

[5] Cf paras 5.12-5.29.

through all the matters which arise. The purchaser's attention should be drawn to any alterations made to the property and any relevant covenants contained in leases on the title. If the client makes any additional points, these should also be raised with the vendor's solicitor. It may be necessary to amend the draft contract. Whether or not this is the case, once everything else is in order and the purchaser is ready to proceed, the purchaser's solicitor should complete in the contract:

- the price to be paid (if it is not already on the contract)
- the deposit
- the completion date
- the amount of any loan and the name of the lender
- price for any fittings and / or furnishings
- any special conditions
- the purchaser's name and address.

The purchaser can then sign the contract which becomes his offer to purchase and his solicitor will send it back to the vendor's solicitor for acceptance by the vendor. The purchaser's solicitor should check at this stage that the purchaser has the amount of the deposit readily available and ask for it to be paid over to him as soon as possible.

Vendor

1.16 The vendor's solicitor will deal with any additional queries raised by the purchaser and consider any amendments to the contract made by the purchaser. He will discuss these with the vendor and then, when the points are agreed, have the contract accepted by the vendor. The vendor's solicitor keeps the original contract and sends back a copy to the purchaser's solicitor. At the same time he requests payment of the deposit.

Purchaser

1.17 On receipt of a copy of the accepted contract, the purchaser's solicitor checks that there are no further unauthorised amendments to the contract and then sends the deposit to the vendor's solicitor. Now that the parties are bound by the contract he has to think about completing the purchase. He has to make arrangements to obtain the mortgage advance and any balance to be paid by his client in good time for completion.

The purchaser's solicitor also drafts the purchase deed. If it is straightforward, the normal practice now is to send an engrossment to the vendor's solicitor for approval and execution by the vendor. If there is any particular difficulty, a draft can be sent for approval first. Often the requisitions on title are sent with the purchase deed for the vendor's solicitor to provide replies.

If the purchaser has a mortgage, his solicitor drafts the mortgage deed and has it executed by the purchaser, reports on title and requests funds from the lender.

The recommended procedure provides for the purchaser's solicitor to request a completion statement from the vendor's solicitor at this stage, but in practice this is seldom furnished in the sale of a domestic property. The parties are normally aware of the amount required on completion and it is usually paid direct to the vendor's solicitor by solicitor's cheque.

The purchaser's solicitor has to check the manner of completion which means that he has to agree with the vendor's solicitor how and when the money is going to be paid over. Arrangements must also be made for the purchaser to collect the keys. Normally they can be picked up from the estate agent, once the vendor's solicitor has confirmed that the money has arrived. Alternatively, the vendor and the purchaser may make their own arrangements to hand them over direct.

The purchaser's solicitor must obtain all the funds required to complete. That is: the mortgage advance, any balance due by the purchaser and sufficient monies to cover Stamp Duty and Registry of Deeds / Land Registry fees. The purchaser's solicitor should advise the vendor's solicitor in advance of any undertakings required on completion so that proper notice of any unusual requests is given. It may also be advisable for the purchaser's solicitor to update the Registry of Deeds search/Land Registry search against the vendor.

Vendor

1.18 On receipt of the deposit, requisitions on title and draft deed, the vendor's solicitor will respond by acknowledging receipt of the deposit, replying to the requisitions and confirming that the deed meets with his approval (or not as the case may be). If the deed is in order he should arrange to have it executed by the vendor, ensuring that the vendor's signature is properly witnessed. He should also obtain a redemption figure (the amount required to repay the vendor's mortgage in full) from the lender as at the completion date (or one or two days after this date) if the vendor has a mortgage to repay. He will confirm the arrangements for completion and handing over the keys when contacted about these points by the purchaser's solicitor. If required, he will submit a completion statement to the purchaser's solicitor.

The vendor's solicitor should also remind the vendor to make arrangements to pay his rates up to the completion date and to inform the Rates Collection Agency of the name of the purchaser who will be responsible for payment of the rates in future.

1.19 The vendor must pay his ground rent to the last gale day before completion (GCS 15.2). In effect that means that it should be paid to the previous 1st November or 1st May as ground rent is payable in arrear. Under the GCS no apportionment of rent is required but many solicitors still expect an apportionment to be done. Under the terms of the GCS the vendor cannot be compelled to pay the ground rent due to completion unless the purchaser's solicitor has added a special condition to this effect.

If the ground rent has not been demanded or the vendor does not know to whom it is payable, the purchaser will commonly ask the vendor to provide an indemnity for an amount equal to six years' ground rent. This is because six years' arrears is the maximum amount that can be claimed under the Limitation (NI) Order 1989.

Purchaser

1.20 On completion the purchaser's solicitor sends a completion letter to the vendor's solicitor with the full purchase money (if no deposit has been paid) or the balance purchase money. The money is generally paid by solicitor's cheque, although sometimes a bank draft may be required. The only advantage of a bank draft is that it is guaranteed funds. Like a cheque, a bank draft has to be cleared.

Under the GCS the purchaser has the right to pay by way of two cheques/drafts: one made out to the mortgagee for the amount necessary to redeem any outstanding mortgage and the other made out to the vendor's solicitor for the balance purchase money.

Vendor

1.21 When the vendor's solicitor receives the money he should immediately telephone both his client and the vendor's solicitor to confirm that it has arrived. He should also advise either the estate agent or his client that the keys may be released to the purchaser.

The vendor's solicitor should reply to the purchaser's solicitor's completion letter as soon as possible, dealing with each of the points and undertakings in it. He should release the executed purchase deed and last receipt for ground rent as soon as practicable. He must also repay the vendor's mortgage immediately and send the mortgage deed to the lender with the redemption money for the vacating receipt to be sealed.

Purchaser

1.22 After completion the purchaser's solicitor dates the purchase deed (and the mortgage, if any) with the date of completion. He then lodges the purchase deed in the Stamp Office and pays the Stamp Duty if the document is liable to it. The next step is to lodge the purchase deed and the mortgage deed in the Registry of Deeds or Land Registry, as appropriate, for registration.

The purchaser's solicitor should notify the ground landlord of the change of ownership and make final searches as required. It is advisable to check through the file and all the documents to make sure that everything is in place before finally scheduling the documents to send to the client or to the lender if there is a mortgage.

Once the deed(s) have been returned by the Registry of Deeds in the case of unregistered property, the purchaser's solicitor should update the Registry of Deeds search to show registration of the assurance to the purchaser and, if appropriate, the purchaser's mortgage. This search should also show registration of a certificate of satisfaction of the vendor's mortgage if he had one.

Vendor

1.23 Meanwhile, the vendor's solicitor registers satisfaction of the vendor's mortgage (the vacate of mortgage) when the deed is returned to him and he sends it on to the purchaser's solicitor. If the title is registered in the Land Registry it may be simpler to send the deed of charge, with the executed release endorsed, to the purchaser's solicitor with a cheque for the appropriate Land Registry fee. Indeed, this is also quite proper in relation to Registry of Deeds transactions if agreed between the two solicitors.

Lastly, the vendors' solicitor should deal with any outstanding queries including any acts appearing on the final search. Again, it is advisable for him to check through his file to make sure that everything is complete. Any outstanding documents should be furnished to the purchaser's solicitor.

The transaction is now complete.

CHAPTER TWO

DUTIES OF THE PARTIES

Introduction

2.01 Duties are imposed on each of the parties in a conveyancing transaction and there is an obligation on the respective solicitors to discharge those duties effectively. There is a duty on the purchaser to make proper investigations in relation to various aspects of the property whilst the vendor has a limited duty of disclosure.

PURCHASER: *CAVEAT EMPTOR*

2.02 One of the basic principles of conveyancing is *caveat emptor* (buyer beware). The purchaser is assumed to take the property at his own risk and a burden is imposed on him to protect his own position before he is committed to a binding contract. Generally, unless the vendor actually misleads the purchaser, the purchaser cannot complain if any difficulties are not disclosed to him.

Physical state of the premises

2.03 *Caveat emptor* is particularly significant in relation to the physical state of the property. The vendor generally has no obligation to disclose any physical defects and is not taken to be giving any warranty. The onus is on the purchaser to satisfy himself as to the condition of the premises. Failure to do so may leave him without a remedy if he discovers the defect later.

Latent physical defects

2.04 Despite the principle of *caveat emptor* a latent physical defect raises a duty of disclosure if it materially interferes with the enjoyment of the property:

    (1) as promised by the contract;

    (2) as promised to induce the purchaser to enter the contract; or

    (3) for a purpose for which the vendor knew it was being purchased.

This is a very limited exception. It applies only where the defect is not reasonably discoverable on inspection. Even if a defect is not discoverable on inspection, there will only be a duty of disclosure if it can be shown that one of the three categories applies.

Inspection and survey

2.05 The purchaser has a duty to protect himself by making an inspection and obtaining a survey of the property. If he is obtaining a mortgage, the lender commissions a valuation which does not amount to a full survey. The purchaser should be advised to obtain a full structural survey. If he has made a cash offer, the purchaser should also be advised to have the property properly surveyed himself before entering into the contract.[6]

The lending institutions are now very cautious in their approach and frequently recommend further specialist reports after their own inspections, although the surveyor appointed by the lender to inspect the property is really only ensuring that it is of sufficient value to cover the amount of the loan.

Latent defects in title

2.06 A vendor has no obligation to disclose in the contract patent defects in title which may be discovered from an inspection of the premises and materials supplied to the purchaser. However, he does have a duty to disclose a latent defect in title, not so apparent, of which he is or should have been aware.

In some circumstances, failure to disclose a latent defect in title may amount to a fraud. For example, where the vendor makes a representation that title is good and then fails to disclose a defect in title known to him.

In practice it may be difficult to distinguish between a physical defect and a defect in title. It may also be difficult to distinguish between patent and latent defects in title.

The difference between a patent and latent defect in title can be illustrated by considering a right of way. If the right is obvious from inspection and appears as a clear path, then it is a patent defect in title and there is no duty of disclosure. If however the right is not discoverable by an inspection of the land, then it is a latent defect in title and must be disclosed.

As a general rule, a vendor of leasehold property is under a duty to disclose onerous (as opposed to usual) covenants in the lease. Defects which prevent the vendor conveying the precise title or estate that he is contracting to sell, notices materially affecting the vendor's position which do not require registration and encumbrances not discoverable from inspection or materials supplied are also all latent defects in title which ought to have been disclosed.

Traditionally, a latent defect was simply one which was not discoverable from an inspection of the property. Nowadays the title deeds are furnished to the purchaser before the contract is signed, and his solicitor has the opportunity to discover any defect disclosed by the deeds which is not apparent on an actual inspection of the premises. This is a departure from an older conveyancing practice under which the title deeds were only provided by the vendor after the contract was formed.

Thus the vendor could argue that he has fulfilled his duty of disclosure without actually pointing out the defects and that the purchaser is fixed with constructive notice of the contents of the deeds. It can also be argued that if the documents have been supplied prior to the contract, any defects contained in

---

[6] In *Smith* v *Bush* and *Harris* v *Wyre Forest District Council* [1989] 17 EG 68 (HL), the House of Lords held that valuers of houses have duties of care to the purchasers and their disclaimers of liability for negligence are subject to, and do not satisfy, the requirement of reasonableness imposed by the Unfair Contract Terms Act 1977.

them cannot be latent. Whatever the position regarding disclosure of latent defects, the vendor also has a duty to properly deduce the title.[7]

Duty of disclosure under the General Conditions of Sale

2.07 The following provisions of the General Conditions of Sale (GCS) are relevant when considering the vendor's duty of disclosure:

(a) GCS 8.3(a)

The purchaser is deemed to have notice of the contents of the lease or grant under which the vendor holds the property if the vendor furnishes a copy of same prior to contract and also of the covenants and conditions in all superior leases and grants.

(b) GCS 3.2

The vendor has a duty to disclose the existence of any lease or tenancy out of his own interest in the property and notices served.

(c) GCS 4.1

The vendor has a duty, prior to the formation of the contract, to disclose all easements, rights and liabilities affecting the property not discoverable on inspection.

(d) GCS 4.3

If the property is sold subject to restrictive covenants the purchaser is deemed to have full knowledge of them.

Consequences of non-disclosure of defects

2.08 It is a criminal offence to conceal with intent to defraud any instrument or encumbrance material to the title or to falsify it to induce the purchaser to accept it.[8] This basically means that a vendor must not hide or tamper with any of the deeds. In some circumstances a failure to disclose a latent defect in title may amount to a fraud, with similar consequences to a fraudulent misdescription.

Where there is no fraud the remedies for non-disclosure of a latent defect in title depend on whether or not the defect is substantial. It is substantial if it can be said that the purchaser is not getting that which it was intended to be sold to him.

Where it emerges that a substantial defect was not disclosed, the vendor cannot enforce the contract. Where the defect is not substantial, the vendor can enforce the contract, subject to a reduction in price. In either case the purchaser can obtain specific performance if he wishes to proceed, subject to a reduction in price.

---

[7] Cf para 2.10.
[8] Law of Property Amendment Act 1859, ss 24-25.

Doctrine of notice

2.09 The doctrine of notice is important in relation to title and other ancillary matters, such as statutory charges, because it determines whether or not a purchaser takes the property subject to prior interests and charges.

Conveyancing Act 1882, section 3(1) provides:

> "A purchaser shall not be prejudicially affected by notice of any instrument, fact or thing unless
> (1) it is within his knowledge, or would have come to his knowledge if such inquiries and inspections had been made as ought reasonably to have been made by him; or
> (2) in the same transaction with respect to which a question of notice to the purchaser arises, it has come to the knowledge of his counsel as such, or of his solicitor, or other agent as such, or would have come to the knowledge of his solicitor, or other agent as such, if such inquiries and inspections had been made as ought reasonably to have been made by the solicitor or other agent."

This means that the purchaser is fixed with actual notice of matters within his own knowledge, with constructive notice of matters which would have been revealed by inquiries and inspections which ought reasonably to have been made and with imputed notice of matters within the actual or constructive knowledge of an agent employed in the transaction.

It effectively imposes a duty to make a proper investigation of title. That involves perusing the deeds furnished by the vendor, raising appropriate objections and requisitions on the title, obtaining satisfactory replies, making all necessary searches and obtaining property certificates.

It is negligence for the purchaser's solicitor to fail to make an investigation of title or not to do it properly. Although the purchaser has a duty to investigate title, the vendor has a duty to deduce title and to establish that the vendor is in a position to transfer the estate in the property he is agreeing to sell to the purchaser.

In theory the duty to deduce title does not arise until the contract is executed. Nowadays, because the title is sent to the purchaser's solicitor in advance as a matter of practice, he may be fixed with constructive notice of the contents. However, GCS 10.1 allows the purchaser ten working days after the title documents have been delivered or ten working days after the contract if later, to raise requisitions on title.

VENDOR : DEDUCTION OF TITLE

2.10 Title is the right to ownership of property.

The objectives of investigating title are to be satisfied that:

(1) the vendor can cause a good title to be vested in the purchaser;
(2) the title is to the property which the purchaser has agreed to buy;

(3) the title that is contracted for;

(4) the title is free from all encumbrances except those to which the sale is expressly subject.

Obligation to show good title

2.11 As a general rule the vendor has a duty to deduce title and to establish that he is in a position to transfer the estate in the property he is agreeing to sell to the purchaser.[9]

He must be able to show that when he conveys his ownership of the property to the purchaser any challenge by a third party can be resisted. The practical test is whether a court would grant the vendor specific performance of the contract and force the title on the purchaser.

In order to deduce title and discharge his obligation in this respect, the vendor should produce copies of all the documents by which dispositions of the property have been made during the period for which title has to be shown, together with relevant supporting documents such as marriage and death certificates.

Traditionally, an abstract of title was furnished by the vendor with the salient information, summarising the title documents and stating facts such as marriages and deaths. The abstract was prepared by the vendor's solicitor and sent to the purchaser's solicitor with copies of the title deeds after the contract was signed.

Nowadays, abstracts of title are seldom prepared. The modern practice is for the vendor to provide the purchaser with the title deeds for inspection at the same time as the draft contract. This puts a greater onus on the purchaser to investigate the title because he does not have statements by the vendor on which he can rely and must satisfy himself as to the contents of each deed.

The *caveat emptor* principle applies to the title because the purchaser has a responsibility to investigate the title deduced by the vendor. The vendor has a duty only to disclose latent defects in title of which he is or should have been aware. It could be argued that any defects contained in the deeds supplied have been disclosed by the vendor.

At one time the contract defined precisely the extent of the vendor's duty in furnishing title and the investigation of title occurred after the contract was signed. Now that the title is invariably furnished before the contract is signed, the vendor may be relieved to some extent of his duty to deduce it.

The advantage to the purchaser of the modern practice is that, where he is not satisfied with the title offered, he can walk away from the transaction before signing the contract. Thus some of the difficulties relating to interpretation of the contractual provisions can be avoided.

---

[9] There has been a divergence of views as to whether the vendor's obligation to show good title rests upon an implied term of the contract for sale or exists as a general rule of law. See Wylie, *Irish Conveyancing Law* (2nd ed) para 14.08.

Only if the purchaser discovers a problem with the title after he has signed the contract do the following definitions become important.

Marketable title

2.12 A title need not be absolutely perfect to be forced on a purchaser so long as it is good enough for a court to grant specific performance to the vendor. The title is considered to be adequate if it is marketable and the purchaser can in turn sell it without any special conditions in the contract to cover defects.

Good holding title

2.13 Where the vendor can establish that he has been in long, undisturbed possession of the land but does not have the usual documentary evidence of title, he has a good holding title. It is arguable whether the vendor may be able to force such a title on the purchaser in the case of leasehold land because of the difficulties of the operation of the doctrine of adverse possession in such circumstances.[10]

Doubtful title

2.14 Where there is uncertainty concerning the title it is a matter of construction for a court to decide whether the title is so doubtful that it would be unfair to force it on the purchaser.

Bad title

2.15 Where the problem is so obvious that a court will have no difficulty in holding that the title is clearly bad, the vendor has failed in his duty to deduce title and it will not be forced on a purchaser even if he has signed the contract.

For example, the question arose in *Mulholland* v *Corporation of Belfast*[11] where the lessor had a right of re-entry for breach of covenant in a lease, which meant that the sub-lessee might be evicted without any breach of covenant on his part. Another illustration is *Boyd* v *Dickson*[12] where the vendor had bought the property on behalf of one of the trustees of the property which was in breach of the trust and consequently could not force the title on the purchaser because it was really no title at all.

Matters of conveyance

2.16 A matter of conveyance is a matter with which the vendor can deal immediately and does not require the co-operation of any third party. For example, discharge of a mortgage. It is quite distinct from a defect in title. When a purchaser discovers a defect in title he can raise objections immediately and resist specific performance; whereas if he finds a discrepancy in the title which is a matter of conveyance, the vendor has until completion to rectify it.

---

[10] See Adverse Possession paras 23.01-23.08.
[11] (1859) Dru temp Nap 539.
[12] (1867) IR 10 Eq 239.

Length of title to be deduced

2.17 Under the Vendor and Purchaser Act 1874, section 1, the vendor must trace the title back for a period of 40 years.[13] However if a good root of title is not shown when 40 years title is deduced, it must be traced back further until one is reached.

The statutory period can be reduced by contrary provision in the contract specifying a more recent deed as a root of title (GCS 8.1). A shorter period is generally acceptable if superior title can be furnished because this traces the title back for a further period. However, a purchaser must remember that if a problem is discovered in the superior title after the contract has been signed it will be extremely difficult to raise requisitions or objections.

In practice there are occasions, if the circumstances allow, when a shorter period may be accepted without superior title. In such a case the purchaser takes a risk that he will be fixed with constructive notice of all interests which would have been discovered from the earlier documents.

Root of title

2.18 The conveyance or other document with which the title commences is called the root of title. In order to be a good root, the document specified as being the commencement of the vendor's title should:

(1) Deal with the whole legal and equitable estate in the property sold. For example, on the sale of the freehold, a lease is not a good root; on the sale of the legal estate, a transfer of the equity of redemption is not a good root.

(2) Contain a description identifying the property.

(3) Not depend for its validity on any other document. For example, a document exercising a power of appointment is not a good root because it depends for its validity on the instrument creating the power.

A satisfactory root of title is normally a conveyance or fee farm grant for a freehold estate and a lease for over 21 years for a leasehold estate. A will or assignment is not usually acceptable. Traditionally a fee farm conversion grant was not acceptable either, but as any such document is now over a century old, there is little justification for continuing objections.

In the absence of any contrary provision in the contract, under the Vendor and Purchaser Act 1874 and the Conveyancing Act 1881, a purchaser is not generally entitled to call for title prior to the lease under which the property is sold. However, the purchaser will be fixed with constructive notice of the content of the superior title. This is reflected in GCS 8.2 with the modification that this condition provides that where the property is held under a fee farm grant or a lease for a term over 21 years which is less than 12 years old, the

---

[13] Final Report of the Land Law Working Group para 2.5.14 recommends reduction to 20 years.

vendor shall deduce title to the lessor's estate for at least another 12 years before that. If the GCS are not used, any root must be at least 40 years old.

There is a risk in accepting a root of insufficient age in that there may be pre-existing third-party rights, exceptions, reservations or burdens, of which there is no evidence in the document furnished but which nevertheless continue to affect the land.

Unless there has been a division of the property, the original root should be with the title deeds, but the purchaser cannot insist on having original deeds prior to completion.

Pre-root title

2.19 By the Conveyancing Act 1881, section 3(3) and GCS 8.1, provided that the root of title specified in the contract is a suitable document of proper age, the purchaser cannot require production of any documents prior to it nor raise any enquiries and objections to prior title. If the purchaser has accepted a specified document as a root of title then, under GCS 8.1, the age and character of the document are not relevant.

This means that the document specified in the special conditions as being the commencement of title shall be conclusively accepted as such. However until he signs the contract the purchaser can insist on any title he likes.

Presumably the root specified need not be a good root, provided the purchaser is prepared to accept it. However the vendor must take care not to mislead the purchaser especially when he is seeking to reduce the length of title to which the purchaser would otherwise be entitled under an open contract.

A purchaser is not bound to complete in any case where specific performance would not be granted by a court and the title is so bad or doubtful that it could not be forced on him. In theory, under an open contract it can be argued that the purchaser may still produce evidence obtained from other sources to show that the pre-root title is defective, but it is arguable that GCS 8.1 precludes this too.

The fundamental principle is that the vendor must show good title and this duty cannot be circumscribed by rules defining the manner of proof. The purchaser may object if latent defects in title come to light about which the vendor knew or ought to have known.

Fee farm grants and leases

2.20 Under an open contract for the sale of property there are particular statutory provisions relating to the deduction of title in leasehold transactions.

The statutory provisions are as undernoted.

Vendor and Purchaser Act 1874, section 2

2.21 Where the contract relates to a grant or assignment of a term of years the intended lessee or assignee is not entitled to call for the title to the freehold.

This applies to:

(1) the grant of a lease by a freeholder;
(2) the assignment of such a lease;
(3) the grant of a sub-lease out of such a lease;
(4) the assignment of such a sub-lease.

Conveyancing Act 1881, section 3(1)
2.22 On a contract to sell and assign a term of years derived out of a lease of land, the intended assignee does not have the right to call for the title to the leasehold reversion.

Conveyancing Act 1881, section 13(1)
2.23 On a contract to grant a term of years out of a leasehold interest with a leasehold reversion, the intended lessee does not have the right to call for the title to the reversion.

Prior to the implementation of the above statutory provisions, the position at common law allowed a purchaser of leasehold property to call for the lessor's title. The vendor could seek to preclude this by an express provision in the contract.

Under an open contract after the passing of the legislation the purchaser is fixed with constructive notice of all matters which he would have discovered by investigating the title he is allowed to see and of all matters he would have discovered by investigating the superior title which the statutory provisions preclude him from investigating.[14]

Consequently by failing to investigate the superior title, the purchaser runs a risk of being affected by matters such as restrictive covenants relating to the freehold interest or a superior leasehold interest of which he is not aware.

For his own protection a purchaser should not leave the contract open. He should modify the effect of the statutory provisions by insisting that the vendor deduce the relevant superior title. This includes the title to the freehold and, in cases of sales of sub-leases, the intermediate title as well. The purchaser should not allow the vendor to restrict his duty by any contractual provision.

Modification by contract
2.24 The position of the parties under the general law relating to the deduction of title is modified by the following provisions of the GCS:

(a) GCS 8.1
The document specified as the root of title is conclusively accepted as such and the purchaser may not require production of any title prior to the root. The purchaser may even be precluded from showing that the pre-root title is defective, by use of information gained elsewhere.

---

[14] *Patman v Harland* (1881) 17 Ch D 353.

This condition may be too restrictive and does not relieve the vendor of the obligation to warn the purchaser of any defect in title of which he is aware arising before the root of title.

(b) GCS 8.3(a)

The purchaser is taken to have notice of the contents of the lease or grant under which the vendor holds the property if he furnishes a copy of it prior to the contract and also of the covenants and conditions in all superior leases and grants.

(c) GCS 4.2(b), (c) and (d)

Without prejudice to the vendor's duty of disclosure, the property is sold subject to all rights affecting it, the purchaser is not to acquire any rights or easements restricting the use of the vendor's adjoining land and the purchaser indemnifies the vendor against all claims arising in respect of any matter contained in any deed or document a copy of which has been furnished to the purchaser prior to contract.

Further limitation by special conditions

2.25 The vendor may attempt to further limit his duty to deduce title by inserting special conditions in the contract restricting or preventing objections or requisitions being raised by the purchaser.[15]

However, he must give warning of the existence of any latent defect of which he is aware and not make any misrepresentation or deliberately mislead the purchaser.

At the same time, the purchaser may not wish to accept the position under the GCS which fixes him with constructive notice of all matters in the superior title which might affect him. He may insert special conditions in the contract amending the vendor's duty to deduce title.

It may be relevant in each case to consider the provisions of the GCS limiting the vendor's duty of disclosure and modifying the general principles. In practice a purchaser may wish to proceed with the transaction despite a defect in title. He is entitled to insist on strict proof of marketable title but may choose to accept such evidence as the vendor can reasonably provide rather than abandon the purchase.

---

[15] Statutory provisions may restrict, to an extent, the conditions which can be included. For example, the Solicitors (NI) Order 1976, art 70, as amended by the Solicitors (Amendment) (NI) Order 1989, art 71(b)(i), prohibits any arrangement for the purchaser to pay the vendor's costs, including outlays; the Stamp Act 1891, s 117, prevents a purchaser from objecting to title on the ground of insufficient stamping; the Commission on Sales of Land Act 1972, s 1(1), makes any agreement for the purchaser to pay the vendor's agents' fees void.

Construction of contractual provisions

2.26 Where misconduct or lack of fairness is suspected or there is a doubt that the purchaser will obtain a good title, a court may refuse to grant specific performance to the vendor. If the vendor is aware of a defect in title there is a limit to the extent which he can preclude all investigation by the addition of restrictive special conditions.

The vendor may restrict his liability under the general law to some degree but must not frame any condition deliberately to mislead or cheat the purchaser. A condition construed against the vendor is not enforccable and the purchaser has a good defence to an action for specific performance of the contract.

CHAPTER THREE

CONTRACT

Introduction

3.01 The contract stage is a very important part of the conveyancing process. A contract to sell or make any other disposition of land is made in the same way as any other contract and must comply with the general principles of the law of contract. As soon as there is an agreement for valuable consideration between the parties on definite terms there is a contract, whether the agreement was made orally or in writing. However, it is important that any contract relating to land complies with the statutory requirements as to written evidence. If it is not it will be unenforceable by action, unless the requirements of equity as to part performance have been satisfied.

FORMATION OF THE CONTRACT

Essential elements

3.02 In accordance with the general law of contract, conveyancing contracts must include:

   (1) An intention to create legal relations;
   (2) Offer and acceptance;
   (3) Consideration;
   (4) Certainty of terms.

For any type of contract to exist there must be a final and complete agreement between the parties as to the terms. Provided the parties intend to enter a legally enforceable contract and there is agreement upon the essential terms made for valuable consideration, a contract is made. The terms agreed must be sufficiently certain to be enforced by the court.

Statute of Frauds (Ir)1695, section 2

3.03 The only special requirement in relation to the sale of land is the requirement that the contract be evidenced in writing. Section 2 does not state that the actual contract has to be in writing but that there must be written evidence of it in the form of a memorandum or note.

Section 2 requires written evidence only to render the contract enforceable by action. A purely oral agreement relating to land which complies with the general law of contract is a perfectly valid contract. Such an oral contract may be enforced in any way other than by proceedings. If one party defaults on the contract, the other can recover or forfeit the deposit. It is even possible to enforce an oral contract by an action as long as the defendant does not plead the Statute of Frauds as a defence.

Section 2 applies to all contracts for sale of land including sales of freehold and leasehold interests, surrender of leases, mortgages, grants of easements and profits.

Written memorandum or note

3.04 This must include the essential terms of the contract of which it is evidence; that is, sufficient information to identify:

(1) The parties;

(2) The property;

(3) The consideration;

(4) Any other essential provisions regarded as important by the parties;

(5) The term and date of commencement of the lease, if a new lease is to be granted.

The writing does not need to be in a particular form but must be signed. Section 2 does not require the signature of both parties, but only of the one who becomes the defendant in any action to enforce the contract, or of some other person authorised by him.

Anyone signing for either of the parties should be lawfully authorised to do so, either orally or in writing. In the absence of express authorisation, it is a question of construction whether the agent has authority to sign a memorandum and implied authority may arise from the circumstances of the case, as where a husband stands by and lets his wife sign.

The memorandum or note can be made up of more than one document if it can be established that the documents are so connected that they can be joined to constitute a memorandum or note; for example, by correspondence. Where each document is obviously connected and is signed by the party to be charged there is no difficulty in establishing a memorandum or note.

Where only one of the documents is signed by the party to be charged, it can be connected only with other documents referred to in it, either expressly or impliedly. Unsigned documents cannot be joined with signed documents except by establishing such a cross-reference. This means that an unsigned document cannot be joined with a signed one unless it precedes the signed document and is either expressly or impliedly referred to in it.

A connection between documents cannot be established by parol evidence but if the connection can be established by other means, parol evidence is admissible to explain the documents. It is usually easier to connect letters, draft contracts, draft agreements, receipts or loan applications together than to connect advertisements or catalogues with any other documents because of the lack of a signature and the difficulty in finding a cross-reference.

Where a contract which complies with the statutory requirements is subsequently varied by oral agreement the variation is not enforceable and cannot be given as an answer by a defendant in proceedings to enforce the original agreement. Specific performance can only be given for the contract as originally written.

Part performance

3.05 It became apparent that the Statute of Frauds (Ir) 1695 was as likely to facilitate fraud as to prevent it because it enabled a party to renege on a firm oral agreement which was not committed to writing. The courts realised that a strict interpretation of section 2 was tantamount to allowing the Statute of Frauds to be used as an instrument of fraud and devised the doctrine of part performance as a counter-balance.

Part performance is an equitable doctrine and may well be confined to cases involving actions for specific performance.[16] It is usually pleaded by the plaintiff to counter a defence, based on the Statute of Frauds, raised by the defendant in an action for specific performance of an oral agreement.

Under the doctrine of part performance an oral contract may be enforced in specific circumstances where the absence of written evidence would be a means of effecting a fraud. The defendant is charged upon the equities which arise from the acts of part performance in which he has acquiesced, so that his conscience is affected in the eyes of equity and a court will not allow him to plead the Statute of Frauds as a defence.

For the plaintiff to succeed the acts of part performance on which he relies must have some reference to the alleged contract and be consistent with it. The acts do not have to be unequivocably referable only to the contract in question. It is sufficient for the plaintiff to establish on the balance of probabilities that it was more likely than not that the acts were performed in reliance on a contract with the defendant which was consistent with the contract alleged.

The traditional view of the operation of the doctrine is that if the acts of part performance prove that there must have been a contract, then the parol evidence as to the existence of the oral contract can be admitted. It is not for the court to look first at the evidence showing the existence of the oral contract and then see whether the acts of part performance are consistent with it.

It depends on the particular circumstances of each case whether or not a certain act is considered sufficient part performance to take the case outside the Statute of Frauds. There may be a single act which is sufficient or a series of acts which, taken together, substantiate the claim. In some cases there may be acts of part performance executed by both parties to the contract so as to render it enforceable by each against the other.

Possession

3.06 Taking possession is generally enough to establish part performance. However if, for example, the contract is for renewal of an existing lease, for the

---

[16] But in *Moritt* v *Wonham* [1993] NPC 2 a trust was imposed by order of the court rather than a decree of specific performance because it was the most viable form of remedy in the particular circumstances. This decision is controversial and may best be interpreted as resting on proprietary estoppel than part performance.

purchase of the reversion or if the purchaser takes possession as caretaker, continuing in possession is not usually enough in itself. There must be some additional act consistent with the new agreement and not explicable merely as a continuance of the position under the existing agreement, such as payment and acceptance of an increased or reduced rent as specified in the new agreement.

Expenditure

3.07 Expenditure incurred in respect of making alterations or improvements to the property has been found in several cases to be a sufficient act of part performance. Taking possession often accompanies the work and this strengthens the plaintiff's claim. However, a tenant who continues in possession under a pre-existing arrangement and makes improvements in the ordinary course of events may not be able to establish sufficient acts.

Money

3.08 Payment of money is not normally considered a sufficient act of part performance because it can be repaid and the parties can be restored to their original positions. It is also an equivocal act for which there may be other explanations. The payment may, for example, be a loan. Nevertheless, there may be cases where the payment of money becomes evidence of the contract and of its nature.

TYPES OF CONTRACT

Open contracts

3.09 An open contract is a contract where only certain terms have been expressly agreed leaving others to be implied by the general law. The simplest possible contract is where only the parties, the property and the price are specified. However there are so many matters which ought to be considered in a conveyancing transaction that it is generally inadvisable to sell land by open contract.

Informal contracts

3.10 A valid informal contract for the sale of land may come into existence through negotiations or correspondence, despite the intentions of the parties, as long as there is sufficient evidence of it to satisfy the Statute of Frauds (Ir) 1695, section 2. Any terms not included are open to implication under the general law.

The inadvertent creation of an informal contract can cause difficulties between parties who consider themselves to be in the early stages of negotiating an agreement, particularly when one party refuses to recognise the agreement. To avoid such a situation and prevent the contract being enforceable sooner than the parties intend, it is advisable to mark all correspondence during preliminary negotiations 'subject to contract'.

Another way of showing that the intention was not to form a binding agreement is to describe the intended transaction as the 'proposed sale' or the 'proposed purchase' and the parties as the 'prospective purchaser' and 'prospective vendor'. Additionally, the heading of any correspondence can be set out with the names of the parties given separately as 'your client' and 'our client' one above the other rather than as 'vendor' - to - 'purchaser'. Any reference to the intended agreement can also be suitably phrased in inconclusive terms so that, on a question of construction, there should be evidence that the final agreement had not been reached.

In complete contrast to the situation where the parties are trying to ensure that correspondence over a period of time does not constitute a binding contract, there may be situations where the parties may wish to make an immediate and unconditional agreement by which they are bound within its terms at once. This is not uncommon and generally happens at sales by auction. It may also arise where the vendor is anxious to have a purchaser totally committed within a very short space of time and has more than one interested party.

Most auction sales are expressly held under and covered by the GCS. By bidding at such an auction a purchaser appoints the auctioneer as his agent to enter the contract on his behalf and cannot withdraw that authority after the fall of the hammer. Similarly, the vendor appoints the auctioneer as his agent and cannot withdraw it once the bidding has passed the reserve price.

Conditional contracts

3.11 Contracts are frequently signed conditionally to commit the purchaser or vendor to an agreement and prevent him from changing his mind, but allowing him to withdraw in the circumstances specified in the condition.

The effect of the condition is a matter of construction in each case. A condition precedent must be satisfied before a contract becomes binding; a condition subsequent causes an existing contract to cease to be binding. Any such clause should be drafted carefully to ensure that it operates as intended and is not void for uncertainty.

For example, if a contract is made subject to the purchaser obtaining planning permission, it should be made clear whether the condition will be satisfied by the grant of outline permission or whether full detailed permission is necessary. The purchaser should also consider whether he intends that a grant of permission subject to conditions be sufficient to fulfil the contractual condition.

Options

3.12 The grant of an option to buy land gives the option holder the right to require the grantor to transfer the land to him, provided the option holder complies with the terms of the option.

There is some dispute as to whether an option is an irrevocable offer or a conditional contract. The differences may have been resolved by Hoffman J's judgment in *Spiro v Glencrown Properties Ltd*.[17] Following that case an option to buy land can be characterised as a unique type of contract coming into existence at the time of its grant. Although there are potentially two stages,

---

[17] [1991] Ch 537.

namely grant and exercise, there is but one contract. That one contract is neither an irrevocable offer nor a conditional contract, though it has elements of both.

The creation of an option is governed by ordinary contractual principles. To be enforceable, an option must be either granted by deed, or evidenced in writing for the purposes of the Statute of Frauds (Ir) 1695, or supported by consideration moving from grantee to grantor. A nominal amount suffices.

The grantor is bound by the option to the extent that he may not dispose of the land to deprive the grantee of his right to exercise it.

The grant of an option confers an equitable interest on the grantee.[18] In the case of unregistered land the option can be registered in the Registry of Deeds to protect the priority of any proprietary rights arising from its exercise. In the case of registered land it can possibly be registered in the Land Registry as a burden to establish priority for the right to exercise the option which is then transferred with the beneficial interest if and when it occurs.

The option agreement should specifically fix the price payable upon its exercise or set out how it is to be determined by reference to a prescribed formula as long as such formula imposes a legal obligation on the grantor to co-operate and the criteria to be applied are sufficiently certain. The option agreement must not transgress the rule against perpetuities.

Formal contracts

3.13 A formal contract is usually created by the parties' solicitors in conveyancing transactions and all the terms of the agreement are explicitly set out. It is normally intended that there be no binding agreement until the contract is signed by both parties and the acceptance has been communicated to the party making the offer.

In the event of a dispute, it is possible that the contract may be seen as a completed contract at an earlier stage of the process or that the purchaser may be bound by an agreement when the vendor is not.

The purchaser's signature alone may be sufficient to bind him if the court decides that an oral agreement has been concluded of which the signed contract is written evidence. Once the purchaser has signed there may be sufficient memorandum to bind him although the vendor is not yet bound because he has not signed.

Alternatively, it may be that when the contract has been signed by the purchaser, it can be considered as his offer to purchase and to bind him as soon as the vendor communicates acceptance, even if the vendor has not signed it. Again, the contract binds the vendor only when he actually signs.

GCS 5.1 provides that the contract shall be formed upon receipt by the purchaser or his solicitor of a copy of the purchaser's offer as accepted by the

---

[18] *Armstrong and Holmes Ltd* v *Holmes and another* [1994] 1 All ER 826.

vendor which puts it beyond doubt that the contract is only formed when the vendor returns a copy of it to the purchaser.

There are some cases where a formal contract may not be considered necessary. For example, where the consideration is small, the transaction is between members of the same family, or there is a short-term lease.

CONTENTS OF THE CONTRACT

3.14 Although the contents of a contract for the sale of land are largely a matter for the parties to determine, as in any contract, it has long been recognised that it is essential to have a formal contract containing much more than the basic requirements of the Statute of Frauds (Ir) 1695.[19]

Until late 1994 the formal agreement used in most domestic transactions was a standard contract prepared by the Law Society of Northern Ireland which consisted of two separate documents. One comprised the General Conditions of Sale (2nd edition) and the other contained the particulars and conditions of sale, the special conditions and the memorandum of sale. The latter was specific to the particular transaction in hand.

The formal contract now commonly used in domestic conveyancing is one document which contains three principal parts: the memorandum of sale, the General Conditions of Sale (3rd Edition Revised) and the special conditions.

Memorandum of sale

3.15 A memorandum of a contract is a note of the particulars of a transaction. No precise form of memorandum is required by the Statute of Frauds (Ir) 1695 but it must contain all the essential elements of the contract (price, parties, property and any other essential provisions) and be a memorandum of the contract.[20]

If this information is contained in the body of the contract a separate memorandum is not necessary. The standard Law Society of NI contract employs a separate memorandum containing:

- a description of the property;
- the parties;
- the agreed price;
- deposit;
- price for furnishings etc;
- date for completion;
- loan details;
- capacity of vendor;
- signatures.

---

[19] Cf paras 3.02-3.04.
[20] *Ibid.*

The remaining essential terms are contained within the GCS and, if appropriate in the special conditions.

Particulars of sale

3.16 The particulars describe the subject matter of the contract. A legal description and a physical description of the property must be included.

Legal description

3.17 The legal description of the property must indicate the estate or interest being sold and the title under which it is held. Thus the vendor should state whether the title is freehold or leasehold. If it is leasehold he should provide brief details of the lease. If the title is registered in the Land Registry the folio number should be provided.

The particulars should also indicate any benefits and burdens attaching to the land. The vendor must take care to include all material facts and avoid a misdescription amounting to a breach of contract.

Physical description

3.18 The physical description must identify the property with certainty. Accordingly the vendor should clearly state its address and location. He may also make reference to a description in a deed.

A map is not usually referred to and included in the particulars unless the circumstances demand that it should be, as where only part of the vendor's property is being sold. In many cases there is already a suitable map in the title deeds which sufficiently delineates the property and does not have to be reproduced.

GCS 12.1 provides that the vendor is responsible for identifying the property with sufficient accuracy as to measurements and quantities to inform the purchaser of what he is proposing to sell. The vendor may describe the property by reference to the title deeds. If he elects to do so by reference to a map this should be prepared at his own expense.

GCS 13.1 states that measurements and quantities, if substantially correct, shall not be the subject of compensation, nor shall any compensation be paid in respect of any mistake in a sale plan furnished for the purpose of identity. However an incorrect statement, error or omission, whether as to

measurements, quantities or otherwise, materially affecting the description of the property may entitle the purchaser to compensation.[21]

Conditions of sale

3.19 The conditions are essentially the terms on which the property is sold. The general conditions are in the standard form which is part of the Law

---

[21] Cf Misdescription paras 4.02-4.08 and GCS 13.

Society of NI printed contract. There is provision for special conditions to be included if required in each particular case, either adding to or varying the general conditions. By virtue of GCS 1.1, in the event of any conflict between general and special conditions, the special conditions prevail.

The courts have recognised that it is invariably the vendor or his solicitor who draws up the conditions of sale. When a question of interpretation arises, the conditions are usually construed against the vendor in favour of the purchaser.

THE DEPOSIT

3.20 Payment of a deposit on entering into a contract for the sale of land is generally regarded as an important part of the transaction. Not only is the deposit a payment towards the purchase price, but it is also regarded as security for the performance of the agreement by the purchaser. If the purchaser defaults on the contract, the vendor can forfeit the deposit.

When the deposit is paid to a third party, for example, the vendor's solicitor, it may be held by him either as agent for the vendor or as stakeholder. The vendor is responsible to the purchaser if the deposit is lost, regardless of the capacity in which it was held by his solicitor.

Contractual provision is normally made for payment of the deposit. GCS 5.2 provides that the purchaser shall pay such deposit as may have been agreed to the solicitor for the vendor who shall hold the same as agent for the vendor. Accordingly, as his agent, the vendor's solicitor is liable to pay the deposit to the vendor on demand and to account to the vendor for any interest earned on it.

If the sale does not proceed, the purchaser can sue only the vendor and not his agent to recover the deposit. The advantage for the vendor is that he can demand the deposit immediately and use it, for example, for the purchase of another house. The advantage for the purchaser is that he has a lien on the vendor's land for the return of the deposit.

On the other hand, in a case where the contract provides that the vendor's solicitor holds the deposit as a stakeholder, he is personally responsible for its safekeeping and must not hand it over to the vendor without the purchaser's permission. In this respect he is agent for both parties, obliged to hold on the deposit until the vendor becomes entitled to it on completion. He does not have to account for any interest due.

Although the purchaser is not obliged to pay a deposit at the pre-contract stage, he may be put under pressure to do so as a gesture of good faith. Where an estate agent is acting in the sale of a new development, a booking fee, which is in reality a deposit, is generally required to secure a site. One of the reasons for this is that the vendor is responsible for paying the agent's fees and the booking fee is a means of obtaining payment without having to wait until completion to receive it from the vendor.

There is no direct sanction against such a practice but the engagement of an estate agent by a vendor does not confer on the agent any implied authority to receive as agent of the vendor a pre-contract deposit from a prospective purchaser. In the absence of any express authority from the vendor the purchaser is at all times, until the contract is entered into, the only person with any claim or right to the deposit and this is a right on demand. It is inadvisable to pay any money direct to the vendor because of the risk that he might disappear with it or become insolvent. If a vendor is adjudicated bankrupt the purchaser is an unsecured creditor with little prospect of recovering his deposit.

Where the vendor is a builder covered by the NHBC scheme[22] the purchaser is protected against the vendor's insolvency provided that the Buildmark cover is operative at the time of payment. Unfortunately it is unlikely that any such cover would be in place at the stage at which a booking fee is demanded.

If for any reason the purchase falls through before a formal contract is signed the question may arise as to whether the vendor may keep the pre-contract deposit. The answer may depend on the terms on which the money was paid.

If there is a written note setting out the circumstances in which it is returnable, then that should be followed. In certain circumstances it may also be argued that a written note constitutes a memorandum sufficient for the Statute of Frauds (Ir) 1695[23] which therefore applies. Where there is nothing in writing the purchaser may possibly have a better chance of his money being returned because the vendor is less likely to be able to justify keeping it.

---

[22] See paras 13.01-13.16.
[23] See paras 3.03-3.04.

CHAPTER FOUR

MISDESCRIPTION, MISREPRESENTATION AND MISTAKE

Introduction

4.01 Misunderstandings can arise between the parties in a number of ways. For the purchaser to invoke a legal remedy he must be able to show that he has entered into a contract to buy or has bought property which is not exactly that which he thought he was purchasing. In practical terms the defect, whatever its nature, must be significant and must have resulted in sufficient loss to the purchaser to justify him seeking to remedy the situation. The problems caused by misdescription, misrepresentation and mistake are considered in this chapter.

MISDESCRIPTION

4.02 Misdescription occurs in the contract and must be a statement of fact, not of law or opinion. It is an inaccuracy on the part of the vendor in either the legal or physical description in the particulars of sale. Misdescription amounts to a breach of contract.

Legal description

4.03 The legal description in the particulars of sale must indicate the title being transferred by describing the tenure together with the benefits and burdens attaching to the property. As well as being a misrepresentation, failure to disclose material facts may be a breach of the vendor's duty of disclosure.[24] If the legal description is not limited, the general law implies that the vendor is contracting to sell the fee simple free from encumbrances.

Physical description

4.04 The physical description in the particulars of sale should describe the property with sufficient accuracy as to inform the purchaser of what the vendor is proposing to sell. It is not necessary to define the exact boundaries, but it is unlikely that the vendor will be able to enforce the contract if the property in sale is not satisfactorily identified.

Fraudulent misdescription

4.05 A misdescription made by the vendor knowing that it is false is a fraud. Fraud entitles the purchaser to rescind the contract, demand the return of his deposit and seek damages for breach of contract.

---

[24] This failure may be remedied by the fact that title deeds have already been furnished.

Innocent misdescription

4.06 Where the misdescription is not fraudulent, the purchaser's remedies depend on whether or not it is substantial.

Substantial misdescription

4.07 A substantial misdescription results where the purchaser did not actually acquire that which he was led to believe he was purchasing, nor what he was contractually entitled to have, either physically or in relation to the title. In such a case, the purchaser is entitled to specific performance of the contract subject to a price reduction, or to rescission of the contract. The vendor cannot enforce the contract even on the basis of an abatement of the purchase price.[25]

If a substantial misdescription has been made GCS 13 allows either the vendor or the purchaser to resist specific performance of the contract, but only if the relevant party can show that he has been prejudiced by the misdescription.

Insubstantial misdescription

4.08 Where the misdescription is insubstantial the purchaser still acquires that which he was led to believe he was to have and that to which he was entitled under the contract, despite the misdescription. The vendor may enforce the contract but the purchaser is entitled to a price reduction. The purchaser may also obtain specific performance subject to such a reduction.

GCS 13 modifies the position under the general law. It deprives the purchaser of the right to compensation for insubstantial errors. The condition also distinguishes between material and substantial misdescriptions, although these are interchangeable in case law. If a misdescription is material but not substantial, it does not annul the sale but entitles the aggrieved party to a reduction in price.

At common law if there is an insubstantial misdescription from which the purchaser benefits, the vendor is not entitled to any compensation. This principle is modified by GCS 13 which extends the right to a reduction in price to the vendor where the misdescription means that the purchaser will get more than that for which he originally bargained.

MISREPRESENTATION

4.09 A misrepresentation is a statement or conduct which conveys a false or wrong impression. It takes place outside the contract, rather than in it and usually occurs prior to the contract. To obtain relief the purchaser must be able to establish that the vendor made a misrepresentation of fact and not of law or opinion. He must also be able to establish that the misrepresentation induced him to enter the contract.

---

[25] The same remedies are available when the vendor fails to disclose a substantial latent defect in title.

Fraudulent misrepresentation

4.10 A fraudulent misrepresentation is one made with knowledge of its falsehood and intended to deceive. A fraudulent misrepresentation of fact made by or on behalf of the vendor inducing the purchaser to enter into the contract entitles the purchaser to rescind the contract before completion.

Damages are available as of right for a misrepresentation which has resulted in loss unless the defendant can prove that he believed and had reasonable grounds to believe that the information he supplied was accurate.

If the fraud is not discovered until after completion, the purchaser may apply to have the transaction set aside or may seek damages on the basis of the difference between what he was induced to pay for the property and what it was actually worth at the date of the contract. The purchaser may also sue in tort for damages for deceit.

The Misrepresentation Act (NI) 1967, section 2(1), places the burden of proving reasonable grounds for belief in the truth of the representation on the defendant, so that the onus of proof is shifted to the vendor. The vendor must prove that he believed and that he had reasonable grounds to believe that the information which he supplied was accurate.

Innocent misrepresentation

4.11 An innocent misrepresentation is one made with reasonable grounds for believing it to be true, as where an honest mistake is made. Prior to the Misrepresentation Act (NI) 1967 a purchaser's remedies for innocent misrepresentation were very limited.

If the misrepresentation induced the purchaser to enter into the contract, he could seek rescission in equity, provided that completion had not actually occurred. There was no right to damages unless the representation became a term of the contract. In many cases this was effectively a misdescription. It may alternatively have been a collateral warranty and consequently a separate but subordinate contract.

The Misrepresentation Act (NI) 1967 widens the scope for action on an innocent misrepresentation. Section 1 allows the purchaser to rescind for an innocent misrepresentation made at the pre-contract stage if the misrepresentation has become a term of the contract or the contract has been completed.

To obtain rescission it is still necessary to prove that the misrepresentation was one of fact and either that it induced the purchaser to enter the contract, or the purchaser was relying on the misrepresentation, for example, a representation that the premises were suitable for a certain purpose. In general, a representation by an agent is regarded as a representation by his principal.

There is a discretion under section 2(2) to award damages in lieu of rescission for an innocent misrepresentation where it is equitable to do so having regard to the nature of the misrepresentation and the loss which it would cause if the contract were upheld, as well as to the loss that rescission would cause to the other party if the contract were not enforced.[26] The amount of damages is likely to be assessed to represent the difference between the value of the land as it stood and the value which it would have had if the representation had been true.[27]

Under section 3 any provision in an agreement purporting to exclude or restrict liability for a misrepresentation made before the contract or the remedies available by reason of the misrepresentation shall have no effect except to the extent that a court feels it was fair and reasonable. It is very difficult to exclude liability for misrepresentation and an exclusion clause attached to replies to enquiries before contract may not be considered to be fair and reasonable.

Enquiries before contract

4.12 The object of the enquiries before contract is to elicit information about a wide range of matters which are of importance to the purchaser, but which the vendor might not otherwise give because of his limited duty of disclosure under the *caveat emptor* principle. The enquiries should, in theory, deal with matters other than title.

It is helpful for the purchaser to have this information at an early stage before he signs the contract because the replies may affect his decision whether or not to proceed. However it does impose a considerable burden on the vendor not to make any false representations or mislead the purchaser. If the vendor provides an inaccurate reply which induces a purchaser to enter into a contract the purchaser will normally be entitled to a remedy for misrepresentation.

The vendor's solicitor must take great care in framing the replies so that he does not make a misrepresentation, particularly where he cannot give a complete and categorical answer. He is placed in a difficult position because he may not have any information about many of the questions asked and the vendor himself may not be of much assistance. The replies should be qualified to ensure that no liability is incurred for inaccurate information unless the information is within the direct knowledge of the vendor.

Where the vendor has no direct knowledge of specific matters, such as easements affecting the property which do not appear on the title, he is expected to make such inquiries about the matter as could reasonably have been expected to be made under the guidance of a prudent conveyancer.[28]

---

[26] Wylie's *Irish Conveyancing Law* at para 6.71 suggests that the discretion to award damages in lieu of rescission is lost once completion has occurred.

[27] *Sindall* v *Cambridgeshire County Council* [1994] 3 All ER 932 (CA). The court went on to point out that where damages are awarded under s 2(1) of the 1967 Act for a misrepresentation not proved to have been reasonably believed by the representor to be true a different method of calculation is used. Subject to rules relating to remoteness of loss, all loss flowing therefrom is recoverable whether or not reasonably foreseeable by the representor. See also *Dodd* v *Crown Estate Commissioners* [1995] EGCS 35.

[28] *Ibid.*

In answering questions such as whether the property is affected by dry rot, wet rot, wood-boring insects, fungi, subsidence or other matters not immediately apparent from an inspection, the vendor's solicitor should suggest that the purchaser satisfy himself by obtaining a survey rather than give a negative answer in case there should be any undiscovered problems of that nature. Other enquiries, such as whether there are any proposals or proceedings affecting the property, may be too wide for a definitive reply and the reply should be phrased accordingly.

If an inaccurate reply is discovered before the purchaser enters into the contract he can withdraw from the purchase entirely or he can negotiate new terms. On the other hand, if the inaccuracy comes to light after the purchaser enters the contract, he may be able to take proceedings for misrepresentation.

Any rights which the purchaser has are usually against the vendor. Where the vendor's solicitor signs the replies to the enquiries before contract he does so as agent of the vendor. The vendor then may be able to recover against his solicitor for negligent answers to the questions on his behalf.

Generally speaking GCS 2 considerably widens the vendor's duties of disclosure to the purchaser. However, GCS 2.4 which limits the vendor's duty to some extent. It provides that the purchaser shall rely on the information contained in the property certificates and searches provided by the vendor and the vendor shall be exonerated from liability in respect of any statement or representation made by him either before or after the date of the contract or in the contract itself in respect of the matters covered by the certificates or searches notwithstanding that any such statement or representation shall be incomplete or inaccurate provided always that such statement or representation shall have been honestly made.

Negligent misstatement

4.13 It is theoretically possible that negligent misstatement is a basis of liability for inaccurate replies to pre-contract enquiries in accordance with the principles established in *Hedley Byrne & Co Ltd* v *Heller*.[29] It is considered unlikely that the duty of care can be extended to the relationship between the vendor's solicitor and the purchaser.[30] Such a duty may exist in the relationship between an estate agent and a purchaser and liability for negligent misstatement may arise in that case.[31] However, in many cases it will be difficult to establish such liability.

---

[29] [1964] AC 465.

[30] In *Gran Gelato Ltd* v *Richcliff (Group) Ltd* [1992] 1 All ER 865 it was held that a vendor's solicitor does not owe a duty of care to a purchaser in ordinary conveyancing transactions. A plea of contributory negligence is available in answer to a claim for misrepresentation under s 2 of the Misrepresentation Act 1967.

[31] *McCullough* v *Lane Fox & Partners* [1996] 18 EG 104.

Property Misdescriptions Act 1991

4.14 This statute was enacted to prevent estate agents and property developers from misleading prospective purchasers by creating a wrong impression of property. A criminal offence is committed where a false or misleading statement about any particular of the property is made in the course of an estate agency or property development business. The provision of conveyancing services is specifically excepted.

The statement can be oral, or in the form of a picture, drawing, or plan. It may be misleading because of an omission. It must be false to a material degree but the test is objective. It is not relevant that no-one has been misled by it. It is a defence to show that all reasonable steps were taken and all due diligence exercised to avoid infringing the statute.[32]

The provisions are strict and go some way towards alleviation of the problem of misstatement. Estate agents now have to be particularly careful not to make any statement about a property they cannot verify.

MISTAKE

4.15 A unilateral mistake does not have any legal effect. The mistake must be common to both parties for relief to be obtained at common law or in equity.

Common Law

4.16 At common law, if the mistake is sufficiently fundamental it renders the contract void. This obviously has consequences for third parties who take interests subsequent to the void agreement. However, because of the difficulty in compensating the purchaser without prejudicing third parties it may not be possible to remedy a mistake made by the vendor if it is discovered after completion.

The mistake must be so fundamental that it negatives consent to the extent that there was never any real agreement between the parties; for example, where unknown to both parties the subject matter has ceased to exist or the land is already owned by the purchaser.

Where a fundamental mistake has been made it is as if no contract ever came into existence. Although mistake is a ground for rescission, the contract in one sense cannot be rescinded if it never existed in the first place.

Equity

4.17 In some cases equity merely follows the law and holds the contract to be a nullity. In other instances, where there are lesser degrees of mistake which do not come within the common law definition, equity may intervene. Without holding that such agreements are void *ab initio*, as would be the case if they were mistakes at common law, equitable remedies may be available because a mistake has been made.

---

[32] See, *eg, Enfield Borough Council* v *Castle Estate Agents Ltd* [1996] EGCS 30.

Specific performance of an agreement may be refused to the vendor because of a mistake, thus forcing him to rely on any common law remedies available. Alternatively, rectification of a document may be ordered so that it accords with the true terms agreed between the parties.

Rescission is another equitable remedy available for mistake. Equity generally follows the law in the grounds for granting rescission on the basis of mistake but is not as strict in its requirements. The question is whether the facts of the case raise a sufficient equity to justify the court in making a decree for the rescission of the contract.

Types of mistake

Mistake as to subject-matter
4.18 This may arise where the vendor is mistakenly attempting to sell property to which he is not entitled, where unknown to either party the property has ceased to exist, or where it is already owned by the purchaser. It is likely to be so fundamental as to render the agreement void at common law.

Mistake as to identity
4.19 A mistake as to the identity of one of the parties is very difficult to establish. It only has effect at common law if it is held that personal considerations were fundamental to the formation of the contract. It is possible that a claim may be more successful in equity if personal considerations formed a material ingredient of the agreement, because equity is more willing to take account of personal attributes. For example, if the purchaser is insolvent equity may refuse specific performance to him if the vendor thought he was selling the property to someone else.

Mistake as to quality
4.20 At common law a mistake as to the quality of the subject-matter will only avoid the contract if it makes the actual subject matter essentially different from that which it was supposed to be. Such mistakes are rarely so fundamental as to be void at law, but equitable remedies may be available.

Mistake in contract
4.21 If the mistake actually finds its way into the contract, there may be a remedy for misdescription.

Post completion remedies

4.22 If a mistake is discovered after completion it is more difficult to remedy the situation. Relief is available where there is total failure of the subject matter which effectively means that the subject matter has ceased to exist or is already owned by the purchaser. For the claim to succeed the mistake must be so fundamental as to render the contract void *ab initio* and therefore any conveyance on foot of it ineffective.

Whether relief is available in respect of fundamental mistakes not resulting in total failure of consideration is less clear. Equity may set aside contracts on the basis of mistake but it is doubtful whether the jurisdiction extends to rescission after completion.[33]

One mistake which may be dealt with after completion is the execution of a document by a party under the mistaken impression that it was a document of a different kind. This is the defence of *non est factum* (it is not his deed). For the claim to succeed the mistake must go to the substance of the whole consideration or the root of the matter.

The relief afforded by this defence was originally intended to protect blind and illiterate people but, if the interests of justice so dictate, it may be extended beyond these narrow categories. The burden of proof of showing mistake lies with the claimant and is exceptionally difficult to discharge; negligence is insufficient and a considerable onus lies on anyone not suffering from a disability.

Rectification

4.23 If through some error in drafting, a written document fails to record accurately the terms of the true agreement, equity will rectify the document to make it accord with the intended agreement. To come within this principle there must have been a prior agreement or accord between the parties and it must have been intended to record all the terms of that agreement in writing.

Generally rectification is only available if the mistake was common to both parties and not if it was made by only one of them. However, rectification for unilateral mistake may be available where one party was mistaken and the other was acting fraudulently, or where one party realises that the document contains a mistake to his advantage but does nothing about it.[34]

If rectification is ordered by a court, the court order is usually endorsed on the deed. The original deed is read as if it had originally been drafted in its rectified form and it does not require fresh execution.

---

[33] *Solle* v *Butcher* [1950] 1 KB 671 suggests that it might, but it is not of persuasive authority.

[34] It has recently been suggested that the jurisdiction to grant rectification for unilateral mistake may be exercised when it would be unconscionable for one party to insist on performance of the strict letter of a contract by the other party if the latter was mistaken as to its effect when he entered into it, *Commission for the New Towns* v *Cooper (GB) Ltd* [1995] 2 All ER 929. Previously where a mistaken impression about the effect of an agreement was held by only one of the parties rescission was considered to be justified, but not rectification.

CHAPTER FIVE

SEARCHES AND PROPERTY CERTIFICATES

Introduction

5.01 There has been an extensive growth in the number of charges and interests affecting land which are not revealed by a traditional investigation of the title, nor by an inspection of the property but which affect successive owners. These relate to, for example, public health, housing, roads, building control and planning matters.

Such concerns do not necessarily affect the physical state of the premises, nor are they really latent defects in title, so there is no duty on the vendor under the general law to disclose them. They can only be discovered by obtaining property certificates and searches against the particular property. Since the introduction of the Home Charter Scheme in late 1994 it has become the responsibility of the vendor to obtain the property certificates and searches.

Where the GCS are used, a duty is imposed on the vendor by GCS 2.1(a) to disclose to the purchaser all matters of which he has or ought to have knowledge, which are registered with any competent authority pursuant to any statutory provision. This duty applies to *all* matters registered with any competent authority up until completion.

Under GCS 2.1(b) the vendor has a duty to disclose all matters of which he knows or ought to know which might reasonably be expected to be disclosed as a result of searches or enquiries which a prudent purchaser would make of any such competent authorities. The vendor's duty under GCS 2.1(b) applies only to the contract and can be discharged by the vendor replying to enquiries before contract and furnishing certain property certificates and searches.

In order to discharge this duty and to ensure that the relevant information is available to the purchaser as early as possible, the vendor is required to obtain the property certificates and searches at the commencement of the transaction.

In all cases, the vendor should furnish to the purchaser DOE and local authority property certificates. If the purchaser requires it, it is for him to obtain a NIHE property certificate, but in many cases this will also be provided by the vendor.

In addition the vendor should obtain a statutory charges search against the property and either a hand search in the Registry of Deeds against the vendor from the date he acquired the property to the date of supplying the search or a Land Registry folio search if appropriate.

Under the Home Charter Scheme the vendor's solicitor is obliged to furnish bankruptcy and enforcement searches against his client. The purchaser's solicitor is also responsible for obtaining the relevant searches against his client, particularly if the purchaser is obtaining a mortgage.

SEARCHES

5.02 It is essential to make searches as part of the investigation of title because of the risk that some other interest in the land may be registered prior to that of the purchaser which will enjoy priority over the purchaser.

Registry of Deeds searches

5.03 Each person appearing on the title should be searched against from the date of the accrual of his title to the date of registration of a conveyance by him which makes all subsequent deeds or documents by him ineffectual.

Searches made in the Registry of Deeds can be official or non-official. The official searches are made by the Registry and are either common searches or negative searches.

Common searches

5.04 A written request is made to the Registry for the search which is made by one clerk of the Registry and signed by an Assistant Registrar. It is not warranted.

Negative searches

5.05 A requisition is completed for the search required which is made by two clerks of the Registry. A certificate of search is issued, signed by the Registrar or the Assistant Registrar, setting out the acts appearing on the register for the period requested. The Registrar is liable for any damage caused by any error in the certificate as a result of fraud, collusion or negligence. A negative search can be kept open until the sale is complete.

Non-official searches

5.06 Any interested person can make a hand search in the books and indexes kept in the Registry of Deeds. On payment of the prescribed fee he is entitled to search the records and documents. He may also examine any original memorial.

A hand search is made at the discretion and risk of the person searching. The firms of law searchers which undertake the great majority of searches on behalf of solicitors have indemnity insurance to cover this eventuality.

Statutory Charges Register

5.07 The Statutory Charges Register Act (NI) 1951 established a central register of different matters affecting land which had previously been recorded in various places. The Act applies to both registered and unregistered land.

The statutory charges register shows registration of charges on land created by or in favour of government departments and public and local authorities under statutory provisions. These include a wide range of matters such as planning restrictions, notices relating to water and sewage, notices relating to roads, turbary regulations, ancient monument preservation orders and statutory conditions arising from home improvement grants.

Designated areas such as areas of special scientific interest and conservation areas should be registered. However, areas of outstanding natural beauty are regarded as being too large to be recorded in the statutory charges register.

Enforcement searches

5.08 All judgments can only be enforced through the Enforcement of Judgments Office (EJO) under the provisions of the Judgments Enforcement (NI) Order 1981, as amended. The EJO has jurisdiction to select the most appropriate method of enforcement of a judgment; for example, by making an order for seizure and sale of the debtor's goods or an order charging land. A purchaser of property need only be concerned about the possibility of the judgment being enforced by means of an order charging land.

An order charging land must be registered in the Land Registry or Registry of Deeds depending on whether the land is registered or unregistered. If it is not registered the charge on the land is not effective and the creditor cannot be repaid out of the sale proceeds.[35]

An enforcement search goes back for a period of six years. It shows judgments repaid in full, part payments received and those which remain outstanding.

When acting for a purchaser it is useful to be provided with an enforcement search against the vendor because it will give prior notice of any judgment which has the potential to be registered as an order charging land before registration of the purchase deed.

An enforcement search should also be made against the purchaser by his solicitor, to check if there are any judgments registered against him. Most lenders insist on this as part of the investigation of the financial status of the purchaser.

Bankruptcy searches

5.09 A search in the Bankruptcy Office in the High Court will reveal whether a bankruptcy petition has been issued against a particular person.

A clear bankruptcy search must also be obtained against the vendor. If a petition has been issued against him, a notice to that effect should be registered by the Official Receiver against his land in the Land Registry or Registry of Deeds as appropriate.

Where there is any doubt as to the solvency of the vendor it is in the interests of both parties to update the bankruptcy search against the vendor at the date of completion and avoid the possibility of the notice being registered before the purchase deed.

It is also essential that a bankruptcy search is obtained against a purchaser by his solicitor and most lenders insist on a clear bankruptcy search before issuing any loan.

---

[35] *NB* An order charging land ceases to have effect 12 years from the date of the judgment by virtue of the Judgments Enforcement (NI) Order 1981, art 47.

Company searches

5.10 Charges created by companies or existing on property acquired by companies must be registered with the Registrar of Companies within 21 days of their creation or the acquisition of the property under the Companies (NI) Order 1986, article 402.

A purchaser buying from a vendor company should make a search in the Companies Registry to check the position regarding loans. It may also be useful to see whether the company has filed up to date returns and to obtain a general impression from the file of the prosperity of the company.

Folio searches

5.11 When the title to the property is registered in the Land Registry the vendor should furnish a folio search. This follows an inspection of the folio in the Land Registry and reveals the name of the current registered owner, any charges registered and details of any transactions pending registration.

A person who has entered into a contract to purchase, take a lease of or lend money on the security of a charge on registered land can also apply for a priority search. On application the Land Registry issues a certificate of search stating that a priority entry has been made on the affected folio for that contract. If the transfer, lease or charge contemplated by the contract is delivered to the Land Registry within 40 days from the date of the certificate it will rank in priority before any other dealing presented for registration during that period.

PROPERTY CERTIFICATES

Department of the Environment

5.12 On the sale of a property, the vendor's solicitor must obtain a DOE property certificate. An application for a DOE property certificate is sent to the central processing unit in Enniskillen. Queries raised on the property certificate are divided into sections for reply by different branches of the DOE.

Roads Service

5.13 The DOE has general responsibility for public roads. A property owner requires confirmation that the road abutting the property is adopted and maintained at the public expense, or alternatively that adequate steps have been taken to ensure that there is no liability on him or a purchaser to meet the expenses of the construction of the road. If there is a rear entry he will also need confirmation as to its status, which is normally unadopted.

New roads

5.14 In the case of a new development, a purchaser needs to know that the roads on the estate leading to his property from the nearest highway maintainable at the public expense are adopted, or will be adopted, in due course, when the estate is completed or earlier if possible. If the roads have not been adopted it is important that a road bond has been obtained from the developer under the provisions of the Private Streets (NI) Order 1980.

The Private Streets (NI) Order 1980, article 24, provides that, where it is proposed to erect a building which will have a frontage on a private street, no building work shall be done until the DOE has received sufficient payment or satisfactory security for the street works from a person having an estate in the land.

Under article 32 the DOE may enter into an agreement under seal with any person to carry out street works in a private street. The developer usually enters into such an agreement with the DOE whereby he agrees to construct and complete the streets. The DOE undertakes to take over the roads when they are satisfactorily completed.

When the work is complete and the road has been maintained by the developer for at least 12 months in accordance with the agreement the DOE will issue a certificate to that effect. After approval the road becomes adopted as a public road maintainable at public expense.

The developer must secure the performance of the agreement under article 24 by way of a guarantee bond or other means acceptable to the DOE. The agreement and guarantee bond ensure that a developer completes the roads to a satisfactory standard without running out of money or disappearing.

Existing roads

5.15 If an existing road is not maintained by the DOE the question is whether it has been determined for adoption and if it has, whether a bond has been obtained from the developer. Where a road has recently been made up without a bond, it is possible that there may be outstanding charges in respect of road making or adoption of sewers affecting the property. The owners of the properties fronting the road are normally responsible for any such charges.

When a property is part of a development there is usually a covenant and indemnity by the developer to make up the roads to the required standard and to be responsible for any road charges. Otherwise the normal clause as to payment of outgoings by the purchaser may well render the purchaser liable to meet road charge expenses.

Where the property is on a private road, which has existed as such for some time, is unlikely that the DOE will make a decision that it should be made up and adopted, although it has power to do so. If anyone does, it is usually the frontagers who request the road be brought up to standard. The cost is generally prohibitive because the work has to be done at their expense.

Road works

5.16 Proposals for road works may affect the property. If so, there may also be proposals for compulsory acquisition of the property or part of it, whether the work is of a major nature, such as the building of a new road or more minor, such as road widening.

Water and sewerage

5.17 The Water Executive of the DOE has responsibility for public water and sewerage supplies and services.

Domestic water supplies are not metered because ratepayers contribute to a regional rate which includes an element for water and sewerage. Metered customers are mainly in the industrial, commercial and agricultural sectors. The cost of sewerage services is also included in the regional rate, except for trade effluent treatment and disposal costs which are recovered through trade effluent charges.

The Water Executive does not keep records of domestic households and therefore is often unable to answer the question as to whether a public sewer is available to serve the property. If a domestic property is not connected to a public sewer it is probably served by a septic tank.

It is essential to know whether the property is on the public water supply. Although most urban and suburban domestic properties are, some houses in rural areas are served by a spring or well. In order to make a mains connection where there is none, a connection fee has to be paid and the plumbing inspected by the DOE water service.

Water Act (NI) 1972, sections 7 and 8

5.18 Consents under sections 7 and 8 must be obtained from the DOE for the discharge of any trade or sewage effluent or any other poisonous, noxious or polluting matter. This includes domestic septic tank systems.

When a consent is required, an environmental health rivers officer sent out by the district council looks at the site. An application for consent is made and the council makes a recommendation to the DOE. If a consent is granted, it permits industrial or domestic discharges to waterways or underground strata, subject to specified conditions, such as type of construction. The discharge is regularly monitored to ensure these are met. Where a discharge would result in an unacceptable amount of pollution, consent is refused.

If an effluent system is operating without consent, the discharge is illegal. The DOE is unlikely to detect it unless there is a complaint or a rivers officer comes across it in his work in the area. The difficulty will only come to light on sale of the property. The problem may be solved by applying for a consent in the same way as for a new system, but there is a possibility that the effluent system already in place will not comply with the necessary standards.

Except for discharges from septic tanks serving single dwelling houses, all applications for consent are now advertised in local newspapers.[36] Some advertisements have resulted in large numbers of public representation but at present there is no power to hold a public enquiry.[37]

---

[36] Under the Water Act (NI) 1972, s 9(3).

[37] Water Act (NI) 1972 has been reviewed. The DOE is considering the introduction of more effective enforcement powers to prevent polluting material entering waterways, to control pollution from farms and from industry, and to improve public consultation procedures.

Water and Sewerage Services Order (NI) 1973, article 22

5.19 Consent from the DOE is required to the new discharge of trade effluent into sewers or sewage treatment works. This is unlikely to be of any relevance in relation to domestic property.

Planning Service

5.20 The Planning Service of the DOE deals with planning applications and has six divisional offices. Planning Service headquarters is responsible for overall co-ordination and policy.

The importance of enquiries relating to the planning position of a property are obvious. A prospective purchaser needs to know whether the property has been the subject of a planning application and that any work done complies with any permission granted. Such an enquiry may also reveal that work done has not been the subject of a planning application and is therefore illegal.

In rural areas planning permission may be granted subject to an occupancy condition.[38] This means that the dwelling for which planning permission has been granted can only be occupied by a person involved in agriculture or by a person retired from the farm. If such a condition is imposed, the property should not be purchased by anyone who does not so qualify.

If the DOE has served any notice or made any order or taken any action under the Planning (NI) Order 1991 in respect of the property other than matters registered in the Statutory Charges Register, this should be detailed in the reply to the property enquiry.

General

5.21 If the DOE has any proposals to acquire all or any part of the property for any of its statutory functions, details should be given in the property certificate. Details should also be provided of any notice or counter-notice served on or by the DOE under the Planning and Land Compensation Act (NI) 1971, the Planning Blight (Compensation) (NI) Order 1981 or the Planning (NI) Order 1991.

Blight notices apply where the landowner is affected by planning proposals and the land is blighted by inclusion in a development plan or scheme. Usually other property owners are similarly affected.[39]

Purchase notices apply where a property owner is affected by a planning decision. This may arise where an application by him for planning permission has been refused, or granted subject to adverse conditions or permission already granted has been revoked or modified.[40]

---

[38] See para 11.35.
[39] See Planning para 11.33.
[40] See Planning para 11.34.

Local District Council

5.22 On the sale of a property an application must be made by the vendor's solicitor for a council property certificate. Information is then supplied in the property certificate from records kept by the council and not usually from an inspection of the property.

Building control[41]

5.23 A query is raised as to whether any notice has been received by the council within the previous 10 years regarding the erection, alteration or extension of the property or any material change of use of any building on it. In the reply details are given of any application for approval. Details of any relaxation or breach of building regulations are also provided. Applications etc more than ten years prior to the property certificate are not disclosed.

The number and address of the property is confirmed.

Public health

5.24 The property certificate will give details of any notice served and not complied with, or the contemplation of the service of any notice under the Public Health and Towns Improvement legislation.

Environmental health

5.25 The property certificate will give details of any charges, notices, orders or certificates against the property either outstanding or being contemplated under Environmental Health legislation for which the council has a statutory responsibility.

It will also give details of any legal proceedings taken or contemplated against the property.

It will state whether any grant in respect of smoke control has been paid or is pending.

Compulsory acquisition

5.26 The council will disclose whether any vesting application has been made or is being considered in respect of the property.

Number and address

5.27 The council will confirm the number and address of the property.

Other

5.28 The council will state whether there are any charges, orders or notices against the property either outstanding or being contemplated, whether any licences have been issued or refused and whether any legal proceedings have

---

[41] See Building Control paras 12.01-12.24.

been taken or are contemplated under legislation listed in the appendix to the property certificate.[42]

Northern Ireland Housing Executive

5.29 On the sale of a property an application may be made to NIHE for a property certificate in answer to the question as to whether the premises are affected by any slum clearance or redevelopment proposals of the Executive. The reply will be negative unless a redevelopment area has been declared or is currently at the proposal stage pursuant to the provisions of the Housing (NI) Order 1981.

It is considered very unlikely that a property less than 20 years old will be affected by any NIHE proposals because planning permission would not have been granted for its construction if there were any such schemes. NIHE is proposing fewer schemes than it previously undertook and there is a trend for housing associations to do more housing redevelopment work.

---

[42] Local Government (Misc Provs) (NI) Order 1985, Petroleum (Consolidation) Act (NI) 1929, Cinemas (NI) Order 1991, Health and Safety at Work (NI) Order 1978, Dogs (NI) Order 1983, Betting, Gaming, Lotteries and Amusements (NI) Order 1985, Caravans Act (NI) 1963 and Access to the Countryside (NI) Order 1983.

CHAPTER SIX

TITLE: (1) REGISTRY OF DEEDS

Introduction

6.01 The Registry of Deeds and the Land Registry are the two systems of registration relating to land in Northern Ireland. The Registry of Deeds provides for the registration of documents dealing with land, whereas the Land Registry provides for the registration of the ownership of land.

The systems run parallel to each other and can both affect a single piece of land. For example, at one time it was possible to carve unregistered subsidiary interests out of a registered folio, with the result that the freehold was registered and the leasehold was not. Also, very occasionally the leasehold may be registered in the Land Registry while the freehold is not. The important point to remember is that the systems are mutually exclusive in relation to a particular estate in land.[43]

The two systems of registration co-exist side by side and will continue to do so until registration of title is made mandatory throughout Northern Ireland. There is no overlap between the systems because all dealings with registered land proceed through the Land Registry and with unregistered land through the Registry of Deeds.

UNREGISTERED LAND

6.02 In Ireland any title which is not registered in the Land Registry is governed by the registration of deeds system and is known as unregistered land. It is generally urban land because most rural land was bought out under the land purchase schemes and the title then registered in the Land Registry.

Registration of deeds is the older system. It was first introduced to make dealings with land a public matter and to protect purchasers from the uncertainty and fraud which could otherwise result. The Registry of Deeds was established in 1707 and the Belfast Registry opened on 1 April 1923. To make a search affecting a property prior to 1923, the registers in Dublin must be inspected.

The land to which the Registry of Deeds relates is unregistered because it is the deeds relating to the land which are registered and not the property itself. The Registry records the existence of any document registered but not its validity or accuracy.

Documents registrable

6.03 The system is now governed by the Registration of Deeds Act (NI) 1970 as amended by the Registration (Land and Deeds) Order (NI) 1992, the Family Homes and Domestic Violence (NI) Order 1998 and the Insolvency (NI) Order

---

[43] Cf Land Registry paras 7.01-7.46 for more detail.

1989. The Registration of Deeds Regulations (NI) 1997 (SR 1997/28) set out the procedures to be followed for registration of documents affecting land. All deeds and conveyances affecting land may be registered and there are some documents which must be registered, for example orders charging land.

A lease for a term not exceeding 21 years, where actual possession goes with the lease, is an exception and is not registrable, nor is an assignment of such a lease but a mortgage of it must be because in that case possession no longer goes with the lease.

Otherwise all deeds and conveyances affecting land, whether voluntary or for valuable consideration, legal or equitable, are within the Act. For the purpose of the Act "conveyance" includes any written document, whether under seal or not, which carries an interest in land from one person to another.

An equitable deposit of deeds without any written memorandum cannot be registered because there is nothing to register. On the other hand, if it is accompanied by a note, the written document can and should be registered.

Priorities

6.04 The primary function of the Registry of Deeds is to govern priorities between documents dealing with the same piece of land. Registration does not confer any additional force or validity on a document. Although there is no compulsion to register, failure to do so may result in loss of priority. This is particularly important in relation to mortgages. Consequently it is standard practice to register deeds and other documents relating to unregistered land.

Responsibility for registration

6.05 A deed may be registered by either party but it is normally the grantee who registers it because it is in his interest to do so. (In the event of the grantee's death, the document may be registered by his heirs, executors, administrators or assigns.) In the absence of any agreement to the contrary, the expense is also borne by the grantee.

Memorials

6.06 A document is registered by lodging the original together with a memorial of it in the Registry of Deeds. A memorial is an abstract of the material parts of the deed. The memorial should be in the form prescribed by the Registry of Deeds and must contain:

(1) The date;
(2) The names, descriptions and addresses of all the parties and witnesses to the document;
(3) Details of the land affected and its postal address.

Certificate of registration

6.07 When the document has been lodged, it is endorsed with a certificate of registration comprising a serial number and date of registration. Since 1 April 1997 the details on the memorials are no longer checked by the Registrar. The deed is returned to the party submitting it for registration and the memorial is retained in the Registry. The certificate is evidence of registration in any court.

Indexes

6.08 The memorials of registered documents are kept in files in the Registry. The names of all grantors specified in the registered documents are entered in alphabetical order in the index of names. It is this which is inspected when a search against the property is made. Originally there was also an index of lands but it is now irrelevant because it was deemed to have closed on 31 December 1944.[44] Abstract books with brief details of all the memorials lodged were kept to 1 April 1997.

CHAIN OF TITLE

Documents of title

6.09 The title to unregistered property normally consists of a bundle of documents which may trace the ownership of the property back over a long period.

The production of the original deeds is regarded in conveyancing practice as sufficient proof of title. In the absence of suspicious circumstances, a deed is presumed to have been duly executed and generally it is accepted that the vendor acquired the deeds by the means by which he purports to have done so. Subject to any contrary provision in the contract the vendor has an obligation to show title going back for a period of at least 40 years under the Vendor and Purchaser Act 1874, section 1.[45] A deed 20 years old or more coming from proper custody proves itself by virtue of the Evidence Act (NI) 1939, section 4.

Under the Vendor and Purchaser Act 1874, section 2(2), recitals, statements and descriptions in deeds 20 years old at the date of the contract are taken, unless proved to be inaccurate, to be sufficient evidence of the truth.

The vendor must do more than produce as evidence of his title to the property the document by which he acquired the title, unless he has held the property under that document for many years. The reason for this is that there may be some defect in an earlier document on which the vendor's title depends.

Although a defect may be cured through the operation of the doctrine of adverse possession, most purchasers are wary of accepting a possessory title based on such a short time as the 12 year limitation period. There is always the danger that there are third parties with interests in the property or with rights over the property who might challenge the right to possession or interfere with the rights which they claim.

6.10 The general rule is that the vendor must show an unbroken chain of title running from the root to the document under which he acquired the interest in the property he is selling. The links in the chain usually consist of various

---

[44] Registration of Deeds Act (NI) 1967, s 1.
[45] See Deduction of Title paras 2.10-2.26.

assurances (conveyances or assignments) and events (marriages or deaths), by which the property is transferred from one person to another. If there is a missing link the title is bad and the purchaser can rescind the contract for failure to show good title, unless the special conditions provide to the contrary.

Conveyances

6.11 Any conveyance of the land in sale is obviously an important link in the chain of title and should be furnished by the vendor. If the purchaser is buying only part of the property comprised in the conveyance the vendor will keep the original conveyance with the title for the land he is retaining and forward a copy of it to the purchaser. When drafting the purchase deed the purchaser's solicitor should include an undertaking by the vendor for safe custody and acknowledgement of his right to production of the original deeds.

Leases

6.12 Where the current transaction involves an assignment of an existing lease, the original lease and previous assignments of it are important and should be furnished. If the lease is quite recent, prior title should be furnished going back for a further period. Contractual provisions normally specify the exact age required. Under GCS 8.2 where a lease is less than 12 years old, prior title should be provided going back a further 12 years. It may be advisable to amend this to provide for title to go back further still.

In a conveyance of the freehold, any existing lease should be disclosed as an encumbrance on the title and the counterpart furnished.[46] Leases which have expired do not affect the purchaser but may nevertheless be produced with the title.

Mortgages

6.13 Any mortgage by a previous owner should be repaid and properly discharged. The receipt should be executed and registered. A discharged mortgage is not part of the chain of title.

It is not essential for the discharge of mortgage to be *registered* prior to the assurance which follows it but the receipt must be *dated* before the subsequent assurance so that the appropriate legal interest in the property vests in the purchaser clear of any prior mortgage.

An existing mortgage is an encumbrance which must be disclosed, although it is usually redeemed out of the sale proceeds. The actual mortgage deed should not be sent with the title to the purchaser but a copy may be furnished for information.

---

[46] The original lease is retained by the lessee, the counterpart by the lessor.

Settlements[47]

6.14 A settlement is the instrument by which land is settled or limited upon trust for any persons by way of succession. The settlement may be a deed, will, agreement or other instrument. A copy of the document creating the settlement should be furnished as evidence of the title of the vendor purporting to sell as entitled under it or as a life tenant.

Trusts[48]

6.15 A trust arises where property is transferred by the owner to trustees who are under an obligation to hold the legal title for and on behalf of beneficiaries or for specified purposes. For example, church and club property is held by trustees on trust for the benefit of its members. The use of the property may be circumscribed either by the deed creating the trust or under the constitution governing the body for whom the property is held.

The legal title under a trust is vested in the trustees and the interest of the beneficiaries is equitable. The legal and equitable interests in the property are separate but there is no fragmentation of ownership.

Where there is a trust on the title it is advisable to check that there is either a trust for sale or a power of sale which has become exercisable. In either case the trustees may sell the property. Under a trust for sale the trustees may sell without the consent of any other person unless the trust instrument provides otherwise. If neither a trust for sale nor a power of sale has been created then the trustees do not have the right to sell the property.

The trust instrument should be produced because it appoints the trustees, contains the power (if any) to appoint new trustees and sets out any powers intended to be conferred under the trust in addition to the statutory powers of the Trustee Act (NI) 1958. Any deeds of retirement and appointment of new trustees should also be furnished.

Trusts are often kept off the title by avoiding reference to them in the assurance which vests the property in the trustees and it is good practice to do so. A separate declaration of trust which is not registered will prevent the trustees from claiming beneficial ownership.

Joint ownership

6.16 Where a joint tenancy exists the interest of each joint tenant is undivided and indivisible. The share of each person passes to the others by survivorship until only one remains in whom the entire interest vests.

Where there is a tenancy in common no right of survivorship exists and the shares devolve separately. This means that the title to each share has to be deduced on its own.

---

[47] See paras 24.01-24.10 on Settlements generally.
[48] See paras 25.01-25.29 on Trusts generally.

Succession

6.17 The estate of a deceased person vests in his personal representatives on his death. The personal representatives may sell the whole or any part of the estate, not only to pay the debts, but also for the purpose of distribution among the beneficiaries. The personal representatives must have regard to the wishes of the beneficiaries, if they are of age, but a purchaser is not concerned and cannot require the concurrence of any beneficiary to the sale. Where a sale is made by personal representatives more than a year after the testator's death, the purchaser's solicitor should enquire whether the administration of the estate is incomplete.

A purchaser in good faith for value from the personal representatives gets the property free from all debts and from all liabilities of the deceased except those charged otherwise than by his will and from all claims of the beneficiaries. The purchaser is not concerned with the application of the purchase money.

Similarly a purchaser from a beneficiary, in whom property has been vested by the personal representatives, takes free of all claims of creditors except those of which he had actual or constructive notice.[49]

When a joint tenant, a trustee or a person with a life interest of any kind in the property dies, a copy of the death certificate is sufficient evidence of the cessation of that interest.

When a beneficial owner or a tenant in common dies, a copy of the grant of probate or letters of administration to the estate is required to prove the succession. If there is a will a copy of it is incorporated in the grant to show the appointment of the executors and the devise or bequest of the property.

Assents

6.18 The Administration of Estates Act (NI) 1955 came into effect on 1 January 1956 and applies in all cases where the death occurred after that date.

Section 34(4) provides that an assent must be in writing to pass an estate in land. An assent can be made by the proving personal representatives only but it does not have to be in the form of a deed. A conveyance or assignment by the personal representatives to the beneficiaries has the same effect as an assent.

The personal representatives have power to execute an assent vesting any estate or interest in the land of the deceased in the person entitled thereto on the deceased's death. This applies to a devise by will and on intestacy.

An assent operates to vest in the beneficiary or other person entitled the legal estate to which it relates, subject to such charges and encumbrances as may be specified. Until then the land of the deceased remains vested in the personal representatives.

The reason for an assent is that, since the executor is answerable to the creditors to the extent of the assets coming into his hands, the legatee cannot

---

[49] This does not extend to registered land.

take possession of his legacy until the executor assents. The title of the devisee is not complete until the personal representatives have assented to it.

Where a testator bequeaths property to his executors upon trust, the law regards them as continuing to act as executors until they have assented. After they have assented to the property vesting in themselves they become trustees. Where the testator died after 1955, it is essential to do so in writing.

The advantage of a written assent which has been registered is that a beneficiary is protected against a later conveyance of the same land by the personal representatives so that his position and that of a purchaser from him are more securely protected.

Before 1 January 1956 an assent of unregistered land could be given orally or even inferred from conduct. Whether or not implied assent was given was a question of fact. It was possible, for example, that a personal representative who was also a devisee could show that he had impliedly assented to the devise of the property in himself. The problem was that it may not have been clear in which capacity he was selling. It may also have been difficult to establish whether to deal with the personal representatives of a deceased or the person beneficially entitled to his property.

The personal representatives generally have a year to complete the administration of the estate. Accordingly, if the property of the deceased is sold within a year of his death it may be permissible for the personal representatives to act as vendors without first vesting the property in the beneficiaries. When a longer period has elapsed since the deceased's death it may be advisable to make enquiries as to why there is no assent on the title.

Possessory title[50]

6.19 A vendor can be in occupation of the land without having title to it, in which case his occupation may be inconsistent with the right of the true owner. If the vendor has no documentary evidence of his title he has to establish his title by other means. He must prove that he has been in occupation in the absence of the true owner for a period sufficient to extinguish the true owner's title and to establish a possessory title for himself.

Controller

6.20 A property will be sold by the controller of the estate of the property owner when the property owner is incapable of managing his own affairs and a controller has been appointed by the Office of Care and Protection of the High Court for that purpose. A copy of the court order appointing the controller and ordering the sale should be on the title. The deed of sale by the controller should have the consent of the Master of the Office of Care and Protection endorsed in the margin.

---

[50] See Adverse Possession paras 23.01-23.12.

Companies

6.21 An extract from the articles and memorandum of association used to be required to show that a company had power to enter into the proposed transaction and to show the method of sealing. By the Companies (No 2) (NI) Order 1990, article 44, amending the Companies (NI) Order 1986, article 45, the validity of an act done by a company is not called into question on the ground of lack of capacity by reason of anything in the memorandum.[51]

The old doctrine of *ultra vires* is abolished as far as third parties are concerned. The new provisions became effective from 19 August 1991, but are not retrospective and do not affect the validity of an act done by a company prior to that date.

A certificate of incorporation should still be furnished as proof of identity and execution of any document should be in accordance with the articles. However failure to do so does not affect the validity of the transaction.

A common seal is not essential.[52] A document signed by a director and a secretary of a company, or by two directors and expressed to be executed by the company has the same effect as a deed.

A contract may be made by a company, by writing under its common seal, or on behalf of a company, by any person acting under its authority, express or implied.

Insolvency and voluntary assurances[53]

6.22 The Insolvency (NI) Order 1989 has increased the powers of the court to set aside transactions where there is no consideration or where there is a transaction at an undervalue. It is therefore important to be aware of the circumstances if any document of title shows the consideration to be less than expected because the donee/purchaser or subsequent purchaser may be effected.

When the donor or vendor becomes bankrupt the trustee in bankruptcy can in certain circumstances seek to set aside a gift or undervalued transaction. If this occurs after a property has been sold or mortgaged by a donee then an innocent purchaser or mortgagee can suffer a financial loss.

Protection for innocent purchasers and third parties is provided by the Insolvency (No 2) Act 1994 to the extent that any interest in property which is acquired from a person other than the bankrupt in good faith for value is not prejudiced.

---

[51] Prior to this provision, under the Companies (European Communities) Order (NI) 1972, art 3 a person dealing with a company in good faith could assume that a transaction decided on by the directors was within the power of the company, free of any limitation under the memorandum or articles and a party to a transaction was not bound to enquire as to the capacity of the company to enter into it.

[52] Companies (No 2) (NI) Order 1990, art 65, amending Companies (NI) Order 1990, art 46.

[53] Cf paras 27.01-27.24.

A bankruptcy search affecting the donor should be obtained when acting for a purchaser from a donee within five years from the date of the gift.

Covenants for title

6.23 Another point to consider when there is a gift on the title is the question of covenants for title. In a conveyance for valuable consideration, statutory covenants are implied. This is not so in the case of a gift.[54] The statutory covenants must be expressly stated in a voluntary conveyance if they are to apply, because they are not implied automatically.

Sale of portion

6.24 If the property has been subdivided, or a portion sold at any stage, there should be proper maps accurately showing the respective boundaries. Traditionally, it was acceptable to apportion a ground rent when a property held under an existing lease or fee farm grant was subdivided in any way. In such a situation the deed should contain proper charging clauses and indemnities.[55]

Since article 29 of the Property (NI) Order 1997 became operative on 10 January 2000 it is suggested that it may no longer be possible to create a rentcharge such as a charge of an apportioned rent on an assignment of part. However it may be arguable that such a situation might come within the exception to article 29(3)(c) which relates to a rentcharge payable under an agreement of indemnity to the owner of a legal estate in land contingently upon a purchaser being made to pay the whole or part of a rent in respect of all or part of that land.[56] In considering if a ground rent can be apportioned one factor to take into account is whether the lease which created the rent is dated prior to 10 January 2000. If the lease is subsequent to that date it could be argued that any scheme to apportion the rent is contrary to the spirit of the legislation intended to prevent the creation of new ground rents.

If copy title is furnished to a purchaser after a subdivision, there should be a clause in the purchase deed granting him and subsequent owners a right of access to the originals.

Purchase of freehold or other superior interest

6.25 The freehold interest or a superior leasehold interest in leasehold premises may sometimes be purchased by the lessee. When the transaction is completed the purchaser should receive the original title deeds to the superior interest in

---

[54] See paras 27.23.
[55] Cf para 20.23.
[56] Property (NI) Order 1997, art 30 prohibits the creation of a new lease for a dwelling house in excess of 50 years. Art 29 prohibits the creation of any new rentcharges. However, it may be possible to argue that an apportionment of a ground rent comes within the exception in art 29(3)(c). This provision permits the creation of a rentcharge which is payable under an agreement of indemnity to the owner of a legal estate in land contingently upon his being made to pay the whole or part of a rent in respect of all or part of that land or in respect of a larger area of land of which that land forms or formed part. Also see para 20.23.

the property. The purchaser already has the original lease and should be given the counterpart so that he then has both copies of it.

Miscellaneous documents

6.26 There are a number of other documents which may be required to establish a link in the title. These include:

(1) Power of attorney if at any time the property was sold under one ;
(2) Marriage certificate as evidence of a woman's change of name and identity;
(3) Death certificate to show cessation of a life interest or joint tenancy.

Lost deeds

6.27 If all or any of the title deeds can be proved to be lost or destroyed and the vendor can deduce adequate secondary evidence of their contents and execution, the purchaser cannot repudiate the contract. In most cases, the purchaser knows prior to the contract that the deeds are lost and is able to walk away from the transaction without signing the contract if he so wishes. In the event of an auction the form of contract and documents of title should have been available for inspection in advance of the auction and the purchaser should have taken the opportunity to inspect same.

The vendor cannot force the purchaser to accept secondary evidence of title unless he can establish clearly that the original deeds are destroyed or, after a proper search, are lost.

The usual secondary evidence provided is:

(1) A certified copy of the memorial obtained from the Registry of Deeds;
(2) A Registry of Deeds search; and
(3) A statutory declaration as to the circumstances in which the missing documents were lost and as to the searches and enquires made to locate them.

The purchaser may request an insurance indemnity in case any claim having priority should subsequently come to light.

Searches[57]

6.28 All acts appearing should be satisfactorily explained and existing searches should be provided with the title against:

(1) Each owner of the property from the date of the deed to him to the date of registration of his deed of sale;
(2) Personal representatives from the date of the deceased's death to the date of registration of the deed by which they dispose of the property;

---

[57] Cf paras 5.02-5.11.

(3) A deceased owner to the end of the month following the month in which he died (at least).

Under GCS 2.3(d) there is an obligation to provide only a search in the Registry of Deeds against the vendor and not against any previous owners of the property. A purchaser should amend the contract as appropriate if he requires further searches which have not been supplied with the title.

General points

6.29 There are a number of general matters which have to be checked in relation to each document.

Description

6.30 The description of the property in the title deeds should be consistent *inter se* and correspond with that in the contract. Maps referred to in documents should be included or attached to the deeds and should be compared with the written description. Normally the description in the body of the deed is taken as correct if it differs from the map but an accurate description in the map prevails over inconclusive or vague wording in the deed. Where the words 'more particularly described on the plan' are used then the plan will take precedence, but if the words 'for identification only' are used with reference to the plan then the words take precedence.

Execution

6.31 Each document should be properly executed by all necessary parties. Generally the grantee need not execute a deed because, having taken the benefit of it, he is bound by it in equity. However if an easement is reserved to the grantor, the grantee should execute the deed so that it operates as a legal regrant to the grantor; otherwise the grantor merely takes an equitable right.

In practice the deed is seldom executed by the grantee despite any reservations, unless it is a grant of an estate such as a fee farm grant or a lease. A deed is a document under seal. Execution of a deed includes the necessity to seal and deliver it. A deed does not need to be supported by consideration.

Attestation

6.32 At common law no witnesses at all are required for a deed to be effective. The Registry of Deeds (Ir) Act 1707 required the execution of the memorial to the deed to have two witnesses for the purposes of registration. It then became the invariable practice for each party to a deed to sign, seal and deliver it in the presence of two witnesses who signed the attestation clause giving their names, addresses and occupations.

The Registration of Deeds Act (NI) 1970, section 2(1) provided that a document lodged for registration must have its execution by the grantor attested by two witnesses. This provision was repealed in the case of unregistered land by the Registration (Land and Deeds) (NI) Order 1992, article 40.

In law there is now no requirement in respect of unregistered land relating to witnesses but GCS 11.5 provides that the execution of any assurance by the vendor or other necessary party shall be witnessed either by a solicitor or two other independent persons.

A party to the deed cannot be a competent witness nor, by tradition, can his spouse.

Attestation is *prima facie* evidence that the deed was duly executed, even if it is not strictly necessary for the deed to be effective.

Stamping[58]

6.33 All the deeds should be properly stamped. Stamping should take place within 30 days of the date of execution and a penalty may be imposed for late submission to the Stamp Office. Failure to stamp a document means that it cannot, except in criminal proceedings, be produced in evidence or be available for any purpose whatever.

Since 4 November 1996, when the consideration shown on a transfer, conveyance or assignment is below the threshold for stamp duty it no longer has to be lodged in the Stamp Office but can be sent straight to the Registry of Deeds or Land Registry along with a completed note of 'particulars delivered'. This means that documents no longer have a 'PD' stamp affixed.

Certain instruments are exempt from Stamp Duty and others are liable to fixed rate duty regardless of the consideration involved in the transaction.[59]

Registration in the Registry of Deeds

6.34 After stamping a document should be lodged in the Registry of Deeds with a memorial for registration. The registrar need not satisfy himself that the execution of a deed or conveyance has been properly witnessed.

Registration merely fixes the priority of a document and does not confer any additional force or validity. Failure to register a document after stamping may cause a loss of priority over subsequent transactions relating to the same land, but is not in itself fatal to the validity of a deed.

It is only the document which is registered, not the title or the land to which it relates. Registration does not guarantee the title nor the validity of the document itself.

Deeds, other conveyances, assents and most other documents even if not under seal, relating to unregistered land may be registered in the Registry of Deeds. Some documents must be registered to be effective, for example, orders charging land. A lease for less than 21 years, where actual possession goes with the lease, is not registrable nor is an assignment of such a lease, but a mortgage of it is registrable.

The certificate of registration is evidence of registration in any court. The certificate usually appears in the margin of the first page of the deed, stating the date of registration and the serial number given to the document. If a photocopy deed has been furnished the details of registration should nevertheless appear legibly.

---

[58] See Stamp Duty paras 16.01-16.40.
[59] *Ibid.*

CHAPTER SEVEN
TITLE: (2) LAND REGISTRY

Introduction

7.01 The Registry of Deeds and the Land Registry are the two systems of registration relating to land in Northern Ireland. The Registry of Deeds provides for the registration of documents dealing with land, whereas the Land Registry provides for the registration of the ownership of land.

The systems run parallel to each other and can both affect a single piece of land. For example, at one time it was possible to carve unregistered subsidiary interests out of a registered folio, with the result that the freehold was registered and the leasehold was not. Also, very occasionally the leasehold may be registered in the Land Registry while the freehold is not. The important point to remember is that the systems are mutually exclusive in relation to a particular estate in land.[60]

The two systems of registration co-exist side by side and will continue to do so until registration of title is made mandatory throughout Northern Ireland. There is no overlap between the systems because all dealings with registered land proceed through the Land Registry and with unregistered land through the Registry of Deeds.

The Local Registration of Title (Ir) Act 1891 first established a proper system of registration of title and the Land Registry is now governed by the Land Registration Act (NI) 1970 ('LRA (NI)'), as amended by the Registration (Land and Deeds) Order (NI) 1992.

Registration of land was introduced to give certainty to the titles bought out under the land purchase schemes and to simplify the transfer of land. The Land Registry was created to maintain the registers of title and all land bought out under the land purchase schemes was compulsorily registered.

Most agricultural land is freehold and registered. Much of the newer residential and commercial property built on land which was previously agricultural is also registered, because it is now compulsory for all leases carved out of a registered freehold to be registered too.

Apart from these cases and the title to land compulsorily acquired by statute, which also must be registered in the Land Registry, registration is generally voluntary.[61] The first area of compulsory registration was designated by the Compulsory Registration of Title Order (NI) 1995 which became operative on 1 June 1996. Within that area which covers part of the local government district of Ards, it is compulsory for all land to become registered on transfer of ownership.

---

[60] Cf Registry of Deeds paras 6.01-6.34 for more detail.
[61] At the time of writing it is envisaged that further compulsory registration may be introduced with compulsory redemption of ground rents under the Property (NI) Order 1997.

REGISTERS

7.02 The basic principle of registration is that title is guaranteed by the Land Registry and entries on the register are proof of the title shown. The problem is that, while the register is conclusive as to matters appearing on it, it is not conclusive evidence of the entire title to the land. Unfortunately it is not safe to assume that unless something appears on the folio it will not bind a *bona fide* purchaser.

The possibility of various matters affecting registered land which are not immediately apparent has to be considered. It is important to realise that the land certificate should not be accepted as conclusive, particularly where the title registered is not absolute. Even where the title is absolute, the entries on the land certificate may not be marked up to date and the title may be affected by interests which do not need to be registered.

7.03 The Land Registry used to maintain three registers of title providing for the ownership of land.[62] These related to: (i) freehold interests; (ii) leasehold interests; and (iii) subsidiary interests, that is, incorporeal rights held in gross and such other rights in land as may be prescribed.[63] The Registration (Land and Deeds) (NI) Order 1992, article 6 provides that the three separate registers shall cease to be maintained and shall now be treated as a single register to be known as 'the title register'.

Folios

7.04 The register consists of a series of folios, each of which relates to a particular property. Each folio is numbered and refers to the county in which it is situated. For example, folio AR 12345 Co Armagh. The full reference is necessary to identify the property. Each folio is also identified on a Land Registry map which shows the physical dimensions and the location of the property.

A new folio is opened when the Registrar has examined the title deeds relating to a property and the title is first registered. The folio contains details of ownership of the registered estate and any registrable encumbrances, exceptions, reservations or other matters affecting it.

The folio consists of a single title deed which is retained in the Land Registry and is guaranteed by it. Once a title has been registered, the entries on the folio take the place of the deeds as evidence of title and the Land Registry is responsible for ensuring that the registers are accurate.

Folios are divided into three separate parts.[64] Part I contains a verbal description of the relevant land with a reference to the appropriate Land Registry map and details of any appurtenances, exceptions and reservations. It also notes mines and minerals affecting the land. In the case of leasehold land,

---

[62] Land Registration Act (NI) 1970, s 10.
[63] None were prescribed.
[64] Folios maintained under the Local Registration of Title (Ir) Act 1891 recorded each dealing with the land in chronological order irrespective of the nature of the transaction involved.

it contains details of the lease under which the estate is held. Part II contains details of ownership and of any cautions, inhibitions and certain other restrictions on dealings with the land. Part III contains information relating to burdens affecting the land.

A lease for a term exceeding 21 years or for a term of life or lives or determinable on life or lives is compulsorily registrable if granted out of registered land and will become void if the appropriate application for registration is not made within three months of the date thereof. The lease is automatically registered as a burden on the folio relating to the lessor's title and is also registered in the register of leaseholders. The registration of the title to the leasehold estate is a first registration since the lease creates a new estate in the land. A new folio is opened for the leasehold estate when it is carved out of the freehold estate.

Other leases, not subject to compulsory registration (i.e. those for 21 years or less without occupation thereunder) can simply be registered as a burden on the lessor's title. In such a case the leasehold estate remains an unregistered estate and a new folio is not opened for it.

When ownership changes, the relevant transfer is completed, stamped as appropriate and forwarded to the Land Registry together with a fee. The new owner is noted on the folio and the transfer itself ceases to be relevant once registration has taken place.

Land certificate

7.05 The owner of registered land proves his ownership by means of a land certificate which is issued to him by the Land Registry and which contains exactly the same information as the folio. The land certificate mirrors the folio and becomes *prima facie* but not conclusive evidence of the title to the land. Any previous title deeds are largely obsolete. There are exceptions. For example, a lease or fee farm grant affecting the land will still be relevant as the covenants, conditions etc contained in it will not be detailed on the folio or land certificate.

The land certificate and the Land Registry map identifying the property together fulfil the same role as the title deeds for unregistered land. A copy of any appropriate registered fee farm grant or lease also forms part of the title and should be retained with the land certificate.

When any transactions or dealings have to be registered the land certificate should be lodged in the Land Registry for the change to be noted so that it continues to mirror the folio.[65]

FIRST REGISTRATION

7.06 An application for registration of land or an incorporeal interest may be made by a freehold or leasehold owner, a mortgagee, a life tenant with statutory

---

[65] Under the Land Registration Rules (NI) 1994 this is now not strictly necessary in certain cases and specified matters can be registered without lodgment of the land certificate.

powers, or any other person authorised by statute. Although a voluntary application for registration can be made at any time, first registration is normally only sought where such registration is compulsory.

The land subject to compulsory registration is:

(1) Freehold land bought out under the land purchase legislation.[66]
(2) Freehold and leasehold land within a compulsory registration area.
(3) Compulsorily acquired land.
(4) Leasehold interests granted out of registered land after 1 October 1977 where the lease exceeds 21 years, or is for a life or determinable on a life.
(5) Perpetual rent charges or fee farm rents issuing out of registered land created by grants made after 1 October 1977.
(6) Fishing or sporting rights granted out of registered land by express grant or reservation after 1 October 1977.
(7) Any estate in land required by any other statutory provision to be registered in the Land Registry.

Compulsory first registration

7.07 The power to require registration of title in a particular area was originally conferred on the DOE by the LRA (NI) 1970, section 25(1), but the exercise of that power has only been made recently. By the Compulsory Registration of Title Order (NI) 1995 part of the local government district of Ards became the first compulsory registration area.[67] All purchase deeds executed on or after 1 June 1996 relating to property within that area have to be registered.[68] It is the purchaser's responsibility to apply for registration. By the Compulsory Registration of Title Order (NI) 1999 compulsory registration was extended to the local government districts of North Down and the remainder of Ards from 1 May 2000.[69] Similarly, all purchase deeds in that area must now be registered. It is proposed that the compulsory registration area be extended further in the near future.

The property remains a Registry of Deeds property until it has actually become registered in the Land Registry. Consequently, it is necessary to complete the

---

[66] To be included in this category the land must have been (on or after 1 Jan 1892) subject to an annuity or rent-charge for the repayment of an advance made under the Land Purchase Acts (19th century legislation enabling tenants of agricultural land to purchase their freeholds).

[67] The wards to which it applies are specified in the Order as Ballyrainey, Bradshaw's Brae, Comber Central, Comber East, Comber North, Comber West, Glen, Gregstown, Lisbane, Loughries, Movilla, Scrabo and Whitespots.

[68] The type of transaction which triggers a compulsory registration is defined by entry 2 of Sch 2 to the LRA (NI) 1970.

[69] The wards to which it applies are specified in the Order as Ballygowan, Ballywalter, Carrowdore, Donaghadee North, Donaghadee South, Portavogie and Portaferry.

transaction under Registry of Deeds procedures before applying to register the title. The purchase deed and any mortgage should first be registered in the Registry of Deeds.

The reason for this is that there will be a gap between the papers being submitted to the Land Registry and the issuing by the Land Registry to the Registry of Deeds of a memorial showing that the title has been transferred. During that period it is still possible to register matters, such as orders charging land, in the Registry of Deeds. Consequently, failure to register the purchase deed and any mortgage would be to assume a considerable risk to the purchaser and his mortgagee.

Under LRA (NI) 1970, Schedule 2, Part I, certain transactions which relate to property within the specified area are subject to compulsory registration.

Freehold

7.08 The following documents in relation to a freehold estate must be registered:

(1) Conveyance on sale;
(2) Conveyance of grantee's interest under a fee farm grant;
(3) Fee farm grant (if appropriate);[70]
(4) Exchange, only where money is paid for equality of exchange.

Leasehold

7.09 The following documents in relation to a leasehold estate must be registered:

(1) Lease for a term exceeding 21 years;
(2) Assignment on sale of leasehold estate where the residue exceeds 21 years at the date of the assignment;
(3) Exchange where money is paid for equality of exchange.

Application for registration must be made within three months of the date of execution of the transaction, otherwise the transaction becomes void from that date. There is provision to make an application to extend time.

An application for registration may be made by way of solicitor's certificate or by affidavit by the applicant. An up-to-date ordnance survey map of the property must be attached regardless of the fact that there are maps on the title deeds.[71]

Depending on the nature of the title the Land Registry may require the completion of rulings on title and/or the service of notices and publications of advertisements.

---

[70] The creation of any new fee farm grant is prohibited from 10 January 2000 by virtue of the Property (NI) Order 1997, art 28.
[71] Scale 1.1250 or 1.500 if an enlargement is required.

Application by solicitor's certificate

7.10 If application is made by solicitor's certificate the solicitor is liable for statements made as to title. The documents required in that case are:

(1) Form 1 and map
(2) Form 100
(3) Original title deeds and schedule in duplicate
(4) Certified copies of root of title, last assurance and any mortgage or charge which is to be registered
(5) Fee

Affidavit by applicant

7.11 When application is made by applicant's affidavit the applicant is effectively certifying that the title is good. The documents required in that case are:

(1) Form 2 and map
(2) A verified statement of title
(3) Form 100
(4) Original title deeds and schedule in duplicate
(5) Certified copies of root of title, last assurance and any mortgage or charge which is to be registered
(6) Up-to-date hand searches
(7) Up-to-date bankruptcy search
(8) Names and addresses of adjoining landowners if boundaries are not clearly identifiable from maps on title deeds
(9) Fee

Existing easements will be registered as Schedule 5 burdens. If a right is to be registered as an appurtenant right, the title of the servient folio also has to be investigated.

Application based on adverse possession[72]

7.12 When there is no evidence of a documentary title, or where the history of the title is confused and uncertain application may be made for registration based on adverse possession, provided that the applicant has been in occupation for a sufficient length of time to defeat competing claims. The documents required in that case are:

(1) Form 3 and map
(2) Form 100

---

[72] See Adverse Possession paras 23.01-23.12 and 7.41.

(3) Supporting affidavit by an independent person

(4) Names and addresses of adjoining landowners

(5) Fee

(6) An advertisement will always be required.

Date of first registration

7.13 First registration takes effect from the date on which the folio allocated to the title is authenticated by affixing of the Land Registry seal. At the same time the Land Registry prepares a memorial giving notice of the first registration to the Registry of Deeds. Thereafter documents exclusively affecting the newly registered title must be registered in the Land Registry and not the Registry of Deeds.

Cautions against first registration

7.14 A person claiming an interest in unregistered land can lodge a caution against first registration of the land. In order to do so, he must claim to be an encumbrancer on the land or to have an interest in the land of such a nature that it entitles him to object to any dealing. Then if an application for first registration is made, a notice is sent to the cautioner giving him the opportunity to object to the registration within a specified time limit.

CLASSES OF TITLE

7.15 The conclusiveness of the registers may be affected by the class of title granted on first registration. The class of title registered depends upon the extent to which the applicant for first registration is able to prove title to the Land Registry.

An applicant for first registration can be registered with one of the following classes of title.

Absolute title

7.16 An absolute title is the best form of title. In the case of freehold land it vests in the full registered owner a fee simple estate in the land whether or not he previously held that estate. A limited owner of freehold land with an absolute title holds the land subject to the terms of the settlement under which he was registered as limited owner. In both cases, the estate of the registered owner is subject to any relevant entries on the folio and any burdens specified in LRA (NI) 1970, Schedule 5.[73]

An absolute freehold title indicates that the registered owner has the full or limited freehold estate in the land, as the case may be, subject only to any registered burdens and burdens affecting the land without registration. If the registered owner is a trustee he is still subject to his duties and liabilities as a trustee.

---

[73] See Schedule 5 burdens below paras 7.39-7.46.

The first registration of a full or limited leasehold estate with an absolute title is similar to the absolute freehold. However, in the case of a leasehold, included in the Schedule 5 burdens which affect title are all express and implied covenants, conditions and liabilities incident to the lease under which the estate is held.

A good fee farm grant or good leasehold title

7.17 These classes of title are the best that can be obtained by a person holding under a fee farm grant or lease who is not in a position to prove the title of his grantor or lessor. They are granted where the title under the fee farm grant or lease can be guaranteed but not the title of the grantor or lessor to make the actual grant or lease itself.

All kinds of superior estates and interests may exist affecting the land and these are protected to an extent. The registration of a good fee farm grant title does not prejudice any superior estate. The registration of a good leasehold title does not affect or prejudice the enforcement of any rights adverse to or in derogation of the title of the lessor to grant the lease.

A possessory title

7.18 Where the applicant cannot produce documentary evidence of title and can show only occupation of the land or receipt of rents and profits, a possessory title is usually registered. This would arise, for example, in the case of a squatter. A possessory title carries no guarantee that the applicant is entitled to be registered as such. Where a note as to equities exists, the title will be deemed to be a possessory title.

Therefore a purchaser of a possessory title should investigate the pre-registration title. Although there is no guarantee that the first registration was correct, if it can be established independently that it was, then the register can be relied upon in respect of its validity from the date of registration.

A qualified title

7.19 A qualified title is subject to the estates or rights in the qualification noted on the register. It is a residuary class of title available where the title cannot be established as absolute to the satisfaction of the Registrar because of a defect; for example, if it can be established for a limited period only or subject to qualifications.

PROOF OF TITLE ON FIRST REGISTRATION

Absolute title

7.20 To be registered with an absolute title an applicant must be able to deduce title to the freehold estate (not under a fee farm grant) for a period of at least 15 years prior to the application, commencing with a good root of title.

Good fee farm grant title

7.21 An applicant normally has to produce the fee farm grant under which the land is held and show title for 15 years going back to a good root. If the fee farm grant cannot be produced, secondary evidence of it may be admissible. If the fee farm grant is less than 15 years old, the applicant has to deduce the title of the grantor for the requisite period going back before the grant or accept a qualified title.

Good leasehold title

7.22 An applicant should produce the lease and title for a period of 21 years commencing with a good root. If the lease is less than 21 years old the prior title to the property is required for a period of at least 20 years prior to the application, commencing with a good root of title.[74]

Possessory title

7.23 Where an applicant seeks first registration of land with a possessory title he has to show sufficient possession to extinguish the title of the rightful owner.[75]

Qualified title

7.24 By virtue of the Registration (Land and Deeds) (NI) Order 1992, article 7, an application can be made for a qualified title to be registered.

Reclassification of title

7.25 Where a non-absolute title has been registered, the Registrar may, either on his own initiative or on application, convert or reclassify the title into one of the better classes. That is, he may convert qualified or possessory titles into absolute or good fee farm grant or leasehold titles. Generally, reclassification is effected because it is justified by lapse of time or on production of new evidence.

Titles subject to equities

7.26 The titles which were originally registered subject to equities under the Local Registration of Title (Ir) Act 1891 are now deemed to be possessory titles by virtue of LRA (NI) 1970, Schedule 13. However, if the registered owner and his predecessors in title have been in sole and undisputed beneficial occupation and possession of the land for at least 12 years the title can be reclassified as absolute.[76] When acting for a purchaser it is advisable to insist that the vendor has the title reclassified as absolute before completion.

Other possessory titles may be reclassified as appropriate on application when a transfer for value is lodged at least 15 years after first registration and there is evidence that the registered owner was in possession of the property immediately prior to the transfer.[77]

---

[74] See para 2.18.
[75] See paras 23.01-23.12.
[76] See LRA (NI) 1970 Sch 3, para 1 and Land Registration Rules (NI) 1994, r 53.
[77] See LRA (NI) 1970 Sch 3, para 2 and Land Registration Rules (NI) 1994, r 54.

CHARGES

7.27 The legislation provides for the creation of charges on registered land and their transfer, transmission and discharge. The creation of informal charges by deposit of the land certificate is also permitted.

On registration of the ownership of a charge, the owner is entitled to delivery of a certificate of charge in the prescribed form from the Registrar.

The only way in which the owner of registered land can create a legal mortgage of the land is to execute a deed of charge or create a charge by his will. A deed of charge for the payment of money may be in such prescribed form as the case requires and otherwise in such form as is sufficient to charge the land.

The LRA (NI) 1970 does not prevent the creation of equitable mortgages by deposit. The deposit of a land certificate or certificate of charge relating to registered land has the same effect as a deposit of the title deeds of unregistered land. It creates an equitable mortgage on the registered land which need not be registered in the Land Registry as a burden on the land in order to secure priority as against subsequent transactions relating to it. Accordingly, it is possible for an equitable mortgage to take priority over a registered charge.

The mortgage is protected to an extent because subsequent transactions relating to the registered land generally cannot be completed by registration in the Land Registry without production of the land certificate, which the mortgagee holds. As a further precaution it is advisable for the mortgagee to lodge a caution with the Registrar against subsequent registered dealings, particularly now that it is not necessary to produce the land certificate or certificate of charge to the Land Registry on registration of orders charging land under Land Registration Rules (NI) 1994, rule 128(1). The mortgagee can also lodge a notice of deposit in the Land Registry stating details of the loan secured so that a subsequent mortgagee will have notice of it.

Registered burdens

7.28 Burdens affecting registered land which may be registered are listed in LRA (NI) 1970, Schedule 6. In most cases the concurrence of the registered owner of the land affected is required for a burden to be registered.

Schedule 6 burdens include charges, fee farm and perpetual rents, any lien on the land for unpaid purchase money, leases for over 21 years, judgments or enforcement orders, pending actions, charging orders, easements or profits created by express reservation after the land has been registered, restrictive covenants created after registration of the land and certain rights of residence.

The registration of a burden secures its priority over subsequently registered burdens, other registrable burdens and unregistrable burdens (but not Schedule 5 burdens), provided that the other burdens were created after first registration of the land. If burdens are registered, a purchaser for value takes subject to them; if they are not registered, he takes priority over them.

Rights of residence

7.29 A right of residence is a burden which may be registered as a general right of residence on the land, an exclusive right of residence on all or part of the land, or a right to use a specified part of the land in conjunction with a right of residence.

Such a right is deemed to be personal to the person to whom it is granted and is not construed as conferring any right of ownership. However, once registered as a Schedule 6 burden, the right is binding upon the registered owner of the land and his successors in title.

Appurtenant rights

7.30 Appurtenant rights are incorporeal interests, such as easements, other than natural rights which have been created and annexed to the land. They are burdens in so far as they relate to the servient land (the land over which the right is enjoyed) and are included in the provisions of Schedule 6 so long as they have been created by express grant or reservation.

At one time such rights could be entered only as burdens on the folio relating to the servient land. Since LRA (NI) 1970 became operative an entry can be made noting the existence of an appurtenance on the folios relating to both the dominant land (the land benefited by it) and the servient land. There may still be appurtenant rights which do not appear on older folios of dominant lands. Any such rights can be discovered by an inspection of the Land Registry maps.

REGISTRATION OF OWNERSHIP

Joint ownership

7.31 Registered land may be owned by two or more persons concurrently in the same way as unregistered land, either as joint tenants or as tenants in common. They are deemed to hold the land as joint tenants unless there is an entry to the effect that they are tenants in common. Any such entry also indicates the extent of each share in common.

Trusts[78]

7.32 Generally trusts, whether express, implied or constructive are not entered in the register. The trustees may be registered as full owners of the land without any indication of the trust appearing on the register. A purchaser for value need not enquire as to whether the land is subject to a trust unless he is fixed with notice of its existence. Beneficiaries however can protect themselves to some extent against fraudulent dealings by trustees registered as full owners by lodging cautions or inhibitions.

Settlements[79]

7.33 In the case of a settlement the life tenant or a person having the powers of the life tenant under the Settled Land Acts 1882-90 can be registered as limited owner of the freehold or leasehold estate. Where there is no-one entitled to be registered as limited owner, the trustees of the settlement are registered as full

---

[78] See Trusts paras 25.01-25.29.
[79] See Settlements paras 24.01-24.10.

owners of the property. This is also the case where the land is held under a trust for sale, unless the life tenant has powers conferred by court order under the Settled Land Act 1884.

LIMITATIONS OF THE LAND REGISTRY SYSTEM

7.34 The difficulty with the registration system is that there may be a number of interests which are not registered but which nevertheless affect the land and bind a transferee. In theory a prospective purchaser should concern himself only with the existing state of the register rather than its previous history and it should not be necessary to investigate the title each time the property is sold. However it is now generally accepted that registration does not remove all the problems of unregistered conveyancing and that the system is not as simple as was originally intended.

There is a danger of relying too heavily on the basic principle of registration and believing that unless something appears on the folio it will not bind a *bona fide* purchaser. It cannot safely be assumed if, for example, an easement, a covenant or a secured loan is not registered and does not appear on the folio, that it does not bind the purchaser.

The possibility of various matters affecting registered land which are not immediately apparent must be considered. Checks and investigations have to be carried out in the same way as with unregistered land.

Land certificate

7.35 It is important to realise that the land certificate should not be accepted as conclusive, particularly where the title registered is not absolute. Even where the title is absolute, the entries on the land certificate may not be marked up to date or the title may be affected by interests which do not need to be registered.

Title partially registered

7.36 It is possible that some estates in a particular piece of land may be registered while others remain unregistered, which creates confusion. The problem has been alleviated to an extent now that a lease carved out of a superior registered freehold title has to be registered and a new leasehold folio opened for it under the provisions of LRA (NI) 1970, Schedule 2.

Formerly such a lease was registered only as a burden on the freehold folio and not as part of the title. The lease and any assignments or mortgages of it were then registered in the Registry of Deeds. The freehold in the property remained registered but the leasehold was unregistered.

Equities note

7.37 Most of the titles registered compulsorily under the Local Registration of Title (Ir) Act 1891 registered the former tenant as owner of the freehold subject to existing burdens and equities held by third parties. The note as to equities preserved them as if there had been no registration and made the title subject to them without specifying their nature or extent. The note remains, whether or not the rights it protects survive and this obviously affects the title of subsequent purchasers.

Folios subject to equities now rank as possessory titles only under LRA (NI) 1970, Schedule 13. Since all such notes are of a considerable age, the effect of any equities is minimal, but it is nevertheless advisable to have the title reclassified.

Unregistered dispositions

7.38 Under LRA (NI) 1970, section 34(4), an unregistered disposition does not generally affect a *bona fide* purchaser of registered land for valuable consideration, but under section 34(5) a voluntary transferee and persons claiming through him otherwise than for value are bound by all unregistered rights affecting the transferor.

Unregistered burdens

7.39 Certain burdens listed in LRA (NI) 1970, Schedule 5, can affect registered land without registration even though no evidence of their existence appears on the registers. The purchaser must raise pre-contract enquiries and inspect the property to ascertain if any such burdens exist.

Although Schedule 5 burdens affect a title without registration, notice of the existence of any of the burdens may be entered on the registers and a notice may also be entered to confirm that a particular title is exempt from or has ceased to be subject to any such burden.

The more common Schedule 5 burdens are considered below.

Rights of occupation

7.40 The possibility of the existence of rights of occupation presents considerable difficulties, particularly to a mortgagee. Any person who has a beneficial interest in registered land and who is in actual occupation when a subsequent disposition is registered cannot be prejudiced by that registration unless he signifies his consent or has been asked previously whether or not he has any rights in the land and has not disclosed any.

The mortgagee normally also makes enquiries of other adult occupiers and obtains their consent to postponing any rights they may have in the property to the rights of the mortgagee. It therefore may be advisable when a couple purchase a property, to have both their names on the title, regardless of their respective financial contributions.

Adverse possession

7.41 Rights acquired or in the process of acquisition by adverse possession affect the land without registration. The provisions of the Limitation (NI) Order 1989 apply to any right of action by the rightful owner to recover possession.

A squatter can apply to be registered as owner of the land under LRA (NI) 1970, section 53, after he has extinguished the title of the previous registered owner. The position of the squatter may be clear in relation to a freehold title but is less so where the squatter displaces a person with a leasehold interest.[80]

Under LRA (NI) 1970, section 53(4), the registration of a squatter must not prejudice any estate of another person in the land which is not extinguished by the adverse possession. The registration of a squatter on leasehold land arguably may prejudice the estate of the lessor and there is some doubt as to the extent to which section 53 is applicable to leasehold titles.

Taking a pragmatic approach, if the lessor is notified of the squatter's application for registration and given the opportunity to object, the problem may be avoided.

Mineral rights

7.42 The registered owner of land does not have title to the mineral rights in that land unless a note to that effect appears on the register in accordance with LRA (NI) 1970, section 11(1). Even if such a note does appear, it does not affect any rights to petroleum or minerals vested in the Department of Economic Development.[81] Normally any rights and privileges connected with the exploitation of mineral rights also affect the title without registration.

Leases under 21 years

7.43 These leases are not registrable, but nevertheless bind a transferee for value if occupation goes with the lease.[82]

Leasehold covenants, conditions and liabilities

7.44 It is essential to examine the lease creating the leasehold estate because all express and implied covenants, conditions and liabilities incident to the lease under which a leasehold estate is held affect the title without registration. The possibility of an outstanding claim for non-payment of rent or breach of covenant should also be investigated. The same applies to fee farm grants.

Unregistered easements and profits

7.45 All easements and profits created in any manner prior to first registration, those acquired by prescription or implied grant after first registration and those registered in the statutory charges register affect the land without registration.

---

[80] Cf para 23.04.

[81] By the Petroleum (Production) Act (NI) 1964 or the Minerals Development Act (NI) 1969.

[82] In *Woolwich Building Society* v *Dickman and Todd* [1996] NPC 22 a house was let to tenants who were required by the mortgagee to sign a document postponing their rights to those of the mortgagee. When the mortgagor defaulted and the mortgagee sought possession the tenants argued that they were entitled to an interest which enjoyed priority over the mortgage. The tenants were successful because they could not exclude their rights under the Rent Act 1977 (which confers similar protection to the Rent (NI) Order 1978) by any agreement and their lease being for a term not exceeding 21 years was an overriding interest (equivalent in NI to a burden affecting the land without registration) unless there was a note to the contrary on the register.

Non-absolute titles

7.46 When land is registered with title less than absolute there may be rights which existed prior to first registration, not noted on the folio, but which continue to be capable of enforcement against the land.

In the case of a fee farm grant title the only right excepted from registration is an estate arising from a superior grant. However the position in respect of good leasehold titles, possessory titles and some qualified titles is less clear. Registration does not prejudice or affect the enforcement of certain vaguely defined rights or estates created or arising prior to first registration.

CHANGES OF OWNERSHIP

7.47 The general principle is that the registered owner alone is entitled to deal with the land by a registered disposition. Changes of ownership may occur by transfer, by transmission or by defeasance of the estate of a registered owner. Anyone who becomes entitled to the land, for example on the death of the owner or by transfer, may also deal with the land by transferring or charging it.

Transfers

7.48 Generally a transfer operates as a conveyance by deed within the Conveyancing Acts 1881-1911, which includes assignments. The transferee is registered with the appropriate title subject to express or implied rights, privileges and appurtenances and registered burdens or burdens affecting land without registration.

If the transfer is not for value, the voluntary transferee is registered subject to all unregistered rights subject to which the transferor held the land and these bind all persons claiming through the transferee otherwise than for value. Such unregistered rights may also be protected by cautions or inhibitions.

A transfer does not vest the land in the transferee but gives him an equitable right to the land. The transfer is only completed on registration of the transferee as owner, and he is then entitled to delivery of the land certificate.

An instrument of transfer of freehold registered land transfers the fee simple or the whole interest which the transferor had to transfer without the need for words of limitation unless a contrary intention appears. In certain circumstances, as where the transferee wishes to have the benefit of the covenants for title implied by the Conveyancing Act 1881, section 7, it may be advisable to include appropriate words of limitation.

The registered owner should transfer the registered land by using the prescribed form in all appropriate cases with such modifications as may be necessary.[83] Where no suitable form has been prescribed the document used to effect the transaction must be acceptable to the registrar.

If only part of the land is transferred, the registrar may either allow the transferor to retain his certificate with an entry in it as to the part transferred or

---

[83] The forms are contained in Land Registration Rules (NI) 1994, Sch 2.

deliver to him a new certificate for the part retained. It is more common for the transferee to be issued with a new certificate for the land he acquires.

Transmission on death

7.49 On the death of a sole full registered owner the deceased's personal representatives are recognised as alone having any rights in the land and dispositions by them have the same effect as if they were by the registered owner. The personal representatives can obtain an entry on the folio providing evidence of their power to deal with the land but cannot be registered as owners merely by virtue of their status as personal representatives.

The beneficiary entitled to the land may be registered as full or limited owner when an assent in his favour from the personal representatives is produced. The personal representatives may be registered as trustees on production of an assent vesting the property in themselves in that capacity in accordance with the will of the testator.

When a joint tenant dies his share in the property is transmitted to the remaining joint tenant(s) by production to the Land Registry of his death certificate or the grant of representation to his estate.

Where a tenant in common dies his share devolves in accordance with his will or on his intestacy and it is necessary to produce the grant to his estate together with an assent in favour of the beneficiary.

On the determination of a limited interest, the ownership is transmitted to the remainderman in accordance with the terms of the settlement. All material facts have to be disclosed together with the information necessary to establish the entitlement of the remainderman to the land. This will be different in each case and should show how the limited ownership has determined and the interest of the remainderman arisen.

Defeasance

7.50 The situations in which the ownership of registered land can pass to another person otherwise than by transfer or death are set out in LRA (NI) 1970, section 36. These include defeasance under a power of sale conferred by a mortgage prior to first registration of the land, a power of appointment, a vesting order, a court order for sale, any statutory provision and any other case which may be prescribed.

The situations where defeasance occurs and which fall within the category of any statutory provision include the following.

Bankruptcy

7.51 Under LRA (NI) 1970, section 59(5), the trustee in bankruptcy is entitled to be registered as owner in place of a bankrupt registered owner.

Sale by owner of a charge

7.52 Under LRA (NI) 1970, Schedule 7 Part I, the registered owner of a charge has all the rights and powers of a mortgagee under a mortgage by deed

Adverse possession

7.53 The LRA (NI) 1970, section 53, confers upon a squatter, who claims to have defeated the estate of a registered owner, the right to apply to the Land Registry for registration of himself as the new owner of the estate.

Bankruptcy of vendor[84]

7.54 The title of a purchaser of registered land who purchased it in good faith for valuable consideration is not affected by a bankruptcy petition or bankruptcy order against the registered owner unless the purchaser had actual knowledge of it, or at the date of registration of his transfer a notice of bankruptcy had been registered. However if the purchaser makes a priority search when the contract to purchase the land is signed, when the transfer or lease contemplated by the contract is delivered for registration it will rank in priority before a bankruptcy petition or order presented during that 40 day period.

Merger and extinguishment of leases

7.55 The owner of a leasehold estate may acquire the fee simple or a superior leasehold title and the inferior estate can merge in the superior one. Alternatively, the lessor may acquire the title of the lessee by assignment, surrender or forfeiture and the title of the lessee is then extinguished.[85]

When a registered estate is involved, merger or extinguishment does not occur automatically, but only when the appropriate cancellations or entries have been made on the affected folios in the Land Registry. It is necessary to complete the appropriate form to extinguish the leasehold estate.

Priorities

7.56 A person who becomes entitled to be registered as owner of any registered land by transfer or otherwise should immediately take steps to procure his registration because, until he does so, his rights in respect of the land are severely restricted. A transfer does not operate to actually transfer the land until the transferee is registered as owner. The same applies to a person entitled to be registered as owner of a burden.

Priority between registered transactions depends upon the order of registration which is normally dependent on the order in which dealings are lodged for registration.

---

[84] See Bankruptcy paras 27.12-27.14.
[85] Cf Merger and Surrender paras 23.13-23.16.

Cautions and inhibitions

7.57 Nothing in LRA (NI) 1970 can prevent a person from creating any estate in registered land which could be created in unregistered land. It is therefore possible for registered land to be subject to interests which cannot be adequately protected by substantive registration. Such interests are vulnerable if the land is transferred for valuable consideration but may be protected by lodging cautions or inhibitions.

Under LRA (NI) 1970, section 66, any person interested in land may lodge a caution so that no dealing by the registered owner may be registered without the consent of the cautioner unless and until the caution lapses. The registrar is required to notify the cautioner of any proposed dealings with the land by the registered owner. The cautioner may then take whatever action is necessary to prevent the registration of such a dealing if it adversely affects his rights.

A caution is intended to be temporary to protect the cautioner until his unregistered interest can be secured by registration. The effect of a caution is limited to dealings by the registered owner. It may be withdrawn at any time.

When a caution is lodged the registered owner must be notified and he may apply for its discharge. If he does so, a notice will be sent to the cautioner warning him that the caution will lapse after the expiration of the period specified in the notice (normally 14 days) unless the registrar makes an order to the contrary. The onus of preventing lapse is placed on the cautioner and he has the opportunity to show cause why the caution should continue or why the dealing should not be registered. The registrar can then order either that the caution should cease to have effect or that it should continue.

An inhibition is of potentially wider effect than a caution. It is an entry on the register forbidding any dealing with lands or charges for a given time, or until further order, or except with the consent of or notice given to some specified person or generally until further order or entry. An inhibition can relate to dealings by persons other than the registered owner and remains effective indefinitely or for whatever period is specified in the relevant entry.

Generally an inhibition imposes greater restrictions on dealings with the land than a caution. Therefore, an inhibition may only be entered by the registrar when he has the consent of all interested parties or is satisfied that there is a *prima facie* case for the making of the entry. It can be withdrawn with the consent of all interested parties or discharged by order of the registrar or the

Searches[86]

7.58 The registers, maps and index of names maintained in the Land Registry and all instruments filed there are open to public inspection on payment of a fee. Members of the public may obtain copies of or extracts from the registers, maps or documents received in the Land Registry on payment of a further fee. The copies can be certified if required. Copies of folios and maps should only

---

[86] Cf paras 5.01-5.29.

be taken as accurate at the date of issue. The possession of a copy folio in no way indicates that a person has an interest in the lands comprised in the folio.

Personal searches

7.59 Anyone wishing to make a personal inspection of any folio, map, index or instrument must attend at the Land Registry's public office, complete a requisition and pay a fee.

Official searches

7.60 When a member of the public, including a solicitor, requisitions an official search it is made by the Land Registry and the result is furnished in a certificate providing the relevant particulars.

A search may provide the details of all registered land held by a particular person or the subsisting entries on a particular folio during a specified period. A search may also confirm whether a piece of land is registered provided that a map is furnished.

Priority searches

7.61 Although a prospective purchaser, lessee or chargee can inspect the land certificate, make a personal search of the folio, or requisition an official search, the information obtained may be out of date when completion of the transaction actually takes place.

There is always the possibility that, between the date on which the state of the title was last verified and the date on which a transaction is registered, some other dealing may have been accepted for registration which could adversely affect the title or security of a purchaser.

To meet this problem the legislation provides for a priority search. It is only available to a person who has actually entered into a contract to purchase, take a lease of or lend money on the security of a charge on registered land.

On application, a certificate of search is issued similar to a normal search, but also stating that a priority entry has been made on the affected folio. The priority entry consists of a note to the effect that if the transfer, lease or charge which is contemplated by the contract is delivered to the Land Registry within 40 days from the date of the certificate it will rank in priority before any other dealing presented for registration during that period.

Telephone searches

7.62 Where it is necessary to obtain information about a registered title quickly, this may be achieved by means of a telephone search. Confirmation can be obtained from the Land Registry that no further entries affecting ownership have been made or are pending on a particular folio since the relevant Land Certificate was last brought up to date or a copy of the folio was last obtained. A telephone search can also be used to confirm that no dealings have been registered or are pending affecting the ownership of a registered charge since such date as may be specified.

Land certificates and certificates of charge[87]

7.63 The registered owner of any registered land may apply for the issue of a land certificate which is to an extent, *prima facie* evidence of his title. The registered owner of a charge may similarly obtain a certificate of charge which will, for most purposes, provide evidence of his title to the charge.

Normally only one land certificate can be issued in respect of any one title. Tenants in common may obtain separate certificates in respect of their individual interests, but in practice this is seldom required.

An application for a land certificate can be made at any time and generally only one land certificate can exist at any given time in respect of a particular title. Except in some special cases, a registered owner can only apply for the issue of a land certificate where one has not been previously produced for a particular title.

Once a land certificate has been issued it should normally be produced for updating each time a dealing affecting the relevant title is presented for registration. There are however some circumstances where a dealing can be accepted for registration without production of all relevant land certificates and certificates of charge, such as orders charging land, in accordance with Land Registration Rules (NI) 1994, rule 128(1).

Replacement certificates

7.64 The registrar has no general power to dispense with production of lost or destroyed certificates, but does have power to issue replacement certificates. The issue of a replacement certificate permanently robs the original of any value. Even if the replacement is subsequently lost and the original is found, the validity of the original cannot be revived and it is necessary to apply for a further replacement.

A replacement certificate should be distinguished from a copy folio. A replacement certificate becomes *prima facie* proof of title. A copy folio is merely proof of the contents of that folio on the date it was issued.

Deposit of certificates

7.65 Since most types of dealing cannot be registered without production of all relevant land certificates, a person having custody of a land certificate can exercise considerable control over the title to which it relates. However, his position is not totally secure because of the transactions which can be registered without the land certificate being produced. These include matrimonial charges, pending actions, cautions, inhibitions, orders charging land, court orders and vesting orders.

---

[87] Cf paras 7.05 and 7.27.

A person with whom a land certificate is deposited as security for the payment of money has an equitable charge on the property to which the certificate relates. The equitable interest may be protected against the possibility of being defeated by a subsequent dealing if a notice is lodged in the Land Registry stating the details of the loan secured.

Lodgment of dealings

7.66 Dealings cannot be accepted for registration unless:

(1) The documents are properly stamped, (or are accompanied by a written undertaking that within a specified period they will be resubmitted properly stamped);

(2) The proper fee has been paid;

(3) Any relevant land certificate or certificate of charge has been produced if required;

(4) The matter is otherwise *prima facie* in order for registration and all documents have been properly executed.

An application for voluntary first registration[88] of the ownership of a freehold or leasehold estate should be accompanied by:

(1) All such original deeds and documents relating to the title as the applicant has in his possession including affidavits, statutory declarations, opinions of counsel, abstracts of title, contracts, searches and requisitions on title as may be required;

(2) A concise statement of title summarising the documents, events and facts on which the claim is based;

(3) An ordnance survey map sufficient to identify the land or a building or development plan;

(4) A schedule of all documents lodged including;
    (i) the assurance to the applicant
    (ii) the fee farm grant or lease under which the land is held
    (iii) any mortgage or charge to be registered
    (iv) any other document which is referred to in the application containing details of a matter which requires to be registered.

Every application or dealing lodged by a solicitor must be accompanied by a statement in writing, which should be in Form 100 containing the following information:

(1) The names of the parties;

---

[88] See paras 7.07-7.14 *re* Compulsory Registration.

(2) Particulars of the registration applied for;
(3) The documents enclosed;
(4) The fee enclosed;
(5) The details of the person to whom the land certificate is to be delivered after registration, if not the solicitor concerned.

Generally, all deeds and documents lodged in the Land Registry in connection with a dealing, other than the land certificate, are filed as instruments and retained. Copies of the documents may be returned on request.

Solicitor's certificates

7.67 To aid the speed of the registration process the Land Registry now encourages the increased use of solicitor's certificates in a wide range of situations as an alternative to affidavits and more formal evidence. For example, on first registration, on modification of a burden and on extinguishment of a lease such a certificate can be produced. In most instances more detailed proofs are no longer required but in particular cases the more formal procedures may still be followed if preferred.

If a solicitor makes an application based on his certificate he is giving a warranty as to the facts stated in it. In a case where the facts are not absolutely certain, the client should complete an affidavit so that the solicitor is not making statements about matters of which he has no personal knowledge.

Execution of documents

7.68 Normally the execution of a deed relating to registered land must be attested by two witnesses, but if it is witnessed by a solicitor, no further witness is required. The execution of other documents such as forms requires one witness. A witness must state his name, address and occupation. A document executed by a solicitor does not need to be witnessed.

Where a document is executed by a blind person or by a person making his mark, an affidavit of an attesting witness or a solicitor's certificate is required verifying the execution.

Execution by attorney

7.69 If a document is executed by an attorney, the power of attorney, or a certified copy of it must be produced to the Land Registry together with evidence of the identity of the donor of the power. This can be provided by solicitor's certificate.

If any transaction between the donee of a power of attorney and the person dealing with him is not completed within 12 months of the power coming into operation, evidence is required that the power had not been revoked at the time of the transaction.

In the case of an enduring power of attorney the evidence that the power has not been revoked can be in the form of a statutory declaration by the person dealing with the donee that at the time of completion of the transaction he was not aware of any revocation of the power.

A solicitor's certificate may be accepted as an alternative to a statutory declaration. It should certify that the document lodged for registration has been executed validly by the donee of the power of attorney on behalf of the donor pursuant to a power in that behalf contained in the power of attorney and that such power has not been revoked or there is a conclusive presumption under the Powers of Attorney Act (NI) 1971, section 4 or, as the case may be, the Enduring Powers of Attorney (NI) Order 1987, article 11, as to the validity of the transaction.[89]

Alteration of instruments

7.70 If alteration is required after an instrument has been presented for registration, it may be withdrawn for alteration. The alteration must normally be re-executed by the parties to the instrument and any other person affected by the alteration. Where a document has been withdrawn for alteration it is deemed to have been received on the date on which it is returned.

If the map of the property annexed to the instrument requires alteration, the amended plan can be signed by all interested parties or their solicitors and it is not necessary for the actual document to be re-executed.

Where a document has been withdrawn for the purposes of an alteration the dealing to which it relates is deemed to have been first received in the Land Registry on the date on which it is returned.

If a mistake is discovered after registration has been effected a deed of rectification is normally required. Under LRA (NI) 1970, section 69, the registrar has a limited jurisdiction to order rectification in respect of an incorrect registration caused by an error made in the Land Registry or by a mistake in a document presented for registration. Except where the error is of a purely formal nature, the consent of all interested parties must be obtained.

---

[89] Under these provisions a third party is entitled to assume that the power is still fully operative as long as it is expressed to be irrevocable and the third party is not aware that the power has been revoked. See Powers paras 25.30-25.35.

CHAPTER EIGHT
TITLE: (3) FLATS AND APARTMENTS

Introduction

8.01 The development and sale of flats has become more common in recent years. Although the physical characteristics of flats are quite different from those of single free-standing dwellings, many of the issues involved in the purchase are the same. For example, the title has to be examined, property certificates obtained and consideration given to the same areas of potential difficulty in both cases.

Obviously, there are other matters which have to be investigated in respect of a flat because of its distinctive physical characteristics. When acting for the purchaser of a flat it is important to check that the position of the flat owner is adequately secured and protected.

Each flat is part of a larger structure and is dependent for support on other flats or parts of the structure. Various parts of the whole building are often shared in common with other occupiers. These may include entrances, stairways, lifts and passageways. The garden and access roads may also be shared in common. Services in respect of the common areas also have to be shared, including electricity, water and heating.

Traditionally, flats have almost universally been sold by way of long lease so that the lessor can impose identical obligations on each flat owner and because it was easier to enforce positive leasehold covenants against successors in title. Following the implementation of the Property (NI) Order 1997 the position is unlikely to change substantially because the grant of a long lease of a flat is one of the few situations where a long lease of domestic property may still be created.

MANAGEMENT COMPANY

8.02 The developer/lessor retains ownership of the common parts of the building and sometimes also of the actual structure. However he may not necessarily wish to get involved managing a block of flats once he has sold all the apartments and it is common for the lease to include a third party, a management company, which takes responsibility for the management of the development.

A management company is a limited company which is initially set up and registered by the developer. Its purpose of managing a particular development will be reflected in its memorandum and articles of association. The number of shares issued in the company is equal to the number of apartments in the development.

The agreement for lease provides that on completion of the sale of each flat the purchaser takes one share in the company, so that when the development is complete all the shares are owned by the flat owners. Provision is made in the lease that on any subsequent assignment of the flat for the share in the management company to be transferred to the assignee.

Interim provisions may be made to run the company until all the flats have been sold. Two nominees of the lessor may take the first two shares in the company and hold them until the last two units are sold, when the shares are transferred to the purchasers. Until all the flats have been sold these nominees will be the only shareholders with voting rights.

Control of the management company is transferred to the flat owners when all the flats have been purchased, so that they can control the common areas and enforce the covenants against any individual owner. The management company usually becomes responsible for the repair and maintenance of the structure and of the common areas. This is financed by the service charge collected from the flat owners. The property is usually insured by the management company taking out a block policy for the entire building.

The management company is then run by the residents who appoint a company secretary, make the annual return to the companies registry, hold meetings, etc. If a management company is involved in this way it is essential that once the last flat in the development has been sold the lessor will then convey his reversion and his interest in the common parts to the management company which will thus also become the lessor of the premises.

If the reversion is not transferred to the management company it could have real difficulties in enforcing covenants against successors in title of the original flat owners. If the management company does not have an estate in the development it could also encounter difficulties in exercising rights over the various apartments.

THE LEASE

The physical perimeters of the flat

8.03 It is important that the precise boundaries of the flat are properly defined. Both a plan of the flat and one of the building or development should normally be provided. It should be clear exactly which walls, floors and ceilings are included in the demise. In most instances (other than very small apartment blocks) it is wise to exclude the roof, exterior and structure of the whole building from the demise as these should remain the responsibility of the management company or developer.

The lessee's rights

8.04 The lessee must have various rights which can be granted as easements.

These include:

    (1)   An easement to gain access to the block of flats;

    (2)   An easement to gain access to the flat via common stairways, lifts, entrance halls etc;

    (3)   The right to use the common areas inside and outside the building, and to use shared facilities;

(4) Any further rights, for example, to use a particular space or area for parking, keep dustbins or hang washing;
(5) The right to support from the rest of the building;
(6) The right to use service media running through the building;
(7) The right to enter other flats and the common parts to maintain the service media and the flat itself.

To be effective the last two rights must have been excepted out of the leases to the other tenants. The lessor cannot grant a right over someone else's property in one lease when he has failed to reserve that right in the original lease of the property.

Responsibility for maintaining the rest of the building

8.05 It is important to ensure that someone is legally responsible for looking after each and every part of the whole building. An obligation should be imposed on each flat owner to keep his premises in good repair and on the developer or management company to repair and maintain the rest of the building, that is, to keep it clean, painted, decorated, and properly lit.

If there is a management company it should be granted an easement to enter the apartments to inspect and ensure that each flat owner is carrying out any repair obligations which could affect the other owners.

Exceptions and reservations

8.06 Whoever is responsible for the maintenance of the structure and service media should have the right to enter all the flats to carry out the necessary works. Exceptions and reservations should also be made by the lessor for the benefit of the other flat owners, such as a right of entry to carry out repairs to services which run through it and serve other flats.

As a matter of drafting, if a management company is involved, the lessor and management company should have identical rights reserved in their favour.

Insurance

8.07 It is essential that an obligation is imposed for the insurance of both the individual apartments and the common parts. The obligation to insure each apartment can be imposed on the lessee with the obligation to use the proceeds of any claim to rebuild and reinstate. The developer or management company should have the right to inspect the certificate of insurance and obtain confirmation that the premium has been paid. This arrangement may be appropriate in small developments where there are no common parts.

The obligation to insure the whole building, that is all the apartments and the common parts, can be imposed on the developer or management company with a similar obligation to reinstate and a right for the lessees to inspect the certificate of insurance. The developer or management company should be given the right to recover the cost of the premiums from the apartment owners.

The management company

8.08 It is important to ascertain:

(1) How the development is managed;
(2) The powers of the management company, by examining the memorandum and articles, to establish that it has all necessary power to manage the development;
(3) That the company is being properly run and that annual returns are being filed in the company's register;
(4) That the vendor's share in the management company is transferred to the purchaser.

Service charge

8.09 The provision for the purchaser to contribute to the costs of common maintenance should be examined. The management company may only be obliged to carry out its obligations subject to the lessee paying his contribution.

In the lease there should be a schedule setting out all the costs and expenses to which the lessee will have to contribute. The expenses and obligations imposed may not appear too great while the building is in good repair but are likely to become more onerous with the passage of time. Questions should be asked regarding the amount of the service charge paid over say, the last three years and any reasons why it may increase in future. In the case of a new apartment, an estimate of the annual charge should be furnished.

Normally a service charge includes such matters as maintenance and repair of the building, refuse disposal, lighting and heating, window cleaning, redecoration and refurbishment of common areas, estate agents' and accountants' fees. The lease should contain clear provision as to how the service charge is to be assessed and collected and how it is to be divided between the various apartment owners. A detailed account of the payments made in preceding years should be furnished.

Usual lessee's covenants

8.10 The covenants in a lease of a flat, both positive and negative, are usually fairly extensive. They vary according to the particular development but normally include obligations to pay rent, rates and outgoings, to keep in good repair, obligations as to decoration and maintenance, restrictions as to user, prohibition of nuisance and prohibition of structural alterations.

Particular obligations

8.11 Additional obligations are often imposed on each apartment owner in order to maintain the standards in the whole building. It is preferable for these matters to be set out in the lease as covenants rather than be left to trust.

For example, covenants:

(1) Not to make too much noise;

(2) Not to hang out washing other than in approved areas;
(3) Not to display signs or external aerials;
(4) Not to decorate the exterior other than in a specific manner;
(5) Not to keep pets;
(6) Not to sublet the flat and not to assign or sublet part of it;
(7) Not to do anything which would invalidate the insurance cover.

It is advisable to ensure that all previous leases in the block have been on identical terms to be certain that there are the same provisions for covenants, exceptions and reservations in them all. All subsequent leases should also be on the same terms and there should be a covenant to this effect in the lease.

Unfortunately, if deficiencies are discovered in a lease, in many cases, the developer will not amend it, especially if many of the other units in a development have been sold. If a solicitor is unhappy with the provisions in a particular case he should explain the position to the client and his lender. If necessary he should advise against purchasing the apartment.

Enforcement of obligations[90]

8.12 At common law a covenant may be enforced where there is privity of contract or privity of estate between the parties. The parties to a deed are able to enforce against each other because there is privity of contract between them. It is essential for the various parties to have actually covenanted with the other parties properly, for example, "the management company covenants with the lessor and the lessee" or, "the lessee covenants with the lessor and the management company".

The successors in title of the lessor and the lessee can enforce the covenants between the original lessor and lessee because there is privity of estate between them. However, if the reversion is not transferred to the management company there will be real problems when trying to enforce covenants against a reluctant flat owner who is a successor in title to the original lessee. As the management company is not the lessor there is no privity of estate between it and the lessee. As the flat owner is now an assignee of the original lessee, nor is there any privity of contract between the parties. In these circumstances the flat owner may also find it difficult to enforce covenants against the management company.

There are a number of ways in which it is possible to overcome a situation where an assignee and a management company cannot enforce covenants against each other.

(1) The management company and lessee can covenant in the original lease that upon any assignment of the property the assignee and management company will enter into a separate deed of covenant reflecting their respective obligations. Alternatively, the covenants could be repeated in

---

[90] Cf Enforcement of Leasehold Covenants paras 20.19-20.24.

the assignment to which the management company is made a party. This will maintain privity of contract but is a fairly cumbersome means of doing so. There is also the obvious problem that if a particular flat owner has failed to carry out this obligation when the assignment of his flat is drafted, then privity of contract is lost.

(2) The lessor can covenant in the original lease that he will be responsible for any of the management company's obligations which the latter fails to fulfil. He can also covenant to enforce all breaches of covenant by the lessee. However, the lessor may not find this option acceptable. Even if this obligation is included in the lease, by the time a party wishes to rely on it the developer may be impossible to trace or insolvent.

(3) Under the general principle set forth in *Halsall* v *Brizell*[91] a landowner may have the burden of covenants enforced against him because this is reasonable in view of the fact that he has a reciprocal right to enforce the benefit of related covenants.

(4) Because there are difficulties and dangers in relying on any of these options the only real solution is for the lessor to agree that on the sale of the final apartment he will convey his interest in the reversion and the common parts to the management company which will then become the lessor, thus maintaining privity of estate between itself and any successors to the lessee. The management company must be given the power to take land in its memorandum and articles of association. If this approach is adopted the lease should be drafted in such a way that all of the management company's covenants are also included as covenants by the lessor. It is also prudent to give the lessor the obligations mentioned in (2) above.

Even if it is possible to enforce a covenant against the management company there is then the question whether the company is worth suing. It may not have sufficient capital to pay costs or damages. If it does not take the reversion in the land its assets are non-existent. All it will have is the power to raise money to maintain and repair.

If the company has the reversion but only a nominal ground rent is charged in respect of each flat its position will be little better. Where a more reasonable ground rent is charged it may be possible to accumulate sufficient funds in reserve to meet the costs of any actions.

Enforcement of covenants between flat owners

8.13 There is neither privity of contract nor of estate between individual flat owners but there are several possible ways in which the covenants can be enforced by the parties against each other.

---

[91] [1957] Ch 169.

Real Property Act 1845, section 5

8.14 This provides that a person may take the benefit of a covenant made in his favour even though he was not a party to the deed in which it was contained. The courts have limited the benefit of the clause, for instance by suggesting that the covenant must touch and concern the land of the covenantee.[92] It has been held that the section does not enable a covenant to be made with a person who does not actually exist and is not capable of being identified at the date of the deed.

In some deeds there are covenants by the lessee with the lessor and the lessees of the other apartments. It is suggested that under section 5 such covenants may enable the owners of flats already leased to enforce against a particular lessee because they could be identified at the date of the lease but may not be effective in favour of persons leasing other flats after the date of the lease.

Rules in Elliston v Reacher[93]

8.15 Tenants in a building scheme such as a new development or block of flats could, in certain circumstances, enforce the restrictive covenants of other purchasers in the development even though the various owners in the development are strangers to each other as a result of rules laid down in the case of *Elliston v Reacher*.

In order to come within the scope of this rule:

(1) Each party must have derived title from the same vendor;

(2) The same restrictive covenants must apply to each dwelling within the development;

(3) The covenants must be for the general benefit of all the owners within the development; and

(4) The covenants must have been intended to be enforceable between the tenants.

The simplest way of protecting flat owners *inter se* is to include in the lease a covenant by the management company or lessor to the effect that all necessary steps will be taken to ensure that the other lessees would observe their covenants.

---

[92] *Lloyd v Byrne* (1888) 22 LR Ir 269.
[93] [1908] 2 Ch 374.

CHAPTER NINE

TITLE: (4) BUILDING AND DEVELOPMENT PROPERTY

9.01 The documentation required for the purchase of new property is not substantially different from that for existing houses and the same general procedures can be followed. Points of particular importance are considered below.

Title

9.02 It is essential to investigate the title in the same way as for existing property. Unless the new building is on one existing site, photocopies only of the prior title are furnished and the purchaser is not generally entitled to the originals. An abstract of the prior title may also be provided.

If the property is part of a development, it was, prior to 10 January 2000, the operative date for the relevant provisions of the Property (NI) Order 1997, usually sold by way of the creation of a long lease. As a result of the prohibition of the creation of long leases of dwelling houses over 50 years and fee farm grants by article 30 and article 28 respectively of the 1997 Order, new sites which have a freehold title are now sold by way of conveyance or transfer. New sites in which the developer only has a leasehold interest are sold by way of assignment of part[94] but covenants may be imposed in the same manner as in a traditional lease.

A draft of the proposed deed is sent with the prior title at the beginning of the transaction. A location map of the development and a map of the site should also be attached. The new assurance (with a counterpart) is usually drafted and engrossed by the vendor but stamped and registered by the purchaser at his own expense after completion.

Contract

9.03 A new property is often sold by means of two separate agreements which together comprise the contract: an agreement for conveyance and a building agreement. The former sets out the details of the title which are to be granted to the purchaser and the latter relates to the arrangements for the actual building of the house. The two agreements may be in separate but interdependent documents or in one amalgamated form.

---

[94] When the provisions for redemption of ground rents are implemented, it will be easier for developers to purchase the freehold of the lands which they own in leasehold and in turn sell the freehold on to the purchasers. At the time of writing (April 2000) the most recent proposals are comprised in the draft Ground Rents Bill. Cf para 6.24.

Other essential documents

9.04 This documentation may not all be available immediately, but it should be furnished before completion. The purchaser should make the contract conditional upon any matter for which the appropriate documentation has not been issued or produced when the contract is signed.

If the purchaser is obtaining a loan to finance the purchase, the lender will probably make the offer of advance conditional on these approvals and certificates being issued.

If an existing property is less than ten years old these matters are still relevant and should be provided with the title.

Planning permission[95]

9.05 A copy of both the outline, (if there is one) and the detailed planning permission granted by the Department of the Environment for NI ('the DOE') for the property should be furnished. All reserved matters and conditions should be checked.

Building control approval[96]

9.06 The plans for the building should be approved. A certificate of approval should be available confirming that the plans comply with building regulations. The construction is also subject to inspection by the local council and a certificate of final inspection is issued on completion of the building works.

Road bond and private streets agreement[97]

9.07 If the road fronting the property has not been made up and adopted and there are more than four houses in the development, a purchaser should satisfy himself that a road bond has been obtained from the developer under the provisions of the Private Streets (NI) Order 1980.

The DOE enters into an article 32 agreement with the developer whereby the developer agrees to properly construct and complete the streets to the satisfaction of the DOE. When the work has been completed and the road has been maintained for at least 12 months in accordance with the agreement the DOE will issue a certificate to that effect. After approval the road is adopted as a public road maintainable at public expense.

The developer must secure the performance of the agreement by way of a guarantee bond or other means acceptable to the DOE in the estimated cost of the street works.

The road is often finished after the building work and by the time of the second sale of the property it should usually be adopted. The road bond is then no longer relevant.

---

[95] See Planning Permission paras 11.01-11.39.
[96] See Building Control paras 12.01-12.24.
[97] See Property Certificates paras 5.12-5.29.

Where there are fewer than four houses in the development it is possible for the road to remain as a private road. In that case the purchaser should ensure that he is granted the necessary rights of way and that there are satisfactory covenants for the repair and maintenance of the road.

NHBC[98]

9.08 The National House-Building Council operates a scheme whereby it inspects the construction of new houses built by all builders registered with it to ensure that the construction is of a required standard. The scheme also provides insurance for up to ten years for specified problems and defects occurring or subsequently discovered.

Where the builder is registered with NHBC, 'buildmark cover' is available to the first purchaser and his solicitor should ask the developer's solicitor to supply the documentation.

NHBC self-build cover is available where a purchaser of a site who is not a registered builder builds the house himself.

Where no NHBC cover is available and an architect is employed, he should furnish a certificate confirming that he has supervised the construction of the house. The certificate should be worded so that it is of some value if it later transpires that there is a structural problem in the building.[99] A solicitor for a subsequent purchaser should establish whether or not the benefit of this certificate can be assigned to the purchaser.

Company

9.09 Where the builder or developer is a company it is necessary to furnish a copy certificate of incorporation.

Water and electricity

9.10 It is essential to ensure that there are mains electricity and water supplies to the property and that there is a connection to the main sewer. The mains may not yet be adopted if the supplies run through the new development.

It is advisable to find out whether the services run through adjoining lands, in which case easements are required. This is particularly important in the case of an individual site. Also ensure that there are no outstanding charges to the statutory bodies for the connections.

Under the Water and Sewerage Services (NI) Order 1973, article 17, as amended by the Water and Sewerage Services (Amendment) (NI) Order 1993 the DOE will agree to proposals for the construction of foul and/or surface water sewers serving a development subject to specified terms and conditions. A copy of the agreement may be requested.

---

[98] See NHBC paras 13.01-13.16.

[99] Building societies will sometimes impose special conditions in relation to the architect's certificate, *eg*, as to his professional qualifications and indemnity insurance.

Septic tank

9.11 Where the property is not connected to a main sewer but is served by a septic tank it is important to establish the location of the tank and its soakaway or effluent pipes. If both are within the boundaries of the property to be purchased there is no problem, but if either or both are on adjacent property the necessary easements should be obtained.

Under the Water Act (NI) 1972, sections 7 and 8 no-one is allowed to discharge sewage effluent into a waterway or underground stratum without the consent of the DOE Water Executive. If such consent is not obtained the discharge is illegal. The property certificate should reveal whether there is a consent. If there is not, it can be obtained at any stage, provided the septic tank and system for discharge meet with the approval of the Water Executive.

CHAPTER TEN

FINANCING THE PURCHASE

Introduction

10.01 Many clients require a loan to finance the purchase of property and the money is usually raised by way of mortgage.[100] There are several types of mortgage now available and it is likely that more variations will develop in the future. The mortgage market has constantly to adapt to changing conditions in the financial world and to the introduction of new government policies.

When considering a mortgage, a borrower has to consider;

(1) The source of the loan;
(2) The amount of the loan;
(3) The method of repayment.

A client should always be advised to obtain independent financial advice as to the most suitable mortgage available for the property in his particular circumstances. If he arranges the purchase through an estate agent he may be encouraged to apply for a loan through a particular institution to which the agency is linked, without realising that there is any alternative.

It is particularly important that anyone involved in mortgage lending advice should provide the client with Consumer Credit Act 1974 documentation which gives details of the annual percentage rate (APR) and the total interest payable over the full term. The interest eventually paid is approximately three times the amount borrowed.

FACTORS TO BE TAKEN INTO ACCOUNT

Ancillary costs

10.02 Buildings and contents insurance may vary from lender to lender. Contents insurance and buildings insurance can be arranged independently of the mortgage package, although the buildings insurance must be to the satisfaction of the lender. The cost of mortgage payments protection which provides cover for sickness, accident and involuntary unemployment can also vary considerably. It is therefore important to check the actual costs of types of insurance before taking out a loan.

Valuation fees

10.03 These are an important factor in obtaining a mortgage and vary considerably from lender to lender. It is essential to realise that a valuation is just that: a valuation and not a survey. Some lenders do not advise the

---

[100] See Mortgages paras 26.01-26.37.

borrower of the identity of the valuer and do not make the valuation report available if the purchase does not proceed, despite the fact that the borrower has paid for it. It is therefore advisable to enquire about valuation fees when calculating the costs of the mortgage application.

Lenders

10.04 The majority of loans for domestic property are obtained from building societies and banks including those banks which are converted building societies. Building societies generally do not consider loans for commercial premises (although there are exceptions) and are only permitted very limited unsecured lending.

Building societies are strictly controlled by statute which ensures that the bulk of a society's commercial assets consists of first mortgages of residential property.[101] This means that some potential borrowers may have to look elsewhere for a loan. If, for example, the purchase includes an area of land and the value of the building on it is insufficient security for the loan required, a building society loan may not be available. The former building societies which are now banks have not significantly extended the range of properties on which they are prepared to offer loans. In the case of a holiday home, for example, a borrower can normally only obtain a loan from a traditional bank.

Other lenders include certain employers, such as insurance companies, who are able to give loans to their employees on favourable terms, but this is obviously a very small part of the market. At one time NIHE also made a significant number of mortgages, but when interest rates rose in the 1980s the borrowers were encouraged to obtain loans from other sources. Private arrangements which in the last century were a common means of financing the purchase of property, are still made occasionally.

Value of property

10.05 The amount which the financial institutions are prepared to advance to borrowers as a proportion of the value of the property varies with the economic climate. Although 100 per cent mortgages are sometimes available, the normal maximum most lenders will consider is 90-95 per cent of the value. The proportional limit is based on the lesser of the purchase price and the valuation.

Mortgage indemnity

10.06 A mortgage indemnity policy is generally required as a matter of practice, rather than of law, for loans exceeding 75 per cent of the purchase price or valuation of the property. This rule is designed to protect the lender if the borrower defaults and the property is sold at a loss. The borrower has to pay a one off premium for the policy which increases with the amount borrowed, but the method of charging varies. It may be added to the loan,

---

[101] Building Societies Act 1986 as amended by the Building Societies Act 1997.

deducted from the advance, requested from the borrower before completion, or converted into extra interest for the first year of the mortgage term.

The fee for the policy is a one-off premium made by the borrower. Some or all of the fee may be used by the lender at its discretion to obtain mortgage indemnity insurance to act as extra security for its sole benefit. The insurance does not protect the borrower if the property is subsequently taken into possession and sold for less than the amount owed. The borrower may be liable to pay all sums owing including arrears, interest and legal fees. If a claim is paid to the lender under this insurance, the insurer generally has the right to recover this amount from the borrower.

Income of borrower

10.07 The income of the borrower is another factor taken into account in calculating the maximum loan available. The loan is limited to a multiple of the borrower's gross annual income, which varies from time to time, but is usually in the region of 2.5 or 3. In the case of a couple, the salary of the highest earner is multiplied by the multiplier and then added to the lower income to assess the amount.

Collateral security

10.08 Additional independent security may be taken by the lender from the mortgagor or a third party to cover the amount of the loan alongside, but subordinate to, the principal security of the property. An alternative is a guarantee by a third party for repayment of the mortgage debt or a mortgage of other property owned by the mortgagor to secure his liability.

The most common example is a mortgage of life policy by the mortgagor on his own life to secure the same amount as that secured by the principal mortgage. Traditionally such a life policy was assigned to the lender, thereby preventing the borrower from using the policy for any purpose other than that of providing collateral security for the loan.

In recent years some lenders have relaxed their requirements and thereby placed the security of the policies at more risk. These lenders now request either that the policies be deposited with the title deeds or that the details are noted at their offices.

MORTGAGE SCHEMES

Capital and interest: Repayment mortgage

10.09 This is the standard traditional type of mortgage. The borrower undertakes to repay the capital lent together with interest over the term fixed for repayment. The payments are made monthly and there is normally very little capital repaid over the early years because the interest is repaid first. Interest rates will fluctuate over the term of the mortgage.

A repayment mortgage is normally protected by some form of life assurance to repay the loan if the borrower dies during the mortgage term. The main types of cover are: decreasing term assurance (mortgage protection); level term assurance; and pension term assurance.

There is no investment element in any of the policies and they do not have a cash value.

Mortgage protection is the cheapest form of life insurance for repayment of the loan because it provides cover which decreases throughout the term as the loan is repaid. The premium is static and does not vary over the repayment period.

Level term assurance also covers the loan in the event of the death of the borrower but the sum assured remains the same throughout the term and is fixed by reference to the amount initially owed. This means that in the event of the borrower's death later in the term there may be a balance payable to his estate. In some cases the premium may be reviewed.

Pension term assurance is similar to level term assurance. It is available to the self-employed and those employees who are not in an occupational pension scheme. Tax relief is available on the premiums paid.

Interest only mortgage

10.10 Under this type of mortgage the monthly payments to the lender consist of interest only and the capital must be repaid at the end of the mortgage term. In order to provide money to repay the capital the borrower can choose to pay premiums to some form of investment or pension which will mature at the end of the mortgage term. The most common ways of providing a lump sum involve making regular contributions to an endowment savings plan, personal pension plan or individual savings account.

Endowments

10.11 By this method a monthly premium is paid into an endowment policy with an insurance company which pays a lump sum either at the end of the mortgage term or earlier on death. The lump sum is designed to repay the capital and there may be a surplus available at the end of the term. While the minimum sum payable on death is guaranteed there is always the risk that the proceeds of the policy may be insufficient to repay the loan at the end of the mortgage term.

Pensions

10.12 Under this type of mortgage the borrower pays only the interest on the loan to the lender over the mortgage term and makes another payment each month towards a pension. The mortgage runs until the borrower reaches retirement age. Then part of the cash sum accumulated in the pension fund pays off the outstanding mortgage. The lender will only accept a proportion, such as 80 per cent, of that cash sum towards repayment of the loan because the fund providing pension benefits is thereby substantially reduced.

A term assurance policy is also required for a pension mortgage because the actual pension cannot be assigned to the lender as collateral security for the loan. Using the cash sum to repay the mortgage decreases the eventual benefits. There is no absolute guarantee that the mortgage will be repaid.

This type of pension is suitable for the self-employed professional person and to a lesser extent, those in non-pensionable employment, because it is flexible. The self-employed pay gross contributions and claim Schedule D tax relief. Employed borrowers make contributions net of basic rate tax.

Individual Savings Accounts (ISAs)

10.13 Contributions to an ISA can be made monthly or by a lump sum and the mortgage is repaid when the plan is encashed. An ISA offers two options: (i) Mini; and (ii) Maxi; both of which provide investment in stocks and shares, life assurance and cash. Since the value of ISAs can go down as well as up there is no guarantee that the mortgage will be repaid.

Interest payments

10.14 The interest payments made to either a repayment or to an interest only mortgage can take several forms and the most common ones are as undernoted.

Variable rate

10.15 When the interest rate set by the lender changes, so does the interest rate payable on the mortgage.

Discounted rate

10.16 The borrower is given a discount off the variable rate for a set period on all or part of his loan. If the variable rate rises, so does the discounted rate. There are substantial penalties on repayment during the discount period.

Fixed rate

10.17 The interest rate is fixed for a period of say two, three or five years. After the fixed-rate term has expired the interest reverts to the variable rate. There is no element of flexibility in the terms of the mortgage and the charges are often higher than normal. There are usually high penalties for early redemption of the loan.

Combination mortgage

10.18 Some lenders are prepared to consider making a loan which is a combination of two of the basic types of mortgage: the repayment mortgage; and the interest only mortgage. The combination mortgage is usually part repayment and part endowment. This suits a borrower who may be able to make occasional lump sum capital payments.

Second mortgage

10.19 When a borrower wishes to increase his borrowing and cannot extend his existing mortgage, he may be able to obtain a second mortgage from a different bank or finance company. He can only obtain a second mortgage up to a maximum of his equity of redemption. For example, if the property is valued at £30,000 and his first mortgage is for £20,000, his second mortgage should be for a maximum of £10,000. If the second mortgage is obtained to finance improvements to the property, the lender will take its increased value afterwards into account.

A second mortgage is charged at a higher rate of interest than the first. It is usually repayable over a shorter term and imposes more severe penalties for default.

Income tax on mortgages

10.20 Individuals who made payments of interest on mortgages were, until recently, entitled to income tax relief for interest paid if the relevant conditions were satisfied under the MIRAS scheme. The MIRAS scheme was introduced by the Finance Act 1982 whereby payments of relevant interest by a qualifying borrower could be made net of basic income tax. This tax relief was politically controversial and was criticised as being too favourable to property owners. The relief was gradually phased out and from 6 April 2000 removed completely. There is now no income tax relief on mortgages used to acquire a main residence. However, relief at the basic rate of tax continues for people aged 65 and over who take out loans to buy life annuities.

CHAPTER ELEVEN

PLANNING PERMISSION

Introduction

11.01 The purpose of planning policy is to control the development and use of land in the best interests of the community. The overall responsibility for planning and development of land and the actual administration of it are vested in the Department of the Environment for Northern Ireland ('the DOE'). The planning function is now carried out by the Planning Service as an agency within the DOE.

The submission of a planning application provides the opportunity for a particular development to be considered against the background of the general interests of the locality. The amenity of the land, the environment and the general economy are factors which are taken into consideration by the DOE in making the decision whether or not to grant planning permission.

DEVELOPMENT

11.02 The Planning (NI) Order 1991 ('the 1991 Order') governs planning in Northern Ireland. Article 12 contains the general principle that planning permission is required for the carrying out of any development of land and that is the case unless the need to obtain permission is specifically excluded or permission is granted automatically.

There is nothing to prevent the construction of unlawful development but there is an indirect sanction in that development without permission may result in enforcement action being taken by the DOE.

The concept of development is defined in article 11(1) as the carrying out of building, engineering, mining or other operations in, on, over or under land, or the making of any material change in the use of any buildings or other land. Development is thus divided into two classes: (i) operational development and (ii) development by a material change in the use of any buildings or other land.[97]

The question whether proposals amount to a change of use or an operational development may be difficult to answer. Where the DOE determines that the proposals do not amount to a development or that planning permission is not required, such determination is equivalent to the granting of planning permission. There is a right of appeal against a determination under the 1991 Order, article 41, to the Planning Appeals Commission, (the 'PAC').

Operational development

11.03 Operational development is activity which results in some physical alteration of the land and has some degree of permanence to the land itself.

---

[97] The distinction was discussed in *Parkes v Secretary of State for the Environment* [1979] 1 All ER 211.

Article 2(2) provides that building operations include rebuilding, structural alterations, additions to buildings and other operations. Engineering operations include the formation or laying of access roads.

The meaning of other operations is in some doubt.[98] It may mean such operations of a constructive character, leading to an identifiable or positive result, as might alter the physical characteristics of land sufficiently substantially to be within the general contemplation of the planning legislation or it may be similar to building operations or engineering operations. The definition of a building extends to any structure or erection.[99] Demolition work may, but does not necessarily, constitute development.[100]

Mining operations are defined as the winning and working of minerals in, on or under land whether by surface or underground working.

Material change of use

11.04 Use of the buildings or land is activity which is done in, alongside or on the land but does not interfere with the actual physical characteristics of the land. The 1991 Order, article 11(3) specifies that the following expressly involve a material change of use:

(1) Subdivision of dwelling house

(2) Deposit of waste on land

Material change of use is not otherwise defined in the 1991 Order and the question is one of fact and degree in each case.[101] Insignificant changes of use may be ignored. There are a number of considerations which the courts have taken into account in determining whether or not a material change of use has taken place.

Intensification

11.05 Intensification of use can amount to a material change, whether it is a primary or an ancillary use.

The planning unit

11.06 The land and planning unit in question has to be defined. A change of use which relates to only a small part of the owner's land may not be material in relation to the land as a whole. The question is whether the smaller area is a distinct planning unit. For example, if one flat in a block of ten is used as a shop, is the relevant unit the whole block, or just the flat which has become a shop?

---

[98] See *eg, Coleshill and District Investment Co Ltd* v *Minister of Housing and Local Government* [1969] 2 All ER 525 for discussion.

[99] See *Barvis* v *Secretary of State for the Environment* (1971) 22 P&CR 710 on the question as to whether the work has resulted in the erection of a building.

[100] See *Cambridge CC* v *Secretary of State for the Environment* [1992] 21 EG 108.

[101] *Marshall* v *Nottingham City Corpn* [1960] 1 All ER 659.

The answer to the question depends on the facts in each case. Where there is clearly a single main purpose of the use of land with incidental secondary activities or where a variety of activities are carried on to a similar degree, it may be possible to consider the whole unit of occupation. However, where two or more physically separate and distinct areas within a single unit of occupation are occupied for substantially different and unrelated purposes it may be that each ought to be considered as a separate planning unit.[102]

Usually the unit of occupation is the appropriate planning unit, unless a smaller unit can be recognised as being occupied for a separate use both physically and functionally. In the case of a dwelling house however it has been said that it can rarely if ever be right to regard one room in it as a separate planning unit.[103] In the case of a block of flats in single ownership but let to different tenants the planning unit will usually be each individual flat.[104]

Primary and ancillary uses

11.07 Planning control is concerned with the primary use of land and not with uses which are considered ancillary to the primary use. For example, a factory may have offices which are ancillary to its primary use as a factory.

A primary use carries with it the right to carry on ancillary uses which may vary in duration and intensity while not amounting to development. If the primary use is unchanged, there is no material change of use. If the primary use disappears, the ancillary use also disappears.

Seasonal use

11.08 Where land is used for one purpose for a period of the year and then for another purpose during another period of the year the land has two uses and the change from one to the other does not constitute development.[105]

ACTIVITIES WHICH ARE NOT DEVELOPMENT

11.09 The 1991 Order, article 11(2) lists a number of acts which are not development for the purposes of the Order:

    (1) Maintenance, improvement or alteration of the interior;

    (2) Maintenance of mains, pipes, cables or other apparatus;

    (3) Incidental uses;

    (4) Use for agriculture and forestry;

    (5) Use for any other purpose of the same class specified in the Planning (Use Classes) Order (NI) 1989 ('UCO').

---

[102] *Burdle* v *Secretary of State for the Environment* [1972] 3 All ER 240. See also statement in *G Percy Trentham Ltd* v *Gloucestershire CC* [1966] 1 All ER 701.
[103] *Wood* v *Secretary of State for the Environment* [1973] 2 All ER 404.
[104] *Johnston* v *Secretary of State for the Environment* (1974) 28 P&CR 424.
[105] *Webber* v *Minister of Housing and Local Government* [1967] 3 All ER 981.

Planning (Use Classes) Order (NI) 1989

11.10 The scheme of the UCO is to list various uses of land in classes as follows:

Class 1	Shops
Class 2	Financial, professional and other services
Class 3	Business not within Class 2
Class 4	Light industrial
Class 5	General industrial
Classes 6 to 10	Special industrial
Class 11	Storage or distribution
Class 12	Guest houses and hotels
Class 13	Residential institutions
Class 14	Dwelling houses
Class 15	Non-residential institutions
Class 16	Assembly and leisure

Class 1, for example, contains seven use descriptions. The UCO provides that the change of use from one of those uses to another is not development, so long as the former and latter uses are in the same class. For example, the change of use from a post office to a travel agency is not development because both uses are within the same class, but change from a post office to an office is development because the uses are in different classes.

The UCO is not comprehensive and certain uses are expressly stated to be outside it. Article 3(5) excludes from any class, use:

(1) As an amusement arcade, centre or funfair;

(2) As a betting office;

(3) For the purposes of a funeral undertaker;

(4) As a hotel;

(5) For the sale of fuel for motor vehicles;

(6) For the sale or display for sale of motor vehicles;

(7) For a taxi business or business for the hire of motor vehicles;

(8) For the sale of food or drink for consumption on the premises or hot food off the premises;

(9) As a scrapyard, or as a yard for the storage or distribution of minerals or the breaking of motor vehicles;

(10) For or in connection with public worship or religious instruction.

11.11 Where the use of land is within one of the exceptions or is not listed in any of the classes, the UCO is of no assistance in determining whether a material change of use has taken place.

Determination of use

11.12 A use may fall within more than one class. The 1991 Order, article 3(3) provides that any use which is ordinarily incidental to a use which is specified in one of the classes in the UCO does not cease to be incidental merely because it is specified in the UCO in its own right as a separate use.

The following approach has been suggested:[106]

(1) Arrive at an accurate description of the actual use;
(2) Decide whether that use fits into one of the classes;
(3) Decide whether the description includes activities which fall into more than one class;
(4) If the activities fall into more than one class, decide which one is incidental to the other.

Permitted development

11.13 The Planning (General Development) Order (NI) 1993,[107] specifies several classes of permitted development which may be carried out without the need to obtain express planning permission. In the case of a listed building, listed building consent may be required for any alteration. There are also special provisions relating to conservation areas. Otherwise permission for such development is granted automatically by the Order itself, subject to specified restrictions, as follows:

Part I - Development within the curtilage of a dwelling house

11.14 It is usually permissible to make small alterations within a house and the area immediately adjacent to it. The Order sets out the restrictions for each particular type of work as classified.

Class A - The enlargement, improvement or other alteration of a dwelling house

Planning permission is not generally required for an extension as long as:

(1) For a terraced house or any house in a conservation area the extension is not more than 50 metres^3 or 10 per cent of the original house volume, whichever is the greater.
(2) For a detached or semi-detached house the extension is not more than 70 metres^3 or 15 per cent of the original house volume, whichever is the greater.

---

[106] *Forkhurst* v *Secretary of State for the Environment* (1982) 46 P&CR 255, *per* Hodgson J.
[107] SR No 278

In all cases size is calculated from external measurement, and there is an upper limit of 115 metres^3.

Any extension built since 1 October 1973 is not treated as part of the original house volume. It is therefore necessary to subtract the volume of any existing extension from the allowances specified.

Further:

(1) The design and materials to be used to build the extension must be in keeping with the main house.

(2) No part of the extension shall be nearer to any road than the part of the original house nearest to the road.

(3) No part of the extension shall be higher than the highest part of the existing roof of the house.

(4) The extension shall not be more than 4 metres high if it comes within 3 metres of the boundary of the property. Height is to be measured from ground level, immediately adjacent to the building, or if it is not uniform, the level at its highest part.

(5) The ground area covered by the extension and any other buildings within the boundary of the property, excluding the original house, must not be more than half the total area, not counting the original house.

In some cases other buildings on the property are treated as extensions and reduce the allowances for extending the house.

NB Building control approval must be obtained from the local district council regardless of whether the work constitutes permitted development under the planning legislation.

If the alterations involve the construction of a new access, or the alteration of an existing access to a road, planning permission is required for both the access and the development. Further, the work carried out must not cause danger by obstructing the view of people using a public road.

(i) A conservatory

Planning permission is not generally required for a conservatory because if it is attached to a house it is treated as an extension and the appropriate rules apply.

(ii) A granny flat

Planning permission is required for a separate and self-contained unit attached to a house. If it is not self-contained it is treated as an extension.

(iii) Conversion into flats

Planning permission is required even though building work may not be involved, because a conversion is treated as a change of use.

(iv) Changing external windows and doors

Planning permission is not required if existing window and door openings are used. However, permission may be required to replace a flat window with a bay or bow window, or to change the style of doors or windows if the house is in a conservation area.

(v) General repairs and internal alterations

Planning permission is not normally required for general repairs and improvements to the house unless the work involves a considerable change to the outside appearance of the house. Nor is it required for internal alterations if the use as a house is not changed.

(vi) Small buildings or structures

To erect a small building or structure less than 10 metres^3 in volume in the garden such as a garage, carport, shed or greenhouse, planning permission is not generally required provided that:

(1) The building is for domestic use only;
(2) The height of the building does not exceed 4 metres if it has a ridged roof, or 3 metres in any other case;
(3) No part of the building extends beyond any wall of the house which faces a road;
(4) The ground area covered is not more than half the total area of the property;
(5) The building is not used for keeping pigeons.

A pigeon loft requires planning permission, as does the use of an existing shed for keeping pigeons.

A building or structure more than 10 metres^3 in the garden is treated as an extension if it is within 5 metres of the house or is in a conservation area. Otherwise the rules for small buildings less than 10 metres apply.

Class B - *Alterations to the roof*

Planning permission is not generally required for the enlargement or improvement of a dwelling house by adding to or altering the roof provided that:

(1) The house is not in a conservation area;
(2) No part of the roof extension projects in front of any existing roof slope of the house which faces onto a road;
(3) The design and materials are in keeping with the main house;
(4) No part of the dormer is higher than the ridge line of the main house;
(5) The size of the roof extension is not more than 20 metres^3 in the case of a terrace or 25 metres^3 in any other case.

Planning permission is not required for re-roofing a house provided that the height of the roof is not increased and the appearance is not significantly altered.

Any internal alterations to convert a roof-space to provide additional living accommodation do not require permission.[108] However, installing dormer windows, or carrying out other works to alter the roof may require permission.

Planning permission is not generally required for roof lights provided that the roof lights do not project beyond the roof slope by more than 150 millimetres.

Planning permission is not required for solar panels on the roof provided they do not project beyond the plane of any existing roof slope by more than 150 millimetres.

If solar panels are erected anywhere on the property other than on the roof, the rules relating to small buildings or structures apply.

Class C - A porch

Planning permission is not required for the erection or construction of a porch outside any external door of a dwelling house provided that:

(1) The floor area is not more than 2 metres^2 measured externally;

(2) The height is not more than 3 metres;

(3) The porch is not closer than 2 metres to any boundary with a road or footpath;

(4) The design and materials are in keeping with the main house.

Class D - A building incidental to the enjoyment of the dwelling

Generally, planning permission is not required for the provision within the curtilage of a dwelling house of a building, enclosure or swimming pool required for a purpose incidental to the enjoyment of the dwelling house, nor for its alteration. The same rules apply as to small buildings, above.

Class E - Hard surface

The provision within the curtilage of a dwelling house of a hard surface for any purpose incidental to the enjoyment of the dwelling house is permitted.

Class F - LPG tank

The erection of a container for the storage of oil or liquefied petroleum gas (LPG) for domestic purposes is permitted development provided that:

The tank is for domestic purposes only

(1) The size is less than 3,500 litres in the case of an oil tank or 2,500 litres in the case of a LPG tank;

(2) The height is not more than 3 metres for an oil tank or 2 metres for a LPG tank;

(3) No part of the tank would be nearer to any road than the part of the original house nearest to the road.

---

[108] Building control approval is required.

Class G - Satellite antenna

The installation of satellite antenna is generally permitted provided that:

(1) The dish is not mounted on the front wall of a house, facing the road;
(2) The dish is not mounted on the roof, facing a road;
(3) The dish is not mounted above the roof ridge;
(4) There is no other dish on the house or within its curtilage;
(5) The dish is not more than 90 centimetres in depth or width;
(6) The house is not in a conservation area.

Planning permission is not required for a television aerial.

Planning permission is required for a radio mast.

Part 2 - Minor operations

11.15 Provisions are also set out in relation to works which have a less fundamental effect on the overall appearance of the property.

Class A - Means of enclosure

The erection, construction, maintenance, improvement or alteration of a gate, fence, wall or other means of enclosure does not generally require planning permission. A wall or fence up to 2 metres high can be built anywhere on the property except where it would be next to a road, in which case the height is restricted to 1 metre.

Hedges are not subject to planning control providing they do not encroach on land cleared for visibility splays as part of an approval for an access.

In an open plan or shared surface development there may be a condition attached to the planning permission for the estate which would override the normal rules for a hedge, wall or fence.

Class B - Access

The formation, laying out and construction or alteration of a means of access to a road which is not a special, trunk or classified road, is permitted where the access is required in connection with development permitted by any class in the Schedule, apart from Class A.

Class C - Painting the exterior

Planning permission is not required provided that the painting is not for the purpose of advertisement, announcement or direction.

Planning permission is required for the provision of exterior cladding.

Part 3 - Changes of use
11.16 Certain changes of use are permitted, generally from a use which has less effect.[109] For example, from a general industrial use to a light industrial use.

The use of any part of a house as an office or for commercial purposes may need planning permission depending on the nature and scale of the use.

Part 4 - Temporary buildings and uses
11.17 The provision on land of buildings, moveable structures, works, plant and machinery required temporarily for operations on that land or adjoining land is permitted without express permission.

The use of any land for any purpose for not more than 28 days in total in any calendar year and the provision of any moveable structure for the purpose of the permitted use does not require planning permission.

Part 5 - Caravan sites
11.18 The use of land, other than a building, as a caravan site in the circumstances specified in the Schedule to the Caravans Act (NI) 1963, paragraphs 2, 3, and 6 to 10 is permitted.[110]

Caravan or boat in the garden
Planning permission is not required to keep a caravan or boat in the garden of a dwelling house provided that the caravan or boat is used for the personal enjoyment of the householder and is simply parked there.

Part 6 - Agricultural buildings and operations
11.19 On agricultural land in an agricultural unit, works for the erection, extension or alteration of a building and any excavation or engineering operations are permitted if reasonably necessary for the purposes of agriculture within that unit. The agricultural land must be more than 0.5 hectares in area.

Permitted development excludes work to a dwelling house and buildings more than 75 metres away from the principal farm buildings. The structure must generally be less than 300 metres^2 and 12 metres in height. It must not be within 24m of a special, trunk, first or second class road or within 9 metres of any other road.

---

[109] See above *re* material change of use.

[110] That means a caravan site licence is not required if the use of the land is incidental to the enjoyment as such of a dwelling house within the curtilage of which the land is situated, for the use by a person travelling for one or two nights, for the use on a site of more than five acres of up to three caravans for a maximum of 28 days a year, for the use as a caravan site by an organisation which bears a certificate of exemption for a meeting for up to five days, for accommodation during a particular season for agricultural or forestry workers, for building and engineering workers or for travelling showmen who have the appropriate certificate.

Part 7 - *Forestry buildings and operations*
11.20 The carrying out on land used for forestry of development reasonably necessary for that purpose, including works to erect, alter or extend a building, the formation, alteration or maintenance of private ways and other operations is permitted development.

Parts 8-20 are less relevant to private dwellings.[111]

MAKING AN APPLICATION FOR PLANNING PERMISSION

Introduction
11.21 The person proposing to carry out the work or make the change of use should make an application in writing to the DOE for planning permission. The application can be made by or on behalf of the person in actual possession of the land or by anyone else as long as the person in possession is notified.

The 1991 Order, article 20(1), provides that an application for planning permission shall be made in the manner specified in the development order or by any directions given by the DOE under a development order. The present regulations are contained in the Planning (General Development) Order (NI) 1993.

The requirements for applications differ according to whether the application is for full permission, outline permission or for approval of reserved matters.

Types of application
11.22 There are two different types of application:

A full application
11.23 For most development by householders this is the most appropriate type of application. The applicant is required to submit a maximum of seven copies of:

    (1)   The application forms;

    (2)   A site location map;

    (3)   Detailed drawings or plans.

An outline application
11.24 If the applicant only wishes to know in principle whether permission will be given for the proposed work and does not wish to prepare detailed plans, an outline application can be submitted. It must be accompanied by a plan sufficient to identify the land. An application for outline permission is often made to obtain permission for the erection of a building.

---

[111] Planning (General Development) (Amendment No 2) Order (NI) 1995 adds a new Pt 21 by virtue of which planning permission is granted for certain closed circuit television cameras used for security purposes.

Reserved matters

11.25 If outline permission is granted it has to be followed by a further application relating to the details, which are known as reserved matters. An application for approval of reserved matters must include details and plans and drawings dealing with the reserved matters.

Fee

11.26 A fee is charged for all planning applications. The amount varies depending on the type of application and the proposed development. Concessions or exemptions may be available.

Advertisements

11.27 On receipt of an application for planning permission, the DOE is required to advertise it in at least one newspaper circulating in the area to which the application relates. Weekly advertisements are placed listing all the applications received in the previous week and indicating the location and type of development proposed.[112] A period of 14 days is allowed within which representations may be made to the DOE by any concerned party.

Neighbour notification

11.28 To ensure that an applicant's neighbours are aware of any proposed development which might affect their amenity, the DOE introduced a scheme in 1985 for neighbour notification. Applicants for planning permission are now required to send to the DOE the addresses of all occupied buildings which are within 90 metres of the boundary of the land to be developed. The DOE then notifies the neighbours that it has received development proposals relating to land adjoining their property and gives them the opportunity to examine the proposals. Owners of land which has no buildings on it do not receive any neighbour notification and are not made aware of the development.

Determination

11.29 In determining the application, the DOE must take into account any representations received in the 14-day period and consult the local district council. The DOE is also under a general duty to have regard to the general development plan and any other material considerations.

The DOE has a discretion to:

   (1) Grant permission unconditionally;
   (2) Grant permission subject to such conditions it thinks fit;
   (3) Refuse permission.

---

[112] Under the Planning Applications (Exemption from Publication) Order (NI) 1999 applications for extensions or alterations to a house and incidental development within the curtilage of a house do not need to be published in the press provided that the development is outside a Conservation Area.

The DOE must give notice of its decision within two months from the date of receipt of the application; or agree an extended period. Failure to notify the applicant causes the application to be treated as refused. There is a written notice of decision. It must state the reasons given for refusal or imposition of conditions.

Time limits

11.30 A grant of planning permission is generally made subject to the condition that the development to which it relates must be begun within five years. If outline permission is granted conditionally on subsequent approval of reserved matters, the application for approval of any reserved matters should be made within three years and the development must be begun by (whichever is the later) five years from the grant of outline permission or two years from the grant of last approval of any reserved matter. Any development commenced outside that period is not authorised.

Enforcement and appeal

11.31 The DOE can serve an enforcement notice requiring a breach of planning permission to be remedied. A breach is carrying out development without permission or not complying with conditions imposed. An enforcement notice may be served only within four years of the date of the breach and must be served on the owner. There is a right of appeal against an enforcement notice to the magistrates' court. It is an offence not to comply with an enforcement notice.

A change of use does not amount to a development so long as both uses are in the same class. If the uses are in different classes there may be development consisting of a material change of use and consent to the change should be obtained. If there is no consent enforcement action can be taken for breaches which have occurred after 25 August 1974.[113]

Appeals

11.32 An applicant can appeal to the Planning Appeals Commission ('PAC') against refusal of planning permission or conditions imposed.

Blight notices

11.33 The Planning Blight (Compensation) (NI) Order 1981 enables landowners whose land is blighted by an authority's planning proposals to serve a blight notice requiring the appropriate authority to purchase the claimant's interest. Such proposals may be, for example, to include the property in a development plan, compulsory purchase order or road scheme.

A blight notice can be served only by a resident owner-occupier, that is, someone who occupies, in right of an owner's interest, the whole, or a

---

[113] *NB* Under the Planning (NI) Order 1991, art 68(4)(b) the four-year rule only relates to operational development, but see para 11.35 in relation to agricultural occupancy.

substantial part of, the hereditament as a private dwelling for six months prior to the service of the blight notice or has vacated it less than a year beforehand.[114] He must establish that he has made reasonable endeavours to sell the property but has been unable to do so except at a price substantially lower than that for which it might reasonably have been expected to sell if not affected by planning proposals.

If the authority agrees that the property has been blighted by its proposals it can accept the blight notice and proceed to acquire the property. A contract is deemed to come into existence two months after service of the blight notice under which the DOE will acquire the owner's interest in the land.

The date for completion of the contract, subject to the parties agreeing otherwise, is three months from the date on which they agree on the amount of compensation to be paid. The purchase price is the amount which the authority would have paid for the property had it been acquired under the relevant statutory provision. Effectively this is the open market value.

On the other hand, when the authority does not accept that the property has been blighted, it has two months to object and serve a counter notice. The claimant then has two months to refer the matter to the Lands Tribunal. [115]

The Lands Tribunal may uphold the objection or declare the blight notice valid. If the notice is valid, the authority is deemed to have entered into a contract to purchase the property and the claimant to sell it. The price is the amount that the authority would have paid if the property was compulsorily acquired on that date. The Lands Tribunal can determine any dispute as to amount.

Purchase notices

11.34 Under the 1991 Order, article 94(1)(a), a landowner affected by a planning decision can serve a purchase notice requiring the appropriate authority to purchase his interest.[116] This may arise for example, where an application by him for planning permission has been refused, granted subject to adverse conditions or permission already granted has been revoked or modified.

A purchase notice is distinct from a blight notice which applies to the effect of a planning proposal. A purchase notice may be served where, because of the decision, the land has become incapable of reasonably beneficial use in its existing state and cannot be rendered capable. This is rare. The procedure is similar to that for a blight notice.

---

[114] Planning Blight (Compensation) (NI) Order 1981, art 4(1) and 4(2). The owner occupier of an agricultural unit and landowner of a hereditament with an NAV which does not exceed £2250 also qualify.

[115] See, *eg, Carrel v London Underground Ltd* [1996] 12 EG 129 where the claimant sold the property after serving a blight notice and receiving a counter-notice, although at the time of the counter-notice the land was no longer blighted. The Lands Tribunal held that the sale of the property was treated as withdrawal of the blight notice and the claimant was not entitled to compensation.

[116] Owner means a person, other than a mortgagee not in possession who is entitled to receive the rack rent (*ie* a rent equal to the full rental value of the land).

Agricultural occupancy

11.35 In such areas as Green Belts, where there is a more restrictive planning policy than in other places, agricultural occupancy conditions can be placed on planning approval for a new house. The conditions usually limit the occupancy of the house to someone wholly or mainly employed in agriculture or who is retired from active farming. A person who farmed the land in his spare time and had another full time or main job would not qualify.

When a solicitor acting for a client who intends to purchase a property finds that such a condition exists, he should not proceed with the transaction unless the client is involved in agriculture.

An agricultural occupancy condition should appear on the DOE property certificate. If the land is registered, the condition should also appear as a charge on the land in the Statutory Charges Register.[117] Consequently it is important to make the appropriate searches.

It may be difficult to obtain a loan for a house with an agricultural occupancy condition affecting it because the property does not have a proper open market value. It is important that the prospective lender is advised of any such condition because, if there is one, financial institutions are generally prepared to lend only up to one half of the amount they would otherwise have lent.

When the occupation of the house is in breach of an occupancy condition the DOE can take enforcement action. There is at present some doubt about the position under the general law because there are two conflicting decisions of the Court of Appeal in England. In the case of *Harvey* v *Secretary of State for Wales* [118] the four-year rule was held to apply, whereas in *Newbury District Council* v *Secretary of State for the Environment* [119] the relevant period was held to be ten years.

The question in this jurisdiction is whether an agricultural occupancy condition falls within the Planning (NI) Order 1991, article 68(4)(b), which gives the benefit of a four-year rule to breach of planning control and whether the DOE is accordingly prevented from taking enforcement action more than four years after the condition has been breached. If the four-year rule does not apply the alternative period in which enforcement action can be taken may be ten years[120].

The PAC in Northern Ireland has followed the earlier 1990 decision of the Court of Appeal in the *Harvey* case and continues to apply the four-year rule to breaches of occupancy conditions. Further, if requested to remove an occupancy condition, the PAC will consider the circumstances and may do so.

---

[117] LRA (NI) 1970, Sch 2 para 30A, as amended.
[118] 1990 JPL 420.
[119] (1993) 67 P & CR 68.
[120] In England the Town and Country Planning Act 1990 as amended by the Planning and Compensation Act 1991, s 171B, provides that enforcement proceedings must be brought within four years of the breach where it consists of either operational development (unauthorised building, engineering, mining, etc) or a change of use to a single dwelling house. All other breaches of planning control are subject to a ten-year limitation period.

However the DOE follows the more recent 1993 decision and applies a ten-year rule.

Historic buildings - listed status

11.36 The DOE is required to list buildings of special architectural or historic interest.[121] It only lists a building after consultation with the appropriate district council and the Historic Buildings Council. The listing appears as a charge in the statutory charges register. There are approximately 8000 buildings listed in Northern Ireland.

The restrictions placed on a listed building include being unable to demolish it, or to do any works to the exterior or interior which would affect its character without seeking consent from the DOE's Town and Country Planning Service. If the restrictions are not brought to the attention of a purchaser, alterations might be carried out which would adversely affect or destroy the character of the building without the required approval being sought.

The DOE has wide powers to make grants and loans for the preservation of listed buildings, to acquire such buildings by agreement or compulsorily and to accept endowments in respect of them.

Tree preservation orders

11.37 Under the 1991 Order, article 64, the DOE may impose conditions when granting planning permission as a means of protecting trees and providing for new planting.

Under article 65, where it appears expedient in the interests of amenity to make provision for the preservation of trees the DOE may for that purpose make an order with respect to such individual trees, groups of trees or woodlands as may be specified. This may not necessarily arise in relation to a planning application but may be, for example, where there is evidence that the trees are in danger of being felled for farming or road development purposes.

A tree preservation order may make provision for prohibiting the cutting down, topping, lopping or wilful destruction of trees except with the DOE's consent, or for replanting. Dead or dangerous trees are excluded. It is an offence to contravene a tree preservation order. The order should be registered in the Statutory Charges Register.

An order takes effect immediately it is made. Notice of it is served on the owners and occupiers of the land and on any other affected person. Anyone on whom notice has been served may object to the order within 28 days of service and be given the opportunity of being heard by the PAC. After considering any objections and representations, the DOE may confirm, withdraw or modify the tree preservation order and notify the persons concerned accordingly.

---

[121] Planning (NI) Order 1991, art 43, replacing earlier provisions in the Planning (NI) Order 1972.

Matters to check

11.38 Before carrying out any construction or improvements to a property it is advisable to check the following:

(a) Legal position

The title should be checked to ensure that there are no restrictions affecting the property or the type of work intended. For example, restrictive covenants or rights of way.

(b) Planning history

The original planning permission for the house may have a condition attached restricting or prohibiting the kind of work proposed.

(c) Traffic safety

The proposed work must not cause danger by obstructing the view of people using a public road.

(d) Listed buildings and conservation areas

Listed building consent may be required for the work proposed if the building is listed as being of special architectural or historic interest. In a conservation area it is advisable to discuss alterations with the local planning office and to contact the Historic Monuments and Buildings Branch of the DOE regarding a Conservation Area Grant or Historic Buildings Grant.

(e) Historic monuments

Work proposed in or near any archaeological site or historic monument may need special permission or certain precautions may be advisable. The Archaeological Survey of Historic Monuments and Buildings Branch of the DOE should be contacted for advice.

Other approvals

11.39 As well as planning permission there are other approvals and consents which may be required.

(a) Development affecting roads

When an application is made for planning permission it is automatically considered by the Roads Service of the DOE. Even where planning permission is not required but work is proposed to create or alter an access to a road or do any work to a road or a footpath, the permission of the Roads Service may be required.

(b) Water regulations

The consent of the Water Executive of the DOE may be needed for plumbing and drainage proposals. It is also required for an extension or garage to be built over an existing sewer or drain.

(c) Effluent disposal

The DOE has general responsibility for water and sewage supplies and services. Under the Water Act (NI) 1972, section 7, the consent of the DOE is required for the discharge of effluent into waterways and under section 8 its consent is required for discharge into underground stratum. Where a property is serviced by a septic tank a consent should be obtained. The DOE property certificate states whether or not any such consent has been granted for a particular property.[122]

The DOE has wide powers and duties under the Water and Sewerage Services (NI) Order 1973 with respect to water and sewerage services, for example, impounding or abstracting water, adoption of works, sewers, pipes or drains and closing of facilities. There are provisions for consents to new connections and agreements works in connection with new developments. Under article 22 the consent of the DOE is required for new discharge of trade effluent into sewers or sewage treatment works and any such consent should also be revealed on a DOE property certificate.

---

[122] Cf para 5.18.

CHAPTER TWELVE

BUILDING CONTROL

Introduction

12.01 Building regulations are intended to ensure good standards of building and are a means of controlling development additional to planning. They are concerned mainly with health and safety issues, although amenity and energy conservation are also important.

The Northern Ireland building regulations are now issued by the Department of the Environment and administered by the district councils.

The Building Regulations (NI) Order 1972 first gave the then Ministry of Finance power to make building regulations to replace local authority building bye-laws. These have subsequently been amended, consolidated and updated. The most recent legislation is the Planning and Building Regulations (Amendment)(NI) Order 1990.

The building regulations currently in force are the Building Regulations (NI) 1994 which came into operation on 28 November 1994. They have been amended by the Building (Amendment) Regulations (NI) 1995 which came into operation on 15 January 1996 and the Building (Amendment) Regulations (NI) 1997 which came into operation on 1 January 1998. Building regulations do not apply to work completed or plans deposited before the date on which they became operative and any previous work is governed by the regulations in force at the appropriate time.

WORK REQUIRING APPROVAL

12.02 Building control approval is normally required for:

(1) Construction of any building;

(2) Structural alteration or extension of a building including a roof-space conversion;

(3) Material change of use of a building;

(4) Installation of certain works or fittings such as a boiler, flue, chimney or drainage.

Exemptions

12.03 Some buildings are exempt from building regulations and others are partially exempt, which means that not all of the regulations apply to them. Detailed descriptions of such buildings are found in Schedule 1 to the 1994 Regulations.

The application of building regulations to some of the more common types of building is considered below.

Agricultural buildings

12.04 Agricultural buildings may be exempt from building control if the buildings are built not less than one and a half times their overall height from the nearest part of a public road or the boundary of the land on which they are sited. Any such buildings intended to be built close to a house may be subject to control. Agricultural buildings to which the public are invited for the purpose of retailing, exhibiting or service provision are not exempt nor are farm buildings used for packing or retail storage. Also, no part of the building is to be used as a dwelling.

Garden sheds

12.05 A detached single storey building not exceeding 30 metres^2 with no sleeping accommodation either constructed substantially of non-combustible material or at least 1metre from the nearest house, road or the boundary of the property is exempt. A detached single storey building not exceeding 15 metres^2 with no sleeping accommodation at least 1metre from the nearest house is exempt.

Storage tanks

12.06 An external storage tank other than a septic tank, settlement tank or liquefied petroleum gas storage tank or tower silo is exempt.

Garages

12.07 A single storey detached garage is similar to a shed, in that if it does not exceed 30 metres^2 in area, has no sleeping accommodation and is either constructed substantially of non-combustible materials or is at least 1metre from the nearest house, road or boundary, it is exempt.

Porches

12.08 A porch with floor area not exceeding 30 metres^2 built as an annexe to an existing building is exempt provided that it is 1metre or more from any boundary.

Greenhouses

12.09 A detached greenhouse 1 metre or more from any boundary which has a floor area not exceeding 30 metres^2 is exempt. An attached greenhouse with a floor area not exceeding 30 metres^2 is also exempt.[123]

Conservatories

12.10 An attached conservatory 1metre or more from any boundary which has a floor area not exceeding 30 metres^2 is exempt.[124]

---

[123] Subject to compliance with the Building Regulations (NI) 1994, Sch 1 para 2.
[124] *Ibid.*

Building (Amendment) Regulations (NI) 1995

12.11 These Regulations provide for the exemption of conservatories and porches under 30 metres,[2] provided that the glazing used complies with current glazing regulations. Prior to this they were partially exempt and an application for approval was generally required.

Summary of the 1995 Regulations

12.12 The Regulations are extremely detailed but are briefly summarised below.

Part A: Interpretation and general

The interpretation and application of the Regulations in various situations is set out together with notices and plans required by the councils. Procedures for relaxation and appeals against council decisions are also detailed.

Provision is made for the issue by district councils of a completion certificate specifying that building work carried out on a building or part of a building complies with the requirements of the Regulations.

Part B: Materials and workmanship

The use of materials is considered and certain unsuitable materials are highlighted. Materials, components and manufacturing products must be fit for their purpose and standards of workmanship should be consistent with health and safety. The quality of finish is not controlled.

Part C: Preparation of site and resistance to moisture

Precautions are required to be taken in the construction of a building to ensure that it can resist penetration of dampness from the weather and from the ground. Provision is made to limit potentially harmful condensation within roof spaces and voids. In specified areas measures must be taken to prevent the ingress of radon from the ground into dwellings.

Part D: Structure

Standards are laid down relating to the structural stability of a building, including elements of the construction such as foundations, walls, floors, roofs and structural framework.

Part E: Fire safety

The Regulations endeavour to ensure standards of safety in the fabric of a building in the event of a fire. The main considerations are fire-resistance, separation, compartmentalisation and spread of flame.

Building design is required to facilitate the escape of people from the building in the event of fire and to provide access and facilities for the fire brigade. Automatic fire detection (smoke alarms) is now compulsory for all new dwellings.

Part F: Conservation of fuel and power

Reasonable standards of thermal insulation to limit heat loss from buildings and conserve fuel and power are laid down. The Regulations have become more stringent because of the need to conserve energy. The insulation requirements relate to walls, roofs, ground floors, glazing, heating and hot water services.

Part G: Sound insulation of dwellings

The construction of certain separating walls and floors is required to provide adequate resistance against airborne sound transmission and impact sound transmission.

Part H: Stairs, ramps and guarding

The design of stairs, ramps and associated guarding must comply with regulations to ensure the safe passage of people moving between different levels in a building. There is provision for safety balustrading to landings, balconies, platforms and for vehicle barriers in certain circumstances.

Part J: Solid waste in buildings

Sufficient storage space must be provided for waste containers and for any waste chute system.

Part K: Ventilation

Adequate ventilation must be provided in buildings including the use of mechanical extraction to remove steam and other pollutants from kitchens and bathrooms.

Part L: Heat producing appliances and liquefied petroleum gas installations

The installation of solid fuel, gas and oil fired heating appliances including the siting of liquefied petroleum gas (LPG) storage tanks must comply with the regulations. Performance requirements are set down for the appliances and associated construction.

Part N: Drainage

Adequate above and below ground drainage systems are required to convey both foul water and rainwater to a suitable means of disposal such as a sewer, septic tank, cesspool or other treatment plant or in the case of rainwater, to a soakaway or storm drainage system.

Part P: Sanitary appliances and unvented hot-water storage systems

Minimum standards are laid down for the provision of sanitary conveniences, washing facilities and bathrooms. The provision of an adequate supply of hot and cold water to the appliances is included.

Part R: Access and facilities for disabled people

Access and facilities for disabled people into and within certain buildings are required to be considered including the provision of suitable sanitary conveniences and the allocation of wheelchair spaces.

Part V: Glazing

Requirements are provided to control glazing with which people are likely to come into contact or collide.

PROCEDURE FOR MAKING A BUILDING REGULATION APPLICATION

12.13 Before any work to which the building regulations apply is begun, an application for approval must be made to the local building control office. It is usually advisable to obtain the services of an architect or building surveyor.

Since the introduction of the Building (Amendment) Regulations (NI) 1997 the application can be made by means of building notice procedure as an alternative to the existing full plans procedure. The building notice procedure is available only for domestic works and ideally suits small uncomplicated schemes.

Building notice procedure initially requires only the submission of a completed building notice application form. It is still necessary to inform the local building control office before work commences on the site. A single fee is payable on submission of the notice and no decision as to approval or rejection is made in relation to the notice.

More emphasis is placed on site inspections to ensure that the works are in compliance with applicable construction performance standards. If work on site is not in compliance it may be required to be altered or removed.

After three years the building notice will expire if works have not commenced. A completion certificate is issued on satisfactory completion of the work.

An application for building control approval made by following the full plans procedure consists of:

(1) Two copies of all the drawings;
(2) A completed notice of intention (application form);
(3) Structural calculations, if appropriate;
(4) The plan fee;
(5) A written estimate of the cost of the work, if required.

The council then examines and assesses the application.

Applicants will be required to submit a full description of the work, facilitate its comprehensive inspection and carry out any additional work required by the district council.

Site inspections

12.14 When work commences the builder is obliged to inform building control at the following stages:

(1) Commencement of operations;
(2) Excavation for foundations;

- (3) Foundation concrete;
- (4) Damp-proof courses;
- (5) Site hardware;
- (6) Site concrete;
- (7) Drainage;
- (8) Completion.

Site inspections are then made at each stage. In instances where the work does not fit into these stages building control will indicate the stages at which it will make inspections.

Building control surveyors may also inspect other aspects of the construction such as fire protection to steel beams, roof structures, thermal and sound insulating measures or facilities for the disabled. Any such interim inspections are usually arranged by mutual agreement with the builder.

An inspection fee becomes payable after the first inspection following commencement of the work and it covers all subsequent inspections.

Relaxation of building regulations

12.15 If an applicant considers that it would be unreasonable for building control to apply some particular requirement of the regulations to his proposal, he may apply for a relaxation or dispensation of that requirement.

The councils have authority to dispense with or relax the requirements of many parts of the building regulations but only the DOE has power to relax the fire precautions in certain large developments.

When considering relaxations, the building control surveyor looks at the reason for the request. He takes into account the likely effect on the building users and fabric in terms of health and safety. Relaxations are usually only granted when it can be shown that a particular regulation may be too onerous for the work in question or when compliance becomes impractical in unforeseen circumstances. Relaxations may have conditions attached to them.

The relaxation procedure is not generally applicable to new building work. Most relaxations involve alteration/extension/change of purpose group applications, such as shops into offices or houses into flats.

Appeal

12.16 An applicant may appeal to the DOE against a decision of a council to:

- (1) Reject plans;
- (2) Refuse to grant an application for relaxation of building regulations;
- (3) Add a condition to the grant of an application for relaxation;
- (4) Serve a contravention notice in respect of defective work.

In respect of (1), (2) and (3) an appeal must be lodged with the DOE within 56 days of the date of notification of the decision.

Contravention and failure to obtain approval

12.17 Contravention of building regulations can generally be classified as follows:

- (1) Failure to deposit plans before commencing building works;
- (2) Failure by the builder to give the required notice at specified stages of the work;
- (3) Failure to comply with the requirements of the regulations in carrying out building work on site.

Contravention of the building regulations is a criminal offence. It may occur during the progress of work but, more often, does not come to light until such time as the property is sold and the purchaser raises enquiries.

The Building Regulations (NI) Order 1979, which continues to apply to work completed prior to 1 June 1990, provides in article 18 that a notice of contravention requiring the removal or alteration of the works cannot be served after the expiration of 12 months, unless the district council considers that it ought to be on health and safety grounds and the DOE consents to the service of the notice.

Article 18 of the 1979 Order was amended by the Planning and Buildings (Amendment) (NI) Order 1990 and a new article 18 provides that if any building work contravenes the building regulations, the district council may serve a contravention notice on the owner requiring him, within a specified period, (normally 28 days) to remove, alter or make good the work.

It further provides that a contravention notice cannot be served more than 18 months after the work has been completed. This does not affect the right of the district council, the Attorney-General or anyone else to apply for an injunction for the removal or alteration of any work on the ground that it contravenes building regulations. However, it is rare for a district council to take legal action and only arises as a last resort if it is not possible to obtain co-operation by other means.

On receipt of a contravention notice the following options are available to the owner, who can:

(1) Comply with it.
(2) Challenge it. This involves obtaining a report from a suitably qualified person setting out reasons why the notice should not have been served. The report is submitted to the council. If the council refuses to accept it there is a right of appeal to the DOE.
(3) Appeal to the DOE.
(4) Apply to the council for relaxation of the regulations which have been contravened. There is a right of appeal to the DOE if the council refuses the application.

COMPLETION CERTIFICATES

12.18 The council issues an approval notice when it receives a satisfactory application for proposed building works. If the work is subsequently inspected by building control officers at various stages of the construction and found satisfactory, it should then be possible, when the building is finished, to obtain a completion certificate.

The certificate gives the date of the final inspection and states that, as far as can be reasonably ascertained, the work carried out conforms to the building regulations. At present the giving of a completion certificate is at the discretion of the district council, but there are proposals for regulations putting an onus on local authorities to issue completion certificates on new properties.

COMFORT LETTERS

12.19 Building control approval cannot be granted retrospectively, even where it is clear that the work in question has been carried out to the appropriate standard, because of the difficulties of inspecting work internally after it has been completed. The requirement for approval continues regardless of the lapse of time.

Technical breaches of building control can cause problems when a property is sold. Although there may be no real physical danger the property still may be difficult to sell because of the attitude of the lender to the situation. Where there is a breach it is possible that the transaction may either not proceed at all or do so at a reduced price. In practice a technical breach should not be important, as long as there is no real threat to health and safety. The emphasis should be on the actual structure of the building rather than on the possibility of enforcement proceedings, which are rarely taken.

Most of the district councils came to recognise the problem with technical breaches and, provided that the work was not considered to be a health and safety risk, the council (prior to 1998) would issue a comfort letter. The issue of a comfort letter was discretionary. It did not certify compliance of the work with required standards but stated that the council had no reason to believe that enforcement proceedings would be brought. That was often sufficient for the purposes of the purchaser and his lender.

The practice of issuing comfort letters was of great assistance in enabling conveyancing transactions to proceed in the absence of building control approval but there was no uniform policy, procedure or fee structure for such letters amongst the councils and they were not universally available.

REGULARISATION CERTIFICATES

12.20 It became apparent that the continuing difficulties caused by unauthorised works had to be addressed. In an endeavour to introduce a consistent approach and to bring the position more into line with that in England and Wales the Building (Amendment) Regulations (NI) 1997 were enacted and came into effect on 1 January 1998. The 1997 Regulations introduced a new power enabling councils to issue a regularisation certificate for works complying with regulation technical performance standards which were carried out without approval and without plans or site inspections being carried out and thus effectively to regularise unapproved work. This power does not detract from existing enforcement powers available to a council, so work completed less than 18 months previously would not be eligible for a regularisation certificate.

There is no obligation on a property owner to apply for regularisation but it may be useful for the purpose of satisfying a purchaser that the work is of the required standard. The council is able to examine work which was done previously without building control approval and certify the extent to which it complies with the building regulations. The building regulations which applied when the work was completed apply to the work in question.

When a regularisation application is submitted a council can require the works to be opened up for inspection, test the materials used in the construction and validate such systems as are considered appropriate to ensure that the issue of a certificate is defensible in the event of a legal challenge.

The cost of a regularisation certificate is 120 per cent of the combined cost of the plan and inspection fee for similar work and consequently it is much more expensive than a comfort letter. The advantage of a regularisation certificate over a comfort letter is that it goes much further towards confirming that there is nothing wrong with the structure in question. It is important to note that the certificate may be issued subject to specified limitations.

Since the facility to issue regularisation certificates was introduced in January 1998 the councils have phased out comfort letters.

MISCELLANEOUS MATTERS

Declarations of no effect

12.21 A council will declare plans to be of no effect, as if they had never been deposited, if work has not commenced on site within three years of the original deposit of plans. This means that an application for building regulation approval has to be made again once the time has expired if the work has not started.

Dangerous places and structures

12.22 It is the responsibility of the owner and occupier to ensure that buildings and other structures are maintained in a safe condition and do not become dangerous to persons using a public road or footpath.

If however, such a danger does arise, or is reported, the council can issue a notice requiring the owner or occupier within a stated period of time to repair, remove, protect or enclose the offending structure and eliminate the source of danger to the public.[125]

Failure to comply with the notice results in the council making an application to the magistrates' court to order the defendant to carry out the works. If the court

---

[125] Public Health (Ir) Act 1878 as amended.

order is disobeyed, the council may have the work carried out and enforce the costs against the defendant.

There are many reasons why buildings become structurally dangerous such as neglect, dereliction, storm, bomb damage or vandalism. The council is not restricted to taking action in respect of structures which are in danger of imminent collapse. It has powers to require that any excavation, land or place adjoining a public street, which might cause a danger to anyone using that street, shall be sufficiently repaired, protected or enclosed. The powers do not extend to alleged dangerous places not adjoining public streets.

Negligent application of building regulations

12.23 In practical terms there is a need for the facility of regularisation certificates. However, the district councils have to be concerned about the possibility of incurring liability for negligence and/or breach of statutory duty as a result. Following the case of *Anns* v *London Borough of Merton* [126] there were many instances where councils were held liable in negligence for failing to secure compliance with building regulations.

Subsequently, the extent of such liability has been limited. A district council is not liable in tort for negligent application of the building regulations where the resulting defects are discovered before there is any physical injury, notwithstanding that there is an imminent risk to health and safety.[127] Consequently a property owner is not entitled to compensation even though he may have to spend money to stop the building collapsing.

Property certificates[128]

12.24 Building control applications during the preceding 10 years are detailed on the district council property certificates. If work requiring approval has been done it is useful to look first at the property certificate to see if there is evidence of any application. If not, the council may be asked to look further back into its records or an application for a regularisation certificate should be made.

---

[126] [1978] AC 728.

[127] *Murphy* v *Brentwood District Council* [1990] 2 All ER 908 (HL). Any money spent in repairing the building must be regarded as pure economic loss, not normally recoverable in an action for negligence against a council even though such loss has resulted from the negligence of a building control inspector.

[128] Cf Property Certificates paras 5.12-5.29.

CHAPTER THIRTEEN

NATIONAL HOUSE-BUILDING COUNCIL

Introduction

13.01 The National House-Building Council ('NHBC') is an insurance company which was set up to control building design, workmanship and materials in the private housing sector.

NHBC is concerned with the maintenance and improvement of standards of construction. It aims to reduce the number and severity of defects in new houses by the imposition of minimum standards.

NHBC provides warranties to ensure that the purchaser does not suffer serious financial loss if the builder fails to comply with NHBC rules and technical requirements. It does not provide guarantees.

The scheme currently operated by NHBC is known as 'buildmark'. It is an agreement between the builder, NHBC and the purchaser. The rights conferred under 'buildmark' are in addition to any contractual, statutory or common law rights which a purchaser may have against a builder.

The cover automatically extends to second and subsequent purchasers of the house. Any owner may claim under the warranty unless the defect or damage should have been reported by the first or previous purchaser.

The scheme provides protection against major defects due to faulty work on the part of the builder but does not compensate for all types of loss. There are various conditions of cover and there are financial limits on the compensation. It is essential to have normal house insurance as well.

Any remedies available under the Defective Premises (NI) Order 1975 are precluded by reliance on NHBC protection.[129]

Mortgagees

13.02 Most lenders insist that the construction of a new house is carried out by a NHBC registered builder or supervised by a qualified architect before a loan can be made to the purchaser. NHBC is the more common, particularly for housing developments.

Self-Build Scheme

13.03 To enable a purchaser to have NHBC cover for a self-built house, NHBC has initiated 'self build' as an extension to the ten-year warranty scheme. In this way NHBC provides cover for a purchaser who is either technically competent himself or employing appropriate supervision.

---

[129] See art 3.

Membership of NHBC

13.04 When a builder applies to register with the scheme, investigations are made to ensure that he can achieve appropriate standards. If these prove satisfactory, the builder is normally offered conditions of registration. He then pays an annual membership fee and a registration fee for each house he builds. This covers the cost of inspection and the insurance premium for 'buildmark' cover. A no claims discount system is operated to encourage the maintenance of high standards.

If a builder fails to correct defects found by NHBC, he faces disciplinary action. A surcharge may be imposed or, in extreme cases, the builder may be deleted from the register.

When a builder is registered, NHBC is able to inspect the work as it progresses to ensure that it complies with the standards imposed. Materials and work done by sub-contractors must also comply.

Procedure for purchaser to obtain warranty

13.05 The NHBC offer of cover is sent by the builder's solicitor to the purchaser's solicitor, usually at an early stage of the construction. It should be passed to the purchaser before completion for safekeeping.

To accept the offer, the acceptance has to be completed by either the purchaser or his solicitor and returned to NHBC. As soon as it is received by the NHBC the purchaser becomes entitled to:

(1) A warranty by the builder that the house will be built.

    (a) In accordance with NHBC requirements.

    (b) In an efficient and workmanlike manner and of proper materials and so as to be fit for habitation.

(2) Compensation from NHBC for any loss if the builder fails, due to his insolvency or fraud, to complete the house in accordance with NHBC requirements.

    (a) If the building has not started, NHBC will reimburse the purchaser any amount paid to the builder under the contract which cannot be recovered from him.

    (b) Where the building has started but is not complete, NHBC will pay either the amount above the original agreed price which is needed substantially to complete the house in accordance with NHBC requirements, plus the cost of putting right any defect or damage; or any amount paid to the builder under the contract which cannot be recovered from him.

    (c) Instead of paying the cost of putting right any defect or damage, NHBC may itself arrange to do the work. NHBC's liability in this context is limited to a maximum of £10,000 or, if greater, 10 per cent of the original agreed price of the house.

Ten-year notice

13.06 When the house is completed in accordance with NHBC requirements to the satisfaction of the NHBC inspector, a ten-year notice is sent to the purchaser. He is then covered by a ten-year warranty.

The ten-year notice verifies that:

(1) The house has been subject to NHBC's system of inspection.
(2) The house appears to have been designed and constructed substantially in accordance with NHBC's requirements. It also brings into operation the ten-year cover.
(3) The protection for the purchaser expires ten years after the date of the notice.
(4) No inspections system can prevent all defects and it is for this reason that 'buildmark' protection is provided. NHBC cannot accept any other liability for the house.

Initial guarantee period (the first two years)

13.07 NHBC makes the builder liable for defects which appear during the initial guarantee period. This normally means two years from the date of the ten-year notice. It relates to defects from failure to comply with NHBC minimum standards for workmanship and materials. The defects must be reported in writing by the purchaser before the end of the period. Otherwise the builder is not liable.

Structural guarantee period (years three to ten)

13.08 From the beginning of the third year to the end of the tenth year the NHBC warranty provides insurance cover against major damage caused by structural defects and against any defects in the drainage system.

Provided that NHBC decides that there is a problem, it will pay the cost of putting right any major damage which is properly reported before the end of the structural guarantee period and is caused by either a defect in the structure or caused by settlement, subsidence or heave affecting the structure. Major damage means that complete or partial rebuilding or extensive repair work is necessary. Where a claim for structural defects is made for a house built after 1 April 1999 during years three to ten NHBC will not pay any claim where the cost of repair is £500 or less. However, if the cost exceeds £500 it will pay the full amount.

Examples of structural defects which could cause major damage are:

(1) Dry rot affecting structural timbers;
(2) Collapse or serious distortion of joists or roof structures;
(3) Serious damp penetration;
(4) Damage caused by chemicals in building materials or in the ground;
(5) Failure of rendering;

(6) Movement resulting from ground settlement, subsidence or heave, provided there is no other remedy or appropriate insurance cover;
(7) Problems with the external envelope of the building, including permanent roof coverings and tiling.

Matters not covered
13.09 Matters not covered include the following:
(1) Defects which are not in the load-bearing structure, for example, doors, door frames, gutters, boilers, plumbing.
(2) Damage which is not major, for example, slight cracks.
(3) Breaches of technical standards which have not and are unlikely to cause major damage, for example, joists theoretically under size.
(4) Damage covered by household insurance.
(5) Damage which was discovered or ought to have been discovered but was not reported during the initial guarantee period.
(6) Anything excluded from cover by an endorsement on the ten-year notice
(7) Any claim caused by defective structural or installation design details provided by or on behalf of the purchaser.

Damage must be notified in writing to NHBC as soon as practicable after it appears and before the end of the ten-year warranty period. If it is not, NHBC may not be liable. The protection afforded is in addition to any other remedies that a purchaser might have.

Making a claim

During the initial guarantee period
13.10 A purchaser can make a claim against the builder as follows:
(1) A written notice must be given to the builder reporting all defects and damage as soon as possible after their appearance.
(2) If the builder fails to deal with the claim satisfactorily, the purchaser may refer the dispute to the NHBC resolution service.
(3) NHBC sends an investigator to look into the list of defects and determine which are breaches of NHBC requirements and are therefore the responsibility of the builder.
(4) NHBC makes a written report which, if appropriate, will require the builder to carry out work or actions within a set timescale.
(5) If either party does not accept the recommendations in the report or, if NHBC is unable to reach a satisfactory solution, the dispute can be referred to arbitration within 28 days of the issue of the report, provided that both parties agree.

(6) If a purchaser accepts the NHBC recommendations in settlement of a complaint but the builder fails to carry them out, then NHBC will take further action to ensure that the recommendations are implemented. NHBC may itself arrange to do the remedial work and is only liable to the extent that the builder fails to pay the cost of the work.

During the structural guarantee period

13.11 NHBC cover applies only where major damage has occurred and extensive repair work is necessary. The damage must have arisen due to the builder's failure to comply with NHBC technical requirements.

If the damage is not covered by the normal house insurance policy, the purchaser can make a claim to NHBC. If it is covered by the house insurance, (subsidence and heave usually are covered) NHBC will assist by paying the excess on the policy which is normally £500 for valid claims.

The purchaser can make a claim as follows:

(1) A written notice of the claim must be given to NHBC as soon as possible after the damage appears;

(2) A completed claim form must be returned to NHBC;

(3) A charge must be paid representing NHBC's reasonable costs of investigating the claim;

(4) NHBC must be given the opportunity to inspect the item and decide what remedial work should be carried out;

(5) All relevant documents requested by NHBC must be furnished.

Arbitration

13.12 During both the initial guarantee period and the structural guarantee period, if the purchaser makes a claim against the builder or the NHBC and disagrees with the NHBC decision, he can go to arbitration, provided that the builder agrees to it. This is conducted independently of NHBC and is carried out in accordance with legal procedures governed by the Arbitration Act 1996. The arbitrator visits the house and takes evidence from both sides.

Under the Consumer Arbitration Agreements Act 1988 the purchaser may have the right to pursue claims in court rather than by arbitration.

Insurance ombudsman bureau scheme

13.13 Alternatively the purchaser can use the Insurance Ombudsman Bureau Scheme. The Ombudsman may try to settle the dispute by giving advice, or by trying to bring the two sides together. If he does not resolve the matter the Ombudsman will make a decision based on the law and good insurance practice. If the purchaser accepts the decision, the insurer must pay any award up to £100,000. If the purchaser rejects it, the decision is suspended and he is free to do as he wishes. A rejected decision does not affect his right to take legal action afterwards.

Bankruptcy of builder

13.14 When the builder becomes bankrupt, NHBC normally compensates the purchaser for any loss within the insurance limits of the scheme.

Compensation from NHBC

13.15 Before the end of the initial guarantee period NHBC will pay the purchaser the cost of rectifying any item which the builder fails to put right if:

(1) NHBC makes a recommendation in relation to a particular item and the purchaser accepts it in full and final satisfaction of his claim against the builder;

(2) The builder fails to honour an arbitration award or judgment to do specified work.

During the initial guarantee period and the structural guarantee period the builder is not liable for, and NHBC will not pay for, the following:

(1) Wear and tear;
(2) Deterioration caused by neglect;
(3) Normal dampness, condensation or shrinkage;
(4) Anything which the purchaser (not being a mortgagee in possession) knew about, or should reasonably have known about when he bought the house;
(5) Anything excluded from cover by an endorsement on the ten-year notice;
(6) Anything caused by alteration or extension to the house after the date of the ten-year notice;
(7) Any defect or damage caused by defective structural or installation design details provided by the first purchaser;
(8) Loss of enjoyment, inconvenience, distress or any other consequential loss;
(9) Increased costs resulting from any unreasonable delay in pursuing a claim;
(10) Any cost or expense in excess of that which a reasonable owner would spend in putting right any defect or damage.

During both the initial guarantee period and the structural guarantee period, if it is necessary for the purchaser to vacate the house while the work is being done, NHBC will pay the reasonable costs of removal, similar quality alternative accommodation and storage.

Limits of compensation

13.16 There are limits on the amount of compensation payable.

(1) NHBC will in total pay up to the maximum insured value set out in the ten-year notice. That liability will be increased by 12 per cent a year compound from the date of the ten-year notice until the date a claim is paid.

(2) NHBC will pay for removal expenses, alternative accommodation and storage up to a maximum of 10 per cent of the limit above.
(3) NHBC will pay such reasonable amount as is necessary to repair an item.

CHAPTER FOURTEEN

FIXTURES, FITTINGS AND CHATTELS

Introduction

14.01 Although the phrase 'fixtures and fittings' is commonly used, the distinction in law is actually between 'fixtures' and 'chattels'. A 'chattel' is not necessarily interchangeable with a fitting because it is a wider concept.

A fixture is anything annexed to the freehold. Whatever is so annexed, as a general rule, becomes part of the realty and the property in it immediately vests in the owner of the soil. The word fixture includes anything which has become so attached to land as to form in law part of the land.

A fitting is not a recognised legal term but usually refers to an item which is attached to the property in some way but not so as to become a fixture, for example, a carpet.

A chattel[130] is any property other than freehold land. Leaseholds and other interests in land less than freehold are termed chattels real because they savour of the realty. Chattels personal are movable, tangible articles of property.

GENERAL RULE

14.02 The general rule as to fixtures is *quicquid plantatur solo, solo cedit*, (whatever is attached to the ground becomes part of it).[131]

If a building is erected on land and objects are permanently attached to the building, then the soil, the building and the objects affixed to it are all in law "land", that is they are real property, not chattels or fittings.[132] Land includes for legal purposes all shrubs, hedges, plants and flowers growing on it, whether cultivated or wild.

As a fixture, the annexed object is regarded as having merged with the land. It then passes with all subsequent conveyances of the realty unless and until it is lawfully severed from the land.[133] This merger of chattel with realty automatically extinguishes any separate title formerly held in the object.[134]

Although a physical object will in law usually be either land (as a fixture) or a chattel, its nature may change according to the use made of it. For example, the materials used for building a house are converted from chattels into land when the house is built. Ownership of the materials passes from the person who owned them as chattels to the owner of the land to which they are attached. Conversely when a house is pulled down, the person who severs the materials from the building converts them from land into chattels.

---

[130] Latin: catulla, cattle.
[131] *Minshall* v *Lloyd* (1837) 2 M&W 450.
[132] See *New Zealand Government Property Corpn* v *HM & S* [1982] QB 1145 (CA). See also Conveyancing Act 1881, s 2.
[133] *North Shore Gas Co Ltd* v *Commissioner of Stamp Duties* (NSW) (1940) 63 CLR 52.
[134] See *Emanuel (Rundle Mall) Pty Ltd* v *Commissioner for Stamps* (1986) 39 SASR 582.

The question whether an object has become a fixture, and so is part of the land to which it has been fixed, is frequently a matter of dispute between competing claimants such as vendor and purchaser, landlord and tenant or mortgagee and mortgagor. In borderline cases ownership may be difficult to determine. "The criteria involved in the identification of fixtures are neither easily ascertained nor easily applied *per* Lord Radcliffe in *LCC* v *Wilkins*."[135]

In principle the question as to whether an article is a fixture and thus passes with the land on transfer depends upon two tests: the degree of annexation and the purpose of annexation.

The classical statement of the law by Blackburn in *Holland* v *Hodgson*[136] is often quoted:

> "It is a question which must depend on the circumstances of each case and mainly on two circumstances, as indicating the intention, *viz* the degree of annexation and the object of the annexation. When the article in question is no further attached to the land than by its own weight, it is generally to be considered a mere chattel .... But even in such a case, if the intention is apparent to make the articles part of the land, they do become part of the land .... Perhaps the true rule is that articles not otherwise attached to the land than by their own weight are not to be considered as part of the land, unless the circumstances are such as to show that they were intended to be part of the land, the onus of showing that they were so intended lying on those who assert that they have ceased to be chattels, and that on the contrary, an article which is affixed to the land even slightly is to be considered as part of the land, unless the circumstances are such as to show that it was intended all along to continue a chattel, the onus lying on those who contend that it is a chattel."

DEGREE OF ANNEXATION

14.03 The degree of annexation was traditionally the primary test of the status of an object as a fixture or chattel. It is not in itself conclusive and is now considered at most to provide a *prima facie* characterisation, which may be reversed by evidence of a contrary purpose. In general, for an article to be considered a fixture, some substantial connection with the land or a building on it must be shown. If it merely rests on the ground by its own weight it is *prima facie* not a fixture.

The more firmly or irreversibly the object is affixed to the earth or to a building, the more likely it is to be classified as a fixture. However, if a chattel is attached in any way such as by nails or screws, it will *prima facie* be a

---

[135] [1957] AC 362, 377.
[136] (1872) LR 7 CP 328.

fixture even if it could easily be removed, for example, a bathroom cabinet, overhead heater or extractor fan.

It is a matter of interpretation in each case. Blocks of stone placed on top of another without any mortar or cement for the purpose of forming a dry stone wall would become part of the land, though the same stones, if deposited in a builder's yard and for convenience's sake stacked on top of each other in the form of a wall would remain chattels.[137]

The fact that a chattel may sink into the ground,[138] or is set in a place prepared for it in the ground,[139] is not sufficient to make it a fixture. But where the article is so firmly fixed in the ground that it cannot be removed except by digging, such as an advertisement hoarding, it has been held that it would become a fixture.[140]

The importance of the degree of annexation varies from object to object. In the case of a large object, such as a house, the question does not often arise. Annexation goes without saying. The question of whether a house can ever be a chattel was considered by the House of Lords in *Elitestone Ltd v Morris and another*.[141] If it is constructed in such a way that it is removable whether as a unit or in sections, it might remain a chattel, even though it is connected temporarily to mains services such as water and electricity. But a house which is constructed in such a way that it cannot be removed at all, save by destruction, could not have been intended to remain as a chattel. It must have been intended to form part of the realty. It is clear that the intention of the parties is relevant only to the extent that it can be derived from the degree and object of the annexation, as the subjective intention of the parties cannot affect the question of whether the chattel has, in law, become part of the freehold.

PURPOSE OF ANNEXATION

14.04 The modern tendency is to regard the purpose of annexation as having greater importance than the degree of annexation and to look at the degree as being evidence of the purpose. Generally the tests of degree and purpose coincide in result, but this is not always necessarily true.

In determining the purpose of annexation, the question to be asked is: was the intention to effect a permanent improvement of the land or building as such or was it merely to effect a temporary improvement or to enjoy the chattel as a chattel?[142] In the first case the chattel is a fixture, in the second it is not.

If the article cannot be removed without great damage to the land or building, this test is conclusive and it is immaterial to enquire into the object of the annexation[143] The more securely an object is affixed and the more damage that

---

[137] *Holland v Hodgson*, Blackburn J at p 335.
[138] *Huntley v Russell* (1849) 13 QB 572.
[139] *Re Richards* (1869) 4 Ch App 630.
[140] *Provincial Bill Posting Co v Low Moor Iron Co* [1909] 2 KB 344.
[141] [1997] 2 All ER 513.
[142] *Hellawell v Eastwood* (1851) 6 Exch 295.
[143] *Wake v Hall* (1883) 8 App Cas 195.

would be caused by its removal, the more likely it is that the object was intended to form a permanent part of the land.

Attachment to the soil or building is not essential to make an article a fixture, if a clear intention can be shown to make the article a part of the land or house. For example, substantial garden ornaments have been held to be fixtures because they were integral to a permanent architectural design or general scheme for the improvement of the realty.[144]

Likewise items which are firmly fixed to the realty may remain chattels if the purpose of the annexation was merely to facilitate enjoyment of them as chattels and if the degree of annexation was no more than was necessary to achieve that purpose. The category of affixed objects which persist as chattels has been held to include tapestries,[145] display cases of stuffed birds,[146] and a private automatic branch telephone exchange switchboard.[147]

Although in these cases there was a substantial degree of annexation, the only way in which the chattels could be properly enjoyed was to attach them to the house in some way, and thus it was easier to infer an intent to affix them for the better enjoyment of them as chattels and not for the permanent improvement of the building.

The relevant intention is usually that of the party who affixes the object to the realty, but this cannot be assessed on a purely subjective basis. Greater weight is given to the objective intention or underlying purpose of the annexation revealed by surrounding circumstances, by the duration of the annexation and shared understandings of the function served by the annexation.

LEGAL RELEVANCE OF DISTINCTION

14.05 The distinction between fixtures and chattels is important for several legal purposes. Fixtures, but not chattels, pass with a conveyance of an estate in the land. Fixtures can be the subject of theft only if severed from the land. An equitable charge over fixtures, but not chattels, must be created in writing since fixtures constitute an interest in land. Perhaps the most significant distinction relates to the circumstances in which they can be removed from the land.

RIGHT TO REMOVE CHATTELS

14.06 A chattel may be removed from the land at any time by the owner of the chattel, subject to any contractual commitment (*eg,* a TV hire agreement or hire purchase agreement) which may regulate the location and use of the chattel.

---

[144] See *D'Eyncourt* v *Gregory* (1866) LR 3 Eq 382.
[145] *Leigh* v *Taylor* [1902] AC 157.
[146] *Viscount Hill* v *Bullock* [1897] 2 Ch 482.
[147] *NH Dunn Pty Ltd* v *LM Ericsson Pty Ltd* (1979) 2 BPR 9241.

RIGHT TO REMOVE FIXTURES

14.07 The right to remove fixtures is more complex. If the article is a fixture, generally it cannot be removed from the land and must be left for the fee simple owner.

Landlord and tenant

14.08 *Prima facie*, all fixtures attached by the tenant are landlord's fixtures and must be left for the landlord. Important exceptions to this rule have been developed and fixtures which can be removed under these exceptions are known as tenant's fixtures. However, the legal title to the fixture remains in the landlord until the tenant chooses to exercise his power and sever it.

The tenant has a right to sever and remove his fixtures during the original lease and any holding over or extension of the term.[148] If the tenancy is brought to an end by notice which does not allow enough time to remove the fixtures, the tenant is allowed a reasonable time to remove them. Once that time has elapsed, the tenant loses his right of removal and the landlord's title to the fixtures is absolute.

The tenant is under no obligation to remove fixtures lawfully attached to the property and if he leaves without removing his fixtures, he may be taken to have abandoned them.

When removing the fixtures, the tenant must make good any damage caused to the property by their removal or by their initial installation, leaving the premises in a reasonable condition.[149]

Tenant's fixtures

14.09 Special rules apply where the fixtures have been attached by the tenant.

(a) Trade fixtures

Fixtures attached by the tenant for the purpose of carrying on some trade, business or manufacture,[150] may be removed although damaging the fabric, together with covering erections.

(b) Ornamental and domestic fixtures

The tenant is permitted to remove in their entirety articles of the nature of fittings rather than additions to the property itself as long as there is no substantial damage to the fabric. This exception appears to be rather more limited than the previous one and seems to extend only to chattels perfect in themselves which can be removed without substantial injury to the building.

---

[148] *Leschallas* v *Woolf* [1908] 1 Ch 641.
[149] See *Mansetter Development Ltd* v *Garmanson Ltd* [1986] 2 WLR 871 as to holes in walls.
[150] *Poole's Case* (1703) 1 Salk 368.

(c) *Agricultural fixtures*

At common law, agricultural fixtures were not regarded as trade fixtures, because agriculture was regarded as a normal use of land and not as a trade.[151] In Ireland the common law position was altered by the Landlord and Tenant Law Amendment Act (Ir) 1860 (Deasy's Act), section 17.

Deasy's Act, section 17 provides that a tenant may remove trade, ornamental, domestic and agricultural fixtures which he has attached to the land as long as they can be removed without substantial damage to the freehold or the fixture. The landlord is entitled to compensation for any damage caused to the premises. The items must be removed during the tenancy or, if terminated by an uncertain event, within two months of termination.

Some points of difference with the common law position should be noted. The section only applies where the fixture is attached at the tenant's sole expense. Damage to the fixture itself is relevant. It is unclear to what extent the common law still applies where the Act does not. It must do to some extent since the Act does not define the terms used in the section and reference would have to be made to the case law if such words as "affixed" or "domestic convenience" were in issue.

Vendor and purchaser

14.10 Without exception, all fixtures attached to the land at the time of a contract of sale must be left for the purchaser unless otherwise agreed. The conveyance will be effective to pass the fixtures to the purchaser without express mention by virtue of the Conveyancing Act 1881, section 6.

When a vendor occupies the property sold, he must not, in the absence of a condition to the contrary, after signing the contract, remove any fixtures from the property, although they may be such as between landlord and tenant could be removed.[152]

There are several ways of providing for payment of articles which are not fixtures, but it is probably best to state in the contract the amount which the purchaser is to pay for the fixtures. It is also advisable to clarify which items are regarded as fixtures.

There may well be differences of view between the parties as to what does or does not constitute a fixture or fitting. The important thing is not to establish who is right but to establish agreement at the outset.

Mortgagor and mortgagee

14.11 A mortgage of land whether legal or equitable includes all buildings and fixtures attached to the land without special mention. The exceptions as between landlord and tenant do not apply. A mortgagor is not allowed to

---

[151] In England, the Landlord and Tenant Act 1851 gave agricultural tenants the right to remove fixtures, subject to the landlord's right to elect to buy them. The position is now governed by the Agricultural Holdings Act 1986, s 10.

[152] *Gibson* v *Hammersmith & City Railway Co* (1863) 32 LJ Ch 337.

remove his ornamental, domestic, trade or agricultural fixtures. He is not even entitled to remove fixtures which he has attached after the date of the mortgage.

Life tenant and remainderman

14.12 On the death of the life tenant, *prima facie* all the fixtures must be left for the remainderman with the common law exception of trade, ornamental and domestic fixtures.

Devisee and personal representative

14.13 If land is given by will, the rule is that all fixtures pass under the devise. The devise naturally carries with it everything which can fairly be said to be part of the land.

Rights of third parties

14.14 The title to chattels may clearly be lost by being affixed to real property by a person who is not the owner of the chattels. However if, for example, equipment or machinery is the subject of a contract for hire or hire-purchase and has been attached to the land of the hirer, the owner of the equipment may reserve a contractual right to remove it in default of payment. This right creates an equitable interest in the land (a right of entry) which may be binding on third parties to whom the land is later conveyed.[153]

---

[153] On unregistered land this right to remove hired fixtures is enforceable against all third parties other than a *bona fide* purchaser of a legal estate for value without notice, see *Poster v Slough Estates Ltd* [1968] 1 WLR 1515 and therefore binds a subsequent equitable mortgagee of the land. On registered land the right to remove hired fixtures cannot apparently be made to bind a purchaser at all.

CHAPTER FIFTEEN

POST-CONTRACT

Introduction

15.01 There may be a considerable time lapse from the date on which the contract is signed until completion. During that period it is possible that because of the occurrence of an event altering his own position or because of something he has discovered about the property one of the parties may wish to withdraw from the contract. It is therefore important to consider the legal position of the parties at this stage and the options available to each of them.

In equity, once the contract becomes binding, the doctrine of conversion operates to treat the purchaser as the owner of the land and the vendor as the owner of the purchase money. The vendor is considered to be the trustee of the property and the purchaser the beneficiary, but a problem then arises in deciding when the beneficial ownership passes.

In general the position of the parties during the intermediate period is as undernoted.

VENDOR

Possession

15.02 The vendor may retain possession of the property until the full purchase money is paid. He has a common law lien on the property for the unpaid purchase money if he retains possession and the right to stay until it is paid, but not to deal with the property in any way. If he leaves, he has an equitable lien on the property for the unpaid purchase money and an equitable charge entitling him to apply to court for an order for sale and payment of the debt out of the sale proceeds.

Rents and profits

15.03 The vendor is entitled to the rents and profits from the property until the time fixed for completion. If completion is delayed, he is a trustee of the rents and profits for the purchaser, who is then entitled to them. This may not apply to a situation where completion is delayed by the purchaser.

Duty to maintain

15.04 The vendor has a duty to maintain the property until completion, as long as he has possession. He must take proper precautions to protect the property from injury by trespassers and he should discharge all outgoings up to completion.

Death

15.05 If the vendor dies after entering into the contract, his personal representatives are bound by it and the contract may be enforced against them.

Bankruptcy[154]

15.06 The important point to consider is whether a binding contract exists before the bankruptcy petition is issued.

Contract before bankruptcy petition

15.07 Where a binding contract exists and a bankruptcy petition is subsequently issued against the vendor, the trustee in bankruptcy takes the land subject to the obligation to complete the sale. If the contract is unprofitable the trustee may disclaim it, but otherwise the purchaser can apply for specific performance against him. The purchaser may apply to the court for an order discharging his obligations under the contract if he does not wish to proceed.

Contract after bankruptcy petition

15.08 The Insolvency (NI) Order 1989, article 257, provides that any disposition of property made by the bankrupt between the date of the presentation of the bankruptcy petition and the vesting of the bankrupt's estate in the trustee is void. This may affect a contract for sale because a contract involves a disposition by the vendor of the equitable interest in the land.

Liquidation

15.09 Where the vendor is a company which goes into liquidation between the contract and completion, the liquidator has power to carry the contract into effect. If the contract is unprofitable he may disclaim it. Otherwise, if the liquidator refuses to complete, the purchaser can seek specific performance or can prove in the winding up.

PURCHASER

Taking possession[155]

15.10 Although the vendor is normally entitled to retain possession of the property pending completion and receipt of the full purchase money, the parties may agree for a particular reason that the purchaser should be allowed into possession prior to completion. Possession may be restricted to a specific purpose, such as carrying out repairs.

Gains and losses

15.11 Under the general law the purchaser takes the benefit of any gains which accrue and suffers any losses relating to the property between contract and completion, subject to the vendor's duty to maintain the property so long as he has possession.

Again this may be altered by contractual provisions. GCS 6.1 provides that the risk of the property remains with the vendor until completion. GCS 6.2 sets out the options available to each party in the event of the property suffering damage

---

[154] See Bankruptcy paras 27.01-27.24.
[155] Cf para 15.42.

and being rendered unusable for the purpose which it had at the date of the contract.

If the property is rendered unusable for its purpose as at the date of the contract the purchaser may rescind under GCS 6.2(a). He may also recover his deposit and any money paid on account of the purchase price but without interest. Alternatively he may affirm the contract, in which case his right to compensation is confined to the cost of making good the damage to the property.

Similarly under GCS 6.2(b), the vendor may rescind the contract where the property has become unusable for its purpose as a result of damage for which he could not reasonably have insured or obtained statutory compensation or where he is legally prohibited from making good the damage.

Under GCS 6.4 if a breach of GCS 6.1 has occurred which is not sufficient to entitle the purchaser to rescind, he is entitled to compensation in the amount required to remedy the damage.

GCS 6.3 states that the vendor is under no legal obligation to the purchaser to insure the property, notwithstanding that fact that he retains the risk. As a precautionary measure it is advisable for the purchaser to have insurance cover from the date of the contract, even if the vendor also has the property insured.

The reason for this is that the purchaser has an equitable interest in the property from the time the contract is entered into. The benefit of the vendor's existing insurance policy does not pass to the purchaser. It is possible for the vendor to collect his insurance money when the property is destroyed and also obtain the purchase money from the purchaser if he is under an obligation to complete. The difficulty may be avoided if GCS 6.2(a), as mentioned above, applies and the purchaser can rescind the contract.

Lien on money paid

15.12 The purchaser has a lien on the deposit and any money paid to the vendor. Consequently, the vendor holds the purchaser's money as security for the performance of the contract. The lien binds the property but does not affect a *bona fide* purchaser for value without notice.

Death

15.13 On the death of the purchaser, his equitable interest in the property vests in his personal representatives who can enforce the contract and have it enforced against them.

Bankruptcy[156]

15.14 Where a purchaser enters into a contract and is subsequently adjudicated bankrupt, the transaction may proceed provided that the trustee does not disclaim it as unprofitable. The vendor may apply to the court for an order discharging the obligations under the contract if he does not wish to proceed but

---

[156] See Bankruptcy paras 27.01-27.24.

he cannot obtain specific performance against an unwilling trustee in bankruptcy even if the transaction is profitable.

The Insolvency (NI) Order 1989, article 257, applies to payments of money in the same way as to dispositions of land. Therefore, the transaction is valid only if the vendor receives the money before the bankruptcy order in good faith and without notice of the petition.

Liquidation

15.15 Where the purchaser is a company which goes into liquidation between contract and completion the liquidator can elect either to complete the contract or to disclaim it.

Registered land

15.16 The purchaser probably has an unregistered equitable interest in the property between contract and completion. Any such unregistered right is subject to defeat by registration of a transfer for value, even if the transferee had prior knowledge of the unregistered interest. The purchaser can protect his interest by registering a caution which entitles him to be given notice of any other transfer.

The purchaser can also make a priority search which consists of an entry being made on the register to the effect that if the transfer, lease or charge which is contemplated by the contract is delivered to the Land Registry within 40 days from the date of the certificate of the priority search it will rank in priority before any other dealing presented for registration during that period.

Priority between registered transactions depends upon the order of registration which in turn normally depends upon the order in which dealings are received for registration.

Once the purchaser has paid over the balance purchase money and the executed transfer deed has been delivered to him, the purchaser has an equity to be registered as owner and has an unregistered right to the land, valid against the registered owner (the vendor) and all others except a registered transferee for value without notice.

The purchaser in such a position has a right which takes priority over almost all others, including anyone claiming the property under a voluntary disposition from the registered owner. Only a person in a similar position to himself, who had purchased the property from the registered owner prior to the purchaser in question, or a subsequent purchaser for value without notice whose transfer is registered first, could take priority.

REQUISITIONS ON TITLE

15.17 In traditional practice, requisitions were not raised until the post-contract stage. Now that there can be a number of interests and charges affecting land which are not easily discoverable by an inspection of the physical state of the property nor by a perusal of the title deeds, preliminary enquiries are made before the contract is signed. Supplementary requisitions are raised before completion to ensure that nothing significant has arisen meanwhile.

Requisitions relate to something the purchaser intends the vendor to explain and put right. Objections are usually made if the title shown is bad and the purchaser does not wish to proceed. The purchaser should not raise requisitions on matters which are of no concern to him nor which will fix him with notice of something that would not otherwise have affected him.

GCS 10.1 requires requisitions to be made within 10 working days of delivery of the title or after the date of the contract, if later. Time is of the essence. If the purchaser does not raise requisitions, he is deemed to have accepted the title and may be construed to have waived any breach of the vendor's duty. If the GCS are not used requisitions should be raised within a reasonable period of the title being received.

Waiver of rights by purchaser

15.18 The purchaser may impliedly waive his right to object to a defect in title after the contract has been signed if he continues to act as if the contract still exists when the defect has been discovered. Failure to request documents or to raise requisitions may also be construed as waiver. GCS 14.3 specifically confirms that a purchaser going into occupation before the completion date shall be deemed thereby to have accepted the vendor's title.

BREACH OF CONTRACT

15.19 A breach of contract occurs when one party fails to comply with, or acts contrary to, his obligations under the contract. There are many ways in which the contract may be breached and a case may turn on the interpretation of a particular clause in the contract.

Time clauses

15.20 One of the most common breaches of contract is failure or refusal by one party to complete on the date agreed. The general rule is that time is not of the essence of the contract unless it can be implied from the conduct of the parties or the special conditions make it so.[157] GCS 19.1 confirms this position.

The disadvantage of time being made of the essence of the contract is that it acts against both parties. The party who originally hopes to take prompt action in the event of default by the other may end up being trapped by it himself if an unforeseen delay prevents him from completing.

As an alternative incentive to the purchaser to complete on time, contractual provisions, such as GCS 16.1, may provide for payment of interest by him in the event of a delay. This raises a presumption that time is not of the essence because it indicates that the parties anticipate the possibility of a delay.

---

[157] In *Union Eagle Ltd* v *Golden Achievement Ltd* (1997), *The Times*, 7 February, a contract provided for completion by 5.00 pm on the completion date, time being of the essence. At 5.01 pm when the money had not arrived the vendor informed the purchaser that he reserved the right to rescind and forfeit the deposit. The money arrived at 5.10 pm, the vendor refused to complete and forfeited the deposit. The court held that time being of the essence has to be applied strictly and there is no room for equity to intervene.

Accordingly, where there is provision for payment of interest each party is allowed to complete within a reasonable time of the completion date without being in breach of the contract.

GCS 16.4 provides for the purchaser, if he so wishes, to impose a financial penalty on the vendor when he fails to complete. This is only the equivalent of a fair rent for the relevant period equal to the rateable valuation of the property and consequently is not likely to compensate the purchaser adequately for his losses.

Completion notices

15.21 In most cases either party may complete the contract after the agreed completion date without being in breach of contract as long as he completes within a reasonable time thereafter.

Under the general law governing an open contract the party who wishes to enforce the contract may issue a completion notice after a reasonable time has elapsed from the completion date without completion actually taking place. The definition of a reasonable time depends on the circumstances in each situation. At common law the innocent party has to wait until that reasonable period has elapsed before seeking any remedy. Then when the notice to complete is issued he must allow the defaulter a further reasonable time to complete.

In other cases the issue of a completion notice, its terms and consequences will be determined by the provisions of the contract. GCS 19.2 provides that if the sale is not completed on the date fixed for completion, either party may on that date or at any time thereafter, give notice in writing to the other party to complete the transaction. The injured party must himself be ready, willing and able to complete when he issues the notice.

Under GCS 19.3 the notice can specify that the transaction shall be completed within five working days of service and that time is to be of the essence in respect of that period, but without prejudice to any intermediate right of rescission by either party.

If the purchaser fails to comply with a notice to complete served by the vendor, the vendor may forfeit the deposit and resell. The contractual provisions of GCS 19 relating to completion notices do not affect the pursuit of any other rights or remedies available to the vendor, such as specific performance of the contract.

Under the general law the vendor may forfeit the deposit as soon as the purchaser defaults. There is some authority for the view that the vendor is even entitled to keep the deposit when it exceeds any loss he may have suffered.

By virtue of GCS 19.4, the vendor may forfeit and retain for his own benefit the deposit paid by the purchaser regardless of any loss and resell the property. If on any such resale within one year he incurs a loss, the purchaser shall pay the amount of such loss to him inclusive of costs and expenses: in this situation the vendor will give credit for any deposit and any money paid on account of the purchase price, but any surplus money shall be retained by him. In practice it may be impractical for the vendor to recover any loss or deficiency on resale from the purchaser.

Under the general law, when the vendor is in default the purchaser may recover his deposit with interest and, in most cases, the costs of investigating title. GCS 19.5 further provides that when the vendor fails to comply with a completion notice the purchaser may, without further notice, enforce such rights and remedies as are available to him.

Alternatively, without prejudice to any right to damages he may have, the purchaser may give notice to the vendor to repay the deposit and any money paid on account of the purchase price. GCS 19.5 states that after requesting the return of the deposit the purchaser is not entitled to specific performance of the contract and must return all the papers to the vendor.

REMEDIES FOR ENFORCEMENT OF THE CONTRACT

15.22 The remedies available to the parties depend on the general law as extended or restricted by the contract. There may be several alternatives but they may not all be consistent with each other, nor necessarily available to both parties. The injured party has to elect which remedy he is seeking and which course of action he wishes to take when the contract has been breached by the other party. This usually depends on the circumstances of the case and the result the injured party hopes to achieve.

The effect of the breach varies according to its severity. If one party repudiates the contract, makes its performance impossible or fails to perform his promises, the other party has the right to treat the contract as discharged and to pursue the appropriate remedy.

Time

15.23 At common law if a party failed to complete by a fixed date he was immediately regarded as being in breach of the contract, because time was of the essence. In equity time was not of the essence and delay alone did not necessarily involve a breach of contract. The defaulting party was allowed to complete within a reasonable time after the completion date. The equitable approach was adopted by the Judicature (Ir) Act 1877 and operates now as the general rule for all contracts.

If the injured party wishes to rescind the contract for delay or claim damages for breach of contract, he cannot do so until a reasonable time has elapsed from the completion date or, if governed by the GCS, the requirements of GCS 19 have been complied with. On the other hand, if the injured party wishes to seek specific performance, he can do so as soon as the delay occurs because of the equitable duty on the other party to perform the contract once it becomes binding. Specific performance may even be sought before completion where, for example, one party repudiates the contract.

Vendor and purchaser summons

15.24 Before applying for a remedy for breach of contract, the parties may attempt to have the dispute resolved under the Vendor and Purchaser Act 1874. This Act introduced a special summary procedure to enable vendors and purchasers of land to settle disputes arising during the course of the transaction without invoking substantive remedies. The procedure is rarely used, perhaps because the summons cannot be used to determine the validity of a contract nor a question of fraud. Its use is confined to the determination of disputes between the parties on matters of interpretation of the contract and related conveyancing matters, such as whether the vendor has made good title or has sufficiently answered a requisition.

Specific performance

15.25 Specific performance is an equitable remedy which lies in the discretion of the court. It compels the party who is not performing his obligations under the contract to do so.[158]

Specific performance is only available if a binding contract exists and a breach of that contract has either taken place or is anticipated. It applies only to contracts for the sale of land and not usually to building contracts or contracts to lend money on the security of land.

Specific performance and damages are not mutually exclusive but one is usually more appropriate than the other in the particular circumstances of each case.

Defences to specific performance

15.26 There are a number of possible defences to an application for specific performance.

Lack of formalities

15.27 Specific performance will not generally be granted where a contract is not fully binding because it lacks some formality. Nevertheless, if there has been part performance of the contract sufficient to take it outside the provisions of the Statute of Frauds (Ir) 1695, specific performance may be granted.

Uncertainty or incompleteness

15.28 Where the contract lacks certainty as to the intention of the parties or as to the precise terms of the agreement, specific performance may be refused.

Lack of mutuality

15.29 If there is a particular reason, such as lack of capacity, which prevents one party from enforcing the contract, the other party cannot enforce it either. There are many recognised exceptions to this rule. For example, if the contract has been signed by one party it can be enforced against the one who has signed, but not against the one who has not.

Hardship or lack of fairness

15.30 If the grant of a decree would cause undue hardship to the defendant, for example, by foisting a bad title on a purchaser, or if the plaintiff has acted

---

[158] For consideration of the issue of the effect of alterations to the contract and a solicitors authority to approve alterations, in the context of specific performance, see *Day and another* v *McCrum and another* [1996] NI 607.

unfairly, the defence may be successful. If the circumstances are sufficiently serious, the defendant may have a counterclaim for rescission of the contract as well as a defence to an action for specific performance. This is the case where the acts involve fraud, duress, undue influence or mistake. Other less serious acts may be a sufficient defence to specific performance, but do not justify rescission. For example, where a bargain has been made at a considerable but not gross undervalue, or an agreement made when one of the parties was drunk.

Laches (delay)

15.31 Delay defeats equity. It is for the court to decide in each case whether the plaintiff has delayed too long in exercising his right to apply for specific performance.

Misdescription

15.32 Misdescription can be a successful defence to a claim for specific performance. However, if there is a misdescription but it is insubstantial, the vendor may still be able to enforce the contract against the purchaser.[159]

Lack of title

15.33 The court will not force a bad title on a purchaser. In some cases the title may be merely doubtful and the doubt can be resolved by the court, for example by determining a question of law on the construction of the title. After resolving the doubt, the court may then grant a decree of specific performance if the result favours good title.

However, the purchaser may elect to take whatever title the vendor has to give subject to a price reduction. If he does so, he may be taken to have waived all objection to the vendor's title and cannot then have a defence to an action for specific performance on the grounds of lack of title.

The special conditions in a contract may prohibit the purchaser from raising any objections to title but the court will scrutinise such conditions carefully. Generally the vendor is not allowed to use the conditions to deliberately conceal defects and to force a bad title on the purchaser. It would be contrary to the basic principles of equity to grant equitable relief to the vendor in such circumstances.

If specific performance is not granted the parties would then be left to their remedies at law. A purchaser may recover his deposit but damages may be restricted.[160] A deposit may sometimes be retained by a vendor who rescinds because it is intended to be security for performance by the purchaser and to be forfeited if he defaults.

Rescission

15.34 Rescission means abrogation or revocation of the contract. After rescission the contract is treated as never having existed.

---

[159] Cf paras 4.02–4.08.
[160] See Damages, below paras 15.38, 15.40.

In its strict sense, rescission is only allowed where restitution is possible and the parties can be restored to their original positions. Rescission puts an end to the contract and must be exercised as soon as the problem giving rise to the right is discovered. The parties should be able to return any gain made under the contract.

Vendor

15.35 Where the vendor rescinds the contract he is entitled to recover possession of the property and any rent or profits received by the purchaser. He may also forfeit any deposit on the basis that it was paid to him as security for the performance of the contract by the purchaser.

Under the general law, because there is no actual breach of contract on rescission, the vendor cannot recover any loss on resale. This position is modified by GCS 19.4 which states that when the purchaser fails to comply with a notice to complete the vendor can recover any deficiency on resale within a year from the purchaser, including the costs of resale. This provision, in effect, does not allow rescission in the strict sense to operate.

In many instances only one party will be entitled to rescind because the other party is at fault.

Purchaser

15.36 Where the purchaser rescinds the contract he can usually recover the deposit and his expenses in investigating the title, but has to account to the vendor for any rents or profits received out of the property. He is not entitled to any damages for loss of bargain.

If the purchaser discovers substantial defects in title he may immediately repudiate the contract and treat himself as discharged from it. He may then sue for damages or rescind the contract. It is questionable whether the court has power to return his deposit unless he has sued for its recovery.

When the purchaser has delayed in exercising his remedy despite the defects in title rescission may only be available in equity. This means that the contract is not put to an end but that the purchaser is entitled to resist specific performance. It also enables the vendor to redeem himself if he subsequently acquires proper title.

Contractual rights of rescission

15.37 The GCS confer certain contractual rights of rescission:

GCS 2.2

Failure by the vendor to disclose all matters of which he has or ought to have knowledge as a result of the normal searches and enquiries etc is a ground for rescission by the purchaser in addition to any other remedy which may be available to him.

GCS 6.2

If the property suffers any damage between contract and completion which makes it unusable for its purpose either party may rescind but the right of the vendor to do so is restricted to specific circumstances.[161]

GCS 8.3(d)

If a required consent to the sale is not obtained either party may rescind.

GCS 18.1

If the purchaser insists on objections or requisitions which the vendor is unable or, on reasonable grounds, unwilling to remove, the vendor may rescind.

GCS 18.2

If rescission occurs on any of the above contractual grounds the vendor must return the deposit to the purchaser but does not have to pay interest and the purchaser has no further claim against the purchaser.

Damages

15.38 Apart from the general law of contract, particular provisions may be applicable under the contract itself, depending on the nature of the breach. Nevertheless damages for breach of contract are always available to the aggrieved party under the general law. Damages may also be awarded in addition to or in lieu of specific performance.

In equity damages can be awarded where the court has jurisdiction to award specific performance. This means that in some instances damages can be awarded where they are not available at common law, such as where the contract lacks a legal formality but is enforceable in equity. In equity the measure of damages is assessed at the date of the judgment whereas at common law damages are traditionally assessed at the date of the breach of contract.

The injured party can only seek damages for breach of contract when he has already elected to affirm the contract. Where he does not affirm the contract but applies for rescission in the strict sense and sues for restitution of his former position, the contract is treated as never having existed. In that case it is not possible to claim damages for breach of contract.

The extent of the damages are such as may reasonably be considered as arising naturally from the breach or may reasonably be supposed to have been in the contemplation of the parties when they entered the contract as the probable result of it. The amount of damages varies according to the circumstances of each case and are assessed at the actual loss suffered. The cost of repairs or work required to the property as a result of the breach is not the basis for assessment.

---

[161] See para 15.34.

Vendor

15.39 On breach by the purchaser the vendor is entitled to be put in the position he would have been in had the contract been performed according to its terms. The general rule is that the damages awarded are the difference in value between the contract price and the value of the property at the date of the breach of contract. When the vendor does not resell the latter value is estimated as that realisable on the sale within a reasonable time of the breach.

The vendor may claim the expenses of the resale but must also account for any deposit forfeited by him, whereas if he rescinds he can keep the deposit notwithstanding a profit on resale.

The vendor cannot sue the purchaser for breach of contract if the purchaser's obligation to perform the contract is nullified because of the vendor's inability to show good title, or being otherwise not able, ready and willing to perform his side of the agreement.

Purchaser

15.40 Where the vendor is in breach of contract, the purchaser is generally entitled to the return of the deposit with interest and, in most cases, damages for loss of bargain. However the recovery of damages by the purchaser on breach of contract by the vendor is subject to the restriction of the rule in *Bain* v *Fothergill*.[162]

The rule states that where the vendor breaches the contract by failing to show good title to the property, then provided the vendor was not fraudulent and did not act in bad faith, the purchaser is not entitled to recover damages for loss of bargain. He is limited to recovery of his deposit with interest and any expenses incurred in investigation of the title.

Where the rule in *Bain* v *Fothergill* does not apply and the purchaser is entitled to damages, then he is entitled to damages for loss of bargain in addition to the deposit plus interest. Loss of bargain is the difference between the contract purchase price and the market value of the property at the date of the breach. In appropriate cases, loss of prospective profits on development may be included. He is not in general entitled to his conveyancing expenses because he would still have incurred them if the contract had been performed.

Where the purchaser is unable to establish a loss of profit and so cannot claim on the basis of loss of bargain, the court may instead seek to restore him to his position prior to the contract as if it had never been made. He is entitled to his legal and other expenses because he would not have incurred had the contract not been made.

Forfeiture and recovery of deposit

15.41 The deposit is usually regarded as part payment of the purchase price and security for performance of the contract. The vendor may be entitled to forfeit the deposit if the purchaser defaults on the contract and the purchaser to

---

[162] (1874) LR 7 HL 158.

recover it if the vendor defaults. Any contractual provision to this effect must not offend against the equitable rule against penalties and manifestly exceed any loss sustained by the innocent party.

Normally, when the purchaser is in default of the contract the vendor forfeits the deposit even if the deposit exceeds his losses or he resells at a profit. However, there is the possibility that a court will apply the law relating to penalty clauses if the question of reasonableness arises.

If the amount of the deposit is reasonable, the vendor is entitled to retain it regardless of actual loss. If it is not a reasonable amount, forfeiture will not be enforced beyond the amount of the actual loss.[163] A reasonable amount is probably 10 per cent or less.[164]

TAKING POSSESSION BEFORE COMPLETION

15.42 The vendor normally retains possession of the property pending completion. However, the purchaser may in certain circumstances require possession before completion and the parties may make an agreement to this effect, for example to carry out improvements or repairs. In each case the dangers of allowing the purchaser into possession before completion should be clearly pointed out to both parties.

The vendor is perfectly entitled to refuse to permit the purchaser to take possession until the purchase price has been paid. Once he has obtained possession the purchaser may lose the incentive for furnishing the purchase money on the agreed date although he is still legally obliged to do so.

The vendor is taking a great risk in allowing a purchaser into possession without paying the full purchase money. He is leaving himself in a vulnerable position by relinquishing possession because he then has neither the property nor the money.

At common law a purchaser in possession may be regarded as being a tenant at will and not merely a licensee. Accordingly he may be construed as having possessory rights. If he can then establish a tenancy within the restrictive criteria laid down by the Rent (NI) Order 1978 it may be possible to acquire security of tenure by that means.

Contractual provisions may modify the position under the general law. GCS 14 states that where the purchaser is authorised by the vendor before actual completion to take up physical occupation of the property, the purchaser shall be in occupation as the licensee/caretaker for and not the tenant of the vendor.

---

[163] See *Workers Trust and Merchant Bank Ltd* v *Dojap Investments Ltd* [1993] 2 All ER 370.
[164] In England there is a statutory jurisdiction conferred by Law of Property Act 1925, s 49(2), for the court to order at its discretion the repayment of any deposit. If invoked, this prevents the vendor from retaining any amount above his legitimate damages for breach of contract.

This is an important distinction.[165] The purchaser being a caretaker protects the vendor against the risk of removing a tenant who has acquired some security of tenure.

By taking possession, the purchaser impliedly undertakes to pay interest on the outstanding balance purchase money, whether or not he derives any profit from his possession. He is entitled to the rents and profits of the property but is also responsible for repairs and outgoings while in possession. This position is confirmed by GCS 14.1. If he makes improvements, the purchaser cannot recover his expenditure from the vendor even if the sale falls through because of the vendor's default.

GCS 14.3 provides that the purchaser shall be deemed to have accepted the vendor's title by taking possession. Presumably he will also have waived any right to make objections or raise requisitions thereto. This would not necessarily be the case under the general law which does not generally regard the purchaser's possession as enough in itself to be treated as waiver or acceptance of title. If construed in the context of other acts of ownership, it might be, for example, actions such as making alterations, or granting a lease.

GCS 14.2 provides that, upon rescission of the contract or upon the expiration of not less than five working days notice given by the vendor to the purchaser, the purchaser shall forthwith give up the property.

Normally, the purchaser also enters into a caretaker's agreement which clarifies the details of his position and confirms that he is in possession as caretaker. In the event of any problem, the vendor should be able to remove the purchaser under GCS 14.2 and the terms of the caretaker's agreement, avoiding the difficulties he would otherwise have in ejecting a tenant. If the purchaser refuses to leave the vendor may still have to take proceedings to recover possession.

Whilst in possession as caretaker the purchaser has to pay and indemnify the vendor against all outgoings including insurance, costs of repairs and any other expenses relating to the property for the period of his occupation. He also has to pay the vendor interest on the outstanding purchase money. GCS 16.1 provides that the rate should be six per cent above the UK clearing bank base lending rate or at such other rate as may be agreed.

If the vendor seeks specific performance of a contract where the purchaser is in possession but has failed to pay the agreed price, the court may allow the purchaser to stay in possession and pay the balance purchase money with interest into court.

---

[165] Cf para 22.09.

CHAPTER SIXTEEN

STAMP DUTY

Introduction

16.01 In this chapter the Stamp Act 1891 is referred to as SA 1891 and all Finance Acts as FA followed by the relevant year.

Stamp Duties are one of the oldest taxes and were first imposed in 1694. Although they produce substantial revenue, their coverage in recent years has become much reduced following simplification and modernisation.

The Stamp Duties Management Act 1891 and the Stamp Act 1891 are consolidating statutes which still constitute the present law on Stamp Duties. Stamp Duties may be varied or abolished in budget resolutions passed by the House of Commons.[166]

The intention of the legislation is to make it obligatory to stamp the most common types of document. Only those relating to land and premises are considered here.

Stamp Duty is a tax on the document itself, not on the transaction or the parties to it. There is no VAT on Stamp Duty of residential properties.

The duty is charged in SA 1891, Schedule 1, which sets out the instruments alphabetically specifying the duty charged on each under different heads of charge. The duty in each case is either *ad valorem* or fixed. There are general exemptions from all Stamp Duties and specific exemptions under particular heads of charge.

One of the most important things to be done by a purchaser's solicitor after completion of the transaction is to have the purchase deed taken to the Stamp Office for stamping.

PRINCIPLES OF STAMP DUTY

16.02 Stamp Duty is revenue raised by means of stamps impressed on certain written instruments. The tax is on documents and not on transactions as such, nor on persons. If a transaction can be carried out orally or by conduct, there need be no instrument and no duty.

Duty is paid in accordance with the substance of an instrument; that is, its intention and operation in law, rather than merely its form. Only instruments which in substance carry out a transaction should be stamped. No stamp is necessary if the instrument precedes the transaction. Nor is there any general statutory provision for stamping written evidence of oral transactions.[167]

---

[166] FA 1973, s 50.
[167] However, there is judicial authority for saying that if the written evidence was brought into existence as a part of the transaction then it should be stamped as if it carried out the transaction. This is known as the "all one transaction rule", see *Cohen and Moore v IRC* [1933] 2 KB 126.

If more than one instrument is written on the same paper, each must be separately stamped.

Method of stamping

16.03 Instruments generally have to be presented for stamping at the Stamp Office. On payment of the appropriate duty, the stamps are impressed by dies, which are usually red (although the stamp on counterparts was blue traditionally). In the past, postage stamps were also used for some duties which have now been repealed, for example, on agreements and receipts.

Adjudication

16.04 Stamping in the ordinary way is not conclusive that the instrument is duly stamped and a further adjudication stamp is required for this purpose, bearing the words "adjudged duly stamped" or "adjudged not chargeable with any duty" as appropriate. Adjudication is desirable to satisfy third parties or where queries are otherwise anticipated, or as the first step in disputing liability to duty.

Adjudication is obligatory in the following cases:

(1) On conveyances in contemplation of sale;[168]

(2) Where exemption or relief is claimed for a conveyance or transfer on amalgamation or reconstruction of a company or between associated companies;

(3) Where any person required to register an instrument chargeable with stamp duty insists.

Appeal

16.05 Any person dissatisfied with an adjudication may, within 21 days and on payment of the duty, appeal to the High Court. On hearing the appeal the court assesses the duty chargeable.

Produced stamp

16.06 Until 4 November 1996 purchasers were required to produce the conveyancing document to the Stamp Office, whether or not duty was payable, together with the particulars delivered ('PD') form which summarised the details of the transaction. The document was stamped with a produced stamp in addition to any *ad valorem* stamp. Without the produced stamp documents were not deemed to be duly stamped.

---

[168] It does not matter that the contract was not binding when the conveyance was executed. Such a conveyance is treated as a conveyance on sale, FA 1965, s 90 (1). A claim for repayment can be made if the sale falls through within two years and there is a reconveyance.

Fast-track

16.07 Under the Stamp Duty (Production of Documents) (NI) Regulations 1996 which came into force on 4 November 1996, documents relating to sales below the threshold for stamp duty can bypass the Stamp Office and go direct to the Registry of Deeds or Land Registry as appropriate accompanied by the completed PD (particulars delivered) form.[169] This procedure is not applicable to a document creating a new estate, such as a lease.

Denoting stamps

16.08 When the duty on an instrument depends in any way on the duty paid on another instrument, then on production of both instruments the fact of payment of duty on the latter will be denoted on the former by a blue impressed stamp. The commonest examples occur with:

(1) Contracts and agreements for lease charged as if conveyances on sale;

(2) Duplicates and counterparts. The stamp now (since 1976) states "duplicate or counterpart - original fully and properly stamped".

Time for stamping

16.09 An instrument does not become stampable until it is complete and has been executed by the last person whose execution is essential for its valid operation.

Execution

16.10 SA 1891, section 122, as amended by FA 1994, section 224, defines execution for these purposes in terms of signature and delivery. This means, not that the instrument must be handed over to the purchaser, but rather that the vendor must indicate by word or action that he is bound by it. Where it is delivered subject to conditions, it will not be treated as executed until those conditions are fulfilled. The date on the instrument must correspond with reality and not be fictitious.

A stampable instrument, in practice, may be stamped or lodged for adjudication either before or within 30 days after its date.[170] The time limit for stamping after adjudication is 14 days.

Since 1 October 1999 the Stamp Office has been much stricter about imposing penalties on documents presented late. It will no longer accept explanations such as a delay in receiving a document from another party as a satisfactory reason for a delay exceeding 30 days.

---

[169] Regulations made under FA 1994, ss 244 and 245. Similar arrangements were already in force in the rest of the UK.

[170] This is part statutory, SA 1891, s 15(2)(a) in relation to a bond, covenant, conveyance on sale, or lease; and part concessionary, in relation to other instruments.

Sanctions for non-payment of duty

16.11 The sanctions are generally passive or indirect because active recovery of Stamp Duty would be impracticable due to lack of knowledge. Instead, the primary aim is to compel stamping by the parties themselves by rendering instruments useless unless and until stamped.

Penalties

16.12 Penalties are imposed on instruments for late stamping and are only passively recoverable through the pressures exerted to have instruments stamped.

It is possible to avoid a penalty for submitting a document late if a cheque for the required Stamp Duty is sent to the Stamp Office within 30 days of the document being executed. The document itself should be submitted as soon as it is available.

Fines

16.13 Fines are imposed on persons for various acts and omissions and are actively recoverable, for example, for fraudulent omission of the consideration or the late stamping of conveyancing instruments.

Evidence

16.14 An instrument which is not duly stamped cannot, except in criminal proceedings, be given in evidence or be available for any purpose whatever. The courts are bound to reject an insufficiently stamped instrument as evidence, except on payment to the court of the duty, the penalty for late stamping and a further penalty of £1. In practice, the instrument can be admitted on the personal undertaking of the solicitor for the party submitting it in evidence to stamp it.

Conveyancing

16.15 The rule affecting the admissibility in evidence indirectly compels the stamping of conveyancing instruments. Since an insufficiently stamped instrument is inadmissible as evidence of title, a purchaser is entitled to insist on every instrument forming a link in the title deduced to him being duly stamped. The vendor cannot exclude the purchaser's entitlement in this respect by contract. However, the onus is on the purchaser to show insufficient stamping.

The stamping of conveyances of unregistered land is ensured by the requisitions of subsequent purchasers and of the Registry of Deeds requirement for proper stamping. Stamping of registered land is ensured by the Registrar's refusal otherwise to complete the transaction by registration.[171]

---

[171] Land Registration Rules (NI) 1994, r 31.

AD VALOREM DUTY

16.16 *Ad valorem* means according to value and the duty varies according to the amount of the consideration involved. If the instrument contains a certificate stating that it is below the threshold for Stamp Duty, no duty is charged.

Conveyance on sale

16.17 The word conveyance is used here in its widest sense to mean any deed or instrument other than a will whereby an interest in property is assured by one person to another to effect a sale.

There is usually no doubt as to whether a particular instrument is or is not a conveyance on sale, but occasionally it may be difficult to decide. The difficulty is accentuated by the general principle that instruments are to be stamped according to their substance not necessarily by their name.

For Stamp Duty purposes a conveyance on sale includes: every instrument and every decree or order of any court or of any commissioners whereby any property, or any estate or interest in any property upon the sale thereof is transferred to or vested in a purchaser, or any other person on his behalf or by his direction.[172]

Stamp Duty on sales of land and buildings is charged on the price paid. Since 28 March 2000 the rates are:

Nil rate of duty

- No duty on a price at or below £60,000.

One per cent duty

- If the price is more than £60,000 but not more than £250,000 (unchanged since 1993).[173]

Three per cent duty

- If the price is more than £250,000 but not more than £500,000.

Four per cent duty

- If the price is more than £500,000.

Since 1 October 1999 the rate of duty is expressed as a percentage figure which is rounded up to the nearest £5.

---

[172] SA 1891, s 54.
[173] Except when by the Stamp Duty (Temporary Provisions) Act 1992 the thresholds for Stamp Duty were temporarily increased for instruments dated from 20 December 1991 to 20 August 1992: (1) On the sale of land and buildings from £30,000 to £250,000; (2) On the average annual rent of a lease from £300 to £2,500.

Certificates of value

16.18 The nil rate is not available unless the instrument has an appropriate certificate of value as follows:

> "It is hereby certified that the transaction hereby effected does not form part of a larger transaction or of a series of transactions in respect of which the amount or value or the aggregate amount or value of the consideration exceeds £60,000." (or the current nil threshold if different).

A certificate is also required certifying that the value is below the other thresholds. To qualify for stamp duty at 1 per cent the instrument must be certified below £250,000 and at 3 per cent certified below £500,000.

The certificate is in practice included as part of the instrument but if it is omitted an endorsement signed by the parties is accepted.

The purpose of the certificate is to discourage the avoidance of duty by the artificial sub-division or separation of transactions and arbitrary apportionments of the consideration. In practice most transactions stand on their own and giving a certificate causes no difficulty.

There is a series of transactions only if they are all sales between the same or associated parties and interdependent, that is integrally and not fortuitously related.

Calculating the consideration

16.19 Most conveyances are made in consideration of an immediately payable money price and there is no difficulty, although the stated consideration is not necessarily conclusive.

The consideration and all other facts affecting the duty must be fully and truly set out in the instrument. If the information is omitted and not otherwise disclosed, with intent to defraud, a fine of £10 is incurred by the parties and the person preparing the instrument (the solicitor)[174]. It is also a criminal offence at common law to conspire to defraud the Inland Revenue.

Duty is payable on whatever sum may be calculable at the date of the instrument as the maximum consideration in any contingency, however unlikely.

Where the consideration is unascertainable the transaction is liable to *ad valorem* duty on the market value of the property immediately before the instrument was executed.[175]

The total price paid for the property passing by the conveyance must be included in the consideration including the value of fixtures, timber, crops in the

---

[174] SA 1891, s 5. It is an offence to prepare or execute a document which does not set out all the facts and circumstances affecting liability for duty if it was intended to defraud.
[175] FA 1994, s 227.

ground or goodwill attached to premises. These are not included in the valuation if they are passed by delivery rather than by the conveyance.

The question whether the consideration includes the cost of the building as well as the price of the site depends on the state of the building at the date of the conveyance and this is considered more fully under the heading of new houses.

Where a NIHE house is sold to a sitting tenant at a discount, the discount is not deemed to be part of the consideration for the purposes of Stamp Duty.[176]

Where a purchaser sub-sells so that the vendor conveys directly to the sub-purchaser, the conveyance is stamped on the consideration paid by the sub-purchaser whether it is more or less than the original consideration. To qualify for the relief, the sub-sale must be of the same property. The duty would otherwise be payable on both the original consideration and the sub-sale consideration.

Conveyances subject to a debt

16.20 Where a mortgaged property is transferred from the sole name of one spouse into their joint names, the transaction may be liable to *ad valorem* duty on the amount of the debt.[177] If the transferee covenants either expressly or impliedly to pay the debt or indemnify the transferor against his personal liability to the lender this constitutes valuable consideration and establishes the transaction as a sale for Stamp Duty purposes.

On the other hand, if the transferee does not assume any liability for the debt, no chargeable consideration has been given and there is no sale. The transfer is then a voluntary disposition and should be certified as category L under the Stamp Duty (Exempt Instruments) Regulations 1987. It is then exempt from the £5 charge that would otherwise arise.

Where a property in joint names subject to a debt is transferred to one of them, for no cash, a covenant by the transferee to indemnify the transferor may be implied even where both parties were jointly liable on the mortgage. Again this constitutes valuable consideration for Stamp Duty purposes.

Leases

16.21 The Stamp Duty on new leases and agreements for leases is calculated on:

- the premium (the capital sum paid by the purchaser) and
- the average annual rent over the term.

On the premium
Stamp duty on a premium for lease is calculated in exactly the same way as on conveyances and transfers of land.

---

[176] FA 1981, s 107.
[177] FA 1891, s 57.

Nil rate of duty

If the premium is £60,000 or less and the rent is £600 or less a year, there is no duty payable.

One per cent duty

If the premium is more than £60,000 but not more than £250,000 duty is payable at one per cent.

Three per cent duty

If the premium is more than £250,000 but not more than £500,000 duty is payable at three per cent.

Four per cent duty

If the premium exceeds £500,000 duty is payable at four per cent.

In each case, unless the premium exceeds £500,000, the lease should contain an appropriate certificate of value.[178]

On the rent

The rate of duty payable on the rent will vary according to the length of the term. It is charged by reference to the annual average rent and is expressed as a percentage. The minimum duty payable is £5.

Stamp Duty on the average rent	
Length of term	Rate of duty
Not more than 7 years	1%
More than 7 years but not more than 35 years	2%
More than 35 years but not more than 100 years	12%
Over 100 years	24%

There is no statutory definition of rent, which therefore has its ordinary meaning of payments reserved out of the land as consideration from the lessee

---

[178] See para 16.18. *NB* if the average annual rent is more than £600 a certificate of value for £60,000 cannot be included in the lease. The certificate of value for £250,000 should be included and duty will then be calculated at 1% on the premium.

to the lessor for exclusive possession of the property. Rents for services, cleaning, insurance etc are disregarded in the calculation of duty.

A furnished letting is a letting agreement for any definite term less than a year of any furnished dwelling house or apartment. Where the rent for the term exceeds £500 it attracts a fixed duty of £5.

The Stamp Duty on a fee farm grant was assessed only on the premium and not on the rent.

Agreements for lease

16.22 Where a new estate is created both the agreement for lease and the lease itself are liable to Stamp Duty; but credit for any duty paid on the agreement is given against the duty payable on the lease, provided that the lease relates to substantially the same property and term as the agreement.

Theoretically, the agreement should be submitted to the Stamp Office first on its own when it has been executed and then again with the lease so that credit can be given for duty already paid. To avoid this duplication, the Stamp Office has relaxed the rules for penalties allowing the agreement to be stamped at the same time as the lease. If both are presented for stamping together within 30 days after the execution of the lease there is no penalty.

It is the agreement which is stamped with the appropriate duty and the lease is then denoted to show that the full amount of duty has been paid on the agreement. The lease itself can only be stamped where there is no agreement. In these circumstances the document should contain a certificate along the following lines:

> "I/We hereby certify that there is no agreement for lease (or as appropriate) to which this lease (or as appropriate) gives effect".

These provisions apply to agreements made after 6 May 1994. Prior to that date, the lease was stamped without the agreement being produced, except as evidence of the total amount paid for the property. Now no lease is treated as duly stamped unless, either it is certified as not being made in pursuance of an agreement, or it is denoted with the duty paid (if any) on the agreement to which it gives effect.

If the basic price for a new property is less than £60,000 and the total consideration, when the extras account is added, will exceed £60,000, then Stamp Duty is paid, based on the overall price. The Stamp Duty is assessed on the amount paid on foot of the final account.

Exchange

16.23 Where the consideration for a transfer of any estate or interest or the grant of a lease includes any property, it attracts *ad valorem* duty based on the market value of property given as consideration immediately before the instrument is executed.[179]

Accordingly, not only are exchanges of interest in land now potentially liable to double *ad valorem* duty, each interest being chargeable consideration for the transfer of the other, but all forms of property given in consideration for transfers of land are stampable consideration. Liability can be reduced where the parties make it clear in the documentation effecting the transfer that the consideration should be apportioned. For example, where a property worth £50,000 plus £50,000 cash is exchanged for a property worth £100,000 the consideration should be apportioned between the cheaper property and the cash. Otherwise the transfer of the cheaper property will be stampable based on the *whole* value of the more expensive property. If, instead of an exchange, the transaction is drafted as a sale of the more expensive property in consideration of a cash sum to be satisfied partly in cash and partly in kind, the transfer of the cheaper property will not be 'on sale' and liable to *ad valorem* duty, but will be chargeable under the head 'conveyance or transfer of any kind not herein before described' with £5.

Surrender

16.24 A surrender of lease is subject to *ad valorem* duty if consideration passes from the lessor to the lessee and is evidenced by deed. Before 8 December 1993, where there was no deed and the lease was surrendered by operation of law, no charge to duty arose. The rule has now changed. Where there is no deed any agreement to surrender is itself chargeable to *ad valorem* duty.[180] This applies to any document evidencing the agreement, however informal, such as a letter outlining the procedure to be followed.

FIXED DUTY

16.25 Certain instruments are liable to fixed rate duty regardless of the consideration involved in the transaction. A duty of £5 is chargeable on each of the following unless the transaction is in effect a conveyance on sale in which case it attracts *ad valorem* duty:

Duplicate or counterpart

16.26 Fixed duty of £5 is charged on the duplicate or counterpart of any instrument chargeable with any duty.

Surrender

16.27 A surrender of lease is subject to fixed duty where there is no consideration or where the lessee pays the lessor to accept the surrender. Where the lessor pays the lessee to surrender it attracts *ad valorem* duty.

---

[179] Prior to 8 December 1993 duty was charged on the difference between the value of the two properties exchanged. If they were of equal value only 50p duty was charged. The position was altered by FA 1994, s 226.

[180] By FA 1994, s 228.

Voluntary dispositions

16.28 For transfers in connection with divorce made pursuant to the Matrimonial Causes (NI) Order 1978 a fixed duty of £5 is payable. Otherwise voluntary dispositions are generally exempt from stamp duty under category L of the Stamp Duty (Exempt Instruments) Regulations 1987.[181] It should be noted that a gift of property subject to a mortgage is not treated as a voluntary disposition and so may still attract *ad valorem* stamp duty.

Other instruments

16.29 Instruments not falling into the foregoing categories may be subject to fixed duty such as:

(1) Conveyance of any other kind;
(2) Declaration of use or trust under hand or seal;
(3) Partition or division;
(4) Release or renunciation.

Instruments formerly subject to fixed duty

16.30 Fixed duties on the following were repealed by FA 1985:

(1) Agreement pursuant to the Highways Acts;
(2) Appointment;
(3) Covenant;
(4) Deeds not liable to other duties;
(5) Power of attorney;
(6) Revocation.

Fixed duties on the following were abolished as from 1 May 1987 in respect of instruments indicated by the Stamp Duty (Exempt Instruments) Regulations 1987:

(A) Appointment or retirement of trustee under which trust property is vested in new trustees.

(B) Conveyance or transfer of property to a beneficiary in satisfaction of a legacy under a will.

(C) Conveyance or transfer of property to a beneficiary on an intestacy.

(D) Appropriation of property within FA 1985, section 84(4), 84(5) or 84(7) being satisfaction of a general legacy of money or any interest of surviving spouse.

---

[181] Under FA 1910, s 74(1), from 29 April 1910 until 25 March 1985, any conveyance operating as a voluntary disposition *inter vivos* was charged with *ad valorem* duty according to the value of the property transferred.

(E) Conveyance or transfer of property to a beneficiary which forms part of the residuary estate of a testator.

(F) Conveyance or transfer of property out of a settlement in satisfaction of a beneficiary's interest.

(G) Conveyance or transfer of property in consideration only of marriage to a party to the marriage or to trustees.

(H) Conveyance or transfer of property on divorce within FA 1985, section 83(1) being transfers in connection with divorce etc.

(I) Conveyance or transfer by a liquidator of property owned by a company to a shareholder in satisfaction of his rights on winding up.

(J) Grant in fee simple of an easement for no consideration in money or money's worth.

(K) Grant of a servitude (easement) for no consideration in money or money's worth.

(L) Conveyance or transfer of property by way of voluntary disposition *inter vivos* for no consideration in money or money's worth, nor in consideration of a debt etc under SA 1891, section 57 (being a conveyance in consideration of a debt).

(M) Conveyance or transfer of property by an instrument within FA 1985, section 84(1) being a variation of dispositions on death.

The documents in this list no longer need to be seen in the Stamp Office and should contain a certificate to the effect that:

"It is hereby certified that this instrument falls within category ... in the Schedule to the Stamp Duty (Exempt Instruments) Regulations 1987."

This certificate should be signed by the transferor or grantor or by a solicitor on his behalf.[182]

NO DUTY

16.31 On certain instruments there is no duty payable, either because it was never chargeable or because it has been abolished.

Assent

16.32 Stamp Duty is not charged on assents as such.[183] An assent under hand is not subject to any duty. An assent under seal was subject to a fixed duty of 50p on the basis that it was a deed, until 25 March 1985, but this is no longer the case. An assent effecting an appropriation in satisfaction of a general legacy

---

[182] An authorised agent may also sign provided he states the capacity in which he signs, confirms that he is authorised and that he has knowledge of the facts of the transaction.

[183] Administration of Estates Act (NI) 1955, s 34(8) provides that s 34 is not to operate so as to impose any stamp duty on an assent. This preserves the pre-existing law.

or the surviving spouse's interest on intestacy is still chargeable with £5 duty. *Ad valorem* duty is charged where an assent gives effect to a sale either by the personal representatives or by the deceased himself.

Companies

16.33 There are some exemptions relating to the amalgamation or reconstruction of companies and to transfers between associated companies under FA (NI) 1954, section 11 as amended, which correspond substantially with provisions in England contained in FA 1930, section 42 as amended.

Charities

16.34 Instruments executed between 1 August 1974 and 21 March 1982, if adjudicated, were liable to a maximum rate of duty of 1 per cent under FA 1974, section 49. From 22 March 1982, no duty at all is payable but the instrument must be adjudicated by virtue of FA 1982, section 129.

Wills

16.35 Wills and other testamentary dispositions are expressly exempt from all Stamp Duties.[184]

Instruments on which stamp duty has been repealed by statute

16.36 Various statutory provisions have abolished the Stamp Duty on certain investments.

	Heading and type of duty	Date of abolition	Statutory provision
(1)	Assent in writing only fixed duty 50p	1 January 1956	Administration of Estates Act (NI) 1955, s 34(8)
(2)	Agreement (under hand not seal) fixed duty 6d	1 August 1970	FA (NI) 1970, Sch 2 Pt I
(3)	Bond *ad valorem*	1 August 1971	FA (NI) 1971 s 5(1)
(4)	Mortgage or debenture *ad valorem*	1 August 1971	FA (NI) 1971 s 5(1)
(5)	Receipt* fixed duty 2d	1 February 1971	FA (NI) 1970, Sch 2 Pt I
(6)	Settlement** *ad valorem*	20 December 1962	FA (NI) 1962 s 3(1)

*   For stamp duty purposes, a receipt was any writing, whether signed or not, acknowledging any payment or settlement.

** An instrument which was both a settlement and a voluntary disposition had, until 25 March 1985, to be charged as the latter.

---

[184] SA 1891, s 1 and Sch 1.

STAMP DUTY ON NEW PROPERTY

16.37 Until 1988 in Northern Ireland it was possible not to pay Stamp Duty on the full consideration of a new house. For Stamp Duty purposes the value taken into account was the value of the property (the land with the building work on it) at the date of the contract. This was usually below the threshold of Stamp Duty.

The Inland Revenue has closed this loophole and now takes the value of the property as the total payable under the contract. Basically the Inland Revenue views a purchase of a site and construction of a building as one complete transaction, unless it can be established to the contrary.[185]

It is possible to establish the existence of two separate transactions. If the vendor and the builder are independent and unconnected persons, the cost of building will not normally be part of the consideration for the conveyance. Even when the builder and vendor are one and the same Stamp Duty may be saved if the purchaser buys a plot of land and enters into a genuinely separate contract for the construction of the house. The builder is paid for the plot and the purchaser pays the Stamp Duty on its value at the time of the purchase. Stamp Duty should not be payable on its subsequent building costs.

In the case of *Prudential Assurance Co Ltd v IRC* [186] two contracts were entered into simultaneously. The building work was half done at the time of the transfer and Stamp Duty was assessed on the total sum payable under both contracts. On appeal it was held that, although the two agreements were part of a single transaction, the sale was completed by the deed of transfer for the expressed consideration in respect of the site and the existing building. Accordingly Stamp Duty was chargeable on that amount only and not on the further sums required to complete the building.

As a result of that decision it is suggested that, provided there are two genuinely independent contracts, the consideration may depend on what is actually there on the ground at the time of the lease or conveyance.

Following the *Prudential* case the Inland Revenue issued a new statement of practice outlining its interpretation of the law, which does not entirely coincide with the actual decision.

The law, according to the Inland Revenue, is as noted below.

Two transactions/two contracts

16.38 Where the purchaser contracts to buy land in consideration of the purchase price and separately contracts for the actual building work, with the vendor or with a third party, Stamp Duty is charged only on the price of the land under the first contract, if the two transactions are genuinely independent.

---

[185] The building agreement and agreement for lease/assignment/conveyance/transfer should be submitted to the Stamp Office as evidence of the total consideration. It is the document itself and not the agreement which is stamped in these circumstances.

[186] [1993] 1 WLR 211.

It does not matter whether any building work has commenced at the date of the conveyance or lease.

One transaction/two contracts

16.39 Where there is one transaction between the parties but there is one contract for the sale of the land and another for the building work, the amount of Stamp Duty charged will depend on the amount of the consideration which in turn depends on whether the two transactions are genuinely independent of each other.

If the two contracts are so interlocked that they cannot be said to be genuinely capable of independent completion, Stamp Duty is charged on the total consideration for the land and the buildings, whether completed or not, as if the parties had entered into only one contract. This will apply whether the purchaser entered into one contract with the vendor of the land and one with the builder or whether he entered into both contracts with the same person.

If the two contracts are shown to be genuinely independent of each other, Stamp Duty is charged on the price paid for the land and the value of any building works on it at the time of the conveyance or lease.

One transaction/one contract

16.40 Stamp Duty is charged on the total consideration paid for the land and for the building.

CHAPTER SEVENTEEN

POST-COMPLETION REMEDIES

Introduction

17.01 If a mistake, misrepresentation or fraud is discovered by the innocent party after completion, it is obviously more difficult to obtain relief than at an earlier stage of the transaction. However, it is not impossible. Rescission, damages and rectification are options which may be considered after completion depending on the particular circumstances of each case.

MERGER

17.02 The first matter to be considered after completion is the doctrine of merger. The general rule is that, on completion, the contract for sale merges in the conveyance and all remedies based on the contract are lost. The parties must rely instead on remedies available under the conveyance which are inevitably more limited.

This means for example, that if the purchaser discovers a defect in title after completion, he cannot sue for breach of contract but must rely on the covenants for title in the conveyance.

The doctrine of merger is based on the presumed intention of the parties and gives way to any indication, express or implied, that no merger took place. GCS 22 confirms that any part of the contract to which effect is not given by the conveyance and which is capable of taking place after completion, remains in full force and effect. In each case it has to be determined which provisions are intended to survive completion and are not given effect by the conveyance.

If the purchaser can prove the existence of a collateral warranty independent of the contract for sale, he can sue on it because it is not affected by merger of the main contract.

There are other remedies which survive completion. Rescission may be available particularly where fraud is involved and, in certain circumstances, on the ground of mistake. Rectification is also a possibility when a mistake has been made.

COVENANTS FOR TITLE

17.03 These are covenants as to title entered into by a vendor in a conveyance of land on sale for valuable consideration. In this context conveyance includes assignment of a leasehold interest. The covenants give the purchaser the right to an action for damages if the title subsequently proves to be bad.

At one time the covenants were set out at length in conveyances. Since the enactment of the Conveyancing Act 1881, section 7, the covenants for title are implied in law by use of the appropriate words.

The covenants for title entered into by a vendor in a conveyance for valuable consideration are implied according to the capacity in which he conveys and is expressed to convey the property. To an extent this protects the purchaser against the consequences of the doctrine of merger because it enables him to sue the vendor for breach of covenant for title if a defect is discovered after completion.

Although the statutory covenants for title are incorporated by use of the appropriate words in the deed, additional express covenants may also be included.

Capacity of the grantor

17.04 The covenants for title implied vary according to the capacity of the grantor.

Beneficial owner

17.05 In a conveyance for valuable consideration, a vendor who conveys and is expressed to convey as beneficial owner implies:

(1) The right to convey;

(2) Quiet enjoyment for the purchaser;

(3) Freedom from encumbrances other than those subject to which the conveyance is expressly made;

(4) Further assurance in that the vendor will execute such assurances and do such things as are necessary to cure any defect in the conveyance.

Further covenants are implied in an assignment of a lease for valuable consideration. These covenants apply only when an existing leasehold interest is sold. They relate to vendor and purchaser not to landlord and tenant. A vendor assigning as beneficial owner implies that:

(1) The lease is valid and subsisting;

(2) The rent has been paid and the covenants in the lease observed and performed.

The second covenant on assignment is limited by GCS 8.7 which provides that any statutory covenant to be implied in an assurance by a vendor conveying as beneficial owner is to be limited so as not to affect him with liability for a subsisting breach of any covenant or condition concerning the state of the property of which the purchaser is deemed to have full notice.

The covenants for title may be varied or extended by deed in which case they operate as if the variation was implied by section 7 of the Conveyancing Act 1881. However the vendor must discharge his duty to show good title and, for this reason, the courts may not allow any restriction purporting to reduce the scope of the covenants for title. Nevertheless the purchaser can, if he so wishes, agree to buy the property subject for example, to an encumbrance which would otherwise be a defect in title and cannot then rely on the covenants for title in respect of that encumbrance. The fact that he is buying subject to the encumbrance must be specified in the deed.

Settlor

17.06 In a conveyance by way of settlement, where the donor conveys and is expressed to convey "as settlor" the only covenant implied is one for further assurance. This covenant binds the settlor and those claiming under him, whether the settlement is voluntary or for value.

Trustee etc

17.07 In a conveyance by a trustee, mortgagee, personal representative or committee of a person of unsound mind, the only covenant implied is that the grantor has not himself encumbered the land. Where the vendor sells in any such capacity the purchaser is entitled only to covenants limited accordingly.

Assent

17.08 In an assent signed by the personal representative, the covenant that there are no encumbrances is implied unless the assent provides otherwise, by virtue of the Administration of Estates Act (NI) 1955, section 34(5).

Lessor

17.09 Covenants for title on the part of a lessor in a lease are implied by Deasy's Act 1860, section 41, which probably also extends to fee farm grants. The Conveyancing Act 1881, section 7, does not apply.

Section 41 implies:

(1) That the lessor has good title to make the lease
(2) Quiet and peaceable enjoyment for the lessee without interruption by the lessor or any person whomsoever during the term as long as the lessee performs his obligations under the lease.

Enforcement of covenants for title

17.10 To enforce the covenants the benefit and burden of the covenant are considered separately.

Benefit

17.11 The benefit of the implied covenants for title runs with the land so that any successor in title of the covenantee may enforce them if he succeeds to the same estate or interest conveyed by the original covenantor.

Burden

17.12 The liability of the covenantor is personal to him and does not run with the land. A successor in title is not liable on the covenants for title of a previous covenantor unless he derives title from such a person otherwise than for value. A successor has to enter into the same covenants himself and convey in the appropriate capacity when he sells the property if the covenant is to be enforceable against him.

A vendor who conveys as beneficial owner personally guarantees the title but his liability is not absolute and extends only to the acts and omissions of persons in the following Classes:

(1) Himself;
(2) Any person claiming by, through, under or in trust for him, for example, a tenant, mortgagee or trustee;
(3) Anyone through whom he derives title otherwise than by purchase for value;
(4) Anyone claiming through or under those in Class 3.

A person conveying as beneficial owner is liable for the acts or omissions of anyone deriving title under him, such as a tenant or mortgagee, but not a person to whom he conveys the property outright.

For example if A conveys land to B for value as beneficial owner and B subsequently discovers undisclosed encumbrances, he can sue A on the covenants for title if those encumbrances were created by A or by a person who left the land to A by will or gave it to him by deed of gift (Class 2) or by A's tenant, mortgagee or trustee (Class 3).

Say B allows his neighbour X to acquire a right over the land by prescription, B then sells to C as beneficial owner who sells similarly to D and X asserts his rights against D. For this defect in title and disturbance of quiet enjoyment D may sue B because D obtains the benefit of B's covenants with C which run with the land.

The only case where on a conveyance for value as beneficial owner the covenantor is liable for the acts of a predecessor is in a conveyance by way of mortgage. Where a person creates a mortgage as beneficial owner the covenants for title implied are absolute and the mortgagor is responsible for the acts of everyone. He makes a complete warranty that the title is good.

The covenants are subject to the usual limitation period of 12 years in relation to any breach and can only be sued on within that period. For example, if the covenant for quiet enjoyment is broken by someone with a valid prior right to an easement, the covenantor can be sued on the covenant at any time within 12 years of the disturbance.

Effect of covenants for title

17.13 The benefit of the covenants runs with the land, but the burden is purely personal. The benefit is passed to a purchaser if he succeeds to the same estate as the original party to the covenant. However, he can only sue on the covenant if each vendor in the chain of title conveyed and expressed to convey in the requisite capacity. The onus of proof in relation to the breach is on the purchaser. It may not be easy to discharge this nor to trace the relevant previous owner.

The covenants

17.14 Four covenants for title are implied by the Conveyancing Act 1881, section 7.

Full power to convey

17.15 When the vendor purports to convey a specified estate as beneficial owner the purchaser may be able to sue for breach of covenant if it turns out that he did not have power to convey it. He cannot sue for breach of covenant in respect of a defect expressly subject to which the conveyance is made.

This covenant is qualified more strictly than the others. The vendor is liable only in respect of the acts or omissions of himself and persons through whom he claims otherwise than for value, not for those of his predecessors. The grantee cannot sue the grantor for breach of covenant on eviction by someone claiming through the act or omission of some previous owner.

Quiet enjoyment

17.16 This covenant is designed to protect the grantee from lawful physical disturbance. If the disturbance is unlawful the grantee is protected by the law of trespass or nuisance. There is no cause of action under the covenant where the disturbance is not caused by the acts of the grantor or persons for whom he is responsible.[187]

Freedom from encumbrances

17.17 This covenant is probably an extension of the covenant for quiet enjoyment. The grantor is undertaking to provide the grantee with an indemnity in the event of disturbance. To succeed in a claim, the grantee must prove that he has actually been disturbed in his possession or had some adverse claim made against him. The mere existence of an encumbrance is not enough. Breach occurs, in conjunction with a disturbance of quiet enjoyment, when use of the encumbrance commences. A right of way is an example of such an encumbrance.

Further assurance

17.18 This covenant requires the grantor to execute such further assurance or to do such further things as are necessary to perfect the title, providing that the outstanding estate or interest is vested in the grantor or some other person for whom he is responsible.

OTHER REMEDIES

Rescission

17.19 Fraud, misrepresentation and mistake are all possible grounds for rescission after completion, although it is obviously much more difficult to rescind a transaction at that stage. Execution of the conveyance is not a bar to rescission but the remedy has more limited effect after completion and it is not always possible to restore the parties to their original position.[188]

---

[187] This differs from the covenant implied for the lessor under Deasy's Act, s 41. In that case the implied covenant covers interruption by "any person whomsoever".

[188] Cf para 4.22.

Rectification

17.20 Where there has been a mutual mistake or improper drafting, equity may order rectification of a conveyance to make it conform with the terms actually agreed between the parties. However, it will not be granted against a *bona fide* purchaser for value without notice. Rectification does not interfere with the actual agreement but alters the instrument to properly reflect it.

PART TWO

LAND LAW

CHAPTER EIGHTEEN

ESTATES AND INTERESTS IN LAND

Introduction

18.01 Land itself is permanent, immovable and virtually indestructible. It has always been of fundamental importance as a source of wealth and security. Although buildings have a more limited existence, they may have a higher value than the land on which they stand. In law buildings are held to go with the land.

Historically, the importance of the ownership of land has contributed to the development of a complicated system of tenure, with a wide fragmentation of ownership. Land can be affected by several different interests, both legal and equitable, existing in it concurrently. The most important interests are estates in land which can be broadly divided into freeholds and leaseholds. There are also various minor interests which can be enjoyed apart from the actual possession of the land which they affect.

This chapter will outline the estates and interests which can be found in existing titles. Although some may be rarely created or used now, they may still be seen in older titles and, for that reason, are of more than purely historical interest.

The concepts exclusively fundamental to freehold estates are 'seisin' and 'words of limitation'. Seisin involves freehold possession. It is difficult to define precisely, because it is a feudal concept which has little practical significance today. Basically, seisin is formal legal ownership as opposed to mere possession or a beneficial interest.

Nowadays, actual possession of land is important because the person in possession is often considered to be the owner regardless of seisin. Seisin and possession are not synonymous and it is possible, for example, for the freeholder to have seisin while the leaseholder has possession.

The concept of words of limitation also derives from the formal approach of the feudal system to transactions regarding land. It relates to the words in a document which determine the duration of the estate. Some freehold estate can only be created if the appropriate words of limitation are used. If appropriate words of limitation are not used, the smallest rather than the greatest freehold estate is passed. This means that only a life estate may be conveyed rather than the fee simple intended.[1]

FREEHOLD ESTATES

Fee simple

18.02 This is the estate nearest to absolute ownership and is the most extensive interest which can be held under the Crown. It was an estate of inheritance

---

[1] See para 18.11.

which could be passed on by the owner to his heirs. It has the potential to last for ever and should usually be created by deed.[2] The owner in general is free to enjoy and use the land as he pleases, but restrictions may be imposed either by the parties to a transaction involving the passing of a freehold estate or by operation of law.

The words of limitation required vary according to whether the estate is created by will or *inter vivos*, To pass the fee simple at common law to natural persons *inter vivos*, the proper words to use are "and his heirs". The Conveyancing Act 1881, section 51, introduced the phrase "in fee simple" as an alternative but the phrase "and his heirs" is still commonly used. It is essential to use one of these two phrases to avoid merely conveying a life estate in the land in question.

In the case of a corporation,[3] the conveyance need only be made to the corporation by name without any words of limitation, except where a corporation sole is involved. Then the words "and his successors" are used because when the person dies or ceases to hold office his office continues.

The courts have taken a more liberal approach to the interpretation of wills seeking as far as possible to give effect to the intention of the parties. Generally the greatest estate of which the testator has power to dispose by the will is passed, unless a contrary intention is shown.

Fee simple absolute

18.03 This is by far the most important type of fee simple and the one most frequently created. The majority of agricultural land is held in this way, free of any restrictions except those relating to the general law on matters such as planning and public policy.

On the other hand, although all urban land is ultimately held in fee simple it is seldom linked to possession. The fee simple may cover a large area and invariably has a multitude of pyramid leasehold titles created out of it.

It is likely that this position will gradually change because, under the Property (NI) Order 1997, articles 28 and 30 respectively, it is no longer possible to create any new fee farm grant at all, nor any long lease of a dwelling house (subject to specified exceptions). In due course when the provisions for the redemption of ground rents contained in the Property (NI) Order 1997 take effect, ground rents will be compulsorily redeemed on sale and a purchaser will become obliged to acquire the fee simple. The intention of the legislation is to simplify urban title and make provision for a lessee in possession to acquire the freehold by means of straightforward procedures.

It has always been possible to create a fee simple absolute subject to covenants and conditions but in the past this has had limited advantages because of the difficulty of enforcing freehold covenants against successors in title. The Property (NI) Order 1997, article 34 introduces provisions for the running of

---

[2] There are exceptions to this principle, *eg*, a possessory freehold would not be created by deed.

[3] A corporation is a body of persons having in law an existence and rights and duties distinct from those of the individual persons who form it. It has perpetual succession, a name and common seal. A corporation sole consists of only one member at a time in succession, *eg* a bishop.

freehold covenants replacing the previous rules of common law and equity.[4] It is not retrospective and does not apply to interests created before the appointed day.

Modified fees simple

18.04 Any fee simple other than a fee simple absolute is a modified fee. By definition this includes determinable and conditional fees, both of which are rare.[5]

A determinable fee simple determines automatically on the occurrence of an event which may or may not happen. When the event occurs the fee simple comes to its natural end and the property reverts to the grantor or his successor.

A conditional fee simple is a fee simple liable to be terminated upon the occurrence of a condition subsequent. The estate comes to an end only when the person so entitled repossesses the property and the grantee may continue in possession until that time.

Fee farm grants

18.05 A fee farm grant is a conveyance of a fee simple subject to payment of a perpetual rent. It has many of the characteristics of the fee simple including, in general, the requirement that the same words of limitation be used.

A fee farm grant confers a freehold estate but creates a leasehold tenure, with the result that it is effectively a hybrid exhibiting both freehold and leasehold features.[6] Covenants in a fee farm grant bind successors in title and can be enforced in the same manner as leasehold covenants.

Today the only significant type of fee farm grant is that which developed under the Landlord and Tenant Law Amendment Act (Ir) 1860, commonly known as Deasy's Act.[7] These grants are peculiar to Ireland, being created by nineteenth century legislation applicable only to Ireland and not being creatures of the common law at all.

The creation of any new fee farm grants is prohibited under the Property (NI) Order 1997, article 28 from the appointed day (10 January 2000).

Fee farm conversion grants

18.06 Fee farm conversion grants may be seen in titles which go back to the nineteenth century. They are fee farm grants converted by statute out of particular leases, for example ecclesiastical leases and leases for lives renewable for ever.[8] It is unlikely that such grants could be created today because the leases from which they arose are largely obsolete.

---

[4] See Freehold Covenants paras 29.10-29.14.
[5] Final Report of the Land Law Working Group para 2.1.14 recommends that the only freehold estate capable of existing at law should be a fee simple absolute in possession.
[6] An estate is an interest in land; whereas tenure is the mode of holding or occupying it.
[7] See Deasy's Act grants para 18.09.
[8] See paras 18.07 and 18.08.

It was not essential to use appropriate words of limitation for the creation of fee farm conversion grants and the courts have treated them as outside the common law rules in this respect.

The enabling statutes usually provided that the fee farm rent was to be recoverable by the same process as the prior leasehold rents, including the remedy of ejectment for non-payment in preference to forfeiture. Nevertheless, a right of forfeiture could be reserved in the grant. Forfeiture for breach of other obligations is governed by the Conveyancing Act 1892 and the Conveyancing Act 1881, section 14.[9]

The covenants created by the lease also continued after the conversion and the law of leasehold rather than of freehold covenants is applied on the basis that the grants originated as leases.[10]

Church grants

18.07 From the late seventeenth century onwards, bishops and other ecclesiastical persons had limited statutory powers to create short term leases of church land. The leases contained covenants for renewal and could be renewed on payment of a fine. Under the Church Temporalities Act 1833 the tenants were later given the right to convert their leases and purchase the fee simple of the property subject to a fee farm rent.

However, the Irish Church Act 1869, which disestablished the Church of Ireland, prohibited any further conversion grants under the 1833 Act from 1874 onwards. Many were later redeemed under the land purchase schemes and the land comprised in the grants became registered. A few still remain in relation to unregistered land which was formerly church property.

Renewable Leasehold Conversion Act 1849

18.08 During the eighteenth and nineteenth centuries it was common for a large landowner to lease portions of his property by lease for lives renewable for ever. The lease contained a covenant for renewal by grant of a lease for a new life, whenever one of those for whose life the original lease was granted died, subject to payment of a fine to the landlord.

The 1849 Act enabled a lessee of such a lease to obtain a fee farm grant from the lessor subject to a fee farm rent. It further provided that any future lease for lives renewable for ever was to operate automatically as a fee farm grant. Any such leases which still subsist and were not previously converted will automatically be converted into an estate in fee simple subject to a fee farm rent by the Property (NI) Order 1997, article 36.

Deasy's Act grants

18.09 Deasy's Act, section 3, provides that "the relationship of landlord and tenant shall be deemed to be founded on the express or implied contract of the parties and not upon tenure or service, and a reversion shall not be necessary to such relation".

---

[9] Cf Forfeiture paras 19.16-19.17.
[10] See Deasy's Act grants para 18.09.

The fundamental importance of this is that the relationship of landlord and tenant is created in fee farm grants as regards the rights, duties and remedies of the parties. Previously at common law a reversion had been necessary to create such a relationship and it was not established exclusively on the basis of contract.

The creation of a fee farm grant operating under Deasy's Act must indicate an intention to create the relationship of landlord and tenant between the parties and an intention to create that particular estate. On the one hand it may be suggested that the words of limitation necessary to create a fee simple at common law may not be required because under section 3, all that is necessary to create a fee farm grant is the intention to create the relationship of landlord and tenant for an estate in fee simple. On the other hand it was held in *Re Courtney*[11] that the proper technical words of limitation are necessary in order to convey a fee farm grant.

In practice the *habendum* invariably includes the words of limitation necessary to create a freehold estate and the grant is made to hold the premises unto the grantee "his heirs and assigns for ever". In all other respects a fee farm grant is generally drafted in very similar form to a lease with suitable modifications in particular clauses.

The law relating to landlord and tenant applies to the action which may be taken for non-payment of rent, forfeiture and for breach of covenant.

Fee tail

18.10 The fee tail is a freehold estate of inheritance which creates very restricted interests in land and passes exclusively to the lineal descendants of the grantee. A fee tail can be general, when the potential beneficiaries are all the descendants; or special, when the potential beneficiaries are limited, for example, to one sex or to the issue of a particular spouse.

Every fee tail has a reversion or remainder following it. On failure of the donee's lineal issue the land reverts to the original donor in fee simple or passes to the remainderman. Notwithstanding any alienation by the donee, the land descends to his issue on his death and ultimately reverts to the donor or passes to the remainderman.

The concept of the fee tail breaches the fundamental principle of free alienation of land by ensuring the succession because, if land is subject to an entail, the tenant in tail has an interest only for the duration of his own life. He cannot dispose of any interest in the property beyond that period. However, under the Fines and Recoveries (Ir) Act 1834, sections 2 and 12, there is a simple means of effectively barring the entail.

A tenant in tail in possession can execute a disentailing assurance enlarging the fee tail into a fee simple by way of conveyance. If he wishes to dispose of it he can make a disentailing assurance in favour of another grantee. On the other hand, if he wishes to retain it, he can make a disentailing assurance to trustees in favour of himself. When the entail is barred, the effect is that the grantee

---

[11] [1981] NI 59.

obtains a legal estate derived from the grantor but enlarged from a fee tail into a fee simple estate.

A tenant in tail who is of age but not entitled in possession can bar the entail, but the effect will depend upon whether he has the consent of the protector of the settlement.[12] If he has the consent, there is a complete bar, as in the case of a tenant in tail in possession. Without the consent, a base fee is created.[13] The base fee may be enlarged into a fee simple estate by acquiring the immediate remainder or reversion in fee simple.

The fee tail estate is of little practical significance today as most entails have been barred. It is unlikely that any new fee tails will arise now because less importance is attached to primogeniture and restrictive settlements have lost their attraction.[14]

Life estate

18.11 This may also be a freehold estate but, unlike the others, is not an estate of inheritance and cannot be passed by the owner to his heirs. It can exist for the life of the tenant himself or for the life of another, which is known as an estate *pur autre vie*.

A life estate exists for a limited, but uncertain, period. The common law developed rules governing the position of the life tenant because of the restricted nature of his estate. On the one hand he was encouraged to make the best use of the property during his period of ownership; on the other, his enjoyment of the property had to be balanced against the interests vesting after the determination of his life estate.

The common law rules were very restrictive but have lost much of their practical significance since the Settled Land Acts 1882-90 provided the life tenant with much more extensive powers.[15]

A life estate can be created in a deed *inter vivos*, by using words of limitation such as "to A for life". It may also be created indirectly, where the incorrect words or no words at all are used to create a fee simple.

When a testator wishes to create a life estate by will he must expressly create a life estate for the intended bequest to take effect. This is because the Wills Act 1837, section 28, provides that his whole estate passes unless a contrary intention is shown.

Lease for lives renewable forever

18.12 The lease for lives renewable forever is an example of an estate pur autre vie and was once very common. There are usually three lives named in the

---

[12] The protector is either the person expressly appointed as such by the settlor or the person who would have had to give consent to the sale before the 1834 Act, *ie* usually the life tenant in possession of the property.

[13] A base fee is an estate which has some qualification and which must cease or be determined whenever such qualification is at an end.

[14] Final Report of the Land Law Working Group para 2.128 recommends the abolition of the fee tail estate.

[15] Cf paras 24.07-24.09.

lease. It differs from the ordinary estate *pur autre vie* in that each person for whose life the estate was granted can be replaced and the estate has indefinite potential. It creates leasehold tenure between the parties but the estate granted to the lessee is a freehold estate. The advantage to the landlord in such a lease is that a specified amount (a fine) has to be paid each time one of the lives is renewed.

By the Property (NI) Order 1997, article 36, a perpetually renewable lease such as a lease for lives renewable forever can no longer be created. Any existing perpetually renewable lease is converted automatically into an estate in fee simple subject to a fee farm rent. Any purported assignment of such a lease has effect as a conveyance in fee simple.

LEASEHOLD ESTATES

Background

18.13 The leasehold estate has been the most common form of grant of title in Northern Ireland, almost universally used in private residential developments and in major commercial developments such as shopping centres.

Historically leaseholds were not recognised as realty and were regarded as personalty. Realty or real property includes lands, tenements and hereditaments. Personalty or personal property includes property unconnected with land.

This premise originated under the feudal system which did not recognise a lease for a term of years as creating any estate in land. It was considered to be a personal contract and only the parties to it could have any rights or obligations under it. Later, when the action of ejectment was developed, the leaseholder was able to protect the lease against adverse claims and it gradually came to have some status as an estate.

However, the new tenure granted by the lease was not feudal tenure. It was regarded as less than freehold and was dependent on the lessor having a reversionary interest, that is an interest longer than the tenant's.

The position is now governed by Deasy's Act. Section 3 provides that the relationship of landlord and tenant

> " shall be deemed to be founded on the express or implied contract of the parties and not on tenure or service and a reversion shall not be necessary to such relation."

The most important consequence of Deasy's Act is that it enables the relationship of landlord and tenant to be created when it could not exist at common law, as in the case of a fee farm grant where the term is for ever. It also enables a landlord to let property for the whole of the term which he himself holds because a reversion is not necessary.

It is essential that a lease specifies the period during which it is to endure as well as the beginning and end of the term. Although a rent is usually reserved by a lease it is not absolutely necessary. If there is no rent the lease operates at common law. It is not affected by Deasy's Act because the relationship of landlord and tenant arises for the purposes of that Act only where there is a rent or return. An example of a lease which does not reserve a rent is a mortgage by sub-demise.

There are several types of leasehold estate and the same law governs them all, regardless of their duration or their nature.[16]

Term certain

18.14 A lease granted for a term certain is a particularly common estate and in Ireland is often granted for a very long period, such as 999 or 10,000 years. It may of course be for any length of time, even for a period as short as a week; the essential point being that there is a limit on its duration. In commercial developments, for example, an 'anchor tenant' might purchase its unit by way of a lease for a term of 125 years at a nominal rent, whereas the tenant of a 'mall unit' would commonly take a lease for a term not exceeding 25 years at a commercial rent with provision for a rent review.

Since 10 January 2000 a lease of a dwelling house for a term of more than 50 years is incapable of creation in law or in equity under the Property (NI) Order 1997, article 30.[17]

Periodic tenancy

18.15 A periodic tenancy is specified as being for a fixed minimum period, such as a week or six months and continues indefinitely after that for successive periods until it is determined by either party. It may be created expressly or by implication if the tenant takes possession with the consent of the landlord and pays rent which the landlord accepts. The type of periodic tenancy created by implication depends on how the rent is calculated rather than how it is paid. If, for example, a monthly rent is paid quarterly, the tenancy is construed as a monthly tenancy.

If a tenant holds over (continues in possession) after the expiration or determination of the lease, for more than a month after a demand for possession from the landlord, the landlord has the option under Deasy's Act, section 5, of continuing the tenancy from year to year on the same terms. Different conditions or terms from those contained in the original lease may be indicated by the conduct of the parties. Where the tenancy is subject to the statutory restrictions contained in the Business Tenancies (NI) Order 1996 or the Rent (NI) Order 1978 inferences cannot be used to opt out of statutory protection.

Tenancy at will

18.16 A tenancy at will arises whenever a tenant, with the consent of the owner, occupies land for an indefinite period as a tenant on the terms that either party may determine the tenancy at any time. Due to the uncertain status of the tenant there is some doubt as to whether such an arrangement has the proper attributes of a tenancy.

A tenancy at will may be created expressly by agreement or by implication, for example, where a tenant whose lease has expired holds over with the landlord's

---

[16] Leases for ever, such as fee farm grants, are very common in Ireland but are really a hybrid exhibiting some features of both the freehold and the leasehold. For this reason they do not really fit into the framework under which leases are generally classified.

[17] See Property (NI) Order 1997 paras 29.01-29.19.

permission, without yet having paid rent on a periodic basis or where a tenant takes possession under an agreement for lease and has not yet paid rent.

Due to the uncertain status of the occupier there is some doubt as to whether the arrangement has the proper attributes of a tenancy and the circumstances may suggest that the occupier is not in fact a tenant but rather a licensee or caretaker. Although Deasy's Act has frequently been held to facilitate the creation of tenancies for periods of uncertain or indefinite duration the factor which may prevent tenancies at will from coming within its scope is the absence of a requirement for payment of any rent. Rent is not usually payable under a tenancy at will because if it is paid the tenancy is generally regarded as being converted into a periodic tenancy.

Tenure is uncertain and insecure. The traditional view is that a tenant at will holds no estate in the land and consequently cannot assign his interest but there is judicial support for the contrary argument based on Deasy's Act, section 9 which provides that:

> "The estate or interest of any tenant in any lands under any lease or other contract of tenancy shall be assigned, granted or transmitted by writing, or by demise, bequest, or act and operation of law, and not otherwise."

It can be determined at any time by any act or words indicating that it has ended. A tenant at will is not entitled to service of a notice to quit. Any act inconsistent with the continuance of the arrangement determines it, such as a demand by the landlord for possession. The death of either party ends a tenancy at will.

Tenancy at sufferance

18.17 A tenancy at sufferance arises where a tenant holds over after his previous tenancy has terminated. It operates where the tenant originally took possession lawfully under a tenancy agreement, regardless of whether the landlord consents to the holding over.

The tenant is not a trespasser because his original entry was lawful under his tenancy agreement. The landlord must re-enter and retake possession before he can exclude all others as trespassers. As long as the tenant remains in possession and the landlord does not accept any rent, his possession excludes the landlord.[18]

However, the landlord has the option by Deasy's Act, section 5, of deeming the tenant's continued possession to be a new tenancy from year to year, subject to the same rent and such agreements in the old tenancy as may be applicable to the new periodic one.

Statutory tenancy

18.18 A statutory tenancy may arise under the Rent (NI) Order 1978 giving the tenant the right to remain in possession after the expiration of a previous contractual tenancy.

---

[18] Cf para 19.27.

Tenancy by estoppel

18.19 There is a general rule that a tenant is estopped from denying his landlord's title, and a landlord from denying his tenant's. The doctrine of estoppel precludes parties who have created a tenancy from denying their respective capacities as against one another. Thus the landlord cannot question the validity of the tenancy that he has purported to grant and the tenant may not question the landlord's title to grant it. Estoppel applies to all types of tenancy, including periodic tenancies, tenancies at will and at sufferance, statutory tenancies and licences. It operates whether the tenancy was created by deed, in writing or orally. Those claiming though the parties concerned are also estopped so that the estoppel binds the successors in title to both landlord and tenant.

A tenancy by estoppel arises where a person with no estate in land purports to grant a tenancy of the land. Although the grant can pass no actual estate and the lessor's lack of title is known to the parties, they and their successors in title will be estopped from denying that the grant was effective to create the tenancy it was intended to create.

If after creating a tenancy by estoppel the landlord later acquires a legal estate out of which the tenancy could be created (as where he purchases the fee simple) this is said to feed the estoppel and the tenant immediately acquires a legal tenancy in place of his tenancy by estoppel.

No tenancy by estoppel can arise if the lessor had any present legal estate in the land when he granted the lease. In that case the lease takes effect in the ordinary way.

FUTURE INTERESTS

18.20 It is possible for several interests to co-exist in land simultaneously. The person currently in possession of the property is generally regarded as the owner, and in most cases may dispose of his own interest without affecting the other interests in the property.[19] A person who holds a future interest has little control over the property because such an interest does not confer possession.

Reversions

18.21 A reversion arises when an owner parts with an interest in his land to another person, but only for a limited period of time. The reversion is that which remains and is not disposed of because possession of the land will revert to the grantor on the determination of the lesser estate. For example, when A who has a freehold interest in property grants a lease for a number of years to B, the reversion is the interest remaining after the lease has expired, which then reverts to A in possession. The reversion lies in the grantor and occurs by operation of law.

---

[19] An exception arises where the property is sold by the life tenant because the interest of the remainderman is thereby affected.

Remainders

18.22 A remainder is a future estate which comes into possession in some person other than the grantor on the determination of a prior estate granted by the same instrument. For example, when C who has a freehold interest in property conveys it to D for life and after his death to E in fee simple, E has the freehold estate in remainder.

Vested interests

18.23 An interest is vested in possession if there is a present right to current enjoyment of the land. For example, before C made his conveyance, his fee simple was vested in possession. After the conveyance D had a life estate vested in possession.

An interest or estate is vested in interest only if there is a present right to future enjoyment of the land, free from conditions or contingencies. For example, E's interest which will vest on D's death. All reversions by their nature are vested in interest.

For an interest to be vested, the holder must be ascertained and his interest able to take effect either in possession at once or immediately on the determination of a prior estate. For example, F conveys land to G for life, remainder to the first child of H to get married. The interest in the remainder does not vest until it is determined which child is entitled to it.

Contingent interests

18.24 An interest is contingent if there is no present right to an estate in the land and there will be none until a condition or contingency is satisfied. If the holder is not ascertained or his interest is dependent on an uncertain event, the interest can only be contingent. For example, until it is determined which child of H marries first, the interest is contingent.

Rules against remoteness

18.25 These rules have evolved in order to preserve a balance between the desire of landowners to control the future ownership of their property and the principle of free alienability which requires that anyone with an interest in land should be able to dispose of it as he wishes. The rules aim to restrict the power to postpone the vesting in interest of property beyond a certain time in the future.

Rule against inalienability

18.26 The statute of *Quia Emptores* 1290 provides that freehold land must not be conveyed subject to a restriction prohibiting the grantee from alienating it.

Whenever lesser freehold estates are conveyed or leasehold estates are assigned subject to any such restrictions, a settlement is automatically created within the meaning of the Settled Land Acts 1882-90.[20] A settlement restricts the disposal of property by creating limited interests, usually because its purpose is to keep

---

[20] Cf Settlements paras 24.01-24.10.

the property in the family for successive generations. However, the life tenant has statutory powers of disposal which may not be curtailed by the wording of the conveyance.

Rule in *Whitby* v *Mitchell*[21]

18.27 The principle is older than the case from which it takes its name. It was developed before the modern rule against perpetuities was devised, to prevent settlors from creating unbarrable entails by a succession of life estates.[22] The effect of the rule is that where an interest in land is given to an unborn person, any remainder over to that person's issue and any subsequent limitations are void. This means that the property reverts to the grantor unless it is valid under the rule against perpetuities, in which case the property will vest in the person intended.

Rule against perpetuities

18.28 Under the feudal system the concept of seisin was fundamental. It meant actual legal ownership and possession; more than mere possession or beneficial interest. It was important to be able to determine, at any one time, who was seised of the land because of the obligation to pay feudal dues. The common law contingent remainder rules were therefore developed to govern the validity of dispositions creating remainders which might not be clear in this respect.

Inventive drafting and the application of equitable rules enabled landowners to avoid the common law contingent remainder rules. Perpetuities were created to dispose of property in such a way that the absolute vesting was postponed indefinitely. They were contrary to the policy of the law because they tied up property and prevented its free alienation.

The rule against perpetuities was then devised to prevent evasion of the rules and also to limit the power to postpone vesting of future interests to a well defined perpetuity period. It is now settled that the period for vesting of any future interest in property, (whether real or personal) at common law is the lives in being plus 21 years, with allowance for any period of gestation.

The rule against perpetuities was developed entirely by the courts until the Perpetuities Act (NI) 1966, ('the Perpetuities Act') modelled on similar English legislation, gave statutory recognition to the common law perpetuity period.

The Perpetuities Act actually supplements the common law rule rather than replacing it altogether. The common law rule should first be applied to a particular disposition and, only if it fails, the statutory rules invoked.

An essential difference between the statutory and the common law approach is that at common law the courts would not allow a wait and see approach to ascertain whether a particular disposition would vest within the appropriate period. Each gift had to be regarded at the time of operation of the instrument concerned and the possibilities taken into account. If there was the slightest possibility that a gift might vest after the perpetuity period had expired it was void *ab initio*.

---

[21] (1890) 44 Ch D 85.
[22] That is, fee tail estates which could not be enlarged into fee simples by execution of the appropriate conveyance.

The Perpetuities Act alters the operation of the rule to the extent that the wait and see principle can be applied to dispositions which would otherwise be void at common law. However, if a disposition could not possibly take effect within the perpetuity period, there is no point in waiting to see. It is void at common law and under the Perpetuities Act. Also within the perpetuity period, if events take place which indicate that there is no further possibility of any vesting, the disposition will fail.

A settlor is allowed under the Perpetuities Act to select an alternative period during which the gift must vest, if it is expressly stated in the instrument and does not exceed 80 years.

If the wait and see approach is adopted, the perpetuity period is determined by reference to the lives in being listed in the Perpetuities Act provided that the individuals can be ascertained at the beginning of the perpetuity period. If there are no lives in being which qualify, the perpetuity period is 21 years both at common law and under the Perpetuities Act.

JOINT INTERESTS

18.29 Joint ownership or co-ownership is the sharing of ownership of property by two or more persons concurrently, as opposed to successively. The only significant categories of joint ownership remaining are joint tenancies and tenancies in common.[23]

Joint tenancy

18.30 This is perhaps the most common type of joint ownership and arises where land is held by more than one person simultaneously in undivided shares. The ownership is treated as a single unit as against third parties and all the shares are regarded as equal.

The central principle of a joint tenancy is that, when one of the owners dies, his undivided share passes to the surviving joint tenants. This is known as the right of survivorship. No joint tenant can defeat the joint tenancy by bequeathing his interest in his will to a third party.

It is convenient for married couples and trustees to hold property as joint tenants because the right of survivorship ensures the automatic vesting of the property in the survivors without the need for any further conveyance.

Where all the joint tenants die together, the common law principle of commorientes is applied. This means that in circumstances which render it impossible to determine who died first, neither is deemed to have survived the other and there can be no survivorship. The respective heirs then succeed to the property as joint tenants.

The four unities of possession, interest, title and time must exist for an estate to qualify as a joint tenancy.

---

[23] Historically, there were also - Coparceny: joint heir, obsolete since the Administration of Estates Act (NI) 1955. Tenancy by entireties: confined to husband and wife, cannot be created *post* the Married Women's Property Act 1882.

Possession
18.31 Each owner has as much right to possession of the property held under the joint tenancy as the others. No joint tenant can exclude any of the others from any part of the land.

Interest
18.32 The joint tenants holding a particular piece of land are regarded as a single unit for the purposes of ownership and they all have to join in any transaction relating to that land if it is to be fully effective. Each joint tenant holds the same interest in land in relation to the nature, extent and duration of the interest.

Title
18.33 All the joint tenants should acquire their interests in the land by the same title, regardless of whether that is a document, an act of another, or even an act of adverse possession.

Time
18.34 The interest of each joint tenant should also vest at the same time. Unity of title on its own without unity of time is not sufficient to create a joint tenancy.

Tenancy in common
18.35 Although tenants in common hold their interests in the property concurrently in undivided shares, the position is different from a joint tenancy. Each tenant in common holds a quite distinct and separate share which may or may not be equal. It is an undivided share capable of being separate. Until the division is made, the particular part of the property to which it relates is not certain.

No right of survivorship
18.36 A tenant in common has a distinct share in the property from the date of the commencement of the relationship and there is no automatic right of survivorship.

Unity of possession
18.37 The only one of the four unities required for a tenancy in common is unity of possession.

Creation of joint interests

Common law
18.38 A joint tenancy is preferred at common law and a presumption arises in its favour in the case of any doubt. This may be rebutted if any of the four unities are not present or if there are words of severance in the conveyance. For example "in equal shares", "equally", "divided between", "between", "respectively". This is largely a matter of construction.

Equity

18.39 Equity leans against joint tenancies and prefers the presumption of a tenancy in common. When it conflicts with the approach of common law the courts have come to accept that there may be a joint tenancy in law but a tenancy in common in equity. This arises in the following situations:

(a) Purchase money in unequal shares

If the purchasers of property provide the purchase money in unequal shares, they are presumed to take the property in equity as tenants in common notwithstanding the fact that they hold it in law as joint tenants. (On the other hand, if the money is provided in equal shares, equity presumes a joint tenancy.) On the death of one party, the survivor takes the entire legal interest himself but must hold part of the beneficial interest, equal to the beneficial share of the deceased owner, for the deceased's successors.

(b) Mortgage loans

Equity considers that mortgagees hold their legal interest in property as tenants in common, whether the money is lent in equal or unequal shares. This enables each lender to be repaid the amount which he lent and prevents the right of survivorship, which seems inappropriate, from applying. The presumption of a tenancy in common is rebuttable.

(c) Partnership property

A tenancy in common is again presumed in equity as the right of survivorship is not considered appropriate to a business relationship.

Married couples

18.40 The common law rule which treated a husband (H) and wife (W) as one legal entity resulted in a rule of construction which, in a conveyance to H and W and a third party, treated H and W as taking one share between them and the third party as taking the other share. The Property (NI) Order 1978, article 13, reverses this by providing that a husband and wife shall henceforth be treated as two persons for all purposes of acquisition of property.

Determination of joint interests

Severance of a joint tenancy

18.41 When a joint tenancy is severed it is converted into a tenancy in common and this may occur either at law or in equity. It can be the result of the acquisition of a further interest in the property or alienation of an interest by one of the joint tenants destroying one of the four unities.

Severance may occur by agreement between the co-tenants but a share in a joint tenancy cannot be bequeathed by will because this would defeat the right of survivorship.

A joint tenancy is severed by an *inter vivos* disposition of one of the joint tenant's interests. It is also severed where the alienation takes the form of a grant of mortgage by conveyance, assignment or demise. It was thought that the creation of a charge by a joint tenant did not constitute an alienation of his interest and could not sever the joint tenancy.[24] Nor did an order under the Judgments Enforcement (NI) Order 1981 charging only the interest of one or some of several joint tenants because article 49 provides that it shall have the same effect as a charge. However under article 50 of the Property (NI) Order 1997, the creation of a charge on the estate or estates of one or more joint tenants (but not all of them) causes (and always has caused) a severance of the joint tenancy.

The bankruptcy of a joint tenant severs the joint tenancy when his estate vests in the Official Receiver or trustee in bankruptcy. An insolvency administration order in respect of the estate of a deceased joint tenancy retrospectively severs the joint tenancy as of the first moment of the day on which the deceased died, with the result that at the actual time of his death he is a tenant in common whose undivided share becomes available for the satisfaction of creditors of his estate.[25]

Partition

18.42 All the co-tenants of a joint tenancy or a tenancy in common may voluntarily agree to put an end to their relationship and to partition the property, which must be done by deed.[26] If there is no agreement, the arrangement cannot be foisted on the dissenters at common law. Under the Partition Acts 1868 and 1876 the court can order a sale instead of actual partition and divide the net proceeds amongst the owners in accordance with their shares.

In a case where the applicant for partition or sale owns at least half the value of the property he is entitled to a direction for sale unless there is good reason to the contrary. Where he owns less than half, the applicant must establish circumstances justifying a sale in lieu of partition showing that it would be in the best interests of the parties concerned to sell. The court has a *discretion* to order partition or sale, but does not have to make an order. If an order is made, it can be postponed pending further enquiries.[27]

An application can be made by a party having an interest in the property, including a mortgagee. Under the Property (NI) Order 1997, article 48, the owner of a charge on land jointly owned can apply for partition or sale in lieu of partition. The operation of article 48 is not retrospective and does not apply to orders charging land created before 1 September 1997.[28]

Union in a sole tenant

18.43 Joint ownership of any nature will be determined when the property becomes vested in one person. This may eventually occur through operation of the right of survivorship in a joint tenancy or when one owner purchases or inherits the interests of the others.

---

[24] *Northern Bank Ltd* v *Haggerty* [1995] NI 211 (Ch D).
[25] *Re Palmer deceased* [1994] 3 All ER 835.
[26] Real Property Act 1845, s 3.
[27] *Northern Bank Ltd* v *Adams,* unreported, 1 February 1996.
[28] *Per* Girvan J in *Ulster Bank Ltd* v *Carter* [1999] NI 93. Art 48 is currently under review by the Office of Law Reform.

Transfer of an interest

18.44 The only manner in which a joint tenant may transfer his interest in property to the other joint tenants is by way of release and any other purported transfer is construed as a release. The significance of this is that a release technically operates to extinguish an interest rather than to convey it and benefits only the party to whom it is made.

If a joint tenant sells or transfers his interest to a third party the joint tenancy is severed and it becomes a sale of a share of a tenancy in common.

A tenant in common cannot release his interest in the property to the other owners. He may however transfer or sell it to them as to third parties by way of conveyance or assignment.

CHAPTER NINETEEN

LEASEHOLD LAW

CREATION OF THE RELATIONSHIP

19.01 When considering the creation of the relationship between landlord and tenant it is important to remember that since 10 January 2000 the creation of a new long lease of a dwelling house (subject to certain specific exceptions) is prohibited by the operation of the Property (NI) Order 1997.

To create a tenancy as opposed to any other type of interest in land such as a licence, exclusive possession must be conferred on the tenant for a term. The agreement must comply with any necessary formalities and the parties should intend that the relationship of landlord and tenant will come into existence between them.

The case of *Street* v *Mountford*[29] established that the most important factor for a tenancy is exclusive possession rather than the professed intention of the parties. In Northern Ireland this decision has to be considered in conjunction with Deasy's Act, section 3, which states that the relationship of landlord and tenant shall be deemed to be founded on the express or implied contract of the parties.

Formalities

19.02 In the case of fee farm grants and of leases not being from year to year or any lesser period Deasy's Act, section 4, requires the agreement to be in writing, and signed by the landlord or his agent previously authorised in writing.[30] To create a lease to which Deasy's Act applies it is also essential that a rent is reserved.

A gratuitous lease may be valid outside the provisions of Deasy's Act if it complies with the requirements of the Real Property Act 1845, section 3, which states that it must be evidenced by deed. If not so evidenced it is void at law.

Periodic tenancies which run from year to year, month to month or week to week, may be created informally and no written record is required. Tenancies for a definite period of less than a year may also be informally created. In both these cases a rent must be reserved.

Any lease covered by Deasy's Act is void under that Act if it does not comply with the required formalities. It can however be saved in a different form, despite the original intentions of the parties. If the tenant takes possession with the landlord's consent, a tenancy at will arises. If rent is also paid and accepted,

---

[29] [1985] AC 809.
[30] There is some confusion as to the precise meaning of "not being from year to year or any lesser period". It clearly excludes periodic tenancies, *ie* tenancies from year to year, month to month or week to week, and those for a definite period of time less than one year, but there has been some controversy over the case of a grant for one year certain.

a periodic tenancy is created, the length of which is dependent on the way in which the rent is calculated rather than on the way it is paid.

If it complies with the formalities laid down by the Statute of Frauds (Ir) 1695[31] an intended lease which does not comply with the necessary formalities to properly create a lease may be enforced as a contract. Alternatively it may be enforceable in equity through a decree of specific performance if there is a sufficient act of part performance to take the transaction outside the requirements of the Statute of Frauds.

ASSIGNMENT AND SUBLETTING

Definitions

19.03 At common law an assignment is a complete transfer of a tenant's entire interest in part or all of the leasehold premises. The assignee takes on all the rights and duties while the tenant retains nothing. On the other hand, a sub-lease involves the tenant subletting all or part of the premises, usually for a period shorter than the term of his own lease and remaining liable on the covenants and conditions of the head lease.

Deasy's Act has blurred the distinction between assignment and subletting because section 3 allows the tenant to sublet for the whole of his term without retaining a reversion. The difference may now be that where the purchaser pays a lump sum he usually takes an assignment; whereas if he pays a rent to the person transferring the interest to him he generally takes a sub-lease. In some cases the distinction does not apply, as where a new rent is effectively an apportionment of an existing rent or a lump sum is paid as a premium on a lease. In many instances the characteristics of the document itself determine whether it is a lease or an assignment.[32]

The words used in the deed may be of some assistance in defining it. In an assignment the parties are usually vendor and purchaser, or assignor and assignee; in a lease, lessor and lessee or landlord and tenant. The property is assigned by an assignment; it is demised by a lease.

A lease has a reddendum which provides for the yielding and paying of a specified amount of rent as well as setting out when and how it is payable. An assignment is made expressly subject to a rent reserved by the lease under which the property is held.

In an assignment the previous title is normally recited, in a lease it is not. An assignment does not contain any new covenants other than indemnity covenants by the purchaser, nor does it contain a proviso for re-entry. A lease generally has both.

The importance of the distinction is that an assignment creates privity of estate between a landlord and a tenant's assignee, but a sub-lease does not create such privity between a head landlord and a sub-tenant. The covenants and conditions in the original lease are enforceable between a landlord and tenant, a landlord and a tenant's assignee, but not between a head landlord and a sub-tenant.

---

[31] See paras 3.03-3.04.
[32] See *eg, Todd* v *Unwin and others* [1994] NIJB 230.

Nevertheless a head landlord can enforce the obligations against a tenant to whom a sub-tenant is answerable.[33]

Assignment

19.04 This is governed by Deasy's Act, sections 9-16. The assignment should be by deed or in writing, signed by the assignor or his authorised agent. It may also be by devise, bequest or act and operation of law. Generally, the benefit and burden of express and implied agreements in the lease are enforceable by or against successors in title of both the original landlord and tenant. This is important because it is more difficult for successors in title to enforce freehold covenants.

Under Deasy's Act, section 10, where a lease contains an agreement prohibiting assignment, whether absolute or qualified, it is not lawful to assign the property or any part of it without the written consent of the landlord or his authorised agent testified either by his being a party to the assignment or by his consent being endorsed on the deed.[34]

Even where there is no prohibition against assignment, if the original tenant wishes to discharge himself from any continuing obligation to the landlord once he has assigned his interest, the same criteria apply by virtue of Deasy's Act, section 16. The consent of the landlord must appear by his being a party to the deed or by endorsement. The consent effectively discharges the tenant from all future liability under the lease leaving him liable only during the period for which he was tenant. Where consent is not obtained, the assignment is not unlawful in itself, but the tenant remains liable at common law to the landlord for breaches of covenant by the assignee. The liability continues because the assignment does not destroy the privity of contract existing between the tenant and the landlord.

The usual method of protection against continuing liability is to insert an indemnity clause in the assignment whereby the assignee undertakes to indemnify the assignor against all future liability. In the case of residential property this is still done despite section 16 because the original tenant seldom actually joins the landlord as party to the deed of assignment or has his consent endorsed on it unless there is a prohibition in the lease of assignment without consent.

Under Deasy's Act, section 14, a subsequent assignee of the tenant may protect himself when he in turn is assigning his interest by giving written notice of the assignment to the landlord. This prevents him from being liable for breaches of covenant occurring after the assignment. If he gave an indemnity when he acquired the property he will also require an indemnity from his own assignee to protect himself in case of any action by an earlier assignee or the original tenant.

In commercial lease cases the tenant assigning would always ensure that the original landlord joins in the deed of assignment or endorses consent upon it so that the original tenant thereby enjoys the protection of section 16.

---

[33] Cf Enforcement of Obligations para 20.19.
[34] See also s 18 *re* subletting, below para 19.05.

Subletting

19.05 Deasy's Act, section 4, is presumed to apply to the creation of a sub-lease because it involves the creation of a new landlord and tenant relationship.[35] By Deasy's Act, section 18, if a lease contains an absolute provision against subletting, it is not lawful to sublet without the express consent of the landlord or his authorised agent testified by his being a party to the sub-lease, by his endorsement on the deed, or by a signed note in writing.

DETERMINATION OF THE RELATIONSHIP

Expiry

19.06 When a lease comes to its natural end the relationship of landlord and tenant is automatically determined unless it has statutory protection, for example under the Business Tenancies (NI) Order 1996 or the Rent (NI) Order 1978.[36] Prior to that it may be determined by any of the following methods.

Notice to quit

19.07 This is the usual means of determining a periodic tenancy which does not necessarily end at the expiration of the original term. It may also be used in relation to a tenancy at will or at sufferance, but is not essential. It is not generally appropriate to a lease for a term of years, although a commercial lease often contains a break clause. A break clause permits the tenant to determine the lease on a particular date provided that the specified notice is given. This notice is similar to a notice to quit.[37]

Form

19.08 In general it does not need to be in writing unless the agreement so provides. If a particular form of writing is required this must be strictly followed.[38]

---

[35] Cf para 19.02: in writing only, signed by the landlord or his authorised agent.

[36] Most commercial leases provide that the tenancy is not to terminate at the end of the stated term but will continue, for example, on a monthly or quarterly basis unless terminated by a specified period of written notice.

[37] In *Mannai Investment Co Ltd* v *Eagle Star Life Assurance Co Ltd* [1997] 2 WLR 945 (HL) a notice to determine the lease was served by the tenant under the break clause but, in error, it was set to expire one day before the specified date. It was held that strict compliance with the term of the clause was not necessary to determine the lease when it would have been obvious to a reasonable recipient of the notice with knowledge of the lease's terms and the date of the break clause that the tenant wished to determine the lease in accordance with the clause but made an immaterial error in wrongly describing the date.

[38] Often the lease in question will have provisions concerning the issue and service of the notice to determine. The notice must be drafted with particular care so as to identify the precise termination date and the party to be served. It must correctly describe the premises and the lease to which the notice relates. Care must be taken as to whether the notice must be signed by the party giving it or may be signed by that party's agent or solicitor. Similarly, care must be taken as to whether the notice must be served direct on the other party or may be served on that party's agent or solicitor.

Contents

19.09 The notice must clearly indicate an intention to determine the tenancy. This may be implied in a demand for a higher rent because it may be treated as an offer of a new tenancy. The original agreement may specify the length of notice required, but if it does not, common law rules apply, as modified by the Rent (NI) Order 1978 and, where applicable, the Business Tenancies (NI) Order 1996.

Length of notice implied at common law for all residential tenancies

19.10 Most leases will contain express provisions for the required period of notice but in the case of omission the length of notice is implied.

Weekly tenancy: a week's notice which can expire on any day.[39]

Monthly tenancy: a month's notice to expire on a gale day or at the end of a monthly period.

Yearly tenancy: six month's notice to expire at the end of a year of the tenancy.

Service

19.11 Service depends on the terms of any provisions in the lease itself. Generally the notice must be served on the tenant, although postal service or putting it through the letterbox is sufficient. The landlord should be able to prove that the notice came to the attention of the tenant, unless there is specific provision to the contrary in the lease.[40]

Waiver

19.12 Waiver of a notice to quit is a different concept from waiver of a breach of covenant or of forfeiture. A notice to quit may be waived either expressly or impliedly by the conduct of the parties. Waiver by implication depends on intention and is not necessarily found where rent is accepted after expiration of notice.

Surrender

19.13 A surrender of lease is usually activated at the instigation of the tenant although in some cases it may be instigated by the landlord. Surrender must operate immediately and not at some future time. Under Deasy's Act, section 7, a surrender may operate by deed, by the tenant in writing, or by act or operation of law, which may be inferred from conduct.[41] The consent of the landlord is required unless the tenant has express power under the lease or by

---

[39] Under the Rent (NI) Order 1978 a landlord must give at least four weeks' notice, although a tenant can give the notice required by the agreement. This applies to all residential tenancies where the property is occupied and not only those governed by the Order.

[40] See *Wandsworth Borough Council* v *Attwell* [1995] EGCS 68 where the tenant was abroad and did not get the notice.

[41] On the question whether the return of keys to the landlord has effected a surrender of the tenancy see *Proudreed Ltd* v *Microgen Holdings plc* [1996] 12 EG 127, *Borokat* v *Ealing LBC* [1996] EGCS 67 and *Filering Ltd* v *Taylor Commercial Ltd* [1996] EGCS 95.

statute to surrender. For example, by Deasy's Act, section 40 if the premises are destroyed by accident.[42]

Forfeiture

19.14 There are several ways in which the relationship of landlord and tenant may be determined by forfeiture.

Right to forfeit

19.15 Forfeiture of a lease occurs when the landlord becomes entitled to retake the premises and prematurely puts an end to the lease. It may take place under the terms of the lease or by operation of law. The courts have a discretion to grant relief from forfeiture. Although the courts do not always favour forfeiture and in many cases the tenant will be successful in an application for relief against it, it can still be a real sanction.

Breach of covenant

19.16 The lease usually contains a list of positive and negative covenants undertaken by the tenant. The landlord only has the right to determine the lease for breach of covenant if it contains an express provision for forfeiture in such event. Consequently, most leases are drafted with an express forfeiture clause.

Breach of conditions

19.17 Some of the tenant's obligations may appear as conditions. A condition is a term of the agreement expressed as being "upon condition that", or "provided always that". The lease is conditional on the tenant performing his obligations. When a breach occurs the lease becomes voidable at the landlord's option. It is not void automatically. The lease can be forfeited on breach of a condition even if there is no forfeiture clause.

Forfeiture clauses

19.18 The majority of the tenant's duties in a lease are usually set out as covenants. A forfeiture clause is always included to provide that if the tenant commits a breach of covenant the landlord may re-enter and the lease is determined. The landlord thereby reserves a right of re-entry and the lease continues unless and until he exercises it. This means that the lease is voidable by the lessor after a breach of covenant and remains valid until he re-enters.

Procedure for re-entry

19.19 If a landlord is entitled to re-enter, he can enforce his right:

(1) By making peaceable re-entry on the land, taking possession and forfeiting the lease. There are very limited circumstances in which a landlord can lawfully make peaceable re-entry. This is always illegal in relation to premises let for residential use and in occupation as in these circumstances the landlord can only regain possession under a court order.

---

[42] See para 19.31.

(2) By commencing an action on the basis that the lease has come to an end, electing immediately to forfeit the lease and claim possession.

(3) By commencing an action claiming either a determination that the lease has been forfeited or enforcement of the covenants in the lease.[43]

For non-payment of rent

19.20 A landlord who has the right to re-enter for non-payment of rent under the lease must make a formal demand before he may re-enter. This means making a demand for the exact sum due, on the day it falls due, upon the demised premises, at such convenient hour before sunset as will give time to count out the money.[44] To avoid these technicalities and exempt the landlord from making a formal demand, a lease should provide for forfeiture if the rent is a specified number of days in arrear "whether formally demanded or not".

The tenant may be entitled to equitable relief against the forfeiture if he pays the rent together with any expenses due to the landlord and it is just and equitable to grant relief. Equity can then restore him to his position despite the forfeiture of the lease.

Other cases

19.21 The Conveyancing Act 1881 Act, section 14, places restrictions on the right of re-entry in cases other than non-payment of rent or breach of covenant against assigning or subletting the leasehold premises.[45] It provides that a right of re-entry or forfeiture shall not be enforceable unless and until the landlord serves on the tenant a notice specifying the breach, requiring it to be remedied and requiring the tenant to make compensation for the breach within a reasonable time.[46]

It is crucial to ascertain which covenants are capable of remedy. Failure to state that such covenants must be remedied and to allow a reasonable time to do so, will not only mean that the notice is invalid, but also any subsequent forfeiture action. Alternatively, if the covenant is irremediable, the notice need specify only the breach.

A breach of a negative covenant against alienation is a 'once and for all' breach which is not capable of remedy at all. Whatever events follow the breach, they cannot wipe the slate clean and the breach remains. However, the court may still, in its discretion, grant relief from forfeiture.[47]

This does not necessarily mean that "once and for all" breaches of positive covenants are never capable of remedy. For example, a breach of covenant to reconstruct premises by a certain date will usually be remediable.[48] The test is whether, for practical purposes, the harm that has been done to the landlord can

---

[43] See *GS Fashions Ltd v B&Q plc* [1995] EGCS 68.
[44] See 1 Wms Saund (1871) 434.
[45] There are some other very limited exceptions under s14(6) as amended, *eg* covenants in mining leases or conditions against bankruptcy of the lessee.
[46] The notice may be invalid if the breaches are incapable of remedy, *Savva v Hussein*, [1996] NPC 64.
[47] See *Scala House & District Property Co Ltd v Forbes* [1974] 1 QB 575.
[48] *Expert Clothing Service v Hillgate House* [1986] 1 Ch 340.

be retrieved within a reasonable time.[49] This approach can be applied to both positive and negative covenants, whether continuous or "once and for all" breaches.

Once the required procedure has been followed and the tenant fails to comply within a reasonable time, the landlord may re-enter, if he can do so peaceably, except in the case of occupied residential premises. If he is unable to gain possession or if he is dealing with occupied residential premises he may take an action for possession by applying for an ejectment on the title or for overholding.

Relief against forfeiture

19.22 The tenant is entitled to equitable relief in cases of non-payment of rent. In other cases, he may take an action for relief if the landlord is seeking to re-enter without a court order for possession or has already effected physical re-entry. Alternatively, he may apply for relief by way of defence or counterclaim in the landlord's action. In his defence he may wish to argue, for example, that a breach of covenant can be remedied or was waived by the landlord.

The court has a general equitable discretion to grant whatever relief it thinks fit, taking the circumstances and conduct of the parties into account, provided that relief is sought before re-entry is completed.[50]

Effect of forfeiture

19.23 Generally forfeiture affects the whole of the premises and renders the lease void. At common law it was also thought that forfeiture normally determined all interests derived out of the lease, such as sub-leases,[51] but now it seems that is not necessarily the case and a sub-tenancy may survive.[52] The Conveyancing Act 1892, section 4, provides that a sub-lessee may apply for relief whereby the lease becomes vested in him. A business sub-tenancy may survive under the statutory provisions of the Business Tenancies (NI) Order 1996.

Waiver of breach of covenant

19.24 The landlord may be unable to proceed with the forfeiture if he waives a breach of covenant. Waiver may take place before the landlord shows that he is treating the lease as forfeited.[53]

Ejectment

19.25 A landlord may take an action for ejectment to recover possession from the tenant, which can take several forms.

---

[49] See *Savva* v *Hussein* [1996] NPC 64.
[50] It may even be possible to apply for relief after forfeiture is effected but the lessee's task will obviously be more difficult the longer he leaves it. Re-entry is not necessarily completed by taking physical possession, and a lessee may apply for relief after such an event. See *Billson and others* v *Residential Apartments Ltd* [1992] 01 EG 91 HC.
[51] *Brown* v *Wilson* (1949) 156 EG 45
[52] *Pennell* v *Payne* [1995] 2 All ER 592.
[53] Cf para 20.17.

Action for possession or ejectment on the title

19.26 This action may be taken where it is alleged that the person in possession has no title and the relationship of landlord and tenant does not exist. This may be appropriate where a tenancy has expired, been determined by notice to quit or where the lessee is claiming that the lease has been forfeited for breach of covenant or condition. It can also be used to eject a squatter from possession.[54]

Overholding

19.27 Alternatively, if the tenant does not give up possession at the end of the lease or has been in breach of the terms of the lease and has had his lease forfeited, the landlord may bring an ejectment for overholding.

Non-payment of rent

19.28 This action is governed by Deasy's Act, sections 52-58 and applies to a tenancy from year to year or longer, which is still in existence and has not yet been determined. The rent must be at least a year in arrear and it is not necessary to await the expiration of the period specified in any re-entry clause before taking action. This action may be taken even if there is no re-entry clause in the lease. A formal demand for rent is not required.

Merger

19.29 Although it is the converse of surrender, merger has the same result, and in each case the lesser interest is absorbed in the greater. Where there is a surrender, the landlord acquires the tenant's interest; whereas if there is a merger, the tenant retains his own interest and acquires the immediate reversion, or a purchaser acquires both.[55]

Enlargement

19.30 There are various statutory provisions enabling a lease to be enlarged into a fee simple. Historically, the Renewable Leasehold Conversion Act 1849 was important in this respect. The Conveyancing Act 1881, section 65 also made provision for a long lease, under which either no rent or a rent having no monetary value was payable, to be enlarged into a fee simple. The more recent Leasehold (Enlargement and Extension) Act (NI) 1971 has been less significant, because there are few leases which comply with its strict requirements.

Frustration

19.31 The traditional view is that the doctrine of frustration of contracts does not apply to leases and the tenant remains liable under the lease whatever happens to the property.[56]

---

[54] Cf Adverse Possession paras 23.01-23.11.

[55] Cf Surrender para 19.13.

[56] It was held in *National Carriers Ltd* v *Panalpina* [1981] 1 All ER 161 (HL) that the doctrine of frustation of contracts is applicable to leases, although the occasions on which it may be applied are extremely rare. In this case the only access to a warehouse was by a

Under Deasy's Act, section 40, there is a statutory right to surrender a lease in the event that the premises are destroyed by fire or other inevitable accident as long as the lease contains no express repairing covenant by the tenant. In practice it would be unusual for section 40 to apply because most leases do contain an express repairing covenant.

---

street which the local authority closed after five years of the term had elapsed, for 20 months. The tenant claimed the lease was frustated but it was held that on the facts, the doctrine did not apply.

CHAPTER TWENTY

COVENANTS AND AGREEMENTS

Introduction

20.01 A covenant is an agreement creating an obligation contained in a deed. It may be positive, stipulating the performance of an act or the payment of money; or negative or restrictive, forbidding the commission of an act.

Covenants may be contained in a conveyance of a freehold, a fee farm grant, a lease, or an assignment. They may also be contained in a deed of covenant. Covenants in leases are naturally more common than freehold covenants.

The rights and obligations of the parties to a transaction include those imposed by any covenants and conditions in the deed affecting it, which may be express or implied. A covenant usually relates to and passes with ownership of the land to which it belongs.[57]

When there has been a breach of covenant the most important question is whether or not the covenant is enforceable. If it is enforceable it normally does not matter whether the covenant affects freehold or leasehold land. In considering whether or not it is enforceable the relevant principles of equity or common law and statutory provisions, either Deasy's Act or the Conveyancing Act 1881 should be applied as appropriate. The position is also affected by the Property (NI) Order 1997, article 34 which provides completely new provisions for the running of freehold covenants contained in a deed made after 10 January 2000. In due course new provisions will come into operation in relation to covenants on land where the ground rent has been redeemed.[58]

Where a landowner owns two pieces of adjoining land and sells one of them, he may wish to impose covenants on the land that he is selling for his own protection. Thus the land he retains enjoys the benefit of the covenants and the land he sells carries the burden. Similarly, a purchaser may insist on the inclusion of covenants creating burdens on the land retained by a vendor for the benefit of the land purchased.

Leasehold covenants are considered here first because of the preponderance of covenants in leases and the amount of material relating to them. Also, it is easier to understand freehold covenants when leaseholds have been examined.

---

[57] If it can be sold separately it may be of a more personal nature, applying to a particular owner, and more in the nature of a licence. This has an effect on its enforceability between successors in title to the original parties.

[58] At the time of writing (April 2000) proposals for a scheme for the redemption of ground rents and consequential provisions are contained in a draft Ground Rents Bill.

LEASEHOLD COVENANTS

20.02 In general the law of leasehold covenants extends to fee farm grants, except where there are statutory provisions to the contrary.[59]

Some covenants may be expressly contained in the lease. Others are implied by common law and by statute in the absence of any express provision.

20.03 Article 25 of the Property (NI) Order 1997 provides that only covenants of the types specified and set out will continue to benefit or burden the land after the ground rent under a long lease or fee farm grant for a dwelling house has been redeemed and the estate enlarged into a fee simple under the provisions of the Order. Consequently, even if the covenants intended to affect a dwelling house are expressly set out or implied at the time the lease is created, they may at a future date cease to have effect under article 25.

Express covenants

20.04 In theory the parties are at liberty to determine the express terms to be inserted in the lease and these will depend upon the particular market factors applicable in each case. In practice, whether it is a short or long term, residential or commercial lease, the agreement is often drawn up by the landlord and presented to the tenant. Although the tenant is discouraged from making any amendments, his solicitor should endeavour to ensure that the terms of the lease are as favourable as possible to his client. If he cannot reach a compromise which adequately protects his client, he should advise against acceptance of the lease.

Landlord

20.05 In residential leases the landlord's covenants are generally fewer than the tenant's and may consist only of one for quiet enjoyment. This means that the tenant will not be disturbed by any acts of the landlord or anyone claiming through him while the tenant is in possession.[60] Other covenants which the landlord may undertake, usually where the lease is for a short term, include responsibility for specific outgoings on the premises, such as insurance, repairs and possibly maintenance and redecoration.

In commercial leases the landlord will have extensive covenants, for example, in relation to management, insurance and service charge provisions. Such covenants would also appear in leases for flats.

Tenant

20.06 Most of the express covenants in any lease will be entered into by the tenant but their exact nature varies according to the characteristics of the particular property, the term of the lease and the type of letting. The positive covenants, requiring action, may relate to matters such as payment of rent, payment of other outgoings, keeping the premises in good repair (in shorter leases this should be qualified as to extent), user and insurance. The negative covenants, restraining activity, may relate to user, structural alterations and additions, assignment and subletting.

---

[59] Cf paras 18.05-18.09.
[60] Cf Implied Covenants para 20.07.

Implied covenants

20.07 All implied covenants are subject to a contrary intention appearing in the lease.

Covenants implied on behalf of the landlord

20.08 The following covenants are implied on behalf of the landlord:

(1) Under Deasy's Act, section 41, the landlord covenants that he has good title to make the lease and will allow the tenant quiet enjoyment.[61] This protects the lessee from physical interference but does not extend to privacy or amenities. It covers interference "by any person whomsoever" and is obviously very wide. Accordingly it is almost invariably replaced by an express covenant limiting the lessor's obligation to the conduct of himself and those claiming through him.

(2) "A grantor may not derogate from his grant" is a common law principle meaning that he may not grant land to another and then interfere with the purpose for which it was granted. It prevents the lessor and those claiming through him, such as other tenants or assignees on adjoining land, from rendering the property less fit for the purpose for which it was known to be let.[62] This obligation can be expressly limited in the lease.

Covenants implied on behalf of the tenant

20.09 The following covenants are implied on behalf of the tenant by Deasy's Act under the sections mentioned:

(1) *Section 42(1)*: That all the rent and impositions due by the tenant on the premises will be paid by him.

(2) *Section 42(2)*: That he will give up peaceable possession of the premises in good repair when the lease determines.[63]

(3) *Section 26*: That he will not cause waste on the property. This means that he must not make any permanent alterations prejudicing the freehold in the way of damage, destruction, neglect, addition or improvement.

Covenants not implied

20.10 It is useful to be aware of covenants which are not implied and which should be expressly stated.

---

[61] *Mulligan v Carroll* in the Republic of Ireland, unreported, 28 July 1995, High Court (RoI) confirms that the terms of the landlord's obligations under s 41 are dependent on the performance of the tenant's obligations.

[62] In *Chartered Trust plc v Davies* [1997] 2 EGLR 83: 49 EG 135 the Court of Appeal held that where a common landlord fails to take steps to prevent tenant A from causing a nuisance to tenant B and the nuisance renders tenant B's land materially less fit for the purpose for which it was let, the landlord will derogate from his grant such that tenant B will be entitled to treat his lease as repudiated.

[63] This may catch a tenant unawares.

On behalf of the landlord

20.11 The following are examples:

(1) In general there is no implied obligation to repair.[64]

(2) There is no implied warranty as to the fitness of the premises for the purposes for which they are let, except the covenant implied at common law, that furnished accommodation is fit for human habitation at the commencement of the tenancy.

(3) Where the landlord's consent to any action is required under the lease there is no implied covenant that such consent will not be unreasonably withheld, except in relation to alienation or improvement by a tenant of business premises under the Business Tenancies (NI) Order 1996, article 26.

On behalf of the tenant

20.12 There is no implied covenant not to part with possession of the premises.

Consent to specific covenants

20.13 An express covenant by the tenant not to assign or sublet may be absolute or may be restricted to obtaining the lessor's consent, which is known as a qualified prohibition.

At common law a covenant not to assign or sublet premises does not preclude the lessee so dealing with part of the premises unless specifically stated. However under Deasy's Act, sections 10 and 18, if there is an absolute prohibition against subletting or an absolute or qualified prohibition against assignment, then neither the premises nor any part of them can be sublet or assigned without the written consent of the lessor.[65]

Other covenants may also provide for the lessor's consent to be obtained, as in the case of restrictive user. In Northern Ireland because there is no implied covenant that consent will not be unreasonably withheld it is essential to make provision for this in the lease wherever consent appears in relation to any covenant.

In the case of a business tenancy, the Business Tenancies (NI) Order 1996 provides that where a tenancy commencing after its implementation contains a covenant against alienation or alterations without the lessor's consent, it is implied that such a consent will not be unreasonably withheld.

Remedies for breach of repair obligations

20.14 In the case of a breach of a repair obligation, the aggrieved party may be able to remedy the stituation.

---

[64] An exception is when individual flats are leased in a building where the lessor retains possession and control of common parts, in which case there may be an implied obligation to keep the common parts in reasonable repair.

[65] See paras 19.04 and 19.05 as to how this consent is evidenced.

Breach by the landlord

20.15 The tenant may carry out the necessary repairs himself after giving notice to the landlord and deduct the cost from the rent as its falls due. Alternatively he may sue for damages or seek a decree of specific performance.

Breach by the tenant

20.16 The landlord may take an action for damages.[66] If the breach occurs during the tenancy the amount is calculated on the decrease in the value of the landlord's reversion caused by the breach. If it occurs at the end of the tenancy, the actual cost of repairing the premises is recoverable by the landlord.

Waiver of breach of covenant

20.17 Waiver of a breach of covenant operates as a disclaimer of the remedy available. It must be distinguished from consent which, if correctly obtained, operates to prevent a particular action from being a breach of covenant.

At common law it is possible for waiver to operate generally in relation to a covenant in a lease for all purposes, in which case the covenant ceases to operate thereafter. Alternatively, it can be a specific waiver of one particular breach of a covenant only, so that the covenant remains as part of the lease and may be invoked in the case of subsequent breaches.

Deasy's Act, section 43, provides that the conduct of the landlord is not deemed to imply waiver unless the waiver is signified in writing. Section 43 appears to reverse the antecedent common law principle whereby receipt of rent amounts to an implied waiver of breach of covenant.

It has been argued that the requirement for writing may apply only to general waivers.[67] If that is the case, an oral waiver of a particular breach would bar the landlord taking action in respect of that breach. However, this has been doubted in later decisions and it is possible a court may find that a specific waiver must be signified in writing.[68] The writing need not mention the breach of covenant. A written demand for rent or a written receipt for rent may be sufficient to act as a waiver.[69]

Deasy's Act, section 18, specifically provides that, in the case of subletting, no receipt of rent by the landlord or his agent is deemed to be a waiver of the agreement against subletting.

---

[66] In *Jervis* v *Harris* [1996] 1 All ER 303 the court held that, where a landlord effects repairs which are the tenant's obligation and the tenant has failed to comply with a notice to repair, the landlord can recover the costs by taking an action for debt rather than damages. It is not necessary for the leave of the court to be obtained because it is not construed as a claim for damages.

[67] See *Foott* v *Benn* (1884) 18 LRT 90 an *obiter* statement by Palles CB.

[68] The case of *Crofter Properties Ltd* v *Genport Ltd*, unreported, (HC, RoI), 15 March 1996 (1988/2225p) in the Republic of Ireland held that the meaning of s 43 is clear: any waiver of covenant, whether general or particular, must be effected in writing.

[69] See the English case of *John Lewis Properties plc* v *Viscount Chelsea* [1993] 46 EG 184 where acceptance of rent did amount to waiver and the decision of the NI High Court in *Duncan* v *Makin* [1985] 2 NIJB 1 where a landlord's receipt of rent was held to act as a waiver of a tenant's forfeiture. *NB*: English cases are not governed by Deasy's Act, s 43.

Deasy's Act, section 22, provides that a subletting with the landlord's consent is not to be deemed a general waiver of the benefit of any agreement against subletting.

Continuing breaches

20.18 Where the breach is of a continuing nature, such as breach of a covenant to repair or to use the premises in a particular way, a waiver extends only to the time when it is given. A breach continuing after the date of the waiver normally gives a fresh right of forfeiture. Therefore it is particularly important to obtain the landlord's consent in writing to signify that the waiver extends for the actual duration of the breach. Even written consent may last only for a limited period if this is indicated by its wording.

Enforcement of obligations

20.19 The remedies generally available for breach of covenant in existing leases depend partly on the terms of the agreement and partly on the general law. Prior to the operation of the Property (NI) Order 1997[70] it was considerably easier for covenants to be enforced between the successors in title of the original parties under a lease than under a freehold title, and this was one of the major reasons for the high incidence of leases in Northern Ireland.

Original parties

20.20 The obligations may be enforced by and against the original parties to the agreement because there is privity of contract between them.

Successors in title

20.21 Once the interest of either of the parties to a lease has been transferred, there is no longer privity of contract because the successor was not party to the original lease. The problem is how to enforce covenants which were not entered into personally by the parties now interested in the land. It is here that the doctrine of privity of estate becomes important. Generally, as long as privity of estate exists between the parties, reflecting the original lessor-lessee relationship, the covenants continue to be enforceable.

At common law generally the benefit and burden of the lessor's and the lessee's covenants run with the land and the reversion respectively. A successor in title to the lessor can sue a successor in title to the lessee on the lessee's covenants and *vice versa*, as long as there is privity of estate and the covenants "touch and concern" the land, thereby excluding those dependent on the personal characteristics of the parties.

Both Deasy's Act and the Conveyancing Act 1881 also make provision for the running of the benefit and burden of covenants. There is an overlap to some extent, but in the context of the landlord and tenant relationship, the 1881 Act applies to leases made by deed only whereas Deasy's Act applies to all tenancies in consideration of a rent which meet with the required formalities, including fee farm grants.

---

[70] See Property (NI) Order 1997 paras 29.01-29.20.

The 1881 Act did not expressly repeal sections 12 and 13 of Deasy's Act and they do not appear to have been repealed by implication. The result is that the two conflicting enactments co-exist, although the courts have generally chosen to prefer Deasy's Act and have ignored the 1881 Act.

(a) Successors of the lessor

Deasy's Act, section 12, provides that the benefit of covenants in the lease can be enforced against the lessee and his successors by the lessor and his successors if this was the intention of the parties. The Conveyancing Act 1881, section 10, states that the benefit only runs if the covenants have "reference to the subject matter of the lease" which means the same as "touch and concern" the land. It is accordingly possible that covenants may bind successors under Deasy's Act which would not do so at common law or under the 1881 Act.

In order to show that it is the intention of the parties that the covenants be enforceable against the successors in title, the wording should include the heirs, executors, administrators, successors and assigns of the parties as appropriate.

(b) Successors of the lessee

Deasy's Act, section 13 and the Conveyancing Act 1881, section 11, provide that the burden of covenants in a lease which "touch and concern" (s 13) the land, or have "reference to the subject matter of the lease" (s 11), may be enforced against the lessor and his successors by the lessee and his successors. Here the statutory provisions coincide and together restrict the running of the burden against an assignee of the lessee. Section 11 has been repealed by the Property (NI) Order 1997.

Duration of liability

20.22 The assignee of a lessor or lessee can recover damages for breach of covenant during his period of ownership only. The lessor's assignee cannot sue for breaches of the lessee's covenants occurring before he took the interest unless they were of a continuing nature.[71]

At common law, a lessee remained liable for all breaches of covenant notwithstanding assignment. Under Deasy's Act, section 16, the original lessee is discharged from such liability after assignment if the lessor's consent is obtained and evidenced by his being a party to the deed or by his endorsement on it. In practice such consent is seldom obtained in the case of long residential leases. Assignments are usually drafted with indemnity covenants included instead to protect the lessee in the event of a breach. Consent to the assignment of commercial leases is usually obtained.

By Deasy's Act, section 14, the lessee's assignee is not discharged from liability until he has given notice of his assignment to the lessor. If he does not do so he should also obtain an indemnity from his assignee instead. Indeed, even if he does give the lessor notice, an assignee should still obtain an indemnity from his assignee if he gave a similar indemnity covenant when he took the property.

If the lessor wishes to take proceedings for breach of covenant, and if the original lessee did not comply with section 16 when he assigned the property,

---

[71] *Doyle v Hort* (1880) 4 LR Ir 455.

instead of suing the present assignee, the lessor may decide to sue the lessee because there is privity of contract between them. The lessee can then sue the assignee under the covenant in the assignment to indemnify the lessee. The assignee can similarly sue the second assignee and the chain of indemnities can be followed to the present assignee. The previous assignees are thus protected from the consequences of any legal actions.

Assignment of part

20.23 Prior to the operation of the relevant provisions of the Property (NI) Order 1997 (10 January 2000) where a lessee assigned only part of the premises, the assignment should have included an apportionment of the ground rent and other covenants between the two parts of the property. The lessor had to join in the deed or consent to the actual apportionment, not just the division, to be bound by it. If he did not the lessor could enforce all the covenants, including payment of rent, against either the lessee or the assignee. This was the case even if the breach had been occasioned by the other party. It was therefore important to include appropriate indemnities and charging clauses if the lessor was not involved in the assignment of part.

Now that the relevant part of the 1997 Order is operative, it is suggested that under article 29 it may no longer be possible to create a rentcharge such as a charge of an apportioned rent on an assignment of part. However, it may be arguable that such a situation might come within the exception in article 29(3) which relates to a rentcharge payable under an agreement of indemnity to the owner of a legal estate in land contingently upon a purchaser being made to pay the whole or part of a rent in respect of all or part of that land. It could also be argued that any such apportionment is contrary to the spirit of the legislation because it is in effect an attempt to create a new rent.[72]

Sub-lease

20.24 Where a lessee sub-leases part or all of the premises he remains liable for all breaches of covenant in the lease, including any by the sub-tenant. There is no privity of estate between the lessor and the sub-tenant. For this reason, the sub-lease should contain the same covenants as the lease. Otherwise the lessee will remain liable to the lessor for breaches of covenant outside his own control, but will not be able to enforce them against the sub-lessee.

Alternatively, the lessor may possibly have the option of enforcing restrictive covenants directly against the sub-lessee under the rule in *Tulk* v *Moxhay*[73] although it has more frequent application to freehold covenants.[74] In that case the general equitable principle was established that the burden of a restrictive covenant will run with the land to which it relates so as to bind all successors in title of the original covenantor, except a *bona fide* purchaser without notice.

---

[72] At the time of writing (April 2000) it is too early to tell how the vexed question of apportionment should properly be interpreted. Already, since 10 January 2000 very different opinions have emerged.
[73] (1848) 2 Ph 774.
[74] Cf para 20.28.

FREEHOLD COVENANTS

20.25 The law of freehold covenants applies to freeholds other than fee farm grants. Freehold covenants should be set out expressly in the deed. The only covenants which may be implied are those which arise under the Conveyancing Act 1881, section 7.[75] In a conveyance for valuable consideration by a beneficial owner expressed as such he is deemed to have covenanted that:

(1) He has the right to convey;
(2) He will allow quiet enjoyment for the purchaser;
(3) The premises are free from encumbrances;
(4) That all necessary acts to further assure the land to the purchaser will be done.

Enforcement of obligations

20.26 The remedies available to the parties for the enforcement of their respective obligations which are considered here apply to those contained in deeds made prior to the operation of the Property (NI) Order 1997. They depend partly on the terms of the agreement and partly on the general law.[76]

Original parties

20.27 When entering into a conveyance of freehold land the parties are bound by the covenants because there is privity of contract between them. The original covenantee can usually enforce the covenant against the original covenantor both at common law and in equity.

Successors in title

20.28 At common law it is difficult to enforce freehold covenants, particularly the burden, against successors in title because privity of contract no longer exists. There can be no privity of estate as it is not an applicable concept.

The situation has been improved by equity which has developed rules providing for the direct enforcement of the burden of restrictive covenants against successors in title, subject to certain requirements.

(a) Benefit

At common law the benefit of a covenant passes to the successors in title of a covenantee if the following conditions are met:

(1) The covenant must touch and concern the land of the covenantee. This means it must relate to the land itself and not merely be of personal benefit to the covenantee.
(2) The successor in title must have a legal estate in the land to be benefited.

---

[75] Cf paras 17.03-17.09.
[76] See Property (NI) Order 1997 paras 29.01-29.20 *re* the operation of art 34 which relates to the running of freehold covenants created by deeds made after 10 January 2000.

(3) The legal estate held by the successor must be the same estate as that held by the original covenantee.[77]

Equity largely follows common law and adopts the same principles. However, there is an additional requirement in equity for a plaintiff seeking to enforce the benefit of a restrictive covenant. To succeed he must establish not only that he holds the property to which the benefit relates, but also that the benefit has actually passed to him. This may be by express assignment or by annexation, express or implied.

(b) Burden

At common law the burden does not pass directly to successors in title of the covenantor. In equity it may do if:

(1) the covenant is restrictive;

(2) the plaintiff is the owner of the land intended to be benefited; and

(3) there is a clear intention that the burden was intended to run.[78]

The possibility of enforcing the burden of a restrictive covenant to bind successors does not extend to a *bona fide* purchaser for value without notice. However such a person may be fixed with constructive notice of matters discoverable by normal searches. Registration of a deed of covenant makes the covenant enforceable against a subsequent purchaser whether or not he has notice of it.[79]

In relation to a positive covenant, the burden does not run with the land at all and it is not possible to directly enforce it against a successor of the covenantor unless, on a true construction, the covenant amounts to a grant of easement.

In any case, when land subject to covenants is conveyed, the deed invariably contains an undertaking by the purchaser to indemnify the vendor against future breaches and in this way the covenant might be enforceable indirectly against the successors in title. This is a cumbersome process which in many instances will not prove practicable, for example because of the death or disappearance of the original covenantor.[80]

There is an argument that any party deriving benefit from a conveyance must also accept any burden created by it,[81] although this principle may be limited to a condition relating to the use of the benefit.

---

[77] Conveyancing Act 1881, s 58 deems covenants to be made with the covenantee his heirs and assigns without any express provision being made. These implied words do not cover persons who do not hold the same estate in the property.

[78] See *Tulk* v *Moxhay* (1848) 2 Ph 774 which sets out the principles and developed the rules relating to the running of restrictive covenants.

[79] Registration of Deeds Act (NI) 1970, s 4.

[80] At common law there are other indirect ways of enforcement, but these are of little practical significance. For example, the purchaser can be granted a determinable/conditional estate or the land can be conveyed to the purchaser subject to a rent charge in respect of which a right of re-entry is reserved for non-payment and breach of any covenant which touches and concerns the land.

[81] *Halsall* v *Brizell* [1957] Ch 169.

Building schemes[82]

20.29 A common situation for the imposition of restrictive covenants is a housing development and, in such a case, it is to the mutual benefit of the site owners for the restrictions to be uniform. When the development is completed, if the developer has disposed of each site by way of conveyance, he no longer retains any interest in the land. Under the normal rules the purchasers would then be prevented from enforcing the covenants against their neighbours unless each expressly covenanted with the others.

In the case of obligations which are not being enforced by a lessor against a lessee the requirements which must normally be satisfied to enable restrictive covenants to be enforced by and against successors in title are modified when the covenants are originally created in a building or estate scheme under the rules in *Elliston v Reacher*.[83] These are:

(1) The plaintiff and the defendant must derive title from a common vendor.

(2) Prior to selling the lands to which the plaintiff and defendant are respectively entitled the vendor must have laid out his land, or a defined part of it, (including the plaintiff's and defendant's plots) for sale in lots subject to restrictions intended to be imposed on all the plots which, though varying in detail, are consistent with a general development scheme.

(3) The restrictions in question must have been intended by the common vendor to be, and must actually be, for the benefit of all the plots intended to be sold.

(4) Both the plaintiff and the defendant, or their predecessors in title, must have purchased their individual plots on the understanding that the restrictions imposed on each sale were intended to enure for the benefit of all other plots included in the general scheme.

Although some of these requirements appear to have been relaxed and modified in subsequent cases,[84] they may still be used as a starting point for consideration of covenants in an estate scheme.[85]

---

[82] See *Rhone v Stephens* [1994] 2 All ER 65.
[83] [1908] 2 Ch 374.
[84] See *eg, Re Dolphin's Conveyance* [1970] Ch 654. Nevertheless the courts have shown themselves willing to grant substantial damages as is illustrated in the case of *Costain Property Developments Ltd v Finlay & Co Ltd* [1989] 1 EGLR 237 and *Transworld Land Co Ltd v J Sainsbury plc* [1990] 2 EGLR 225. The House of Lords subsequently decided on appeal (1997) 23 EG 141 not to compel the tenant to operate a business which, from the tenant's point of view was unsound. Although a landlord may still make a claim in damages, it is difficult to quantify the amount. However, the landlord was successful in obtaining a decree of specific performance.
[85] See *eg, Emile Elias & Co Ltd v Pine Groves Ltd* (1993) 66 P&CR 1.

REMEDIES FOR BREACH OF COVENANT

Action for damages

20.30 At common law, the covenantee can normally sue for breach of contract and recover damages but if he has parted with the land he is unlikely to obtain more than a nominal amount. He may also seek an equitable remedy such as a prohibitory or mandatory injunction or, in the case of a positive covenant, an order for specific performance. Damages can also be awarded in lieu of an injunction under the Judicature (NI) Act 1978, section 92.

When the court refuses to grant an injunction to restrain breach of a restrictive covenant damages may be awarded in lieu.[86] The measure of damages is calculated by estimating the amount which the plaintiff might reasonably have been expected to receive for the release of the covenant. Where the court has no jurisdiction to entertain an application for an injunction, as in a case where it is too late to seek such relief, damages may be calculated by reference to the extent to which the plaintiff's interests have been adversely affected by the breach.[87]

The Property (NI) Order 1997, article 45 confirms that an action for sums due under the covenant and an action for damages, both pecuniary and non-pecuniary, are available for breach of a covenant to which article 34 applies. That is a covenant of a type specified contained in a deed of conveyance of a fee simple made after 10 January 2000. Article 45 does not affect the remedies available for breaches of covenants in conveyances made before that date.

Injunction

20.31 A plaintiff attempting to enforce the burden of a restrictive covenant against a successor in title of the original covenantor has to rely on an equitable interest, so the remedy available to the him is also equitable. He can seek a prohibitory injunction to restrain a threatened breach or to have the defendant desist from acting contrary to his obligations. For example, where a tenant is breaching a user covenant. Alternatively, the plaintiff can seek a mandatory injunction requiring a breach which has already occurred to be remedied and to compel the defendant to take the action required by the covenant. Damages may also be available in addition to or in lieu of an injunction. An injunction may be more appropriate, depending on the circumstances of the case.

---

[86] The question of the supposed settled practice of the court to award damages rather than specific performance or an injunction in the case of breach of a "keep open" covenant was considered by the House of Lords in *Co-Operative Insurance Society Ltd* v *Argyll Stores (Holdings) Ltd* [1997] 3 All ER 297 when a supermarket was closed in breach of a 'keep open' covenant. It was held that there was a settled practice that mandatory injunctions requiring a tenant to carry on a business would not be granted. Whilst the decision on whether to grant specific performance was always for the judge's discretion, the settled practice should only be departed from on special occasions.

[87] See *Jaggard* v *Sawyer* [1995] 1 All ER 189 and *Gafford* v *Graham and anor* TLR 1 May 1998.

An injunction is a discretionary remedy. The court may take into account the characteristics of the land and the surrounding circumstances in considering whether to grant it.

The Property (NI) Order 1997, article 45 confirms that proceedings for an injunction or other equitable relief are available for breach to which article 34 applies. That is a covenant of a type specified contained in a deed of conveyance of a fee simple made after 10 January 2000. Again this will not affect the law relating to covenants contained in conveyances made before that date.

Remedies relating to leases and fee farm grants

20.32 These are considered under leasehold law.[88]

MODIFICATION AND REMOVAL OF COVENANTS

20.33 The Property (NI) Order 1978 provides for the modification or extinguishment of impediments to the enjoyment of land. Impediments are defined in article 3 to include restrictive covenants and positive covenants to pay for or execute works on land.

An application may be made to the Lands Tribunal to modify or extinguish a relevant impediment by anyone interested, including a prospective purchaser. Under article 5(5), in determining whether to exercise its powers the Tribunal takes into account factors such as change in the character of the locality and public interest.

The tribunal has power to modify or extinguish impediments if satisfied that they unreasonably impede the enjoyment of the land, and to order payment of compensation to the covenantor. Any order made binds all persons interested in the impediment and must be registered in the Land Registry or Registry of Deeds as appropriate.

The provisions apply to both freehold and leasehold estates but under article 5(2), no application may be made to the Lands Tribunal if the relevant covenant is contained in a lease which has run less than 21 years, except with the permission of the Tribunal. It should also be possible to make an application in relation to covenants which are enforceable under the Property (NI) Order 1997.

The provisions have proved significant because before the introduction of the 1978 Order it was possible for ground landlords to extort significant amounts of money for agreeing the removal or relaxation of restrictive covenants where there was no valid interest to protect. Now, if a landlord can establish a valid subsisting interest such as ownership of neighbouring property, the Lands Tribunal will not make an order.

---

[88] Cf paras 19.14-19.28.

CHAPTER TWENTY ONE

INCORPOREAL HEREDITAMENTS

Introduction

21.01 A corporeal hereditament is a physical object generally consisting of land and buildings. An incorporeal hereditament is an intangible right which does not confer ownership of land.

Incorporeal hereditaments are minor interests in land which were originally recognised as being part of real property and governed by the feudal law of inheritance. They were said to lie "in grant" which meant that they could be created by deed only.

Incorporeal hereditaments are legal rights recognisable at common law and enforceable against successors in title of both parties. They do not physically exist at all but nevertheless may have some value independently of the land which they benefit. Where they do exist they may be of critical importance to the enjoyment of the land which they benefit. In particular circumstances an incorporeal hereditament may command a relatively high price, for example, when a right of way is purchased to provide an essential means of access.

EASEMENTS

21.02 An easement is a right which is enjoyed by an owner of land over land of another. While there are a number of well recognised rights which may qualify as easements, the law is continually evolving and new situations may arise in which new types of easement may be created.[89]

An easement has the following four essential features.

Dominant and servient tenement

21.03 An easement involves two pieces of land. The land which enjoys the benefit of the easement is known as the dominant tenement. The land over which the easement exists and is exercised is known as the servient tenement. For example, the owner of land A may have a right of way over land B owned by a neighbour. Land A is the dominant tenement and land B the servient tenement.

An easement can exist only if it is appurtenant (annexed) to the land comprised in the dominant tenement. This means that it must benefit the land and be more than a right available to the owner in a personal capacity. An easement, unlike a *profit à prendre*, cannot exist in gross (independently of land) without a

---

[89] "The category of servitudes and easements must alter and expand with the changes that take place in the circumstances of mankind" per Lord St Leonards in *Dyce* v *Lady James Hay* (1852) 1 Macq 305.

dominant tenement and cannot simply be for the benefit of a particular person or group.

Accommodation of dominant tenement

21.04 The easement must benefit the dominant land and improve it in some way in terms of amenity, utility or convenience. The servient tenement must be in sufficient proximity to the dominant tenement to confer a practical benefit on it. A right which confers a personal advantage only on the owner for the time being of a particular piece of land is not an easement, but merely a licence. This is often a matter of interpretation.[90]

Ownership or occupation by different persons

21.05 The dominant and servient tenements should usually be held under separate ownership; although an easement may exist where one person owns both properties, provided that the occupation of them is not common.

Subject-matter of a grant

21.06 The right must be capable of forming the subject-matter of a grant. Hypothetically all easements must be created by deed, so every purported right must belong to a category of interests which are capable of being conveyed. This means that the right must be of a type which can be transferred by deed from one person to another and is broadly in line with a group of rights already recognised as easements, such as rights of way, light, support and water.

Common types of easement

Rights of way
21.07 These are perhaps the most common type of easement. They may be either general, in that they can be used at any time in any way, or limited by some restriction, such as being on foot only.

Rights of light
21.08 These rights can be acquired only in respect of a window or aperture in a building. The amount of light to which a dominant owner is entitled by way of easement is fairly limited. He can successfully claim only light necessary for the use of the building for its particular purpose at the time it was built. However, the right to a higher degree of light may be acquired by prescription.

Rights of water
21.09 There are many kinds of rights concerning water which are capable of being recognised as easements. Some rights, such as the right to a flow of water from other land or a right to draw water from a well, are similar to natural rights. In other cases the right, for example, to a flow of water through an artificial watercourse or the right to water cattle in a stream has been upheld as an easement.

---

[90] Cf Licences paras 22.02-22.08.

Rights of support

21.10 A natural right of support exists only in respect of the land itself, and a right of support for a building must be acquired as an easement. Mutual rights of support probably exist where buildings keep up each other. Where there is an easement of support, the servient owner has no duty to keep the supporting building repaired, but must not damage it.

PROFITS À PRENDRE

21.11 A profit is a right to take something from the land. Generally a profit relates to part of the land itself, such as minerals, turf or creatures living naturally on the land, like game or fish.

A profit may be created appurtenant to a dominant tenement like an easement. If so, it has to comply with the features necessary for an easement as described above and is then known as an appurtenant profit. Unlike an easement, a profit can also be enjoyed in gross independently of any dominant tenement.

Common types of *profit à prendre*

Pasturage

21.12 Pasturage is the right to graze animals on land belonging to another person and may be held in common with others. It is distinct from agistment under which only rights of grazing are conferred on the grantee and not possession of the land itself.[91]

Turbary

21.13 Turbary is the right to dig and take away turf from land. It is generally limited to personal use of turf for fuel. Common turbary rights enable a grantee to take turf from anywhere in a bog without being confined to a particular part.

Mines and quarries

21.14 Historically the right to mine and quarry was another common form of *profit à prendre* although its scope has been considerably curtailed by the Minerals Development Act (NI) 1969 which vests in the Crown most mines and minerals existing in a natural condition in land and the working of all mines.

Fishing rights

21.15 The private right to fish in inland rivers and lakes may be granted in the form of a profit. Such a right is distinct from the public right to fish in the sea and tidal waters.

Other sporting rights

21.16 The grant or reservation of sporting rights is subject to legislation relating to the protection of game.[92]

---

[91] Cf Conacre para 22.16.
[92] *Eg*, Game Preservation Act (NI) 1928 as amended, the Protection of Animals Acts (NI) 1952 and 1961, Wildlife (NI) Order 1985.

Timber

21.17 The right of estovers is an ancient right to take wood from the land of another and is usually restricted as to extent. It is possible to acquire wider timber rights subject to forestry legislation.

ACQUISITION OF EASEMENTS AND PROFITS

Statute

21.18 After the confiscation and resettlement of Irish land during the seventeenth century when statutes were passed to confirm the titles of grantees it was more common than it is now to create incorporeal hereditaments by this means. Nevertheless, statutory rights equivalent to easements or profits can still be created today when public bodies are charged with execution of public undertakings, for example in relation to water and electricity supplies.

Express grant or reservation

21.19 Easements and profits may be created in a deed by direct grant or express reservation and may be made independently of any conveyance of the land. For example, a deed which merely grants a right of way.

If a vendor sells part of his land to a purchaser he may grant easements or profits to the purchaser as part of the sale. These rights may then be enjoyed by the purchaser over the land retained by the vendor. In this way, grant favours the grantee (the purchaser).

Alternatively, the vendor may reserve easements or profits for himself when selling part of his land to a purchaser and those rights may then be enjoyed by him over the part of his land sold. In this way, reservation favours the grantor (the vendor).

There is a technical difficulty in the concept of exception and reservation of easements and profits. At common law a grantor cannot make a simple reservation to himself and can only except from his grant a part of the land itself or a pre-existing right over it, such as the right to mines and minerals. The creation of new easements and profits cannot form the subject matter of an exception because the rights come into operation only when the grant of the land is made.

One way in which the problem can be resolved is for the purchaser to actually execute the deed of conveyance to him from the vendor.[93] A conveyance containing a reservation in favour of the grantor and executed by the grantee operates as a grant of the land to the grantee followed by a regrant of the reserved right to the grantor. Even if the purchaser does not execute the deed the vendor still has an equitable right to the intended easement or profit, even if not a legal one.[94]

---

[93] It is not common practice to have a purchaser execute a deed of conveyance.

[94] Alternatively, by virtue of the Conveyancing Act 1881, s 62(1) X can convey part of his property to Y and his heirs to the use that X should have the easements and profits and, subject to that provision, to the use of Z and his heirs. The use in favour of X relating to the easements and profits is executed so as to vest the legal title to them in X.

Implied grant or reservation

21.20 If the creation of easements or profits is not expressly mentioned in a conveyance, it is possible that they may be created by implication on a true construction of the deed in the following circumstances:

Easements of necessity

21.21 An easement of necessity only arises where a landowner sells part of his land to another and there is no other access available to the part so sold. It does not arise where there is access, but that access is not deemed sufficient for development purposes in cases such as where planning permission is required for a new use.

Easements intended by both parties

21.22 A common intention must be established and this may be inferred from the circumstances.

Rule in Wheeldon v Burrows[95]

21.23 This applies only to the grant of new easements out of existing quasi-easements. Quasi-easements are rights which a grantor has exercised over one part of his land in favour of another part. If this latter part is sold to another person these rights have the potential to become full easements exercisable by the purchaser and his successors over the land retained by the vendor.

The rule lays down that, on the grant of part of the land owed by a grantor, there is an implied right for a grantee to have the benefit of all those easements over the land retained by the grantor which are necessary to the reasonable enjoyment of the lands transferred to the grantee provided that these easements relate to rights which qualify as quasi-easements.

For a right to qualify, it must have been:

(1) Continuous and apparent; this means that the right should have been used by the vendor on a permanent, rather than a temporary, basis and be discoverable by inspection;

(2) Necessary to the reasonable enjoyment of the land granted to the grantee; which is a less strict requirement than that the right be absolutely essential; and

(3) Used by the grantor up to the time of the grant for the benefit of the part of the land granted.

Conveyancing Act 1881, section 6

21.24 This also creates easements out of quasi-easements, but does so by extending the meaning of words used in an express grant, rather than by way of implied grant. It provides that a conveyance shall be deemed to include with the land all privileges, easements, rights and advantages etc, appertaining to it, or any part thereof, or at the time of the conveyance enjoyed with the land or any part thereof.

---

[95] (1879) 12 ChD 31.

Although section 6 may seem to be potentially capable of applying to all quasi-easements and profits, as long as they strictly qualify as such and the rights appertain to or are enjoyed with the land granted, its scope is actually fairly restricted. The main limitation on its operation is that the dominant and servient tenements must have been held under separate ownership or occupation prior to the conveyance.[96]

Presumed grant or prescription

21.25 If a right has been enjoyed for a long period there is presumption that it had a lawful origin. The courts have recognised in theory that easements lie in grant without requiring documentary evidence of their creation. The underlying policy is of "quieting titles". The factors to be taken into account in considering whether a prescriptive easement exists are:

(a) User as of right

The claimant must show that he has used the easement or profit as if he were entitled to it and it had a lawful origin. User by licence or permission will not suffice. The claim will fail if he acts in a manner to suggest that the user is not lawful or if his conduct was prohibited by statute. The user must have been *nec vi, nec clam, nec precario*, (without force, without secrecy and without permission). The claimant must also show that the servient owner acquiesced in the user as if the right were established.

(b) Continuous user

The user must be continuous for the claim to succeed. In the case of certain easements, for example a right of way, this has been interpreted as requiring regular user as opposed to intermittent user.

(c) Tenure

In England the doctrine of prescription is generally confined to freeholds on the basis that prescription involves a permanent right which is inconsistent with the concept of a lease. In Ireland prescription can be claimed against a limited owner. The courts in Ireland have taken a quite different attitude, perhaps because of the preponderance of long leases.

Acquisition by prescription

At common law

21.26 The courts are prepared to presume that a grant of the easement or profit claimed has been made if user as of right can be shown to have continued from time immemorial, which is fixed at 1189. This is clearly impossible in most cases and so the courts have adopted the rule that if user as of right for 20 years or more is shown, it will presume that user has continued since 1189. The courts may also make this presumption if user as far back as living memory can be shown.

Serious obstacles remain. The presumption of user from time immemorial can be rebutted by showing that at some time since 1189 the right could not or did

---

[96] See *eg, Long* v *Gowlett* [1923] 2 Ch 177.

not exist. Thus an easement of light cannot be claimed by prescription at common law for a building which is shown to have been erected since 1189. Again, if it can be shown that at any time since 1189 the dominant and servient tenements have been in the same ownership and occupation, any easement or profit would have been extinguished and any claim at common law would fail.

Lost modern grant

21.27 To avoid these difficulties the doctrine of lost modern grant was devised. Under this doctrine the courts are prepared to indulge in a fiction that the easement or profit claimed was the subject of a grant executed since 1189 but which has been lost and cannot be produced. The presumption of a lost grant can be invoked after a period of 20 years from the date the prescriptive user starts or by establishing user for as long as living memory.

The presumption will not be made if the grant was clearly impossible, for example where it is known that the servient owner was under a legal disability and could not have made the grant. Nor can the presumption be made in favour of a tenant making the claim against his own landlord.

Prescription Act (Ir) 1858

21.28 This statute was intended to resolve the difficulties produced by the doctrine of lost modern grant and the operation of the common law. It provides an additional basis for a claim to an easement or profit by prescription and does not exclude the other two alternatives. Usually, more than one method is pleaded.

An easement acquired by prescription cannot be finally established without going to court. The Act can only apply when such action is taken.

The claimant may bring an action for infringement of the alleged right or apply to the court for a declaration that he is entitled to the easement or profit. Alternatively an action can be taken by a landowner against the user of the alleged right for trespass.

The period for consideration by the court is that immediately proceeding the action. Therefore, in order to rely on the Acts, the claimant must be able to establish both the statutory period of user and that the user took place immediately prior to the action.

Periods of user

21.29 The Act provides for two different periods of user whereby easements and profits may be acquired. The shorter period is 20 years for an easement (not of light) and 30 years for a profit. If this period of user can be established the Act merely provides that a claim to a right cannot be defeated by showing that it was first enjoyed at any time prior to that period or that it has not existed since time immemorial or 1189. This is not of great assistance to a claim and removes only one of the common law barriers to establishing a right.

The longer period of user is 40 years for an easement other than of light and 60 years for a profit. Where a claimant can establish use for the longer period the Act provides that the easement or profit is deemed to be absolute and indefeasible unless it has been enjoyed with written consent.

User as of right

21.30 The Act provides that the user of the easement or profit must be as of right, *nec vi, nec clam, nec precario*, which same test applies to a claim at common law and under the doctrine of lost modern grant. However, the Act further provides that a claim under the longer period can be absolute only if it was not enjoyed with written consent.

To reconcile this with the common law rule that even oral consent prevents the user from being as of right, it has been suggested that oral consent defeats a claim only if it is given or renewed during the statutory period. If the consent is given at the beginning of the period, it must be in writing to defeat the claim.

Without interruption

21.31 An interruption involves at least interference, and possibly discontinuance, of the right. It must last for one year to be effective in defeating the claim; but time does not begin to run until the claimant has notice of the interruption and the identity of the person making it.

The claimant can still establish his right by prescription despite an interruption if he can show that he has not submitted to or acquiesced in the interruption for a period of one year, for example by protesting about the interruption or by taking an action.

Deductions

21.32 Section 7 requires deductions to be made from the shorter period of user for any time during which the servient owner was under a disability or during which there was an action pending relating to the alleged right. The owner is under a disability if for example, he is an infant, lunatic or life tenant.

Where the claim is based on the longer period of user, section 8 provides that the term of any tenancy in the servient tenement longer than three years may be deducted in some cases provided that the person holding the reversion of the lease resists the claim within three years of determination of that term. Periods of infancy or insanity are not deducted.

Easements of light

21.33 The Act contains special provisions relating to easements of light which were the most difficult to establish at common law. An easement of light may now be acquired more easily because, if it can be shown that the right was enjoyed for 20 years without interruption and without express written consent, it is deemed to be absolute and indefeasible. This gives it the same status after 20 years as other easements enjoy after 40 years. However, it is not possible to acquire easements of light over Crown land.

There are no deductions for periods of disability. Further, an easement of light does not require user as of right and can be acquired by a tenant against his own landlord or against another tenant of the same landlord.

A defence to a claim for a right of light can be made if the user has been interrupted for a year. A notice registered pursuant to the Rights to Light Act (NI) 1961 constitutes a notional obstruction. If the notice is submitted to for 12 months this prevents a claim to an easement arising.

Existing easements

21.34 Although it is advisable to refer to easements in the deed in all cases, particularly where only part of the land is being transferred, the Conveyancing Act 1881, section 6, provides that any easements already established in relation to a particular piece of land are automatically deemed to be transferred with the land when it is sold unless a contrary intention is expressed in the deed. Accordingly if the property already enjoys the benefit of an easement, such as a right of way over adjoining land, the easement automatically passes with the property.

Section 6 can also operate to convert into easements rights which did not exist as easements prior to the conveyance. Further, it may apply where part of the land enjoying the easement is being conveyed. In that case, there should be evidence that the easement was intended to benefit the part conveyed and no contrary intention is expressed in the conveyance.

EXTINGUISHMENT OF EASEMENTS AND PROFITS

Statute

21.35 A statute may extinguish an easement or profit expressly or by implication, for example by compulsory acquisition of land under the Local Government Act (NI) 1972.

Release

21.36 The owner of an easement or profit may release it expressly or impliedly. An express release has to be executed by deed at common law. Equity may allow an informal release where the dominant owner has by words or conduct led the servient owner to act on the belief that a release has been made, so that it would be inequitable for the dominant owner to rely on the informality.

An implied release may arise where an intention to abandon the easement or profit is established. Mere non-user is never enough in itself. It has to be inferred that the dominant owner had shown an intention that neither he nor any successor would thereafter make use of the right of way.

Nevertheless non-user for a long period may raise a presumption of abandonment. Such an intention may be presumed from non-user for a long period, such as 20 years. This will depend on the facts.[97] The presumption is rebuttable if there is some other explanation.

It is possible that abandonment may also be presumed where an alternative right is granted or where a substantial alteration is made to either the dominant or the servient tenement so as to make the use of the right impossible or no longer necessary.

If the right is a public right, such as a public right of way, it cannot be released by deed and generally can only be determined by statutory procedures, *eg* under the Roads (NI) Order 1993, article 68.

---

[97] In *Benn v Hardinge* (1993) 66 P&CR 246 the right of way had not been exercised for 175 years but abandonment was not established.

Unity of ownership and possession

21.37 If the dominant and servient tenements come into the ownership and possession of the same person, any easement or profit annexed to those lands is extinguished. Unity of one without the other is not enough.

SIMILAR CONCEPTS

21.38 There are several other concepts which share characteristics of easements and profits, but which are quite distinct from them.

Natural rights

21.39 Natural rights are protected by the law of tort. They exist automatically and are easier to prove than easements which have to be acquired.

The right to support is a common natural right and it can also be acquired as an easement. The natural right is confined to support for land in its natural state, and does not exist in respect of buildings. No natural right of support exists in respect of buildings on the land and such a right must be acquired as an easement.

The right to water flowing in a defined channel is another common natural right which may be enjoyed for example, by the owners of land on the banks of a river. It is a right which can be protected if the water is dammed or diverted. There is no natural right to water flowing in a channel which is not well defined.

Public rights

21.40 A public right can be exercised by anyone at all, whether he owns land or not, and a dominant tenement is not required.

There is a public right to fish in the sea and tidal waters but the right to fish in rivers is generally subject to private agreement.[98]

The land over which a public right of way exists is known as a highway. It can be created either by statute or at common law by dedication and acceptance. Today public rights of way are created by statute when the Department of Environment adopts roads, for example under the Roads (NI) Order 1980.

To establish a highway at common law it must be shown that the landowner dedicated the way to the public either by express words, by writing or by conduct. User of the right of way by the public is strong, but not conclusive evidence, of dedication. Failure by the owner of the land to prevent the public from using the right of way is not to be interpreted as an intention to dedicate.[99] Dedication is usually inferred rather than expressly granted. To raise the presumption of dedication the user must have been as of right for a long time,

---

[98] Cf *Profits à Prendre* paras 21.11-21.17.
[99] For a discussion of the requirements see *Ards Borough Council* v *Franklin and another*, Cty Ct (Judge Hart QC) 1 July 1996 (Access to the Countryside (NI) Order 1983, art 3).

without interruption.[100] The public must then be shown to have accepted the right, normally by long usage.

User with the landowner's permission is not user as of right. It acknowledges that the way is being used not because the public has the right to do so but because the landowner has agreed not to treat it as a trespass in the particular case in question. In order to disprove any intention to dedicate it is a frequent practice for the landowner to close the way for one day in each year because this asserts his right to exclude the public at will.

Once a highway has been established, it can be extinguished only if it is closed or diverted by an order made under statutory provisions.[101] Obstruction of the highway or failure by the public to use it does not destroy the rights of the public. Natural destruction of the road or pathway itself will extinguish the right.

Local customary rights

21.41 These are rights confined to members of a local community, regardless of ownership of land and independent of a dominant tenement. The rights can be exercised by anyone who comes within the custom of the locality, as where parishioners exercise a right to use a path to their church. The rights are recognised at common law if they satisfy the four requirements of being ancient, certain, reasonable and continuous.

Restrictive covenants

21.42 These are similar to easements in that both allow the person benefiting from them to impose restrictions on another person's enjoyment of land. However, a restrictive covenant is a negative right, whereas an easement has a positive nature. Rights of light, water, air and support may be acquired as easements or by the imposition of restrictive covenants on the servient land.

The concept of a dominant and servient tenement, which is essential to an easement, is also relevant to a restrictive covenant if it is to be enforceable against successors in title of the parties to the original deed.[102]

Unlike an easement, a restrictive covenant cannot be acquired by long enjoyment. Further distinctions are also important. Easements have long been recognised at common law and are usually legal interests binding all successors in title. Restrictive covenants only achieved recognition in the last century and are enforceable against successors in title of the covenantor in equity only.

Consequently, a restrictive covenant is a less secure interest. It is not enforceable against a *bona fide* purchaser with no actual or constructive notice of the covenant and its enforceability against a successor in title of the covenantor is dependent on the discretionary exercise of equitable remedies.

---

[100] Cf Acquisition of Incorporeal Hereditaments paras 21.18-21.32.
[101] Roads (NI) Order 1993, art 68.
[102] Cf Enforceability of Covenants paras 20.19-20.22, 20.26-20.28.

Licences

21.43 A licence is a permission to do something in relation to land which would otherwise be a trespass.[103]

A licence is similar to an easement to the extent that it can confer rights over another person's land. However the differences between the two concepts are fundamental. A licence may exist in gross, independent of any dominant tenement and may confer exclusive possession or a general right to occupation of property, rather than simply the right to use it in a particular manner.[104]

---

[103] See Licences paras 22.02-22.08.
[104] *NB* if a purported licence gives exclusive possession for a term and at a rent it is more likely to be a tenancy.

CHAPTER TWENTY TWO

OTHER RIGHTS IN LAND

Introduction

22.01 There are several varieties of lesser rights relating to the possession of land which may affect the title. Although none of these interests can be properly classified as tenancies, their exact status may not be absolutely clear because the boundaries between the different rights are not distinct and the interests are not mutually exclusive. In the event of any dispute, if the person exercising the right is not a tenant, it may be important to consider the position of the parties and the nature of the right conferred.

LICENCES

22.02 A licence is a permission to do something in relation to land which would otherwise be a trespass. At common law it is regarded as nothing more than that and is not seen as capable of creating an interest affecting third parties.

A licence often involves personal relationships and may be a family arrangement. It is frequently informal and may not even be in writing. This can cause problems for anyone investigating the title because there may be no documentary evidence of the licence and it will certainly not be registered.

Features of a licence

22.03 The general principle is that a licence does not create any legal interest in the land, although it may be linked to an interest. A contract to grant a licence does not need to meet the requirements of the Statute of Frauds (Ir) 1695.[105]

The licence does not usually bind successors in title of the licensor. However, if the licensee has acquired an equitable right to the property, for example by constructive trust or estoppel, a successor of the licensor may be bound by the licence unless he can establish that he is a *bona fide* purchaser for value without notice of the licensee's rights.

A licensee uses or occupies land with the consent of the licensor and time does not run under the limitation legislation to establish adverse possession for the licensee against the licensor.

Licence or lease?

22.04 The distinction between a lease and a licence is important because a lease may attract certain statutory protection whereas a licence will not. The case of *Street* v *Mountford*[106] established that the most important factor is

---

[105] See paras 3.14-3.15.
[106] [1985] AC 809.

whether exclusive possession is granted, rather than the professed intention of the parties.

If an agreement confers exclusive possession for a term at a specified rent with an intention to create legal relations between the parties, a tenancy is created and the arrangement cannot be interpreted as a licence. However, if there is clearly no intention to create a tenancy, for example where a charitable, family, master and servant or vendor and purchaser relationship exists, a licence may be created notwithstanding the fact that exclusive possession is conferred with it. If the length of period of occupation is indeterminable and is not fixed by reference to periodic payments it is not possible to create a lease.[107] Further, if there is no right of re-entry and no provision for the landlord to have the right to enter and inspect (all of which would only be consistent with a lease) the agreement may be a licence.[108]

Bare licences

22.05 A bare licence is permission to do something not involving any contractual arrangement. It may be revoked at any time by the licensor and thereafter the licensee becomes a trespasser provided that he is given reasonable notice to leave.

Licences coupled with an interest

22.06 A licence can be included in a grant of a proprietary interest in land. An obvious example arises where a licence to enter land accompanies a profit, such as shooting or fishing rights. Such a licence is not revocable at will, nor by the licensor's death and continues as long as the proprietary interest lasts. If the profit is appurtenant to land it may be assigned to a third party with the interest in the land.

Contractual licences

22.07 A licence can be the subject of a contract which governs the terms of the agreement, including the licensor's power of revocation. It is possible that a contract may be implied, if it is not express, but a court requires clear evidence of a contractual relationship. When the existence of a contract conferring a licence has been established, it binds the licensor and he cannot revoke it contrary to the terms of the agreement. If he does so the licensee is entitled to damages for the breach or, if appropriate, an injunction to restrain revocation.

Estoppel licences

22.08 There is authority to support the view that the licensor and his successors may, in an appropriate case, be estopped from revoking a licence relating to land, even where there is no contract or grant of a proprietary interest. The licensee may acquire an equitable right by constructive trust or by estoppel. If the licensor induces the licensee into acting in relation to the land, for example by building on it, the licensor and his successor in title in certain

---

[107] *Onyx (UK) Ltd* v *Beard* [1996] EGCS 55.
[108] See *Venus Investments Ltd* v *Stocktop Ltd* [1996] EGCS 173.

circumstances may be estopped in equity from revoking it in a manner inconsistent with the understanding between the parties.

CARETAKERS' AGREEMENTS

22.09 A caretaker's agreement is often used to allow a person into occupation of property on a temporary basis. It is a useful arrangement pending finalisation of a full tenancy agreement or sale to the caretaker but must be carefully drafted to ensure that it does not defeat its purpose by creating a landlord and tenant relationship.

It is generally accepted that a caretaker's agreement does not confer any estate or interest in the land, but is a bare licence to occupy the property on behalf of the owner. The agreement may contain provisions requiring the caretaker to maintain the property and to deliver up possession on demand. It may even allow payment for the occupation without the caretaker necessarily becoming a tenant.

TIED ACCOMMODATION

22.10 The exact status of a servant or employee who occupies property owned by his employer is determined by his contract of employment. He is usually considered to be a licensee on the basis that possession is in law retained by the employer.

LODGERS AND GUESTS

Lodgers

22.11 A lodger in a house is not entitled to the same rights as a tenant because the terms of his occupation are determined by a contract rather than by a lease. The house and the lodger remain under the control of the owner. The lodger has no exclusive possession or interest separate from the owner and this prevents him from being a tenant.

Guests

22.12 The same applies to hotel residents, guests (paying and non-paying) and other similar occupants. Although a guest may have the exclusive use of a room as against third parties, the owner concurrently occupies and uses the premises for the purposes of his business and therefore the guest does not enjoy exclusive possession.

RIGHTS OF RESIDENCE

22.13 Rights of residence can be created by a deed, such as a deed of settlement, or by will and are generally intended to allow the surviving spouse of an owner to remain in occupation without conferring actual ownership of the property. It is important to consider the exact nature of the right conferred in each case.

Life estates

22.14 If the right of residence confers an exclusive right in a particular piece of land, it may create a life estate. The consequences of this interpretation are far-reaching because a life tenant has extensive powers under the Settled Land Acts 1882-90.[109]

However, in relation to registered land, the grantee of a right of residence is unlikely to be able to exercise the statutory powers of a tenant for life. The Land Registration Act (NI) 1970, section 47, provides that where a right of residence, whether general or exclusive, is granted by deed or by will, such right shall be deemed to be personal to the grantee.

This means that the benefit of the right does not run with the land and can only be exercised by the grantee, but the burden binds the successors in title of the grantor who are obliged to recognise the right during the lifetime of the grantee.

Licence

22.15 If a right of residence is not created in such a way as to be a life estate it may be construed as a licence. There is little authoritative support for this view but it does seem to be consistent with the real nature of the right intended. The alternative suggestions of it being a trust, lien or annuity charged on land, would confer on it anomalous characteristics, such as requiring it to be defined in monetary terms that are unlikely to accord with the intentions of the grantor.

AGRICULTURAL ARRANGEMENTS

Conacre

22.16 Conacre is a popular system of farming land which does not amount to a tenancy agreement. It confers the right to till land, sow crops, and harvest them, amounting to a licence. The owner of the land retains the occupation while the licensee has the right to farm the land and access to it for that purpose. Conacre agreements often operate for 11 months from 1 November each year and may continue for successive seasons.

There is no necessity to create a conacre agreement by deed and it is normally created by contract. Although it may in practice be created orally, written evidence may be required to enforce it.[110]

Conacre does not involve any sub-letting or disposal of land and does not infringe any covenant against sub-letting or otherwise parting with possession binding the owner.

Agistment

22.17 Agistment is the right to graze livestock on the land of another. It is not a tenancy agreement and does not constitute a demise of the land or a parting with possession. It is not a letting of land itself but a grazing of the grass only, more in the nature of a *profit à prendre* than a tenancy.[111] The occupation of the land remains with the owner.

Agistment is created by contract which confers a licence on the grantee to use the land and may not be revoked at will. It also may be created orally, but again

---

[109] For full consideration of the arguments see *Dent* v *Dent* [1996] 1 All ER 659.
[110] The provisions of the Statute of Frauds (Ir) 1695 do not apply to a conacre agreement.
[111] Cf paras 19.01-19.02.

there may be enforcement problems. The contract is normally for 11 months duration from 1 November and may be for several years in succession. In these respects it is similar to a conacre agreement and also does not need to be created by deed.

Possession of the land remains in the owner and, consequently agistment does not constitute a sub-letting. Nor can the payments made for it be interpreted as rent.

PROPRIETARY ESTOPPEL

22.18 Estoppel in equity usually works only defensively so as to prevent a party asserting his rights. As such it does not operate to perfect an imperfect gift. However estoppel can in some cases be used offensively in order that the imperfect gift can be perfected. Proprietary estoppel is one of the qualifications to the general rule that a person who spends money on improving property of another has no claim to reimbursement or to any proprietary interest in the property.

Proprietary estoppel is permanent in effect and it is also capable of operating positively so as to confer a right of action. It arises when a person is encouraged to act to his detriment by the representation or encouragement of another so that it would be unconscionable for that other to insist on his strict legal rights. The doctrine appears to be of early origin but has been resurrected in recent years and its scope is not decisively determined.

A straightforward example of a case where proprietary estoppel arose is *Dillwyn* v *Llewelyn*[112] where a father put his son into possession of land without a conveyance. It was intended that the son should build a house on the land. The son successfully claimed that the land should be formally conveyed to him. In expending a large sum of money on building the house with the encouragement of his father, the son acquired a right to call on his father to perform the contract and complete the imperfect obligation that was made.

The doctrine has also been used successfully to obtain relief by disappointed beneficiaries who believed that they would inherit property from testators but found that their expectations were not realised on the death of the testator.[113]

In the case of *Wayling* v *Jones*[114] the principle was further developed:

(1) There must be a sufficient link between the promises relied on and the conduct which constitutes the detriment;

(2) The promises relied on do not have to be the sole inducement for the conduct; it is sufficient that they are an inducement;

(3) Once it has been established that promises were made and that there has been conduct by the claimant of such a nature that inducement may be inferred then the burden of proof shifts to the owner to show that the claimant did not rely on the promises.

---

[112] (1862) 4 De GF&J 517.
[113] *Durant* v *Heritage* [1994] EGCS 134 and *Wayling* v *Jones* (1993) 69 P&CR 170 (CA).
[114] (1993) 69 P&CR 170 (CA).

The extent of the equity is to have made good, so far as may fairly be done between the parties, the expectations of the claimant which the owner has encouraged. If, for example, the claimant's expectation is that he could stay in a house for the rest of his life, this may not be given effect in such a way as to confer a life tenancy upon him which would confer rights under the Settled Land Acts 1882-90 and give him a greater interest than he was entitled to expect.

Accordingly, the claimant may have to be content with something less than his expectations, for example, some form of lease at a rent.[115] In other cases it is possible that a full life interest may be given.[116] It is important to remember that the position of the owner also has to be considered in the court's search for the minimum equity to do justice to the claimant.

If the equity is established, effect is given to it in whatever is the most appropriate way. It may suffice merely to dismiss a claim for possession brought by the owner to enforce his legal rights or to restrain the owner by injunction from interfering with the possession of land. It seems that the equity created in such cases can bind purchasers and successors in title to the party whose conduct gives rise to the estoppel.[117] In relation to registered land the right comes within the Land Registration Act (NI) 1970, Schedule 5, Part I paragraph 15 and, as such, affect the land without registration.

In many cases justice cannot be done by the mere use of the doctrine by way of defence and the claimant has to be granted some right. Thus if the owner has made an imperfect gift of the land to the claimant and has not completed a conveyance, the court will compel him to perfect the gift by conveying the land. The result is similar to specific performance of a contract.

The appropriate form of relief has to be considered in each case. For example, the circumstances may suggest that the claimant is to have a lease, a life interest, a licence or an easement. In *Baker v Baker*[118] the only way in which the equity could be satisfied was by payment of money and *In the Matter of JR, a Ward of Court*[119] in the Republic of Ireland the court ordered that the property in which the respondent had successfully established an equity should be sold because it was in such a dilapidated state, but that another house suitable to her needs should be purchased.

The case of *Sledmore v Dalby*[120] shows that in some instances any equity found by the court to exist in cases of proprietary estoppel may have a limited life. The owner, Mrs Sledmore, was granted possession of the property on the basis that the minimum equity to do justice to Mr Dalby on the facts was an equity which had expired. The needs and interests of Mrs Sledmore were held to outweigh those of Mr Dalby.

---

[115] *Griffiths v Evans* (1977) 248 EG 947.
[116] See *Ungurial v Lesnoff* [1990] Ch 206.
[117] *William A Lees (Concrete) Ltd and others v Lees and others* [1992] 11 NIJB 44. See also the English case of *Matharu v Matharu* [1994] EGCS 87, where an equity arising by estoppel was held to be binding on a third party but the extent of the equity was limited to a licence to remain in the house for life.
[118] [1993] EGCS 35.
[119] [1993] ILRM 657.
[120] [1996] NPC 16.

In that case it was pointed out that the doctrine of estoppel exists for the purposes of enabling courts to do justice, modifying what otherwise might be the strict legal rights of the parties. If the supposed application of such a doctrine produces injustice, not justice, then something has gone wrong.

CHAPTER TWENTY THREE
EXTINGUISHMENT OF INTERESTS
ADVERSE POSSESSION

23.01 Adverse possession means occupation of land inconsistent with the right of the true owner. It is actual possession in the absence of the owner for a period sufficient to extinguish his title and create a possessory title for the new owner.

The doctrine operates under the Limitation Order (NI) 1989 ('the Limitation Order') to limit rights of action to recover land to a definite period, under article 21; generally 12 years, beyond which they are statute barred. It applies to both legal and equitable interests in land.

The intention of the doctrine is to quieten titles and confirm long established interests which cannot be proved by documentary evidence. It may also legitimise intentional dispossessions by squatters, although the courts in recent years have inventively interpreted the limitation legislation to overcome this difficulty.[121]

Intention to dispossess is not necessary. All that a squatter needs to show is that he made it clear to the world that he enjoyed physical control and intended for the time being to possess the land to the exclusion of all others including the owner with the paper title.[122] He must be able to show that he enjoyed *de facto* possession throughout the period upon which he relies. Title will not be acquired by the squatter if the owner, while having no present use for the land, had a purpose in mind for its future use and the squatter was aware of his intended purpose.

A person who assumes possession of land in the mistaken belief that he is the owner can, when the mistake comes to light, claim that possession has been adverse to that of the documentary owner for the purposes of the legislation.[123]

A documentary owner and a squatter cannot both be in possession at the same time. Where there is room for doubt the law attributes possession to the documentary owner provided that he retains some semblance of control and there is evidence of him having a continuing intention to possess. Activities by the squatter such as exercising ponies on the land, grazing animals occasionally, cutting trees, erecting or mending fences and clearing fallen timber for firewood may not be sufficient to constitute dispossession of the true owner, even though he made no use of the land. However, it seems to be a

---

[121] Cf para 23.04.
[122] *Buckinghamshire County Council* v *Moran* [1989] 2 All ER 225, *per* Slade J, followed in *Belfast City Council* v *Donohue and others* [1993] 5 BNIL 83.
[123] *Hughes* v *Cork* [1994] EGCS 109.

strong factor in the trespasser's favour if the only access to the disputed land is through his property and he is able to acquire exclusive physical control of it.[124]

Unregistered land

23.02 A person who has dispossessed the rightful owner of a fee simple absolute in possession may be able to establish that there are no third parties at all who have any claims to the property which could take priority over his own. In the case of someone dispossessing a leaseholder the position is not as simple. Although it is accepted as a general rule that a possessory title can be substituted for a documentary title, the nature of the estate established is not necessarily the same as that of the true owner.

Freehold in possession

23.03 The title of the legal owner is extinguished under the Limitation Order according to the relevant limitation period, but the possessory owner does not obtain a conveyance of the title. The reasoning is explained below where the courts have considered the point in relation to leases.

Leases

23.04 It is particularly important to determine the precise nature of the title acquired by the squatter in leasehold cases. After the Statute of Limitations was first introduced in 1833, judicial authority favoured the theory that a parliamentary conveyance or statutory transfer of the dispossessed owner's title was effected. The idea was that there was no actual conveyance; but the estate and interest of the original owner became vested in the squatter, whatever its nature. The fictitious transfer was then explained as a parliamentary conveyance or statutory transfer.

This argument was later rejected by the courts on the basis that the right of the lessee was probably extinguished and destroyed. Accordingly, it could not be transferred to the squatter.[125]

In a number of subsequent decisions, the courts followed a line of reasoning which operated against the squatter, taking the view that although the lessee's estate is extinguished by statute as against the squatter it can still be surrendered to the lessor because it remains in existence between the lessee and lessor. The lease itself is not extinguished.

When the lease is surrendered the lessor has a reversionary right to possession and may then eject the squatter because the squatter's possession becomes adverse in relation to him.[126] This decision enabled the lessor and the dispossessed lessee to legally manoeuvre the removal of the squatter when all hope of recovery of the property seemed lost. It even allowed the lessor to regrant the property to the lessee.

---

[124] See *Powell* v *McFarlane* (1979) 38 P&CR 452, *Tecbild Ltd* v *Chamberlain* (1969) 20 P&CR 633 (CA), *Wilson* v *Martin's Executors* [1993] 24 EG 119 (CA), *Redhouse Farms (Thorndon) Ltd* v *Catchpole* (1976) 244 EG 295 and in the Republic of Ireland, *Doyle* v *O'Neill*, Irish Current Law Digest 106, February 1996.
[125] *Tichborne* v *Weir* (1892) 67 LT 735, an authority which has been accepted, though generally *obiter*, in Ireland.
[126] *Fairweather* v *Marylebone Property Co Ltd* [1963] AC 510.

Further, the lessor could forfeit the lease for non-payment of rent by the dispossessed lessee leaving the squatter with no right to claim relief against forfeiture, as long as the lessor had not accepted rent from the squatter.[127]

By deeming the title to be extinguished and not transferred these decisions prevented the limitation legislation having anything but a negative effect. They also failed to implement the policy of quieting title.[128]

To resolve these difficulties the courts have developed a compromise estopping a squatter on leasehold land from denying that he has become an assignee of the lease, so as to be bound by the covenants. By implication, the lessor is then similarly estopped from denying the tenancy of the squatter by his acceptance of the rent and performance by the squatter of other obligations under the lease.[129]

Time does not begin to run against the lessor until the lease ends and there can be no adverse possession by the lessee against the lessor during the term of the lease.

Where the ground rent under a lease is not collected for six years or more, only the right to the arrears of rent for that period is extinguished and not the title. A fresh right of action accrues on each occasion that the tenant defaults and never becomes statute-barred. Even if the rent has not been paid for say 20 years, a landlord may at any time enforce payment of the last six years of rent and any future rent as it falls due. He may also bring an action to forfeit the lease for any non-payment of rent within the previous 12 years. However, the right to collect a fee farm rent does become statute-barred after 12 years non-payment.

---

[127] *Tickner* v *Buzzacott* [1965] Ch 426. However, in the Republic of Ireland the Supreme Court took a different view in *Perry* v *Woodfarm Homes Ltd* [1975] IR104, holding that the squatter is entitled to possession for the unexpired term of the lease. There is no assignment of the lease to him, but it remains an encumbrance preventing the lessor from entering into immediate possession. A dispossessed lessee who has lost his estate cannot surrender or assign it.

[128] Final Report of the Land Law Working Group para 2.14.19 recommends the operation of a parliamentary conveyance of the disentitled owner's title to the squatter with qualifications dependent on whether the squatter knows with certainty the title so acquired.

[129] In the English case of *Central London Commercial Estates Ltd* v *Kato Kagaka Ltd* (*AXA Equity and Law Life Assurance Society plc, third party*) [1998] 4 All ER 948, Sedley J considered whether after surrender of the lease by AXA (the dispossessed lessee) Central (the freeholder) was entitled to possession of the property by Kato (the squatter) which had been in occupation for more than 12 years. He held that any surrender by a dispossessed lessee is ineffective to allow a lessor into possession because the lessee's entire estate is held on trust under the Land Registration Act 1925, s 75(1) for the squatter. All that surrender is effective to do is to pass trusteeship from the dispossessed lessee to the lessor. Once the trust has arisen, the squatter has an overriding interest under the Land Registration Act 1925, s 70(1)(f) which binds the lessor on disposition of the leasehold. This decision provides a squatter on registered land in England with all the benefits and burdens of a lessee's estate under the protection of a trust. There is no similar provision in the Land Registration Act (NI) 1970 to the English provision allowing for a trust to arise after 12 years occupation by a squatter. Thus, where a dispossessed lessee seeks to surrender the lease to the lessor prior to an application for registration by the squatter, it is unclear what effect, if any, the surrender will have.

A right of re-entry under a forfeiture clause for breach of covenant is a right to recover land and is therefore barred if not exercised for 12 years. A fresh right of re-entry arises every time there is a breach which would entitle the landlord to exercise the forfeiture clause. In the case of continuing breaches of covenant such as failure to repair or user for a prohibited purpose, time continually begins to run afresh and forfeiture can be claimed at any time.

Even if the right to re-entry becomes barred, this does not affect the landlord's title to the reversion because he will have a fresh right of action when the lease expires. However, payment of the rent to the wrong person bars the title of the real landlord after 12 years.

Future interests

23.05 Time runs from the date on which the reversion or remainder falls into possession by determination of the preceding estate. If the previous owner has been dispossessed, the person holding the future interest must sue within 12 years from the adverse possession or six years from the new interest vesting in possession, whichever is the longer. Otherwise the squatter will succeed in establishing adverse possession against him.

Mortgages

23.06 A mortgagor's right to redeem is barred if the mortgagee has been in possession for 12 years, without acknowledgement of the mortgagor's title or any payment on account.

The mortgagee's right of action to sell the land or to sue for possession is barred 12 years from the date repayment became due and his title is extinguished. The right of sale arises when the power of sale becomes exercisable.[130]

The right to sue for recovery of principal monies is barred 12 years from the date the repayment became due, and for arrears of interest six years after it became due.

Estates of deceased owners

23.07 An executor or administrator in his capacity as personal representative can establish a title by adverse possession against those beneficially entitled to the estate which it is his duty to administer. However, an express trustee cannot do so against those beneficially entitled under a trust.[131]

A beneficiary entitled to a share in an intestate's property may bar the rights of the other beneficiaries by adverse possession. This may occur, for example, when a farmer dies intestate or no grant is taken out to administer his estate and one son takes possession of the farm to the exclusion of the deceased's other children. Taking possession in itself is not enough to put the occupier in the

---

surrender the lease to the lessor prior to an application for registration by the squatter, it is unclear what effect, if any, the surrender will have.
[130] Cf para 26.15.
[131] Limitation (NI) Order 1989, arts 44 and 43(1)(b) respectively.

position of an executor *de son tort* in respect of the property and does not prevent him acquiring the title.[132]

Registered land

23.08 In general the Limitation Order applies to registered land as to unregistered in relation to adverse possession. Rights acquired or in the course of being acquired are burdens which affect registered land without registration.[133] However, the Land Registration Act (NI) 1970, section 53(2), also confers upon a squatter, who claims to have defeated the estate of a registered owner, the right to apply to be registered as the new owner of the estate.

It is expressly stated in section 53(4) that the registration of a squatter must not prejudice any estate of any other person in the land, being an estate which is not extinguished by the operation of the Limitation Order. The registration of a squatter as owner of a leasehold estate arguably prejudices the ground landlord and there is some doubt as to the extent to which section 53 applies to registered leasehold titles.

In practice, the problem can be avoided by notifying the landlord of the squatter's application and giving him the opportunity to object to the registration proposed.

When the squatter's title to an estate is registered in the Land Registry it is registered in the same folio as the dispossessed owner's title, as if in effect there had been a transfer of title.

Limitation periods

23.09 Any action taken after the expiration of the limitation period is statute barred. Articles 20-27 of the Limitation (NI) Order 1989 relate to land. Generally, the limitation period is 12 years, but in the case of recovery of the foreshore it is 60 years, recovery of ground rents six years and recovery of land by the Crown 30 years.[134]

Running of time

23.10 Time does not begin to run against the owner until a right of action accrues. Abandonment or leaving land vacant is insufficient because, until someone else goes into adverse possession, the documentary owner has no right of action against anyone. Taking possession is only part of the evidential requirement to establish a claim. There must also be acts of ownership adverse

---

[132] *Pollard v Jackson* (1994) 67 P&CR 327.

[133] Land Registration Act (NI) 1970, Sch 5, cf paras 7.39-7.46.

[134] *Central London Commercial Estates Ltd v Kato Kagaku Ltd Ltd (AXA Equity and Law Life Assurance Society plc, third party)* [1998] 4 All ER 948 (Ch D Sedley J). if however a squatter does not register his possessory title and the dispossessed lessee purports to surrender the residue of the lease to the lessor it is not extinguished but it is deemed to be held by the lessor on trust. The lessor cannot disregard the interest of the squatter which ranks as an overriding interest equivalent to that under LRA (NI) 1970, Sch 5. It is recognised that this objective could not be achieved if the title is unregistered. See *Marylebone Property Co Ltd v Fairweather* [1963] AC 510 (HL).

to those of the owner and all others. For example, fencing the land, cultivating it, cutting hedges or stocking it may be sufficient when added to possession.[135]

Periods of adverse possession can be aggregated if the squatter transfers his interest to another. Time during which the lawful owner is under a disability or where fraud or mistake have occurred may be discounted.

Fresh accrual

23.11 Once the right of action has arisen, time may begin again if there is an acknowledgment of the owner's title. This may be in writing, by part payment, or inferred from conduct. It cannot be revived under any circumstances if the limitation period has expired.

Adverse possession on sale

23.12 The problem of adverse possession often arises on sale of land when a vendor is required to produce evidence of his title to a purchaser. Where a vendor has been in occupation of the land without having title to it and has no documentary evidence of his interest he has to establish his title by other means.

The vendor must prove that he has been in occupation in the absence of the true owner for a period sufficient to extinguish the true owner's title and to establish a possessory title for himself.

Where the vendor's title is entirely possessory it may be unwise for a purchaser to accept 12 years adverse possession and even 40 years may not be enough in some cases. Possession by the vendor bars only the rights of those to whom his possession is adverse and there may be others with an interest in the land unaffected by the dispossession. For example, remaindermen or reversioners.

The purchaser may require the vendor to trace the title back to a good root preceding the adverse possession, from there to the dispossession and then to at least 12 years possession thereafter. If the vendor foresees difficulties he may attempt to preclude these requirements by inserting special conditions in the contract stipulating that possessory title for the specified period of years only will be shown. Such a stipulation should be treated with great caution by a prospective purchaser.

If a purchaser is prepared to accept possessory title he should at least require some independent proof of the vendor's possession in addition. For example, he may request a statutory declaration from a person with specific knowledge of the situation over a number of years.

MERGER

Distinction between merger and surrender

23.13 This occurs by operation of law when an estate in land is acquired by a person already holding a lesser estate in the same piece of land. The lesser

---

[135] *Boosey* v *Davis* (1988) 55 P&CR 83, a trespasser cleared the land of scrub and occasionally grazed goats on it, but this was insufficient to constitute possession. Also cf para 23.01.

estate thereby merges with the greater one. If the lesser one is an interest or encumbrance only, the process may be referred to as extinguishment.

The distinction between surrender and merger is that surrender occurs where the holder of the greater estate acquires the lesser estate whilst merger occurs where the circumstances are reversed or where a third party acquires both. The distinction is less significant than the similarity as in both cases the lesser estate is extinguished.

Common law

23.14 A merger occurred at common law provided that the requisite conditions were satisfied, regardless of the intention of the parties.

The conditions required were:

(1) Unity of possession of the two estates in the same person;
(2) The person in whom the estates vested holding them in the same capacity;
(3) The estates both being legal estates.

Equity

23.15 A merger occurred in equity if it was the intention of the parties, particularly the one acquiring both estates, that it should do so. Where a merger occurred automatically in law, equity would give effect to an express or presumed intention to the contrary and keep the lesser estate alive.

Judicature (NI) Act 1978

23.16 Under this Act there is no difference between the approaches of common law and equity and merger does not occur if the common law conditions are not met nor if there is any intention to the contrary.[136]

---

[136] Originally comprised in the Judicature (Ir) Act 1877.

CHAPTER TWENTY FOUR

SETTLEMENTS

Introduction

24.01 A settlement is concerned with the successive ownership of land as provided in the particular instrument creating it. The essence of a settlement is a series of interests created by a single gift, whether by deed or by will. The legal title is fragmented in succession. Settlements are usually confined to members of the same family and are not commercially orientated.

Land is settled as long as there is a succession of ownership, either by strict settlement or by trust for sale. The word "settlement" is used both generally to apply to all kinds of arrangements whereby property is given to particular persons in succession and more specifically to any settlement which is not a trust for sale.

A settlement can exist in the form of a trust when land is given to trustees to hold on behalf of beneficiaries. Obviously, not all trusts are settlements because many types of trust do not apply to land or do not create the necessary fragmentation of interests in land.

Until modern times settlements were a popular and successful means of preserving property for future generations. Historically, the most usual occasions for making settlements were death and marriage, but new marriage settlements are rare nowadays.

The creation of strict settlements has declined for both social and economic reasons. Although landowners may be less concerned about primogeniture there is still a market for settlements today. Settlors remain anxious to preserve their land for the future by the most tax advantageous means.

STRICT SETTLEMENT

24.02 This was the classical type of landed settlement created to preserve a family estate through successive generations. A life interest followed by an entail was the most effective limitation since anything more restrictive would violate the perpetuity rules. The disadvantage was that no-one had an interest of commercial value and the life tenant was very restricted in his powers of management.

A landowner left his land by will to his eldest son for life and then to that son's eldest son in fee tail with provision made for the other members of the family, including his widow and younger children, by securing charges on the property.[137] A marriage settlement could be created upon similar lines, with limitations of a life interest to the intending husband or wife and successive entails to the children of the marriage.

---

[137] Cf para 18.10.

The restrictive position in relation to alienation and powers of management under a settlement was improved by the gradual introduction of powers for limited owners of land. The Incumbered Estates Court was set up by the Incumbered Estates (Ir) Act 1855 to supervise the sale of incumbered property and pass an absolute title to the purchaser. Any encumbrancers or creditors were repaid out of the sale proceeds and the balance was paid to the vendor or held on trust for those with interests under the settlement.

The most revolutionary provisions were introduced by the Settled Land Acts 1882-90 (SLA 1882-90) giving the limited owner power to sell the land free of all the interests under the settlement. Land is settled within the meaning of the SLA 1882-90 as long as there is an element of succession to its ownership. The SLA apply to both strict settlements and trusts involving land held in succession.

Infants

24.03 The SLA 1882-90 apply where land is granted to an infant. An infant can hold an estate in land but he is deemed to be the tenant for life regardless of his actual interest. The statutory powers of the life tenant may be exercised on the infant's behalf by the trustees of the settlement.

Rights of residence

24.04 There has been some controversy as to whether a life estate and consequently a settlement exists when a right of residence is granted. It may be that, unless it is expressly stated as such, a life estate is not created and the SLA 1882-90 do not therefore apply. It is possibly a form of licence.[138]

Where the land is registered, both a general right of residence on the land and an exclusive right of residence on part of the land are deemed to be personal to the persons to whom they are granted and are not to be construed as conferring any rights or ownership on them.[139] However, once registered as Schedule 6 burdens under the Land Registration Act (NI) 1970, the rights are binding upon the registered owner of the affected land and his successors in title.[140]

Tenant for life

24.05 The life tenant is the person who is beneficially entitled under a settlement to possession of settled land for his own life or for any other limited period. His interest is limited. It ceases on his death and does not pass to his personal representatives but under the terms of the settlement.

The SLA 1882, section 58, lists the various limited owners who are given the powers of the tenant for life but the list is not exhaustive. A settlement can exist without a life tenant and with no-one to exercise the powers of the life tenant. For example, where the land is settled by way of discretionary trusts and no beneficiary is entitled to any income.[141]

---

[138] Cf Licences paras 22.02-22.08 and Rights of Residence paras 22.13-22.15.
[139] LRA (NI) 1970, s 47.
[140] Cf paras 7.28-7.29.
[141] See para 25.14 on Discretionary Trusts.

When there is no-one to exercise the powers of the life tenant the land cannot be dealt with at all unless the trustees hold under a trust for sale or the beneficiaries are all *sui juris* (of full legal capacity) and agree to join in the transaction.[142]

The life tenant cannot assign or release his powers and in exercising them he must have regard to the interests of all concerned. If he sells his interest in the land the life tenant continues to be a trustee of the powers.

The settlor cannot restrict the powers of the life tenant but may confer additional or greater powers if he so wishes. In any conflict between the settlement and the SLA 1882-90 in relation to the powers of the life tenant, the SLA 1882-90 prevail.

Power of sale

24.06 It is important to appreciate that the position where a power of sale is conferred on trustees of a settlement is distinct from the position under a trust for sale.[143]

POWERS OF THE TENANT FOR LIFE

Power to sell

24.07 Under SLA 1882, section 3, the life tenant has power to sell the settled land or any part of it by way of conveyance or assignment, but not by sub-grant unless the practicalities of the situation so demand. He has power to convey all the estate and interest which is the subject of the settlement.

After the sale the land is freed and discharged from all the estates and interests attaching to it under the settlement.[144] They attach instead to the sale proceeds which are invested. This process is known as overreaching.

Power to lease

24.08 Under SLA 1882, section 6, the life tenant has various powers to lease settled land or any part of it. The lease can survive for its full term despite the death of the life tenant or other termination of his interest. The maximum term of any such lease is 99 years for building leases, 60 years for mining leases and 35 years for other leases. The life tenant's power to lease is now curtailed by the Property (NI) Order 1997, article 30 which prohibits the creation of any new long leases of dwelling houses (subject to certain specified exceptions) and by article 39(3) which provides that any power to create a lease shall cease to have effect save to the extent necessary to give effect to an obligation assumed before the appointed day, 10 January 2000.

Power to mortgage

24.09 Unless the settlement confers wider powers, the life tenant can usually mortgage only his own interest. There are limited statutory exceptions giving

---

[142] A trust for sale exists when the trustees are under an obligation to sell the property and to invest the proceeds on the same trusts as applied to the land see para 25.13.
[143] Cf para 25.13.
[144] SLA 1882, s 20.

the life tenant power to bind his successors.[145] In those cases the interests of the other beneficiaries are overridden.

Power to make improvements

24.10 Under SLA 1882, section 25 as amended, some works may be executed using capital money including the erection of buildings, making alterations to existing property, drainage schemes and road building. These items involve making actual improvements and are not merely repairs which should be met out of the life tenant's income. Under SLA 1882, section 26, if the life tenant wishes to make any improvements he must submit a detailed scheme for the approval of the trustees. By SLA 1890, section 15, the court has power to authorise expenditure without a scheme being submitted.

TRUSTEES OF THE SETTLEMENT

24.11 To identify the trustees of the settlement the following statutory provisions are applied in the order in which they appear.

The trustees can be:

(1) The persons with a power of sale, or power of consent to a sale, of the settled land (SLA 1882, section 2(8)).

(2) Any persons expressly declared by the settlement to be the trustees "for the purposes of the Settled Land Acts 1882-90." It is important to use the appropriate wording. In practice this is the most common category.[146]

(3) The persons who have a power of sale or are trustees for sale of other land comprised in the settlement subject to the same restrictions (SLA 1890, section 16(i)). This provision makes those trustees the trustees of the whole settlement.

(4) Any trustees with a future power of sale or trustees under a future trust for sale of the land (SLA 1890, section 16(ii)).

(5) If no-one qualifies as a trustee under any of these provisions, an application has to be made to court for the appointment of trustees. However, in the case of a settlement by will this is not necessary because under the Administration of Estates Act (NI) 1955, section 40(5) the personal representatives are deemed to be trustees of the settlement for all purposes until trustees are appointed. This appears to give the personal representatives power to appoint new trustees of the settlement. There must be a minimum of two trustees.

The trustees were left with largely supervisory functions by the SLA 1882-90 because of the policy to allow the life tenant to deal fairly freely with the land. The trustees retain a protective role in ensuring that the life tenant does not harm the interests of the beneficiaries.

The Trustee Act (NI) 1958 in general applies to all trusts and trustees, including settlements and trusts for sale within the SLA 1882-90. It does not affect the powers of the life tenant and does not prevent the impositions of special restrictions on the trustees.

---

[145] *Eg*, SLA 1882, s 18 power to raise money for equality of exchange or partition by mortgage.
[146] Nowadays most wills provide trustees with a power of sale in any case.

One of the main responsibilities of the trustees is the receipt of capital money and its application in proper forms of investment. The trustees are not answerable to the beneficiaries or third parties for any other dealings with the lands.

The power to receive capital money includes proceeds of sale or mortgage. The money must be paid to at least two trustees unless the settlement itself authorises receipt by a sole trustee. Under SLA 1882, sections 39-40, it is essential for the trustees to issue a receipt to give good title to a purchaser. This generally means that the trustees join in the deed for that purpose.

Another function of the trustees is to prevent the life tenant from completing a transaction which may prejudice the settled land or the interests of the beneficiaries. The life tenant must give a month's notice in writing of any such proposals to at least two trustees. If necessary, an injunction may be obtained to prevent the transaction proceeding.

The purchaser has no obligation to ensure that the appropriate notice has been given to the trustees and it is not for him to check that all the formalities have been complied with.

The trustees must invest or apply the money according to the direction of the life tenant and cannot change the investments without his consent.

CHAPTER TWENTY FIVE

TRUSTS AND POWERS

TRUSTS

Introduction

25.01 By definition a trust is a relationship between one person and another, based on confidence, by which property is vested in or held by one (the trustee), on behalf of and for the benefit of the other (the beneficiary). A trust can apply to any nature of property, not only land.

A trust exists where the legal and equitable interests in property are separate. It may be created *inter vivos* or by will. The settlor or testator gives the legal interest to the trustees and the equitable interest to the beneficiaries. The three parties are not mutually exclusive, but their roles are distinct and beneficiaries may, for example, be animals or charities rather than individuals.

The trust developed from the concept of the use. A use was a conveyancing device which could relate only to land. It was originally employed to enable interests in land to be created outside the rigid framework of the common law and as a means of avoiding feudal dues. Land was conveyed to A to be held by him to the use (the benefit) of B. At common law A had the legal title and B had no interest at all; but equity regarded A as the nominal owner only and required him to exercise his legal ownership for the benefit of B, the equitable owner.

The trust has proved to be a flexible alternative to the strict settlement and has adapted better to changes in taxation. There is sometimes confusion between a settlement and a trust. Although a trust was once regarded as a useful device for settling any kind of property on successive owners, any disposition which creates a succession of interests in land must now be regarded as a settlement.

If a disposition is a settlement, the provisions of the Settled Land Acts 1882-90 apply, the life tenant has fairly wide powers and the trustees have a limited role. On the other hand if it is a trust, (i.e. there is no succession of interests among the beneficiaries) the disposition is potentially more flexible, there are fewer statutory restrictions and the trustees can exercise a broad range of powers. In all cases the conflicting vested interests have to be balanced against each other.

CREATION OF TRUSTS

Statutory trusts

25.02 A statutory trust arises automatically by virtue of certain statutory provisions. For example, under the Administration of Estates Act (NI) 1955, section 2(3), the personal representatives of a deceased person hold his estate as trustees for the beneficiaries.

Express trusts

25.03 Most trusts fall into this category. Under the Statute of Frauds (Ir) 1695, section 4, to create an express trust of land, written evidence is required to prove its existence and the essential terms.

Three certainties are generally required.[147]

(a) Words

The settlor or testator must use words which indicate sufficiently his intention to create a trust rather than simply transfer the property to the donees.

(b) Subject-matter

The property and the precise beneficial interest to be taken by each beneficiary must be clearly defined.

(c) Objects

The beneficiaries must be clearly identified or identifiable when the trust comes into operation.

Wills

25.04 To create a trust by will, the will must comply with the formalities required by the Wills Act 1837 as amended by the Wills and Administration Proceedings (NI) Order 1994.

Secret trusts

25.05 If the testator wishes to conceal the trust by omitting reference to it or to conceal the identity of the beneficiaries, he may create a secret trust.

A fully secret trust arises where a testator leaves property in his will to a donee, with no trust appearing on the face of it, but communicating it to him independently of the will without complying with the formalities. It is essential that there is the intention to create a trust, that it and its terms are communicated to the donee before the testator's death, and that the donee acquiesces in its existence.

A half-secret trust also operates outside the will and arises when the donee is designated as trustee of the property by the will but the objects of the trust are communicated to him independently. Again, communication must be made before the testator's death with the acquiescence of the donee to the trust.

Implied trusts

25.06 A trust may come into existence by implication to give effect to the intention of the parties. Presumptions may be raised when intentions are difficult to determine. There are specific situations where an implied trust is presumed.

---

[147] But see Discretionary Trusts para 25.14 where the principles are slightly different.

Purchase in name of another

25.07 Where ownership is transferred to one person but the purchase money is supplied by another, the presumption is that a resulting trust exists by implication. This can be rebutted by evidence. For example, if property is bought in the name of the wife or child of the purchaser, there is a contrary presumption of advancement, because a husband will be presumed to be making a gift to his wife and a father to his child.[148] The result is arguably inequitable in cases where the advancement is made between other parties where no such presumption exists.

Joint purchase and/or joint mortgage

25.08 Normally where the legal title to the property is taken in the names of all the parties contributing to the purchase money, a joint tenancy exists and the survivor will succeed to the entire property.

However, equity leans against joint tenancies. When the parties contribute unequal shares of the purchase money and one dies, equity requires the survivors to hold the legal title to part of the property on trust for the estate of the deceased co-tenant to the extent of his share. If they contributed equal shares, no such presumption of a trust arises and the deceased's share vests in the survivors in the normal way.

In the case of money advanced jointly on mortgage, the presumption of an implied trust arises whether the money was advanced equally or not so that the lenders eventually get their own money back.

Mutual wills

25.09 Two people, usually husband and wife, each agree to make mutual wills leaving their property to the survivor and thereafter to named beneficiaries, in most cases their children.[149] When the first party dies, equity implies a trust to give effect to the intention of the parties. The prior agreement between testators not to revoke their wills without notice to the other is the essence of mutual wills.

The trust covers the property the survivor had at the deceased's death and that which he receives under the deceased's will. It may even extend to property acquired later. Any new will must take effect subject to the trust. Even when

---

[148] It was thought that this presumption was losing its relevance and was considered to belong to the propertied classes of a different social era, *Pettitt* v *Pettitt* [1970] AC 777, but in *Tinsley* v *Milligan* [1993] 3 All ER 65 the ancient presumptions were confirmed and it was held that a man who makes a gratuitous transfer of property to another for an illegal purpose is not allowed to rely on his purpose in making the transfer in order to rebut the presumption of advancement.. Then in *Tribe* v *Tribe* [1995] 4 All ER 236 the English Court of Appeal decided that there is an exception to this principle which applies where the transferor withdraws from the transaction before any part of the illegal purpose has been carried into effect.

[149] There were no reported decisions in which there were not mutual benefits conferred on the testators until *Proctor* v *Dale* [1993] 4 All ER 134, which interestingly suggests that a personal benefit to the second testator is not a pre-requisite for the application of the doctrine of mutual wills.

the surviving testator subsequently remarries the floating trust which arises on the death of the first party is not destroyed by the marriage of the survivor.[150]

To create mutual wills it is not sufficient that the wills are identical in terms. There are considerable evidential difficulties in establishing mutuality and it is advisable to ensure that any such agreement is included in the body of the instrument.[151] Any alteration made by the first testator to his will destroys the mutual effect and the second testator is not bound by the agreement.[152]

Resulting trusts

25.10 Where an express trust fails or does not exhaust the entire beneficial interest in the property, a resulting trust arises in favour of the settlor. For example, where S conveys property in fee simple to trustees on trust for B for life the trustees hold the fee simple on a resulting trust for S.

A resulting trust is founded on the intention of the parties and gives way to a contrary intention, if such can be shown. In the case of a voluntary conveyance for no consideration, it is inferred that the grantee holds the property on a resulting trust for the grantor. This means that where S conveys property to B without being paid for it, B holds it on trust for S. The presumption may be rebutted, as where the contrary presumption of advancement arises.

Constructive trusts

25.11 A constructive trust arises by operation of law regardless of intention. It may be imposed to prevent fraud or unfair advantage in respect of property and may be founded on a fiduciary relationship.

A constructive trust arises in specific situations and is imposed on the following persons:

(a) Vendor

When a contract for sale exists the vendor becomes a constructive trustee of the land for the purchaser. The purchaser is regarded as the equitable owner of the property until completion takes place and the legal ownership is passed.

(b) Mortgagee

When a mortgagee exercises his power to sell the land he is obliged to hold the surplus of the proceeds on trust for subsequent mortgagees and ultimately the mortgagor by virtue of the Conveyancing Act 1881, section 21(3).

---

[150] For a full discussion of the issues see *Goodchild* v *Goodchild* [1996] 1 All ER 670.

[151] In *Goodchild* v *Goodchild* the Court of Appeal was unable to infer any agreement between a husband and wife that would prevent the survivor from interfering with the succession. Nonetheless there was the plainest possible basis for concluding that the wife intended to impose on the husband a moral obligation to leave both estates to their son. The son established a need for reasonable financial provision and his claim on the husband's estate succeeded under the Inheritance (Provision for Family and Dependants) Act 1975, s 2.

[152] *In re Hobley deceased, The Times*, 10 June 1997.

(c) Fiduciary

Any profit or advantage secured by a person in a fiduciary position must be held on a constructive trust in accordance with the equitable principle that he must not profit from his position.

(d) Stranger

A person who is a total stranger to any trust or to any person holding property in a fiduciary capacity may become a constructive trustee if he interferes with the trust property or intermeddles with the trust affairs.

Void and voidable trusts

25.12 A trust may be invalid for a variety of reasons. If it is void *ab initio* it never commences and the trust property is held on a resulting trust in favour of the settlor. For example, if it does not comply with the rule against perpetuities, is illegal, immoral or offends against public policy.

If it is voidable, the trust remains in force until action is brought to have it avoided. It may be voidable if, for example, it has been created by duress, mistake, innocent misrepresentation, fraud or undue influence. Also, by the Insolvency (NI) Order 1989, a trust is voidable under article 328 if it was created within five years of the settlor being adjudicated bankrupt or under article 367 if it was intended for the purpose of defrauding creditors.

COMMON TYPES OF TRUST

Trust for sale

25.13 It is important to distinguish a trust for sale from a power of sale.[153]

A trust for sale exists where the trustees are under an obligation to sell property at the earliest convenient time, invest the proceeds and hold the investments on the same trusts as applied to the land. Usually a power is conferred on the trustees to postpone the sale at their discretion.

The full legal title to the property is vested in the trustees and can be passed to a purchaser. The beneficial interests are overreached and attach instead to the sale proceeds. The purchaser takes the property free of the beneficial interests.

Unfortunately where the land is held in succession a trust for sale is deemed to be a settlement and is subject to the provisions of the Settled Land Acts 1882-90 (SLA 1882-90) which place restrictions on its operation. The legislation was not originally intended to apply to a trust for sale and when it was realised that the provisions of the SLA 1882 were defeating the object of a trust for sale, special provisions were made in the SLA 1884.

These provisions allow the trustees to exercise their trusts to the full, including the sale of the land without the consent of the life tenant or the beneficiaries, provided that the life tenant has not obtained a court order and registered it against the trustees.

---

[153] Cf para 24.06.

It is therefore important to determine whether or not settled property is subject to a trust for sale. If there is a trust for sale it is advisable to search for a *lis pendens*. Where the life tenant has registered a court order he has the power of sale and the procedures of the SLA apply.

Where the trust instrument confers a *power* of sale on the trustees but there is no *obligation* to sell, there is no trust for sale. Again the trust is subject to the provisions of the SLA 1882-90 if the beneficial interest in the land is held in succession. In that case if a power of sale is granted to trustees they will automatically be converted into trustees of the settlement and the life tenant will exercise the power of sale with all the other powers under the SLA 1882-90.

Discretionary trusts

25.14 Under a discretionary trust the trustees have power to distribute income or capital to the beneficiaries at their discretion. No beneficiary has the right to any part of the trust property and receives only that which the trustees see fit to give him. The beneficiaries need not be named if they are a specified class, for example, a settlor's grandchildren.

An accumulation and maintenance trust is a discretionary trust for the benefit of minors where the trustees have power to make payments out of income for the maintenance, education and advancement of the beneficiaries and to accumulate the balance. The beneficiaries must take a fixed absolute or limited interest between the ages of 18 and 25.

A protective trust gives the beneficiary an interest in possession which ceases if he attempts to alienate his interest, becomes bankrupt or any other specified determining event occurs. The trust then becomes discretionary for the class of beneficiaries set out in the trust instrument.

Charitable trusts

25.15 A charitable trust is aimed to benefit society in general rather than definite persons. It has no precise legal definition but there are tax advantages attached to a charitable trust and it may be important to establish whether or not one exists. To assist in determining the question, Lord MacNaghten in *CIT v Pemsel*[154] classified charities as being in four categories:

(1) For the advancement of religion;

(2) For the advancement of education;

(3) For the relief of poverty; and

(4) For other purposes beneficial to the community, not falling within the other categories.

These are not mutually exclusive and a public benefit element should be present in most cases. This element is an objective question of fact rather than a subjective view of the donor.

The rule against perpetuities is modified in relation to a charity. Normally a trust cannot have the potential to last forever but this is allowed in the case of a charitable trust. However the initial vesting must take place within the statutory

---

[154] [1891] AC 531.

perpetuity period, which can be either 80 years or lives in being plus 21 years.[155]

Cy-près doctrine

25.16 A charitable trust will not fail for want of certainty because the requirement of certainty of objects is not as strictly applied as to private trusts and charitable objects may be purposes rather than individuals. If the trust is clearly intended to apply to charitable purposes only and such purposes fail, the court will ensure that a similar application occurs and will direct a scheme for the money, if necessary.[156] This is known as a cy-près application of the funds. In framing a cy-près scheme it is important to adhere as far as possible to the donor's intentions.

The Charities Branch in the Voluntary Activity Unit of the Department of Health and Social Services controls the administration of charities in Northern Ireland. There is no official register of charities but a register is maintained on a voluntary basis by the Northern Ireland Council for Voluntary Action.

Trusts of imperfect obligation

25.17 A trust which does not have a beneficiary, or is not enforceable by the beneficiary is a trust of imperfect obligation. In certain circumstances such a trust may be valid, for example, for the work of a particular institution, the erection of a particular monument or for the maintenance of a particular animal.

In these cases although the trust cannot be enforced and the trustees cannot be compelled to perform it, a court will not forbid its performance if the trustees wish to perform it. Effectively, such a trust is operative at the discretion of the trustees. Imperfect trust provisions which would otherwise be invalid may also be saved if the gift can be used for charitable purposes.[157]

ADMINISTRATION OF TRUSTS

25.18 Once a trust has been created the settlor, unless he has specifically reserved powers to himself, has handed to his trustees complete control over the trust property. The administration of trusts is now governed by the provisions of the Trustee Act (NI) 1958 and the Trustee (Amendment) Act (NI) 1962 which relates to investments.

Position of trustees

25.19 The appointment, retirement and removal of trustees are matters of prime importance for everyone connected with the trust.

Appointment

25.20 Any adult who can hold property can be appointed as a trustee although he should preferably be a suitable person for the position with no conflict of interest. Usually at least two trustees are appointed but a trust corporation may

---

[155] Cf Rule against Perpetuities para 18.28.
[156] Charities Act (NI) 1964, s 22.
[157] *Ibid*, s 24.

act alone. In some situations, for example, in giving a receipt for money, at least two are required unless the settlement provides otherwise or the sole trustee is a trust corporation. There is no limit to the maximum number, but too many may cause administrative problems.

The settlor or testator normally appoints the original trustees and the executors under a will are often also the trustees. The property is vested in the trustees as joint tenants. When the sole surviving trustee dies the trust property devolves upon his personal representatives (the executors or administrators) as trustees pending the appointment of new trustees.

Additional or replacement trustees may be appointed by the persons nominated in the trust instrument, the existing trustees, the personal representatives of the last surviving trustee or, as a last resort, the court.[158] If the beneficiaries are all *sui juris* and absolutely entitled to the trust property they may make the appointment. New trustees may be required where an existing trustee ceases to act through death, incapacity, absence, bankruptcy, or refusal. They act as if originally appointed under the trust instrument.

The method of exercising the appointment is governed by the terms of the trust instrument. The statutory power of appointment is required only to be in writing. However, in most cases it is desirable to make the appointment by deed because under the Trustee Act (NI) 1958, section 39, a deed of appointment operates automatically to vest the appropriate estate in the trustees without any separate conveyance or assignment.

When the court appoints the trustees or where trustees have been appointed out of court under any statutory or express power, the court may make an order vesting the land in the trustees.[159]

A trustee does not formally have to accept his appointment but acceptance may be implied from conduct. If a trustee wishes to disclaim he should do so by deed as early as possible. If he accepts he remains in office until he retires, is removed, dies, or the trust is completed.

Retirement

25.21 Retirement can be achieved under an express clause in the trust instrument or by obtaining the consent of all the beneficiaries. Failing that there is statutory provision for retirement under the Trustee Act (NI) Act, section 38 and again, as a last resort, the trustee may seek a court order.

Removal

25.22 A trustee may be removed in the circumstances specified under an express power in the trust instrument and by the beneficiaries. Under the Trustee Act (NI) 1958, section 35, a trustee who dies, remains outside the United Kingdom for an unbroken period of 12 months, desires to be discharged, refuses to act, is unfit to act or is incapable of acting, may be removed and replaced by the person nominated for the purpose of the trust instrument, or if there is no such person, by the surviving or continuing trustees. The court has

---

[158] Trustee Act (NI) 1958, s 35.
[159] *Ibid*, s 43.

an inherent jurisdiction to remove trustees in cases of dishonesty or incompetence. The welfare of the beneficiaries is the overriding consideration.

Powers of trustees

25.23 The statutory powers conferred by the Trustee Act (NI) 1958, sections 12-34 are additional to any express powers conferred by the trust instrument and are subject to any contrary intention expressed in it.[160]

There is no automatic power of sale but where a trustee holds property upon trust for sale or has been given a power of sale under the trust instrument, there are fairly extensive statutory powers relating to the conduct of the sale.

The receipt in writing of a trustee for any money or other personal property shall be a sufficient discharge to the person paying or delivering the same. The receipt effectually exonerates that person from seeing that the trustee applies the money correctly.

A receipt given by a sole trustee for the proceeds of sale or for other capital money does not discharge the purchaser except where the sole trustee is a trust corporation, a personal representative or is authorised by the trust instrument to receive capital money. Where there are several trustees they should normally all join in the receipt, although the signatures of two trustees are a sufficient discharge to a purchaser.

Duties of trustees

25.24 In the absence of any provision to the contrary in the trust instrument the duties of trustees follow well established principles. In general, a trustee must exercise the same degree of care as in his own affairs and must not profit from his position. There is a duty of loyalty to the trust itself and not to favour one beneficiary against another.

A trustee may not purchase the trust property nor receive remuneration unless expressly authorised, but is entitled to his expenses. Proper accounts must be kept and the beneficiaries given the information they require. Reasonable care must be exercised in making the investments authorised by statute.

Delegation

25.25 Generally a trustee must act personally and not delegate his powers and duties to others. He must look after the affairs of the trust himself and in particular be responsible for the receipt of trust monies. However, delegation may be expressly authorised by the trust instrument and in certain circumstances is inevitable, as where expert professional advice is sought.

The Trustee Act (NI) 1958, section 24, confers certain powers to delegate the administration of the trust to agents, even to the extent of the receipt and payment of money. This provision does not affect the principle that a trustee cannot delegate his discretion and if he does so delegate, will be responsible for any negligence of the agent. He must also keep a watch on the application and receipt of money.

---

[160] Some statutory powers cannot be removed by the trust instrument, *eg* s 16, power to raise money.

The Trustee Act (NI) 1958, section 26, also permits delegation by way of power of attorney for up to 12 months.

Variation of trusts

25.26 Normally a beneficiary cannot interfere in the administration of the trust. Nevertheless, if there is only one beneficiary who is *sui juris* or if there are two or more beneficiaries and they are all *sui juris* and in agreement, they can vary the terms of the trust or wind it up irrespective of the wishes of the trustees or of the creator of the trust.[161] Similarly, an adult life tenant can surrender or assign his interest.

Where there are unborn or infant beneficiaries it is necessary that an application be made to the court for a variation of the trust. There is a limited inherent jurisdiction to sanction a variation of administrative powers in an emergency situation to save the trust from destruction or considerable damage. The court's sanction can also be sought in cases of compromises of disputes as between the claims of various beneficiaries.

The inherent jurisdiction has been largely superseded by the Trustee Act (NI) 1958, sections 56 and 57. Both sections apply to trusts or settlements of any property, whether real or personal. To an extent there is an overlap between the provisions.

Section 56 provides in effect that the court may empower trustees in the management or administration of the trust property to perform any act which is not authorised by the trust instrument if in the opinion of the court it is expedient. The court may by order confer on the trustees the necessary power for the purpose of any particular transaction affecting the trust property including a sale, lease, partition, surrender, release, purchase, acquisition, covenant, contract, option, compromise or arrangement.

Section 57 enables the court to sanction a variation of the beneficial interest or to enlarge the trustees' powers of management or administration. The basis of the court's jurisdiction under this section is the approval on behalf of persons unable to do so themselves of arrangements to which all the parties who are able have already consented. The court will not assent on behalf of a person who can do so for himself. Anyone legally able to consent should do so because otherwise one dissenter can block the whole scheme.

There is another statutory power of variation under the Matrimonial Causes (NI) Order 1978, article 26. A wide power is conferred on the court to vary trusts in a settlement made for the benefit of the parties or their children.

BREACH OF TRUST

25.27 It is the duty of the trustee to act prudently, to comply with the general law of trusts and to comply with the terms of the trust instrument. Breach of trust includes negligence, taking a profit and making unauthorised investments. Some breaches are criminal, such as theft.

---

[161] *Saunders* v *Vautier* (1841) Cr & Ph 240.

The extent of a trustee's liability for his breach of trust is generally the direct or indirect loss caused to the trust estate, even if he made no gain.[162] Any profit made must be surrendered to the trust.

Where more than one trustee is involved in a breach of trust, the liability is joint and several. If one trustee has to pay more than his share of the liability, he may claim a contribution from the co-trustees involved. Where only one trustee is in breach, he alone will be liable against his co-trustees.

A trustee may be protected from being held personally liable for breach of trust if he acted reasonably, honestly and fairly. If the beneficiary was involved in any way his interest is then used to indemnify the trustee and may even be impounded.[163]

Remedies for beneficiaries

25.28 Whenever a breach of trust has been committed the beneficiaries are entitled to take action. There is a general right to recover trust property or to bring an action in respect of a breach of trust for a period of six years from the date on which the right of action accrued, under the Limitation (NI) Order 1989, article 42(1). In the case of breach of trust, this is the date on which the breach occurred and not when the loss was sustained. If a beneficiary has a future interest the right of action does not accrue until his interest falls into possession.

Trustees are considered to bear a special responsibility to both the trust property and the beneficiaries. The beneficiary's right to complain has been treated as persisting indefinitely unless the doctrine of laches applies so that in all the circumstances it would be inequitable to allow him to enforce his rights.[164]

By virtue of article 43 of the Limitation Order, no time limit applies to an action against a trustee where the claim is founded on any fraud or fraudulent breach of trust to which the trustee was party or privy, or where the claim is to recover trust property or the proceeds thereof retained by the trustee or converted to his own use.

Where the Limitation (NI) Order 1989 lays down other periods for bringing specified types of action those periods prevail. Under article 12 an action for the recovery of land may be brought within 12 years from the date when the cause of action arose.

In the case of fraud or retention of any capital of the trust by a trustee there is no statutory defence and no limitation period on a right of action. Instead the equitable doctrine of laches may apply. For the trustee to establish this defence to a claim it is necessary to show that the beneficiary has known of the breach of trust for a substantial period of time and has acquiesced in it.

---

[162] See *Target Holdings Ltd v Redferns (a firm) and another* [1995] 3 All ER 785 (HL). The question of the liability of a trustee who commits a breach of trust to compensate beneficiaries for that breach was considered and it was held that the trustee was not automatically liable for loss where the evidence in retrospect suggests that the beneficiary would have suffered such loss anyway.

[163] Trustee Act (NI) 1958, s 62.

[164] Questions of limitation and laches were considered in *Nelson v Rye* [1996] 2 All ER 186.

The remedy for breach of trust is account and restitution. The common law rules of remoteness are not relevant.[165] If, for example, a trustee transfers trust property to an unauthorised person who suffers the loss of that trust property due to some wholly unforeseen and unexpected circumstance, the trustee is liable.

It seems that considerations of causation require a distinction between a breach arising from an omission to act and a breach arising from positive action.[166] A positive action resulting in immediate loss constitutes an actionable breach *per se*, particularly where the breach is caused by trustees divesting themselves of the subject matter of the trust.[167] Where a breach results from an omission loss must be established and questions of causation may also arise.[168]

An honest trustee, who is deemed to have abused his position of trust, is a constructive trustee of his profits.[169] A trustee is not allowed to keep for his own benefit any unauthorised profits or advantages made in his position as trustee, even if he acted in good faith.[170] He is required to hold the property as a constructive trustee.

However, where a trustee accepts a bribe he has been allowed to retain the profit, notwithstanding the fact that he acted dishonestly and contrary to the interests of his principal, because the principal's own money has not been used in any way.[171] This is most unsatisfactory and is not consistent with the principle that a fiduciary must not be allowed to benefit from his own breach of duty.

It has been suggested that a different conclusion can be reached by following equitable principles. Equity will treat a trustee as having acted in accordance with his duty even where that duty conflicts with his own interest. Where a trustee has obtained a profit for himself or accepted a bribe, (neither of which equity allows him to do) equity treats it as a legitimate payment intended for the benefit of the principal.[172]

Tracing

25.29 When the beneficiaries have the right to make a claim they always have a personal remedy against a trustee, subject to any protection the trustee may

---

[165] See eg *Nestle v National Westminster Bank* [1994] 1 All ER 118 where the beneficiary was unable to show that the trustee had committed any breach of trust resulting in loss.

[166] See *Target Holdings Ltd v Redferns (a firm) and another* [1994] 1 All ER 118 (CA); [1995] 3 All ER 785 (HL).

[167] As in *Bishopsgate Investment Management Ltd (in liquidation) v Maxwell (No 2)* [1994] 1 All ER 261.

[168] It may be that the absence of the requirement to prove causation is limited to breaches in which trustees divest themselves of the subject matter of the trust rather than to any other or all cases of positive breaches by trustees. Although equity will look to the substance rather than the form, it may be advisable for an alleged breach to appear to be positive rather than to be an omission.

[169] *Keech v Sandford* (1726) Sel Cas Ch 61.

[170] See *Boardman v Phipps* [1967] 2 AC 67.

[171] *Lister v Stubbs* [1890] 45 Ch D 1 which is no longer considered to be good law.

[172] *Attorney General for Hong Kong v Reid* [1994] 1 All ER 1 followed this line of reasoning but took it further by imposing a trust remedy.

be able to claim in a particular case. This may be of little use if the trustee is in financial difficulties. The beneficiaries also have a remedy to follow the misappropriated property to wherever it can be found. This is known as the right of tracing.

At common law tracing can proceed against the vendor of land and a constructive trust is imposed on him in relation to the sale proceeds. Once the money from the property becomes mixed with other money or property it ceases to be identifiable and the remedy is lost.

However, equity recognises the right to trace property into an unmixed fund and further into a mixed fund if it can be identified. An innocent volunteer whose money has been mixed with another's may trace his money into the mixed fund or assets acquired with it although the mixed fund is held by another innocent volunteer even if the mixing has been done by him.[173] A beneficiary's right extends to anyone into whose hands the trust property comes unless he is a *bona fide* purchaser for value without notice.

POWERS

Introduction

25.30 A power is an ability conferred on a person by law to determine the legal relations of himself and others. It is the right to exercise, in respect of property belonging to another, one or more of the rights which are the normal incidents of ownership. A power may exist without any interest in property.

A power is the converse of a disability. By traditional definition a power is discretionary, not obligatory and there are no accompanying duties.

The distinction between a trust and a power is fundamental. A trust is necessarily equitable. Historically, the common law also had a limited view of powers but recognised a few, for example, powers of attorney. However, nowadays powers are more commonly created by statute, as under the Settled Land Acts 1882-90 and the Trustee Act (NI) 1958.

The primary basis of the distinction between a trust and a power is that a trust is imperative but a power is not. This can be illustrated by contrasting a trust for sale and a power of sale.

If land is given by will or by deed *inter vivos* to trustees on trust for sale there is a binding obligation to sell and the land will be treated as being converted into money (even if not in fact converted) on the death of the testator or on execution of the deed. This is still the position even if there is a power to postpone the sale and that power is exercised.

On the other hand, where there is merely a power of sale, whether in a will or deed, the land will only be converted into money when the power itself is

---

[173] This principle was established by Sir George Jessel in *Re Hallett's Estate* (1880) 13 Ch D 696 where a trustee mixed the trust money with his own and then purchased property with the mixture. The beneficial owner could not elect to take the property because it was not bought with trust money only, but he was entitled to a charge on the property purchased in the amount of trust money used in the purchase.

exercised and the person in whom the power is vested will not be compelled to exercise it.

It is recognised that the distinction between a power and a trust has become somewhat blurred over the years. A fiduciary power or a power in the nature of a trust, for example, cannot properly be brought within the narrow description. The question as to whether there is a trust or a power is essentially one of construction of the instrument creating it.

Power of appointment

25.31 This is a power given to the donee by will or by deed to create or modify estates or interests in property. It confers a right of alienation as opposed to that of enjoyment. The donee can declare in whom and in what manner the property is to vest, but he has no right of ownership over it.

A general power of appointment is created when the donee may make any appointment, including one in favour of himself. A special power of appointment is one where the donee is restricted in the exercise of the power in that he may appoint among a certain class of persons only or even be restricted to one person only.

A bare power is conferred where the donee has complete discretion in its exercise. A fiduciary power is conferred where the donee is put under some fiduciary obligation in relation to its exercise. The mere fact that the power is conferred on a trustee does not of itself make a power fiduciary, the trustee must have a duty imposed on him with respect to the power for it to be so. A fiduciary power may be exercised by the successors of the original donee.

In the case of a power of appointment of property, as in the case of a power of sale, the donee of the power, in the absence of fraud on his part, will not be liable if he fails to exercise it, nor will he be compelled to do so, except where the power has been given to a trustee in his fiduciary capacity. However, if there is a trust and the trustee fails to perform it, he will be liable for breach of trust and the court will also compel its performance.

A trust instrument may give what on the face of it appears to be a bare power of appointment allowing the donee complete discretion, but which is in fact a trust. Such a power is known as a power in the nature of a trust. It is construed and takes effect as a trust.

A general power of appointment is incapable of being a power in the nature of a trust. A general power confers on the donee a power to make any appointment he chooses. There is no defined class of persons in whose favour it can operate and it is incapable of enforcement by the court, so it cannot be a trust.

Only a special power of appointment where there is a power to appoint among designated persons or classes of persons is capable of taking effect as a power in the nature of a trust. The question is one of construction as to the donor's intention.

It cannot have been the donor's intention for the power to be in the nature of a trust if he has made express alternative provision to take effect in default of appointment. That means that he has made an alternative gift in the event of the donee failing to exercise the power. The mere absence of such provision is not conclusive evidence that the power is in the nature of a trust, though it may be indicative of such an intention.

Creation

25.32 There are no special formalities for the creation of a power of appointment but the validity of the power is determined by the validity of the will or deed creating it. A power of appointment is also subject to the rule against perpetuities which applies to determine both the validity of the power itself and appointments made under a valid power.[174]

Additionally a power is subject to requirements of certainty. The donor should provide sufficiently clear criteria by which to judge whether a claimant can be an object of the power. The rules do not seem to be as strict as in the case of a trust and it may not matter if the class of objects is so wide and fluctuating that at any given time it is not possible to make a complete list of all the objects.

Exercise

25.33 The donee in exercising his power of appointment must follow the conditions laid down by the donor and the general law. When the donee fails to comply with the formalities governing exercise of his power the appointee may be able to have the exercise upheld by reliance on equitable remedies.[175]

Where a donee has by his actions shown that he intended to exercise his power but has failed because the execution is defective for want of some formality or technicality, equity will try to give effect to it. However, equity will not execute a power which the donee fails to execute and will only intervene on behalf of certain persons, for example, creditors or purchasers for value from the donee, not volunteers.

Where the donee in exercising the power exceeds the limits set by the donor or by the general law, for example, by appointing to non-objects or giving larger interests than permitted, the courts try to save the appointment if at all possible.

The failure to exercise a special power of appointment or the exercise of it in a manner inconsistent with the purposes the donor had in mind may amount to a fraud on the power. Any appointment made for improper motives is regarded as a fraud on those entitled in default of appointment. Fraud usually affects the whole appointment which thus fails, leaving the donee free to make a new appointment.

The donee of the power, in the absence of fraud on his part, will not be liable if he fails to exercise it, nor will he be compelled to do so, except in cases where the power has been given to a trustee in his fiduciary capacity.

Determination

25.34 A power of appointment may be determined expressly if the donee executes a release or enters into a contract not to exercise it. Such a release or contract should be by deed.[176] A power in the nature of a trust may not be released because this would be a breach of trust and it is possible that a fiduciary power may not be released either.

---

[174] See para 18.28.
[175] Limited statutory relief may also be available *eg* under the Leases Acts 1849 and 1850.
[176] Conveyancing Act 1881, s 52(1).

A donee of a power may disclaim it by deed which does not destroy the power but renders that donee incapable of exercising it.[177] The power may still be exercised by other donees or their survivors unless the contrary is expressed in the instrument creating the power.

A power of appointment may also be determined impliedly due to actions by the donee inconsistent with further exercise of it, or where the purposes for which the power was created cease to exist.

Power of attorney

25.35 A power of attorney operates where one person authorises another to perform certain acts for him and can be either in the form of a general authority or for specific purposes. A power of attorney was recognised at common law and is now governed by the Powers of Attorney Act (NI) 1971.[178]

Creation

25.36 An instrument creating a power of attorney has to be signed and sealed by the donor. Thereafter the donee may execute documents and do whatever is required, in his own name, by the authority of the donor. He is not allowed to exercise the power for his own benefit. The acts of the donee are effective in law as if they had been done by the donor.

Exercise

25.37 So if the donee does execute a deed in his own name he should make it clear that he is acting under a power of attorney or he is at risk of incurring personal liability. Otherwise he can execute the deed in the donor's name and after the signature add that it is done by the donee under power of attorney. The purchaser of unregistered land is entitled to delivery of the instrument creating a power of attorney.

Revocation

25.38 At common law a power of attorney was revoked automatically by the donor's death, insanity, marriage or bankruptcy. In many cases it could also be revoked by the donor without informing the donee, leaving him in a vulnerable position if he was not notified accordingly. The Powers of Attorney Act (NI) 1971 altered the common law position to provide that the donee in such a situation incurs no liability. However if the donee is aware of an event, such as the death of the donor, which has the effect of revoking the power, he is deemed to know that the power has been revoked.

There are provisions particular to powers of attorney given by way of security which are distinct from other powers of attorney. A security power which is expressed to be irrevocable cannot be revoked without the donee's consent while the donee retains the interest in the property or the obligation under the power remains. A third party, including a purchaser, dealing with the donee is

---

[177] *Ibid* s 6(1).
[178] S 9 of this Act substitutes a new s 26 of the Trustee Act (NI) 1958 and confers a new wide ranging power to delegate by power of attorney, for a period not exceeding 12 months, all or any of the trusts, powers and discretions vested in trustees of a trust.

entitled to assume that the security power remains operative unless he knows it has been revoked.

In respect of all other powers of attorney, a degree of protection is also conferred on any third parties who have dealings with the purchaser. Where the power has been revoked but the third party has no knowledge of that fact, the transaction retains its validity. However, if the third party is aware of an event, such as the death of the donor, which would automatically cause revocation, he is deemed to be aware of the revocation. A purchaser from the third party can presume that the third party was not aware of the revocation as long as the transaction with the donee occurred within a year of the date of operation of the power. If it was outside that period the third party can make a statutory declaration to the effect that he was not aware of the revocation.

Enduring power of attorney

25.39 Enduring powers of attorney, intended to survive the mental incapacity of the donor, are governed by the Enduring Powers of Attorney (NI) Order 1987. An enduring power of attorney must comply with the detailed provisions of the legislation as to its form and execution. It must be executed by both the donor and the donee (the attorney).

An enduring power of attorney enables a person, while mentally competent, to create a power which will not be revoked by subsequent mental incapacity. If the attorney has reason to believe that the donor is or is becoming mentally incapable, he is required to apply to the court to register the instrument creating the power. The power does not come into force until it is registered. Any revocation of an enduring power of attorney has to be confirmed by the court.

CHAPTER TWENTY SIX

MORTGAGES

Introduction

26.01 The person who mortgages his property as security for the mortgage debt is known as the borrower or the mortgagor. The person to whom the property is mortgaged is known as the lender or the mortgagee.

At common law the mortgagee is regarded as the owner of the property, whereas in equity the mortgagor is regarded as the owner and the mortgagee is considered as an encumbrancer. The essential feature of a mortgage is the concept of security.

Legal and equitable

26.02 A legal mortgage is a transfer of a legal estate or interest in property to secure the repayment of a debt. The mortgagee takes a legal interest in the property because an estate is transferred to him.

An equitable mortgage is one which passes only an equitable estate or interest. This may be either because it is in an equitable form, such as a deposit of title deeds, or because the mortgagor has only an equitable estate, as may be the case with a second mortgage.

An equitable mortgage by deposit of title deeds can be created in respect of both registered and unregistered land. If the land is registered such deposit will create an equitable charge. The mere act of deposit is regarded as *prima facie* evidence of an equitable mortgage, unless it is expressly stated to be specifically for another purpose. It is not essential to lodge all the deeds and no written formalities are required. The mortgage thereby created relates to the land, rather than to the deeds.

Equity established several principles which remain important in the law of mortgages, both legal and equitable. For example, the principle that a mortgagor should not lose the property merely because of delay in repaying the loan and is allowed to redeem it long after the date on which the mortgage is required to be repaid.

Mortgage and charge

26.03 It is important to appreciate the difference between a mortgage and a charge. The distinction usually drawn between the two concepts is that a mortgage involves the conveyance of some rights of ownership to the lender, whereas a charge does not and merely confers rights over the property as security.

REGISTERED LAND

26.04 The registered owner can only mortgage registered land by means of a registered charge under the provisions of the Land Registration Act (NI) 1970.

An informal equitable charge can also be created by deposit of the land certificate, or where an attempt to create a legal charge has failed for want of some formality.

UNREGISTERED LAND

26.05 A charge cannot be created over unregistered land and a loan should be secured by either a legal or an equitable mortgage. Freehold property can be mortgaged by conveyance of the fee simple or by demise, which is a grant of a term of years.

The mortgage is subject to a proviso for redemption under which the mortgagee covenants to reassign the property on repayment of the monies due.

The Conveyancing Act 1881 provides a statutory form of mortgage for both freehold and leasehold land in which various covenants are automatically implied but it is rarely used.

Where the mortgage is by demise the mortgagor retains the freehold or leasehold, whichever estate he holds. In such a case, the mortgagor usually appoints the mortgagee his attorney to convey the reversion so that the mortgagee can sell the superior estate if so required.

It is convenient to create a mortgage by demise where the property is held under a fee farm grant since this avoids imposing on the mortgagee any liability in respect of the fee farm rent and other covenants and conditions attaching to the estate held by the mortgagor. In practice, most building society mortgages demise the property even if it is held in fee simple absolute.

Where the borrower holds a leasehold estate in the land, it can be mortgaged by assignment or by sub-demise. A mortgage by assignment involves a transfer of the lessee's interest in the lease to the mortgagee, subject to a proviso for redemption. This form of mortgage is rarely used because it has the effect of making the mortgagee liable to all the obligations in respect of rent and repairs imposed on the lessee by the lease.

A mortgage by sub-demise means that instead of parting with his entire estate in the land, the mortgagor sub-demises it in favour of the mortgagee for a term slightly shorter than the term of the lease. The sub-demise is made expressly subject to a proviso that the term will end on redemption of the mortgage. The mortgagee is under no liability in respect of the original lease as there is no privity of contract nor privity of estate between him and the lessor.[171] Again, the mortgage deed usually contains an appointment of the mortgagee as attorney to assign the remainder of the original leasehold term to enable the mortgagee to sell the whole of the mortgagee's interest if this proves necessary.

The Property (NI) Order 1997, article 30(5)(c) states that the creation of a long lease by way of mortgage is an exception to the prohibition of any new long leases of dwelling houses.

The Property (NI) Order 1997, article 24, provides that where a leasehold estate is enlarged into a fee simple, any existing mortgage continues to have

---

[171] Cf Enforcement of Covenants paras 20.19-20.21.

effect as if it had originally been created as a mortgage of the fee simple. Where the mortgage was by way of assignment of the leasehold estate it has effect as if it were a conveyance of the fee simple. Where the mortgage was by way of sub-lease it has effect as if it were a lease for a term equivalent to the term of the sub-lease.

FEATURES OF A MORTGAGE

Legal date for redemption ('the redemption date')

26.06 This is the date specified in the mortgage instrument for repayment of the loan, usually three or six months from the date of the mortgage. The mortgagor has a legal right to redeem on this date, neither before nor after. This is exercisable as of right, irrespective of any equitable considerations.

Equity established that the mortgagor is not expected to repay the loan on the redemption date and the main significance of the date is that it governs the availability of the mortgagee's remedies to realise his security in the event of a problem arising in the operation of the mortgage.

Equitable right to redeem

26.07 The mortgagor has an equitable right to redeem the mortgage at any time after the legal date for redemption. This is exercisable only on terms considered proper by equity.

Equity of redemption

26.08 The equity of redemption is the equitable estate of the mortgagor in the mortgaged property, which includes the right to redeem the mortgage. It is equitable ownership of the property subject to the rights of the mortgagee and has a monetary value.

Although at law the mortgagor has parted with his land and has only a limited right to recover it, in equity he is the owner of the land subject to a mortgage. In law the mortgagee is the owner but in equity he is a mere encumbrancer. Thus the mortgagor's equity of redemption is an interest in the land which he can convey, devise, settle, lease or mortgage, just like any other interest in land.

Enforcement of security by mortgagee

26.09 A mortgagee, like any other lender of money, is owed a contractual debt and is entitled to sue for it if it is not repaid. In practice, the mortgagor is rarely able to repay the mortgage in full on demand. Consequently the scope of this remedy is severely limited and it is seldom a practical option.

An alternative course of action for the mortgagee is to enforce his security against the land to recover payment of the capital. The various remedies are available simultaneously provided that the mortgagee does not act inconsistently. This is not the case in England.

REMEDIES AGAINST THE LAND

Common law right to possession

26.10 The position depends on whether the land in question is registered or unregistered.

Unregistered land

26.11 Historically the mortgagee, as owner of the legal estate in unregistered property, has had an automatic and immediate right to possession.[172] Unless restricted by contract or by statute, a legal mortgagee's right to possession is absolute.[173] However, the strict rule has, in recent years, been judicially questioned.[174]

It has also been restricted by statute in relation to possession of a dwelling house by the Administration of Justice Act 1970, section 36, as qualified by the Administration of Justice Act 1973, section 8, which relates to instalment mortgages. Section 36 enables the court to grant some relief to a mortgagor in an action for possession where he is likely to fulfil his commitments within a reasonable period, by adjourning the case, staying or suspending execution of judgment or postponing the date for delivery of possession.[175 & 176]

In the case of certain small mortgages (not exceeding £15,000) not granted by an exempt lender (such as a building society or insurance company) where the mortgagor is a private individual, the Consumer Credit Act 1974, section 126, makes any enforcement action subject to the control of the court and the court is also given a wide discretion in allowing the mortgagor an extension of time for making payments.

Enforcement of a judgment for possession may be stayed under the Judgments Enforcement (NI) Order 1981, article 13, and it is not restricted to property on which there is a dwelling house. The discretion to stay proceedings under that provision is not expressly limited to cases where the mortgagor appears likely to be able to remedy his default within a reasonable period, although it has been suggested that the power thereby conferred should be exercised as if restricted in substantially the same manner as that conferred in respect of dwelling houses by the Administration of Justice Acts.[177]

---

[172] Survey of Land Law of NI 1970 para 209 proposed that a mortgagee should no longer have power to go into possession at will and this proposal is supported by the final report of Land Law Working Group at para 2.6.5.
[173] *Midland Bank plc v McGrath* [1996] EGCS 61.
[174] See H Wallace "Mortgagees and Possession" 37 NILQ p 336.
[175] See *eg, Target Home Loans Ltd v Clothier and another* [1994] 1 All ER 439.
[176] Even when a mortgagee's right to possession is suspended or deferred under s 36 he retains an independent right to a money judgment in respect of all moneys owed by the mortgagor.
[177] See *Allied Irish Banks Ltd v McAllister* [1993] 5 NIJB 82. *NB* that decision was made before the *Cheltenham & Gloucester Building Society plc v Norgan* which places it in a different light.

It was widely assumed that adjournments, suspensions or deferrals granted under the Administration of Justice Acts should be of reasonably limited duration, commonly of periods between two and four years. However, the decision in *Cheltenham & Gloucester Building Society plc v Norgan*[178] has radically altered the position. In that case the Court of Appeal concluded that the starting point should be the full term of the mortgage and the question should be asked as to whether it would be possible for the mortgagor to pay off the arrears by instalments over that period.

Accordingly relief should normally be granted to a mortgagor who is likely to be able to pay off accumulated arrears over a period not exceeding the term of the mortgage. If this is likely, the mortgagor should be denied relief only if some special factor makes it unreasonable to expect the mortgagee to wait for so long as this to recover the arrears. It is even possible that, in appropriate circumstances, the time allowed for discharge might actually extend beyond the full term contemplated by the mortgage.

From the subsequent decision of *Bristol & West Building Society v Ellis and another*[179] it seems that *Norgan* is applicable only to cases where a mortgagor is expected to be able to make good his default within the period allowed without having to sell the mortgaged property so to do.

The NI Court of Appeal considered exercise of its powers under the Administration of Justice Acts in *National and Provincial Building Society v Lynd and another*.[180] The court confirmed that the point of the statutory provisions was to give some relief to those in temporary financial difficulties as distinguished from those of a more lasting nature which would require restructuring of the mortgage. The Court disagreed with *Norgan* and distinguished it on the facts as in that case the mortgagee's security was not at risk.

The NI Court of Appeal did not accept that the reasonable period is the term of the mortgage. The court would consider all the circumstances of the case without any predisposition for or against any relevant period being the balance of the term. It is for the mortgagor to adduce a justifiable basis for the court to exercise its discretion in his favour. Courts should first focus on how much the mortgagor can pay and assess how long it will take. To start with the full mortgage term could result in the mortgagor paying considerably smaller payments than he can afford.

In *National and Provincial Building Society v Williamson and another*[181] it was held that before exercising its discretion to suspend the execution of an order for possession under the Administration of Justice Act 1970, section 36, it must appear to the court that the mortgagor is likely to be able, within a reasonable period, to pay any sum due under the mortgage. This is a matter for the court to decide on the evidence before it.

---

[178] [1996] 1 All ER 449.
[179] [1996] EGCS 74.
[180] [1996] NI 47.
[181] [1995] NI 366.

The taking of possession does not of itself put an end to the mortgage and secure payment. It is often invoked prior to exercise of the statutory power of sale to remove the mortgagor when he has ceased to make mortgage payments satisfactorily. Unprecedented use has been made of this remedy in the last decade because of problems experienced by mortgagors resulting from high interest rates and static or decreasing property values.

Where a legal mortgage of a freehold or leasehold estate is created by conveyance, assignment or demise, the mortgagee is theoretically able to claim possession as soon as the mortgage is created. Normally the mortgagor is allowed to remain in possession as a tenant at sufferance.

However, the mortgage may contain an attornment clause by which the mortgagor attorns (acknowledges) himself to be the tenant of the mortgagee, thereby creating the relationship of landlord and tenant between them and facilitating the running of covenants. This may be useful if it becomes necessary to determine which party is responsible for particular obligations.[182]

When the mortgagor refuses to allow the mortgagee to take possession, the mortgagee may take proceedings for ejectment or make a summary application for an order for possession. The summary procedure is more commonly used and renders the existence of an attornment clause in the mortgage deed unnecessary.[183]

Nevertheless, the clause may still be relevant if it provides that the mortgagor's tenancy cannot be determined except by the mortgagee giving a certain period of notice. It thus restricts the mortgagee in claiming possession.

If the mortgagee remains in possession for sufficient time, (which nowadays seems unlikely as most mortgagees are lending institutions), he may eventually acquire full title by adverse possession and extinguish the mortgagor's right to redeem.

Registered land
26.12 The charge does not confer an estate in registered land on the owner of the charge and he does not have a common law right to possession without the permission of the chargor or the consent of the court.[184]

Equitable mortgages
26.13 An equitable mortgagee has no right to possession at law but can apply to the court for an order for possession, at the court's discretion.

---

[182] Cf Enforcement of Obligations paras 20.19-20.22.
[183] An attornment clause enables the mortgagee to take proceedings for ejectment on the basis that the mortgagor is a tenant.
[184] See LRA 1970, Sch 7. The Final Report of Land Law Working Group para 2.6.3 recommends that there should be uniformity as between registered and unregistered land; that mortgagors and mortgagees should have the same rights under a charge by way of legal mortgage as under a mortgage by conveyance.

Court order for possession and sale out of court

26.14 This common law remedy was developed by the courts. At one time it was commonly used by the mortgagee when he was unable to obtain vacant possession of the property. The court has an inherent jurisdiction to put a mortgagee into possession and such an order can also be made by a judge exercising bankruptcy jurisdiction. The mortgagee can apply to court for a declaration that the amount secured by the mortgage is well charged on the mortgagor's interest, for possession and for a sale. However the mortgagee cannot proceed with the sale unless the mortgagor fails to pay the sum due within three months of service of the court order on him.

Athough the common law position has been preserved by the Judicature (NI) Act 1978, section 86(3) it is seldom invoked because of other statutory provisions, such as the Consumer Credit Act 1974 and the Administration of Justice Acts 1970 and 1973.

If the land is registered the power to award possession of the property on the owner of a charge is conferred by the Land Registration Act (NI) 1970, Schedule 1, Part I, paragraph 5 (2).

Sale

26.15 A statutory power of sale arises under the Conveyancing Act 1881 and is governed by the provisions of sections 19-22. The power of sale is conferred on all mortgagees, provided the mortgage was made by deed after 1881. The statutory power is only relevant to legal mortgages and would not, for example, apply to equitable mortgages by deposit of title deeds.

The power of sale is exercisable without recourse to the courts. In practice it may be difficult for a mortgagee to exercise the power of sale without having possession as no buyer would be interested with the mortgagor in occupation.

Sometimes the mortgagor leaves of his own accord when he cannot keep up with the mortgage payments. By doing so the responsibility for the property is imposed on the mortgagee. The mortgagee can then sell it because he has both possession and a power of sale. On the other hand, if the mortgagor remains in the property, the mortgagee may have to get a court order to obtain physical possession.

The statutory power of sale does not arise until the mortgage debt becomes due. This generally means when the legal date for redemption has passed, or in the case of a mortgage paid by instalments, it may mean as soon as any instalment is in arrear.

In practice, the mortgage deed may provide that the instalments have to be two or three months in arrears before the power of sale becomes exercisable. It normally also provides that, after the redemption date, the power of sale will not be exercised if the mortgagor continues to make the repayments and abide by the terms of the mortgage.

There is also statutory protection for the mortgagor in the Conveyancing Act 1881, section 20 which provides that the power of sale cannot be exercised until one of the following conditions is met:

(1) Notice requiring payment of the mortgage money has been served on the mortgagor and default has been made in payment of the mortgage money for three months after such service, or
(2) Some interest under the mortgage is in arrear and unpaid for two months after becoming due, or
(3) The mortgagor has breached a provision in the mortgage deed or the Act, other than payment of the money.

The distinction between when the mortgagee's power of sale arises and when it becomes exercisable is important. If the power of sale has not arisen, the mortgagee has no power at all. Unless he has an express power under the deed he can only transfer his interest under the mortgage, subject to the mortgagor's equity of redemption.

On the other hand, once the power has arisen and the mortgagee purports to exercise it, even though it is not yet exercisable, a purchaser has good title. A receipt in writing by the mortgagee is a sufficient discharge for any money arising under the statutory power of sale. The purchaser is not even concerned to inquire whether the sale has been authorised, notice given or the power properly exercised.[185]

This provision simplifies the enquiries expected of a purchaser who is only obliged to satisfy himself that the power of sale has arisen by the passing of the redemption date. He does not have to look at the relations between the mortgagor and the mortgagee during the currency of the mortgage, although the courts will not allow the mortgage to be used as an instrument of fraud.

The advantage for the mortgagee in selling the property under the statutory power of sale is that he can exercise his power without applying to the court for any order and has a wide discretion as to the means of selling it.[186]

Once the power becomes exercisable, the mortgagee can demand and recover all the deeds and documents relating to the mortgaged property and the title (except in relation to any interests having priority to the mortgage) which a purchaser is entitled to recover from a mortgagee exercising the power of sale.[187]

The statutory power is exercised when the mortgagee enters into a contract to sell the property. When the contract comes into existence, the mortgagor loses his right to redeem the mortgage and cannot prevent the sale proceeding by paying the money due.

The extent of the duty of care imposed on the mortgagee exercising the power of sale has been the subject of some controversy because the statutory provisions are uncertain. The courts have accepted that the mortgagee is not a trustee for the mortgagor. The power is conferred on the mortgagee primarily to

---

[185] Conveyancing Act 1911, s 5(1).
[186] Conveyancing Act 1881, s 19.
[187] *Ibid*, s 21(7).

realise his own security and although he must act in good faith, he cannot be attacked for his motives in selling.

While the mortgagee is not a trustee of his power of sale, he is a trustee of the proceeds of sale and must apply them under the Conveyancing Act 1881, section 21(3) in the following order:

(1) To discharge prior encumbrances;
(2) To pay all costs, charges etc. incurred by the sale;
(3) To discharge the mortgage with interest and costs;
(4) To pay the residue to the person entitled to it.

To protect the interests of the mortgagor and any subsequent mortgagees the mortgagee who is selling is subject to an equitable obligation to obtain the best price reasonably available.[188]

By virtue of the Judgments Enforcement Order (NI) 1981, article 51, where there is an order charging land for rates it takes priority over all other debts and encumbrances except those due to the Crown.

The sale of the mortgaged property under the Conveyancing Act 1881 enables the mortgagee to convey to the purchaser such estate and interest as is the subject of the mortgage, free from all estates, interests and rights over which the mortgage has priority, but subject to all those which have priority over it.[189]

This means that where the mortgage is by conveyance of the fee simple, the fee simple is sold to the purchaser and where the mortgage is by demise, the purchaser can only take the term of years in the mortgage.

However, the mortgagor will usually have given the mortgagee power of attorney to act on his behalf in the sale of his interest. Similarly, the mortgage deed may contain a declaration of trust to the effect that the mortgagor holds the equity of redemption (that is, the difference between what he himself holds and the term of the mortgage) on trust for the mortgagee and this enables the mortgagee to sell the whole of the mortgagor's title.

Where the land is registered, the power of sale includes power to sell the estate or interest subject to the charge.[190]

Court order for sale

26.16 If the mortgagee cannot or does not wish to bring proceedings for possession and if he cannot sell without the intervention of the court he may apply for a court order for sale. The sale is carried out under the control of the court with the mortgagee as the vendor and the proceeds applied in discharge of the mortgage. If the mortgagor remains in possession after the sale it is the duty of the mortgagee to apply for an order that the purchaser then be put into possession.

---

[188] *Parker-Tweedale v Dunbar Bank plc* [1990] 2 All ER 577.
[189] Conveyancing Act 1881, s 21(1).
[190] LRA 1970, Sch 7.

Taking possession

26.17 Where a legal mortgage is created the mortgagee is entitled to claim possession of the property as soon as the mortgage is created because he is the holder of a legal estate. If the mortgagor does not allow the mortgagee to exercise his right to take possession, the mortgagee may initiate an action for ejectment or make a summary application for an order for possession.

Taking possession does not of itself put an end to the mortgage or secure repayment of the capital debt. It may be invoked preliminary to exercising a power of sale but, unless there are problems the mortgagee is generally content for the mortgagor to retain possession.

A chargee on registered land has no estate in the land but may be awarded possession by court order under the Land Registration Act (NI) 1970, Schedule 7, Part I, paragraph 5(2). An equitable mortgagee can also apply to the court for an order for possession and the only restriction is that all equitable remedies are discretionary. An equitable chargee has no legal or equitable interest in the property mortgaged and therefore cannot claim possession.

Appointment of a receiver

26.18 After considering the practical problems of the mortgagee himself taking possession, particularly in relation to commercial properties, it may be more appropriate to appoint a receiver as manager of the property. A mortgage deed may contain a clause reserving for the mortgagee the right to appoint a receiver as the agent of the mortgagor.[191]

The power to appoint a receiver is conferred on mortgagees whose mortgages are created by deed, that is, most legal mortgagees and chargees of registered land. The power arises when the mortgage money has become due, but does not become exercisable until one of the three events specified in the Conveyancing Act 1881 for exercise of the power of sale occurs.[192]

Foreclosure

26.19 When a mortgagor has failed to pay off the mortgage debt within the proper time, (that is, by the redemption date) the mortgagee is entitled to bring an action requesting that a day be fixed on which the mortgagor is to pay it. In default of payment, the mortgagor may be foreclosed of his equity of redemption, which means that it is extinguished. Accordingly, the mortgagee could become owner of a property worth more than the amount due to him. Mortgagees of subsequent charges are not likely to receive anything because the first mortgagee after foreclosure takes the property free of all subsequent interests.

---

[191] There is also a limited statutory power under the Conveyancing Act 1881, s 19(1) extended by the Judicature (NI) Act 1978, s 91 to give the court jurisdiction to make appointments on such terms as it thinks fit.

[192] Cf para 26.15.

Although the jurisdiction to order foreclosure exists, the remedy has not been granted in Ireland for centuries. The courts have been careful to state that there is jurisdiction to order foreclosure but that this power will be exercised in exceptional circumstances only.[193] This may be because second and third mortgages are traditionally more common in Ireland and the only way to safeguard the interests of all concerned is by selling the property.

RIGHTS OF THE MORTGAGOR

Possession

26.20 The mortgagee generally has a right to take possession of the mortgaged property. However, the mortgage deed usually provides that the mortgagee will not exercise that right unless the mortgagor has defaulted for a specified time in making a payment of money under the mortgage or has breached some other obligation under the mortgage.

Actions

26.21 While the mortgagor was in possession he had the right at common law to protect that possession against third parties, such as trespassers. He could also bring an action to recover the land against anyone other than the mortgagee and was able to apply for equitable remedies.

Title documents

26.22 The mortgagee is usually entitled to retain the title deeds of the property, but the mortgagor has the right to inspect them.[194] Most mortgages are to lending institutions which always like to keep the deeds unless there is a good reason for them being elsewhere on a temporary basis, for example, pending resolution of a particular problem. On redemption of the mortgage the mortgagor is entitled to have the deeds restored to his possession and can claim compensation if the mortgagee is unable to provide them.

Sale of property

26.23 The mortgagor can sell the property and repay the mortgage out of the sale proceeds, which is common practice. He can also sell free from the mortgage with the mortgagee's consent, which may be given if other sufficient security is provided for the loan. Further, under the Conveyancing Act 1881, section 5(1) and (2) the mortgagor can sell free from the mortgage upon payment of sufficient money into court to obtain a declaration by the court that the property is free from encumbrance.

---

[193] See, *eg, Bruce* v *Brophy* [1906] 1 IR 611, *McDonough* v *Shrewbridge* (1814) 2 Ba & B 555.
[194] Conveyancing Act 1881, s 16(1).

Sale of equity of redemption

26.24 Alternatively, the mortgagor can sell his equity of redemption, which is his interest in the property, subject to the mortgage. This is only done in specific situations, such as a transaction between joint owners of the property or members of the same family. In most cases the mortgage deed provides that the mortgagor cannot make the transfer without the mortgagee's consent. In the absence of any express provision, the mortgagor is free to deal with the equity of redemption as he pleases.

The mortgage may provide that consent to the transfer will be forthcoming if the transferee enters into a covenant for payment with the mortgagee. A transfer without consent does not invalidate the transfer but is a breach of the terms of the mortgage and gives the mortgagee the right to call in the money.

The property is transferred subject to the mortgage. If the mortgagee is not a party to it, the assignee should covenant with the assignor (the mortgagor) to pay the principal and interest due under the mortgage, to observe and perform the other covenants in the mortgage and to indemnify the assignor. Even if he does not, a purchaser for value will be under an implied obligation to indemnify the mortgagor.

An assignee of the equity of redemption generally steps into the shoes of the mortgagor. The mortgagee should agree to release the original mortgagor from the mortgage and all the obligations arising thereunder.

Redemption

26.25 This is the most important right of the mortgagor and involves the full repayment of the mortgage debt. On the date for redemption specified in the mortgage deed the mortgagor has a legal right to redeem and thereafter has an equitable right indefinitely. Following redemption the legal title to the property is returned to the mortgagor, freed and discharged from the mortgage.

It is fundamental that the property should ultimately return to the mortgagor unconditionally and the courts protect the rights of mortgagors by not allowing any clogs or fetters on the equity of redemption.[195] There can be no restrictions on the right to redeem and the courts have been wary about clauses purporting to postpone the redemption date beyond the usual six month period after the mortgage commences.

The courts have also refused to enforce mortgage clauses which are *"in terrorem"* of one of the parties, that is, intending to frighten or intimidate. Any provisions which secure additional financial advantage for the mortgagee in the form of penalties (*eg*, increasing the rate of interest charged if the repayments are made late) are also prohibited if the courts see them as unconscionable or unreasonable.

---

[195] Meaning that no mortgage deed may contain provision impeding the right to redeem, *eg*, by delaying the time for redemption or being unfair or inconsistent with the right to redeem.

The mortgagor may redeem the mortgage on the legal date for redemption without giving notice, but thereafter the right to redeem is equitable only and must be exercised reasonably, that is, reasonable notice must be given. Commercial practice does not warrant the strict enforcement of this rule.

To redeem the mortgage the mortgagor must repay the principal debt, the interest due and the mortgagee's reasonable costs. Usually the mortgagee can provide a redemption statement showing these amounts, on request.

On the other hand, the mortgagor may actually lose his equity of redemption by releasing it, by sale of the property, by lapse of time under the Limitation (NI) Order 1989 where the mortgagee is in possession, or by merger. The doctrine of merger applies where ownership of two estates or interests in the same land becomes vested in the same person. It operates to extinguish the lesser estate in the greater one, provided that is the intention of the parties.[196] This means that where one person acquires both the equity of redemption and the mortgagee's interest in the mortgage, the mortgage is extinguished.

The actual discharge of the land from the mortgage follows from redemption. Where a legal mortgage has been created by conveyance of the fee simple, assignment of a lease or demise, it can be discharged by receipt endorsed on the mortgage deed following repayment of the amount due.

Under the Property (Discharge of Mortgage by Receipt) (NI) Order 1983 a receipt executed by the mortgagee operates as a discharge of mortgaged property from all the principal money, interest and claims under the mortgage. It is commonly called a "vacate". Prior to that Order, only building society mortgages could be vacated in this manner and all other mortgages had to be discharged by the appropriate deed of reconveyance, reassignment or surrender.[197]

The vacate of mortgage should be dated prior to or on the same date as any subsequent conveyance so that all the interest and estate of the mortgagee in the property is vested in the mortgagor in time for him to convey it to a purchaser. Otherwise it is only the equity of redemption which can pass. It is not necessary for the vacate to be registered prior to a subsequent deed.

Where a mortgage has been created by sub-demise, (a term of years for the purpose of the mortgage), the Satisfied Terms Act 1845 also applies. Provided that where the purpose for which a term was created is fulfilled it becomes a satisfied term and automatically merges with the reversion expectant upon it.

An equitable mortgage can be discharged by ordinary receipt in the normal way.

---

[196] Cf Merger paras 23.13-23.16.
[197] See Building Societies Act (NI) 1967, s 37.

RIGHTS COMMON TO BOTH PARTIES

Leases

26.26 There was a limited power to grant leases at common law but now both parties have a statutory power to lease while in possessions under the Conveyancing Act 1881, section 18. The power may be exercised for example, by a builder or developer selling the mortgaged property by way of leases of individual sites with the consent of the mortgagee.[198] This power is curtailed by the Property (NI) Order 1997, article 30 which prohibits the creation of any new long leases of dwelling houses (subject to certain specified exceptions) and article 39(3) which provides that any power to create a lease shall cease to have effect save to the extent necessary to give effect to an obligation assumed before the appointed day, 10 January 2000.

Transfer of rights

26.27 The various rights of a mortgagor and mortgagee may be transferred to third parties.

Mortgagor

26.28 A mortgagor can make an *inter vivos* transfer of his equity of redemption subject to the mortgage but this is only realistic in specific circumstances.

To sell free from the mortgage, the mortgagor has to repay the debt or have the mortgagee join in the conveyance, which he may do if alternative security can be provided.

Where a mortgagor dies and his interest passes to a successor, the charges and mortgages on the property generally have to be repaid out of the property itself, with the result that it will probably have to be sold. If a contrary intention is expressed in the will the charges may be repaid out of other funds and a sale of the property avoided.

Mortgagee

26.29 A mortgagee may transfer both the debt owed and the security in the property to another or may create a sub-mortgage. Although relatively common in the past neither right is exercised very frequently nowadays except where a financial institution transfers its whole mortgage portfolio.

The security in the property and the debt owed pass to the personal representatives on the death of a mortgagee who is a private individual.

SECOND MORTGAGES

26.30 A legal second mortgage can be created in the same way as a first mortgage: by conveyance, assignment or sub-demise of unregistered land and

---

[198] Conveyancing Act 1911, s 3. Either a mortgagor or a mortgagee in possession may accept a surrender of a lease of the mortgaged land for the purpose of granting a new lease.

by charge on registered land. It is usually made for one day shorter than the previous mortgage.

The first mortgagee generally has the title deeds, but if he does not, the second mortgagee should obtain them. The second mortgagee has the right to inspect and make copies of the deeds in the custody of the first mortgagee.

On completion of the second mortgage, the second mortgagee should give notice of the second mortgage to the first mortgagee. This prevents the first mortgagee making further advances to the mortgagor which would rank in priority to the second mortgagee.[199] The first mortgagee then has no excuse, if on discharge of the first mortgage, he delivers the deeds to the mortgagor instead of to the second mortgagee.

Remedies

26.31 The second mortgagee generally has all the remedies of the first mortgagee but is not usually able to exercise them while the first mortgagee is doing so. He cannot take possession if the first mortgagee is already in possession or has appointed a receiver.

If the second mortgagee sells he must do so subject to the first mortgage unless the first mortgagee agrees to join in the deed and receive part of the purchase money sufficient to discharge the first mortgage. Alternatively, the second mortgagee can take a transfer of the prior mortgage.

If the first mortgagee sells the mortgaged property, he should pay any surplus funds to the second mortgagee.[200]

Discharge

26.32 A second mortgage is discharged in the same way as a first mortgage.[201]

Disadvantages of subsequent mortgages

Tacking

26.33 There is a theoretical possibility of tacking. This is a process by which the normal priority of mortgages being in the order in which they are made is disturbed. It can be upset either by adding a subsequent mortgage or a further advance to an earlier mortgage.

Thus a third mortgagee with no notice of a second mortgage at the time his mortgage was made might subsequently acquire the first mortgage and postpone the second mortgagee. This doctrine is known as *tabula in naufragio* (plank in the shipwreck). It rarely has practical effect because it cannot operate where priorities are governed by the Registry of Deeds system. It can only arise where priorities are governed by the general principles of equity, for example

---

[199] Confirmed by Land Registration Act (NI) 1970, s 43.
[200] See *Thomson's Mortgage Trusts* [1920] 1 Ch 508, but the matter is not entirely free from doubt.
[201] See above paras 26.23-26.25.

where the third mortgage is unregistrable or the second mortgage is unregistered.

When a further advance is made, the advance can be tacked on to a first mortgage if the second mortgagee has agreed to it. In the absence of agreement it cannot be tacked on if the first mortgagee had notice of the second mortgage at the time of the further advance. Registration in the Registry of Deeds does not in itself constitute notice and express notice must be properly given to avoid the possibility of tacking.

In the ordinary case of a second mortgage of a private dwelling house, the risks of tacking are slight and the second mortgagee can obtain some protection by registering his mortgage and giving actual notice of it to the first mortgagee.

Consolidation
26.34 This is an equitable doctrine designed to protect the mortgagee, under which a mortgagee who holds several mortgages by the same mortgagor on different properties can insist on the redemption of all if the mortgagor seeks to redeem any of them. Again, the risk of it actually being invoked is minimal. To protect the priority of his right to consolidate against subsequent dealings, the mortgagee must see that all the mortgages involved are registered. (As a general precaution, he should also search in the index of names of grantors in the Registry of Deeds to ascertain whether there are any other mortgages created by the mortgagor.)

Absence of title deeds
26.35 The disadvantages of this are fairly obvious, in that in the event of default by the mortgagor, the subsequent mortgagee would have difficulty in selling the property.

Danger of sale by the first mortgagee
26.36 The risk of sale can be minimised by obtaining a proper valuation to ensure that the property provides adequate security. The second mortgagee should ascertain the amount due on foot of the prior mortgage. He should thus ensure that there is sufficient equity to enable an appropriate second mortgage to be taken.

Foreclosure
26.37 This remedy available to a first mortgagee has not been invoked in Ireland for a long time, partly because of the injustice it does to subsequent mortgagees. When a mortgagee takes proceedings for foreclosure he seeks to have the mortgagor's equitable right to redeem the mortgage extinguished so that the mortgagee becomes the full owner of it. It is then possible that the mortgagee could become the owner of a property worth much more than the amount of the mortgage. It also means that subsequent mortgagees are not paid anything because the first mortgagee takes the property free of all subsequent mortgages.

CHAPTER TWENTY SEVEN

BANKRUPTCY AND VOLUNTARY CONVEYANCES

27.01 Bankruptcy jurisdiction is exercised by the High Court only. The law of insolvency is governed by the Insolvency (NI) Order 1989 ('the 1989 Order') and the Insolvency Rules (NI) 1991 as amended.

BANKRUPTCY PROCEEDINGS

27.02 A bankruptcy order is generally sought by means of a petition presented to the court either by the debtor personally or by one or more creditors.

Debtor's petition

27.03 A debtor's petition may be presented to the court only on the ground that the debtor is unable to pay his debts and he must demonstrate an inability to pay the debts currently due. If the unsecured debts do not exceed the small bankruptcies level (currently £20,000) and the value of the bankrupt's estate is at least equal to the minimum amount (currently £2,000) the court may issue a certificate for the summary administration of the estate rather than full bankruptcy.

The court may appoint an insolvency practitioner to investigate the debtor's circumstances and prepare a report as to whether a voluntary arrangement might be concluded. Alternatively, direct steps may be taken to conclude a voluntary arrangement and avoid full bankruptcy.

Creditor's petition

27.04 The petitioning creditor must establish that the debt owed to him is in excess of the bankruptcy level (currently £750). The debtor must also appear to be unable to pay that debt or to have no reasonable prospect of being able to pay it. The debt must be for a liquidated sum, payable immediately or at some future time and be unsecured.

In order to establish that the debtor is unable to pay the debt it is necessary for the creditor to serve a statutory demand on the debtor. This requires the debtor to pay the debt referred to in the demand, to provide security for it or come to some arrangement with the creditor for the payment of it.

The debt must be one in respect of which no *bona fide* dispute exists as to liability or as to quantum. If, three weeks after the demand has been served, the debtor is unable either to have the demand set aside or to make some proposal to the satisfaction of the creditor complying with the demand, he is deemed to be unable to pay the debt.

A creditor's petition can be issued on the ground that the debtor has failed to comply with the statutory demand. The petition should be issued within four months of service of the demand.

When the petition is issued by the court, the time, date and place of the hearing are set. The petition cannot generally be heard until at least 14 days have elapsed since it was served, unless the circumstances demand that it should be heard earlier. The debtor can oppose the petition.

On the hearing of the petition, the petitioning creditor must satisfy the court that the debt is still owing by furnishing a certificate of debt.

Bankruptcy order

27.05 For a bankruptcy order to be made, the court must be satisfied that the debt has not been paid and that no satisfactory arrangement has been made to pay it. When the bankruptcy order is made the bankruptcy commences and the bankrupt is not released from it until he gains his discharge or the bankruptcy is annulled.

The Official Receiver functions as receiver and manager of the bankrupt's estate from the time that the bankruptcy order is made until the formal appointment of a trustee in bankruptcy. The Official Receiver must decide whether or not to summon a meeting of creditors for the purpose of choosing a trustee and must hold the meeting within 12 weeks of the bankruptcy order.

It may not always be worthwhile appointing a trustee from the private sector. If, for example, the value of the assets is very small and the Official Receiver decides not to call a creditors meeting, he must serve notice to that effect. The creditors can then require the meeting to be held if they so wish and appoint a trustee. Alternatively, the Department of Economic Development can appoint a trustee or the Official Receiver can become the trustee himself.

When a trustee is appointed he becomes trustee from the time specified in his certificate of appointment and the bankrupt's estate vests in him by automatic operation of law.

Protection of the bankrupt's estate

27.06 The bankrupt's estate consists of all property belonging to him when the bankruptcy order is made, all rights of action and powers exercisable over property and any property which he acquires after the commencement of the bankruptcy order. A duty is imposed on the bankrupt to notify the trustee of the acquisition of any after-acquired property.

From the moment of the presentation of a bankruptcy petition a moratorium is imposed over the debtor's affairs. If a bankruptcy order is made, statutory restrictions apply retrospectively back to the time the petition was presented and all dispositions of property made by the bankrupt during the interval are void unless made with the consent of the court.

Certain items of the bankrupt's property which *prima facie* belong to his available estate are excluded therefrom and are exempt from the effects of bankruptcy. The bankrupt is allowed to retain such items of equipment as are necessary for use personally by him in his employment or business as well as such clothing, bedding, furniture, household equipment and provisions as are necessary for satisfying the basic needs of him and his family.

Investigation of affairs

27.07 The investigation of the bankrupt's affairs begins with the bankrupt preparing a statement of affairs setting out all his assets and liabilities. If the bankrupt cannot prepare a proper statement of affairs, the Official Receiver may employ someone to do so.

In the case of a debtor's own petition, the statement of affairs is included with the papers lodged in court when the petition is issued. In other cases, the statement must be submitted to the Official Receiver within 21 days of the making of the bankruptcy order.

The Official Receiver then investigates the affairs and conduct of the bankrupt and prepares a report which is submitted to the court setting out the circumstances and probable reasons for the bankrupt's failure.

If the Official Receiver or one half in value of the creditors applies to the court the bankrupt may then be subject to a public examination at a public hearing before the court. This provides an opportunity for creditors, the Official Receiver and trustee in bankruptcy to appear or be represented and to question the bankrupt regarding his affairs, dealings and property.

Realisation and distribution of the bankrupt's estate

27.08 The trustee has comprehensive powers of management, control, realisation, sale and disposition in relation to the bankrupt's estate. Essentially, the trustee has power to do whatever is necessary to convert the bankrupt's available property into cash ready for distribution to the creditors. To participate in the distribution, all creditors are required to prove their debts.

The nature of the debt and the basis of the liability must be determined so that it can be allocated to its proper category in the prescribed hierarchy of distribution. Any security for a debt must be valued or estimated. If a creditor realises his security he can lodge proof for the unsecured balance. If the security is worthless, the creditor can surrender it to the trustee and can prove for the full amount of the debt.

The provisions governing the sequence and order of priority of the distribution of the bankrupt's estate are contained in the 1989 Order, articles 295-305 together with Schedule 4.

Conclusion of administration

27.09 A trustee other than the Official Receiver has to summon a final general meeting of creditors to receive his report on the administration of the estate and to determine whether he should be released as trustee. The final meeting cannot be concluded until any final distribution has been made and the administration of the estate is for all practical purposes complete. Even after his affairs have been administered, the bankrupt remains undischarged until the relevant time limit has expired.

Discharge from bankruptcy

27.10 Generally for a first time bankrupt an automatic discharge takes place three years after the making of the bankruptcy order. It can be two years in the case of summary administration of a debtor's petition where the liabilities do not exceed £20,000. The court has power to order that the right to automatic discharge be suspended.

A person who has previously been bankrupt within the last 15 years or who has been made criminally bankrupt has to apply to the court to be discharged and such application cannot be made until five years have elapsed since the making of a bankruptcy order.

When a bankrupt is discharged the court must, at the request of the bankrupt, issue a certificate of discharge. When a bankrupt is discharged he is released from all obligations in respect of his pre-bankruptcy liabilities.

BANKRUPT'S HOME

27.11 The realisation of a bankrupt's interest in a dwelling house is subject to statutory restrictions which give limited rights of occupation to the bankrupt's spouse and to the bankrupt. These restrictions may delay, but will not prevent, the ultimate sale of the property to realise the bankrupt's interest.

Where the bankrupt has a beneficial interest in a house, any charge on it acquired by his spouse under the Family Law (Miscellaneous Provisions) (NI) Order 1984 or under the Family Homes and Domestic Violence (NI) Order 1998[202] continues to subsist after the bankruptcy and binds the trustee and his successors in title.

No such rights of occupation may be acquired by the spouse between the presentation of the petition and the vesting of the bankrupt's estate in the trustee. Where the spouse enjoys a registered right of occupation or a registered matrimonial home right, the legislation prevents the spouse being evicted or excluded from the house without a court order.

Where the house is owned jointly or as tenants in common by the bankrupt and his spouse the trustee can only sell it, in the absence of agreement with the owners, by an order for sale in lieu of partition under the Partition Act 1868. On making an order the court has to consider the interests of the creditors, the conduct of the spouse in contributing to the bankruptcy, the needs and financial resources of the spouse, the needs of any children and all the circumstances of the case other than the needs of the bankrupt.

When the application to the court is made more than a year after the first vesting of the bankrupt's estate in the trustee the court is to assume, unless the circumstances are exceptional, that the interests of the creditors outweigh all other considerations. Consequently, an application for sale after one year will usually be successful. It is nevertheless possible for the spouse to buy the bankrupt's interest from the trustee so that the family can remain in occupation.

---

[202] See paras 28.32-28.34.

Where the bankrupt has a beneficial interest in a house and a person under the age of 18 occupied it with him as his home, the bankrupt has rights of occupation in the house, whether or not the spouse also has rights of occupation. These rights extend to protect minor children living with a single, divorced or separated bankrupt. The bankrupt has the right against the trustee not to be evicted or excluded from the house, except with the leave of the court.

The bankrupt's rights are a charge on the interest in the house vested in the trustee, having the priority of an equitable interest created immediately before the making of the bankruptcy order. Such rights should be protected by registration in the Registry of Deeds or the Land Registry as appropriate.

When the trustee has completed the administration of the estate he can vacate his office and obtain a release even if the house has not been sold. Where the house is legitimately occupied by the bankrupt or his spouse and the trustee is not in a position to realise the bankrupt's interest in it, the trustee can apply to the court for a charge to be imposed in relation to any sum still due out of the bankrupt's estate. The charge is enforceable in an amount up to the value of the property on an application for possession or on sale.

EFFECT OF BANKRUPTCY ON CONVEYANCING TRANSACTIONS

Bankruptcy of vendor

27.12 When the vendor is adjudicated bankrupt the effect on a sale of property and on the purchaser has to be considered and is dependent upon the stage of transaction reached.

Contract before bankruptcy petition

27.13 Where a binding contract exists for a vendor to sell property to a purchaser and a bankruptcy petition is subsequently issued against the vendor, the trustee in bankruptcy takes the land subject to the obligation to complete the sale. If the contract is unprofitable or if the property is unsaleable or not readily saleable, the trustee may disclaim it. Otherwise, if the purchaser wishes to proceed, he can apply for specific performance against the trustee. If he does not wish to proceed the purchaser may apply to the court for an order discharging his obligations under the contract.

Contract after bankruptcy petition

27.14 Any disposition of property made by the bankrupt between the date of the presentation of the bankruptcy petition and the vesting of the bankrupt's estate in the trustee is void under the 1989 Order, article 257. This may affect a contract for sale because a contract involves a disposition by the vendor of the equitable interest in the land.

Any property transferred during this intervening period forms part of the bankrupt's estate and may be recovered by the trustee. The trustee is not bound to complete the sale unless the contract was made, or the property received, in good faith, for value and without the other party having notice that the bankruptcy petition had been presented.

It is unlikely that a purchaser could successfully claim to be unaware of a vendor's bankruptcy once notice of the bankruptcy petition has been registered in the Registry of Deeds or Land Registry because it will appear on a normal search which a purchaser should have made prior to the contract. It will also appear on a bankruptcy search.

Property acquired by a bankrupt after a bankruptcy order has been made against him does not vest in the trustee until the trustee serves a notice claiming it. Even if such a notice has been served and the bankrupt transfers the property to another person who acquires it in good faith for value and without notice of the bankruptcy, the title of that person is protected.

Searches[203]

27.15 A purchaser or mortgagee of unregistered land should search in the Registry of Deeds shortly before completion so that if the search is clear he can ensure priority over any bankruptcy petition or order registered in the meantime.

Under the Registration of Deeds Act (NI) 1970, section 3A, a bankruptcy petition does not affect a purchaser in good faith of unregistered land unless either he has actual knowledge of it or more than 21 days have elapsed since the petition was registered in the Registry of Deeds. Under section 3B, the title of a trustee in bankruptcy is void as against a purchaser of unregistered land in good faith without actual knowledge of the bankruptcy order claiming under a conveyance registered in the Registry of Deeds before the expiration of 21 days from the date on which the bankruptcy order was registered.

A purchaser or owner of a charge of registered land should procure a priority search and lodge his transfer or charge within the period of operation of the certificate of that search so that his interest takes precedence over any bankruptcy petition or order.

In all cases a purchaser or mortgagee should make a bankruptcy search against the vendor or mortgagor.

Liquidation

27.16 Where the vendor is a company which goes into liquidation between the contract and completion, the liquidator has power to carry the contract into effect. If the contract is unprofitable he may disclaim it. Otherwise, if the liquidator refuses to complete, the purchaser can seek specific performance or can prove in the winding up.

Bankruptcy of purchaser

27.17 When a purchaser enters a contract and is subsequently adjudicated bankrupt, the transaction may proceed provided that the trustee does not

---

[203] Cf paras 5.01-5.06.

disclaim it as unprofitable. The vendor may apply to the court for an order discharging the obligations under the contract if he does not wish to proceed but he cannot obtain specific performance against an unwilling trustee in bankruptcy even if the transaction is unprofitable.

The 1989 Order, article 257, applies to payments of money in the same way as to dispositions of land. Accordingly, the transaction is valid only if the vendor receives the money before the bankruptcy order in good faith and without notice of the petition.

Where the purchaser is a company which goes into liquidation between contract and completion the liquidator can elect either to complete the contract or to disclaim it.

Property acquired after bankruptcy order

27.18 Property acquired by a bankrupt after a bankruptcy order has been made against him does not vest in the trustee until the trustee serves a notice claiming it. Even if such a notice has been served and the bankrupt transfers the property to another person who acquires it in good faith for value and without notice of the bankruptcy, the title of that person is protected.

TRANSACTIONS AT UNDERVALUE

27.19 Under the 1989 Order, article 312, where the bankrupt has, up to five years before the filing of the bankruptcy petition, entered into a transaction with anyone at an undervalue, the court may on the application of the trustee make such order as it thinks fit to restore the position to what it would otherwise have been.

A transaction is treated as being at an undervalue where the bankrupt makes a gift or enters into a transaction either for no consideration or for a consideration which is significantly less valuable than that provided by the bankrupt. The fact that an undervalue results from a court order, such as a property adjustment order in a matrimonial cause, does not prevent it from being adjusted in subsequent bankruptcy proceedings.

The undervalue transaction may only be adjusted by the court if it was entered into within five years of the presentation of the bankruptcy petition. If the transaction was entered into less than two years before that date an order may be made whether or not the bankrupt was insolvent at the time of the transaction, but if it was entered into between two and five years of the presentation of the petition an order can only be made if the bankrupt was insolvent at that time or became insolvent in consequence of the transaction.

Where the other party to the transaction is an associate of the bankrupt the trustee does not have to prove such insolvency. It is presumed unless the other party can prove to the contrary. Insolvency here means that the bankrupt is unable to pay his debts or that the value of his assets is less than the amount of his liabilities.

An associate is a spouse, a relative, a spouse of a relative, a business partner, a business partner's spouse or relative, an employer or an employee of the bankrupt.

The court has wide power to adjust the undervalue transaction. An order may be made to impose an obligation on the party with whom the bankrupt entered into the transaction and on any other person. The position is ameliorated to some extent by the Insolvency (NI) Order 1989, article 315(2), as amended by the Insolvency (No 2) Act 1994 which provides protection for *bona fide* purchasers from the donee. Basically, as long as a prospective purchaser makes proper enquiries and searches the property cannot be subsequently recovered from him if he was not aware of the surrounding circumstances or of any bankruptcy proceedings.[204]

PREFERENCES

27.20 Under the 1989 Order, article 313, where the bankrupt has given a preference to any person, the court may on the application of the trustee make such order as it thinks fit to restore the position to what it would have been if the preference had not been given.

The bankrupt gives a preference to a person if that person is one of his creditors, or a surety or guarantor for any of his debts or liabilities and the bankrupt does something which puts the person preferred in a better position in the subsequent bankruptcy than he would otherwise have been. The bankrupt must have intentionally put that person in a better position than he would otherwise have been. Again, the fact that an act has been done under a court order does not prevent it from being a voidable preference.

The court may only make an order in respect of the preference if it was:

(1) a transaction at undervalue within five years of the bankruptcy petition;

(2) given to an associate of the bankrupt within two years of the bankruptcy petition;

(3) a preference not within either of the two previous categories but made within six months of the bankruptcy petition.

Unless the preference constituted a transaction at an undervalue given within two years of the bankruptcy petition, in which case an order may be made without proof of insolvency, the trustee must prove that the bankrupt was insolvent at the time he gave the preference or became insolvent as a result of it. However, where the preference constituted a transaction at an undervalue and was given to a person who was an associate of the bankrupt, such insolvency is presumed unless the contrary is shown.

The Insolvency (NI) Order 1989, article 315(2) as amended by the Insolvency (No 2) Act 1994 provides protection for *bona fide* purchasers from the person preferred. As in the case of a transaction at an undervalue, property cannot be recovered from a subsequent purchaser acting in good faith without notice of the surrounding circumstances nor of any bankruptcy proceedings.[205]

---

[204] Cf para 27.24.
[205] *Ibid*.

TRANSACTIONS DEFRAUDING CREDITORS

27.21 Under the 1989 Order, articles 367-369, a defrauded creditor can apply for relief even where the transferor is not a bankrupt or a company being wound up. Relief is not limited to insolvency proceedings and may be available outside the time limits applying to applications in respect of transactions at an undervalue or preferences.

Where the transferor is not bankrupt an application for relief can be made to the court by any person prejudiced by the transaction. Where the transferor is a bankrupt an application may be made by the Official Receiver, the trustee or the victim of the transaction.

To be set aside, the transaction must have been entered into at an undervalue for the purpose of putting assets beyond the reach of a person making a claim, or otherwise prejudicing the interests of such a person in relation to the claim.[206] Creditors may be actual, contingent or unascertainable future creditors. The court may make such order as it thinks fit to restore the position to what it would have been if the transaction had not existed and to protect the interests of the victims of the transaction. The interests of *bona fide* third parties are protected by the Insolvency (NI) Order 1989, article 369(2) and are not subject to any subsequent amendment. For a purchaser to be protected he has to show that he acted in good faith, for value and without notice.

ORDERS

27.22 The 1989 Order contains a number of provisions under which property formerly owned by a bankrupt may be recovered by the trustee in bankruptcy to form part of the bankrupt's estate or used to reduce the liabilities.

The court has very wide powers to adjust undervalue transactions and preferences. The order may affect both the party with whom the bankrupt entered the transaction and any other person. The property or the relevant sum of money may be recovered by the trustee.

Some provision is made for the protection of *bona fide* purchasers. The order must not prejudice any interest in property which was acquired from a person other than the bankrupt in good faith and for value. Nor shall the order require a person who received a benefit from the transaction or preference in good faith and for value to pay a sum to the trustee of the bankrupt's estate, except where he was party to the transaction or was a creditor of the bankrupt.

GIFT ON TITLE

27.23 When a gift, preference or transaction at an undervalue appears on the title it is important for a prospective purchaser to consider the position in relation to the possible insolvency of the donor, particularly if the voluntary deed is dated after 1 October 1991 and before 26 July 1994.

---

[206] In *Midland Bank plc* v *Wyatt* [1995] 1 FLR 696 the bank succeeded in establishing that Mr Wyatt had set up a trust to transfer beneficial ownership of his property with a fraudulent motive and it was accordingly set aside.

Before the main provisions of the Insolvency (NI) Order 1989 became operative on 1 October 1991, if there was a gift on the title, it was generally only necessary for a statutory declaration as to the solvency of the donor to be furnished together with a clear bankruptcy search against him. This was usually sufficient to satisfy a prospective purchaser that there was no danger of the property being affected by the subsequent bankruptcy of the donor.

After 1 October 1991 the position of a purchaser from a donee became far less secure. The 1989 Order, article 312, provides that where the bankrupt has entered into a transaction at an undervalue within the previous five years, his trustee may apply to the court for an order to restore the position to what it would otherwise have been.

Article 315(2) provides that the court may make an order which may affect the property of or impose any obligation on any person whether or not he is the person with whom the bankrupt entered into the transaction. Thus the position of third parties can be affected.

Originally, article 315(2) further provided that an order should not prejudice any interest in property which was acquired from a person other than the bankrupt in good faith, for value and without notice of the relevant circumstances (the gift).

This conferred very limited protection for a purchaser from a donee because he normally would have been aware of the gift. Consequently it was advisable for him to be provided with indemnity insurance until the expiration of five years from the date the gift was made. As all gifts made before article 315 was amended are now more than five years old this should no longer present a difficulty for a purchaser from a donee of such a gift.

In the case of registered land the position was governed by the Land Registration Act (NI) 1970, section 11(1), which provides that, in the absence of actual fraud, the title of a registered purchaser is not affected in consequence of his having notice of any deed, document or other matter relating to or affecting the title.[207]

Then section 67A of the Land Registration Act (NI) 1970 was added by the 1989 Order with specific reference to the effect of the bankruptcy of the registered owner. It provides that a purchaser in good faith for valuable consideration can be registered as the new owner even if the vendor is bankrupt unless, at the date of registration of the transfer, notice of the bankruptcy petition or bankruptcy order has been registered. However a purchaser with actual knowledge of the bankruptcy petition or bankruptcy order is deemed not to take in good faith.

As a result of this provision the 1989 Order offered a greater degree of protection to a purchaser of registered land than to a purchaser of unregistered land. In the case of registered land, mere knowledge of the gift was not a

---

[207] There are exceptions, *eg*, s 34(4), registered and unregistered burdens, duties and liabilities of trustee, mineral rights can affect a purchaser on registration.

sufficient ground for the transaction to be subsequently set aside, whereas in the case of unregistered land it was sufficient.

Insolvency (No 2) Act 1994

27.24 The Insolvency (No 2) Act 1994 (the '1994 Act') which came into effect on 26 July 1994 attempts to improve the situation and ensure that the position is the same for both registered and unregistered land. It amends the provisions of the 1989 Order relating to orders avoiding transactions at an undervalue and preferences. Greater protection is conferred on a purchaser from a donee but the position of a donee remains the same.

The 1989 Order, article 315(2), has been amended to remove the requirement that, for protection from a court order avoiding a transfer at an undervalue or a gift, an interest in property should be acquired without notice of the gift. Now, if such an interest is acquired in good faith for value from a person other than the bankrupt, even if the purchaser was aware of the gift, that interest shall not be affected by any court order.[208] Nor can a court order prejudice any interest deriving from such an interest.

If a purchaser from the donee has notice of the surrounding circumstances and of the relevant proceedings he is assumed to be acting otherwise than in good faith. The surrounding circumstances are knowledge that the transaction was an undervalue or preference. The relevant proceedings are either presentation of the bankruptcy petition or adjudication of the bankrupt.

The 1994 Act is not retrospective but has effect in relation to all interests acquired or benefits received after 26 July 1994 when it became operative. A purchaser from a donee has the protection of the 1994 Act where his interest is acquired after that date, even if the gift was made prior to it.

If the gift was made after 1 October 1991 the property could potentially be recovered from the donee any time up to the expiration of five years from the date of the gift. It could also be recovered from a purchaser from a donee if he acquired his interest after 1 October 1991 and before 26 July 1994 unless he qualifies for the limited protection afforded by the 1989 Order. Now that over five years has passed since 26 July 1994 any property which was the subject of a gift made between 1 October 1991 and 26 July 1994 cannot be recovered from a donee's successor under article 315(2) of the 1989 Order as long as the property was acquired in good faith for value.

The potential risk is now confined to cases where insufficient enquiries are made about a donor who made a gift less than five years previously. If a purchaser from a donee acquires an interest in the property after 26 July 1994 it cannot be recovered from him even if he was aware of the gift, unless he had knowledge of bankruptcy proceedings affecting the donor. Accordingly, it seems that a purchaser is safe in completing if he has a clear bankruptcy search against the donor and thus can satisfy himself that a bankruptcy petition has not been presented.

---

[208] Similar provision is made in respect of a purchase from a donee who received the property by a conveyance at an undervalue made by a company which later became insolvent.

There is no longer any need for a purchaser from the donee to take out insurance against the donor becoming bankrupt.

Other considerations

27.25 One of the difficulties with a voluntary conveyance or transfer at undervalue on the title is that a transaction may be set aside if the donor subsequently is adjudged bankrupt. The title of subsequent purchasers in good faith is now protected to an extent but the problem with the donee remains and a court has power to recover property from him if the donor becomes bankrupt within five years. A declaration of solvency is not a satisfactory solution because of its dubious nature and an insurance policy can be expensive.

The position of any mortgagee lending to a donee to build on or to extend existing buildings on the property transferred is also vulnerable during this five year period.

When acting for a potential donee it is important to advise him of the potential risks of the property subsequently being taken from him. The possibility of the donor or a third party alleging oppression or undue influence against the donee should also be explained.

CHAPTER TWENTY EIGHT

MATRIMONIAL AND OTHER INTERESTS

Introduction

28.01 At one time, when the husband was usually the breadwinner in the family, the matrimonial home in which he lived with his wife was generally held in his sole name. The wife did not work and was unlikely to have a legal or equitable interest in the property. Even if she made a financial contribution to the price, her name might not have appeared on the title. Nowadays, the title to the matrimonial home is usually held in joint names and the wife often makes a direct financial contribution towards the property.

GENERAL PROPERTY RIGHTS

Title in joint names

28.02 Where the title to the matrimonial home is held in the joint names of both spouses, the wife has a legal interest in the property and will not have any difficulty in establishing her rights to it. Under a joint tenancy the ownership is treated as a single unit as against third parties and the shares are regarded as equal. Under a tenancy in common the shares, though undivided, are not necessarily equal. The purchase deed should specify the extent of each share as a portion of the whole.[209]

Title in husband's sole name

28.03 Where the title to a matrimonial home is held in the sole name of the husband, the wife does not acquire any proprietary interest merely through having the status of spouse, apart from the rights of occupation conferred by the Family Homes and Domestic Violence (NI) Order 1998.[210] Nevertheless, an interest may be acquired by other means and exist independently of such status.

The general legal principles which apply to married couples usually also apply to unmarried couples and other home-sharers who have acquired property as their home by joint efforts.

Where a wife does not have a legal interest, equity may imply the existence of a beneficial interest in the matrimonial home, as established in *Gissing* v *Gissing*.[211] A beneficial interest can be created for a spouse by a direct cash contribution to the purchase price, the deposit, mortgage repayments or even legal charges, of a not insubstantial amount. The court attempts to calculate proportions of contributions where possible.

---

[209] Cf paras 18.29-18.44.
[210] Cf para 28.32.
[211] [1971] AC 886 (HL).

The position where there have been indirect cash contributions to the purchase was left in some doubt by *Gissing* v *Gissing*. Since then different judicial approaches have been taken which are not always easy to reconcile and there is some authority for two opposing views.

One theory is that there is no distinction between direct and indirect contributions, either is sufficient to establish an interest in the property.[212] The other theory is that for indirect contributions to create an interest there must be evidence of intention to do so.[213]

In *Lloyds Bank plc* v *Rosset*[214] it was said that the fundamental question is whether, independently of any inference to be drawn from the conduct of the parties, there has at any time been any agreement, arrangement or understanding reached between them that the property is to be shared beneficially.

The finding of such an agreement can only be based on evidence of express discussions between the parties. Once a finding to this effect is made, if the wife asserting a claim to a beneficial interest has acted to her detriment or significantly altered her position in reliance on the agreement, a constructive trust or proprietary estoppel arises and the husband is unable to deny that he holds a portion of the property on trust for his wife.

On the other hand, where there is no evidence to support a finding of an agreement or arrangement to share, the court must rely entirely on the conduct of the parties to give rise to a constructive trust. In this situation direct contributions to the purchase price will readily justify the inference necessary to the creation of a constructive trust, but it is extremely doubtful that anything less will do.

It is interesting to note that *Rosset* was ignored by the Court of Appeal in *Midland Bank plc* v *Cooke*[215] which seemed to suggest that conduct alone can infer an equitable interest even without prior discussion. In that case it was held that having established some direct contribution it was open to the court to calculate the extent of the wife's beneficial interest otherwise than in proportion to that direct initial contribution, which is also contrary to previous authority.

In the Northern Ireland case of *McFarlane* v *McFarlane*[216] (which was expressly approved by the House of Lords in *Rosset*) following *Gissing* v *Gissing,* it was held that the indirect contributions of a spouse must, if they are to earn or generate a beneficial interest in property acquired, be the subject of some agreement or arrangement between the spouses sufficient to show a mutual intention that the indirect contributions will benefit the contributor. In

---

[212] See *Falconer* v *Falconer* [1970] 1 WLR 1333, *Hazell* v *Hazell* [1972] 1 WLR 301, *Midland Bank plc* v *Dobson* (1985) 135 NLJ 751 (CA).
[213] See *Cowcher* v *Cowcher* [1972] 1 WLR 425, *Lloyds Bank plc* v *Rosset* [1990] 2 WLR 867 (HL) *McFarlane* v *McFarlane* [1972] NI 59.
[214] [1990] 2 WLR 867 (HL).
[215] [1995] 2 FLR 915.
[216] [1972] NI 59.

Britannia Building Society v *Johnston*[217] Carswell LJ sought a definite agreement between the parties which may make it even more difficult to establish beneficial rights.

As a result of the courts' adherence to the policy of trying to establish an agreement, arrangement or understanding between the parties, an occupying spouse who has made an indirect, rather than direct, contribution to the matrimonial home is in a worse position on the bankruptcy of her husband than on divorce. In divorce proceedings a wife's endeavours in looking after her family and home can be recognised by the court in adjusting the property rights, but this is not relevant in bankruptcy.[218]

This can give rise to unfair and unsatisfactory results. The Law Commission has consistently recommended that a house owned by one or both spouses which becomes the matrimonial home, in the absence of agreement to the contrary, should be subject to statutory co-ownership, that is, shared equally between them.[219] A different view was taken in *Midland Bank* v *Cooke* (see above) by Waite LJ who considered that it would be anomalous to create a range of home-buyers who were beyond equity's assistance in formulating a fair presumed basis for the sharing of beneficial title.

If the Law Commission's recommendation is accepted, the position will be clarified. In the meantime, an application for determination of the interests of each spouse has to be made under the Married Women's Property Act 1882, section 17, in the event of a dispute.

Married Women's Property Act 1882, section 17

28.04 Where the interests in property are not clearly defined and there are conflicting claims between husband and wife, either party may make a summary application to court for determination of any dispute affecting the title or possession of property. The court may make such order as it thinks fit.

There has been controversy as to the scope of the court's discretion in this respect, especially as to how far it can vary substantive legal or equitable rights to matrimonial property. It now seems settled that a restrictive view has to be taken.[220]

This means that section 17 is procedural only and cannot operate to confer on a spouse a beneficial interest he does not otherwise have. It confirms that the court has no jurisdiction to change the property rights of spouses. There must have been a mutual intention on the part of the spouses to create such interest and it must arise by agreement between them or through a presumption recognised by the law or equity, such as a resulting trust.[221]

---

[217] [1994] NIJB 21.
[218] See *In the matter of James Wills, bankrupt*, unreported, 30 November 1992.
[219] This is supported by the final report of the Land Law Working Group para 2.2.13 and the Law Reform Advisory Committee for NI in the First Programme of Law Reform LRAC No 1.
[220] *Pettitt* v *Pettitt* [1970] AC 777, *Gissing* v *Gissing* [1971] AC 886.
[221] *McFarlane* v *McFarlane* [1972] NI 59 Lord MacDermott LCJ.

Disputes between spouses most usually arise on divorce and the limitations of section 17 are of less importance now that there are wider powers under the Matrimonial Causes (NI) Order 1978 to make property adjustment orders on breakdown of marriage. However, the question of beneficial ownership of the matrimonial home still remains important in other contexts, such as bankruptcy and third party interests or pre-divorce disputes.

The best way of concluding the question of title between spouses is to expressly declare trusts of the beneficial interests in the conveyance. In the absence of fraud or mistake at the time of the transaction the parties cannot go behind the declaration even on death or break-up of the marriage.

An application under section 17 may be registered in the Land Registry or the Registry of Deeds as a *lis pendens*.

Matrimonial Causes (NI) Order 1978

28.05 By virtue of the provisions of article 26 the court has power, on granting a decree of divorce, to make an order for an interest in property to be transferred, settled, varied, extinguished or reduced for the benefit of the other party or for the children of the marriage.

RIGHTS OF OCCUPATION

Protected rights of occupation

28.06 Before *Williams & Glyn's Bank* v *Boland*[222] it was possible to take a title held in a husband's sole name, which then was a more common occurrence, at face value without the consequences being too serious. There are still cases where property purchased some years ago in the sole name of a husband comes on to the market, but it is now essential to look beyond the interest of the husband to that of the wife and any other occupiers or persons in receipt of rents and profits who might have a relevant interest.

Registered land

28.07 It is particularly important to enquire about rights of occupation in relation to registered land because such interests are not always capable of being disposed of or created by registered dispositions. They can generally be overridden and most do not affect a purchaser whether or not he has notice of their existence.

The rights of a person in actual occupation of the land or in receipt of rents and profits from it are protected by the Land Registration Act (NI) 1970, Schedule 5, Part I paragraph 15 and can affect the land without registration.[223] Any such right is protected unless upon inquiry it is not disclosed or can be classified as a Schedule 6 burden capable of registration.

---

[222] [1980] 2 All ER 408 (HL).
[223] Cf paras 7.39-7.40.

In England the Land Registration Act 1925, section 70, makes similar provisions. The matters which affect land without registration, equivalent to Schedule 5 burdens, are known as overriding interests because they override the registration of ownership and can affect the subsequent purchaser for value.

The provision relating to rights of occupation in particular has produced many difficulties, as is evidenced by *Williams & Glyn's Bank* v *Boland*.[224] In that case the House of Lords held that the beneficial interest of a wife who had contributed directly to the purchase price of a matrimonial home, registered in the sole name of her husband, took priority over the interest of the bank to which the husband had mortgaged the property without the knowledge of the wife and without any enquiry as to her interest. There was no suggestion that the parties were not living together amicably.

The basis for the decision was that the wife was in actual occupation, notwithstanding that the husband was also in occupation. Although the interest of the wife was a minor equitable interest only, the fact of actual occupation enabled that interest to became an overriding interest not capable of defeat by a transfer to a subsequent purchaser or a mortgage.

The concept of the potential beneficial interest was not new in itself but the *Boland* case extended the principle beyond matrimonial claims to parties who are not married, parents and children, friends and anyone purchasing a house together. It cannot now be safely assumed that an occupant of full age has not made some contribution to give himself a proprietary right in any type of real property.[225]

It would therefore seem that any person who has a beneficial interest in registered land and who is in actual occupation at the date of registration of a subsequent disposition relating to the land cannot be prejudiced by that registration unless he has been asked previously whether or not he has any rights in the land and has not disclosed any nor given his consent.

For any rights to be even *prima facie* overriding interests the person concerned must be in actual occupation of the property or in receipt of rents and profits from it. Clearly mere occupancy does not in itself confer any right and a proprietary right of some nature must also exist. Rights together with occupation protect the occupant of registered land.

The *Boland* decision is fully applicable to registered land in Northern Ireland but it does not rest easily on the system. It does not allow a purchaser for value to buy property from a registered owner without having to make investigations beyond the actual register of title.

---

[224] [1980] 2 All ER 408 (HL).

[225] It is interesting to note that in the English case of *Woolwich Building Society* v *Dickman and Todd* [1996] 3 All ER 204 the Court of Appeal went still further by holding that a form of consent and postponement executed by tenants in possession of the premises did not have its intended effect. The only way to prevent the tenant's interest from achieving overriding status is to place a provision on the register of title to that effect.

Unregistered land

28.08 The *Boland* case is equally applicable to unregistered land but there the position is more complex. The difference is the application of the doctrine of notice. In unregistered cases, the purchaser's obligation depends on the matters of which he has actual or constructive notice.

The common law rule is that a purchaser has constructive notice of anything detectable from an inspection of the property and in particular of anything that would be revealed by reasonable enquiry of any occupier.[226] Consequently a *bona fide* purchaser for value of a legal estate takes it free of any equitable interest of which he does not have actual or constructive notice.

An intending purchaser probably has constructive notice only of matters that would come to light after making such enquiries or inspections as are reasonable in the circumstances. If he acts in this fashion and does not find a spouse or any other adult in occupation or evidence which would give him notice of her occupation, he is protected against her interest. On the other hand, if he does find such evidence and fails to make proper enquiries, the interest he takes will be subject to that of the spouse.

A purchaser will normally have constructive notice of the rights of any person in occupation of the land. The fact of occupation gives notice that rights may exist and the rights of any such persons must be considered.

The case of *Ulster Bank Ltd v Shanks*[227] considered the question of notice of the wife's interest. The title to the house was in the husband's name only but it was agreed between husband and wife that by the date of the second mortgage to the bank the wife had acquired a one-third undivided equitable share in the house. Although the wife was present during part of the discussions between the bank manager and her husband relating to the second mortgage she gave no indication that she had any interest in the house nor that her consent was necessary to give any security. It was held that in the circumstances it could not be said that the bank ought reasonably to have made inquiries of the wife as to whether she had an interest in the house and accordingly the bank did not have constructive notice of the wife's interest.

In the more recent case of *Britannia Building Society v Johnston*[228] the result was the same, but it was decided on the basis that the wife had failed to establish an equitable interest which would take priority to the mortgage. The husband inherited the entire legal interest in the property on his father's death and subsequently mortgaged it to the building society without the knowledge of his wife. She had not made a direct contribution to the purchase of the property. Further, there was nothing approaching a definite agreement between the spouses to the effect that the wife was to have an interest nor proof that she had acted to her detriment in reliance on any such agreement.

---

[226] *Hunt v Luck* [1902] 1 Ch 428.
[227] [1982] NI 143.
[228] [1994] NIJB 21.

In *Allied Irish Banks Ltd v McWilliams and another*[229] the bank was less successful. The husband and wife were joint legal owners of the house but the wife paid the deposit and made the mortgage repayments to the building society. The bank was the owner of a charge created by the Enforcement of Judgments Office on foot of a judgment against the husband. There was no express agreement between the spouses concerning the equitable ownership in the house. Ownership therefore resulted to the wife as the person who paid for the property. Since no attempt had been made by the bank to prove that it had no actual or constructive notice of that ownership, the wife's equitable interest had priority over the subsequent legal charge of the bank.

Difficulties of the *Boland* decision

28.09 It is not always easy to identify a potential overriding interest. The courts are inclined to infer a resulting trust in favour of any contributor to the purchase price other than a contributor against whom the presumption of advancement applies, but it is seldom immediately apparent that there has been such a contribution. It is also unlikely that any formal arrangement as to contributions by a non-owning spouse will have been reduced to writing.

There is the additional potential hazard of a couple defending a claim for possession of their home conjuring up a direct contribution made by the wife without any acknowledgment on the title and this would be particularly difficult to disprove.

When a purchaser and a spouse are caught up in the financial manoeuvres of the husband, a decision has to be made as to whose rights take precedence. In the absence of any consent by the spouse or denial of any interest, there is a conflict between the interests of two innocent parties. It appears from the *Boland* decision that the rights of the non-owning spouse (*ie*, the spouse without the legal title) take precedence in such a situation, contrary to the general principles of conveyancing.[230]

Possible legislative solutions

28.10 The particular difficulty caused by overriding interests is the fact that they may exist without being discovered. In order to make them more obvious it has been suggested that they could be registered in the Statutory Charges Register.[231] For registered land, there is also the possibility of bringing the rights in question within the ambit of Schedule 6 rather than Schedule 5. An alternative proposal is to register any such right on the title in a form similar to a matrimonial charge.[232]

---

[229] [1982] NI 156.
[230] This conflict between the interests of a lender and the interests of an occupying spouse is currently the subject of a consultation paper issued by the Office of Law Reform with a view to drafting legislation to clarify the position.
[231] See James Russell NILQ Vol 32, Spring 1981, at p 13.
[232] Recommended by the final report of the Land Law Working Group para 2.2.34.

Registration of an equitable interest in any of these forms would protect it against a purchaser or mortgagee whose interest would then be subject to it, whether or not any enquiries had been made. In some respects the *status quo* is preferable because spouses who are not involved in matrimonial conflict do not want to register interests based on mutual trust. From this point of view, registration might be acceptable so long as it does not prejudice the position of the innocent spouse, just as the existing position does not do so.

Unprotected rights of occupation

28.11 Since the *Boland* case the courts appear to have been trying to keep a sense of balance to ensure that a law designed to protect the vulnerable does not render the matrimonial home unacceptable as security to financial institutions.

Two trustees for sale: interests overreached

28.12 The case of *City of London Building Society* v *Flegg*[233] illustrates that there are limitations to the rights which can be protected against purchasers and mortgagees. A property in which four people were to live was purchased in the names of two of them, although the non-owning occupiers had contributed to the purchase price and were entitled to a beneficial interest. The owners later mortgaged the property to the Society, which sought possession when they defaulted. It was held that, although the non-owning occupiers had a right to occupy the house as against the owners, they had no such right as against the Society.

The rights of the beneficiaries were in the sale proceeds held by the two trustees (the owners) and no longer in the property itself. The equitable interest was overreached and there was no interest in the property remaining for the right of occupation to protect. The Society was protected by having paid the sum borrowed to the two trustees.

The original conveyance contained an express trust for sale and a declaration that the joint proprietors, as trustees, were to have all the powers of mortgaging of an absolute owner. The capital money arising was paid to two trustees for sale and the occupying beneficiaries' interests were thereby overreached.

Once the beneficiaries' rights have been shifted from the land to capital monies in the hands of trustees, there is no longer an interest in the land to which the occupation can be referred or which it can protect. If the trustees sell in accordance with the statutory provisions and so overreach the beneficial interests, nothing remains to which a right of occupation can attach.

The charge created in favour of the Society overreached the beneficial interests of the occupiers. There is nothing which has the effect of preserving against the Society any rights of the occupants to occupy the land by virtue of their beneficial interests in the equity of redemption which remains vested in the trustees.

---

[233] [1987] 3 All ER 435 (HL).

This decision confirms that the problem for the mortgagee in the *Boland* case arose because the husband created the mortgage as sole owner and was regarded as a sole trustee for sale. If there were two trustees for sale and the money had been paid to them, the wife's equitable interest would have been overreached and postponed to the mortgagee.

The principle of overreaching is that where land subject to a trust is sold and the proceeds are paid to at least two trustees, the beneficial interests under the trust shift from the land to the proceeds of sale.

Accordingly it is safer for a purchaser or mortgagee not to deal with a sole vendor and to insist on the appointment of a second trustee to receive capital money.[234] In practice it may be difficult if the legal estate is vested in one spouse only. He is unlikely to appoint the other spouse as trustee if he had not, for whatever reason, wished her name to be on the title in the first place. If obliged to appoint a co-trustee, it is perfectly possible that he may choose to appoint one who is in collusion with him to further his own ends.

In Northern Ireland there are no statutory trusts for sale and it is not normal to declare trusts for sale in a conveyance.[235] Nevertheless the principles of the *Flegg* case may be applicable in this jurisdiction because the concept of overreaching is recognised.

Insufficient occupation

28.13 Following the *Boland* case, one of the potential dangers for a prospective purchaser or mortgagee was that, despite making all conceivable enquiries, he may be bound by an interest claimed by an occupant coming onto the land between completion and registration of the purchase deed.

This possibility was considered in *Abbey National Building Society* v *Cann*.[236] A house was purchased with a mortgage by a single owner who did not occupy it himself, although he told the Society that it was for his sole occupation. The potential occupiers arrived on the premises with workmen about an hour before the transfer to the owner and the charge were created.

When the owner defaulted on the loan and the Society sought possession, it was held that in order to assert an overriding interest against the purchaser, the claimants must have been in occupation at the date of completion and presumably also at the date of registration. The claimants' presence at the material time was not sufficient to constitute proper occupation and was no more than preparatory activity leading to the assumption of actual residential occupation later.

For the beneficial interest of the occupier to be successfully asserted it must exist before completion. If it arises between completion and registration, the

---

[234] Cf para 25.23.
[235] Final report of the Land Law Working Group at para 2.215 supports the proposal of the Survey of Land Law of NI 1971 to impose a statutory trust but not a trust for sale in all cases where co-ownership appears on the title.
[236] [1990] 1 All ER 1085 (HL).

purchaser's equitable interest which arises by the payment or advance of money on completion will take priority over it.

Accordingly one of the hazards of the *Boland* case is reduced, but there is still a risk that a claimant may come into occupation during the delay between inspection by the purchaser or mortgagee and completion of the transaction. There is a greater risk of this happening on a mortgage of the property than on sale.

Definition of occupation

28.14 In the *Cann* case the meaning of actual occupation was defined. The term is said to be synonymous with reside and should be given its ordinary meaning of possession or presence on the land. It is physical possession as distinct from legal possession by receipt of rents and profits. Although involving physical presence, it does not connote continuous and uninterrupted presence. It can exist through the agency of another person but regular car parking, for example, is not occupation. Even with these guidelines, there may still be difficulty in deciding what amounts to actual occupation in a particular case.

Lloyds Bank plc v Rosset[237] illustrates the problem. Semi-derelict property was purchased in the sole name of the husband and possession was given prior to formal completion. The wife was on the property every day with the builders and sometimes slept there. The majority of the Court of Appeal found that her actual physical presence was sufficient to constitute occupation.[238]

Like possession, occupation involves some form of continuity rather than periodic visits and should be unambiguous. Temporary absence cannot bring occupation to an end and a spouse's intermittent occupation poses a further hazard to the purchaser.

In *Kingsnorth Finance Co Ltd v Tizard*[239] the marriage was in difficulties and although the wife came to the house each day, she only slept there when the husband was away. The husband removed all traces of his wife's presence when enquiries were made by the mortgagee but she was still held to be in occupation.

Occupants with the vendor

28.15 It has become common practice for spouses purchasing a property to do so in joint names. However it is not unusual to find a vendor, who purchased a property some years ago, holding it in his sole name. If the vendor's solicitor finds there is a potential conflict of interest between the parties it may be advisable for the other spouse to be independently advised.

---

[237] [1988] 3 All ER 915(CA), [1990] 1 All ER 1111 (HL).

[238] The dissenting judgment of Mustill LJ in the Court of Appeal on this point accords more with the reasoning in the *Cann* case. The House of Lords, having held that the wife acquired no beneficial interest, did not consider whether she was in actual occupation when the charge was created.

[239] [1986] 2 All ER 54.

In most cases there is no difficulty between the spouses, but the solicitor must be careful not to fraudulently misrepresent the ownership of the property. He also is normally required on completion to procure vacant possession and to remove all charges and other encumbrances affecting the property.

The enquiries in use endeavour to put on the vendor the responsibility of identifying the occupants and of obtaining their consent to the sale or mortgage. Therefore on taking instructions, the vendor's solicitor should ascertain the position and make enquiries regarding the spouse, any other occupants and the possibility of anyone being in receipt of rents and profits. If he does not make a proper investigation there is a danger of being found negligent for failing to discover a proprietary claim.

In view of the widespread development of shared interests of ownership, it is now considered essential for lenders of money on the security of matrimonial homes to make enquiries as to the rights of occupants, particularly of a wife where the legal title is not in joint names.

Until the *Boland* case, enquiries were not normally made beyond that of the vendor and the risks of this practice were generally accepted. The *Boland* case caused a reassessment of conveyancing practices and since then more careful enquiries have been made as to the rights of occupation of spouses, other members of the family, and even of persons outside it.

In the case of unregistered land, if there is any document in writing relating to an interest in the property which has not been registered, a later *bona fide* purchaser without notice will obtain priority over it, assuming he has made all necessary enquiries and inspections. Accordingly it is important for the owner of the interest to ensure that any such interest is brought to the purchaser's attention.

The position as to occupants and any other persons with potential rights should be stated as at the date of acceptance of the contract with confirmation at a later date. This prevents the vendor facing a claim for full damages under the Misrepresentation Act (NI) 1967 and prevents the purchaser being denied specific performance.

Conveyancing procedures

28.16 The purchaser's solicitor must, where appropriate, stipulate in the contract that the property is to be free of any occupation rights or satisfy himself prior to contract of the position.

If it appears that there is anyone other than the vendor in actual occupation or in receipt of rents and profits of the premises, the purchaser should ask the vendor to obtain a letter of acknowledgment from any such person stating that he has no right in or claim to the premises or any part thereof. The vendor should also warrant that those who sign the letter are the only relevant persons having any rights. The acknowledgment and warranty should be updated at completion.

In the event of an adult occupier failing to sign the acknowledgment, a letter can be sent to him requesting him to furnish full particulars of any claim within seven days or acknowledge that he has no such claim. He should also be advised that if nothing is heard from him within, say seven days, the transaction will proceed on the basis that he has no sustainable claim and any rights he has will cease. The letter should recommend that he contact his own solicitor.

In the purchase deed the vendor should where appropriate to his capacity convey or assign as beneficial owner because the full covenants for title are then implied.[240] If another person later turns up with a right or claim to the property during the vendor's period of ownership the purchaser has a claim against the vendor.

Occupants with the purchaser

28.17 In the case of a purchaser husband buying the property in his name only, it may be prudent to enquire as to whether there are any particular reasons for it. The most obvious example of the application of the *Boland* case is between spouses so they should be encouraged to vest property in joint names and prevent an interest in property being held without appearing on the title.

For various reasons it is now common practice for property to be purchased and a mortgage to be obtained in joint names of the spouses. They usually hold the title as joint tenants which means that they each have an equal undivided share in the property. Where it is held by them as tenants in common it may be advisable to state the actual beneficial portions in which the property is held in the case of any doubt at a later stage.

However, where instructions are given that the title is to be vested in the sole name of one of the spouses, usually the husband, no serious problems should arise where the parties are happily married. The solicitor's duty in that case is to inform the wife of her statutory rights but not necessarily to go on and register a matrimonial home right.[241]

As soon as the matrimonial affairs reach a stage where there appears to be any risk of dealing with the home to the disadvantage of the occupying spouse, a precautionary registration should perhaps be made. By then there may be a conflict in the duty a solicitor owes to each party separately and they should be independently advised to avoid any such difficulty.

CONSENT

28.18 There is another restriction on the potential for a wife's beneficial claim to override that of a purchaser or mortgagee where she has given her consent to a transaction. She then cannot argue that any interest she may have in the property takes priority. When a wife knows that the house is being bought with the help of a loan and genuinely supports her husband's proposal to this effect, it is taken that their common intention was for the charge to take priority over both beneficial interests.

---

[240] Cf paras 17.03-17.09.
[241] See paras 28.32-28.34.

There is a greater likelihood of a wife's interest creating problems for a mortgagee. To secure a position of priority, a mortgagee may insist on the wife being a party to the mortgage and this will in any event be necessary if the legal estate is vested in both spouses jointly. It is advisable to ensure that a wife has proper advice and avoid the obvious risks in leaving her husband to procure her signature to the deed.

In practice the difficulties are most likely to arise if the husband seeks finance for a business and the only security he can offer is his home. If he knows that his wife does not agree, the husband may resort to undue influence or misrepresentation to obtain her consent. Then if he is acting as the agent of the mortgagee in procuring the signature, the mortgagee will be left unable to enforce the security against the wife and take subject to her interest. In this context the husband is the mortgagee's agent if the mortgagee entrusts to the husband the task of having the mortgage deed executed.[242]

UNDUE INFLUENCE

28.19 The consent of the wife may be invalid and the transaction to which it was given set aside if it was procured by undue influence. The relationship of husband and wife does not of itself give rise to a presumption of undue influence and, as a rule, no presumption arises when a gift is made by a wife to her husband. However the courts tend to scrutinise very carefully the conduct of the husband to ensure that the wife gave a true and informed consent to the transaction.

There are no precise limits to the court's jurisdiction to relieve against undue influence but if it is presumed, rather than actual, the claim to have the transaction set aside can only succeed if the transaction was manifestly disadvantageous to the wife.[243]

Third party

28.20 The position relating to undue influence is further complicated where the transaction is made by the wife in favour of a third party but for the benefit of the husband. This commonly arises where the wife charges her interest in the matrimonial home to a bank to secure her husband's business debts. She may subsequently seek to avoid the charge as against the lender on the grounds that it was procured by undue influence or misrepresentation by her husband.

The question of whether a bank is entitled to enforce against a wife an obligation to secure a debt owed by her husband has come before the Court of Appeal on several occasions in recent years but differences of opinion have emerged.

---

[242] *Kingsnorth Trust Ltd* v *Bell* [1986] 1 All ER 423 (CA).
[243] *National Westminster Bank plc* v *Morgan* [1985] 1 AC 686 (HL).

The agency theory
28.21 One approach, which is known as the agency theory, favours the lender and essentially treats a wife in this position in the same way as any other surety is treated. It considers that the rights of the bank are not affected unless the husband was acting as the agent of the bank in procuring the surety to join or the bank had knowledge of the relevant facts.

The special equity theory
28.22 The alternative approach, known as the special equity theory, is more favourable to the wife. It considers that equity affords protection to a special class of surety where the natural features of the relationship between the surety and the debtor include influence by and reliance on the debtor. Here the obligation is unenforceable by the bank if the relationship was known to the bank and the consent was obtained by undue influence, misrepresentation, or without a proper understanding of the transaction and the bank failed to take reasonable steps to ensure that the surety had given a true and informed consent.

Classification of undue influence
28.23 In *Bank of Credit and Commerce International* v *Aboody*[244] undue influence was classified as follows:

Class 1: *actual undue influence*. There must be proof that undue influence was exerted to induce the claimant to enter into the transaction.

Class 2: *presumed undue influence*. If a relationship of trust and confidence can be shown, which was abused when the claimant was induced to enter the transaction, there is no need to prove actual undue influence.

Such a confidential relationship can be established in two ways:

Class 2A: certain relationships for example, solicitor and client, medical adviser and patient, as a matter of law raise the presumption that undue influence has been exercised.

Class 2B: if the complainant proves the *de facto* existence of a relationship of trust and confidence, the existence of such a relationship raises the presumption of undue influence.

There is no Class 2A presumption of undue influence as between husband and wife but, where a wife relies in all financial matters on her husband and simply does what he suggests, a presumption of undue influence within Class 2B can be established solely from the proof of such trust and confidence without proof of actual undue influence.

The matter has now been considered by the House of Lords in two cases.

---

[244] [1982] 4 All ER 955.

Application of the agency theory

28.24 In *Barclays Bank plc v O'Brien*[245] it was accepted that the risk of undue influence affecting a voluntary disposition by a wife in favour of a husband is greater than in the ordinary run of cases where no emotional ties affect the free exercise of the individual's will.

However it was thought there is no basis in principle for the special equity theory and, if the doctrine of notice is properly applied, there is actually no need for it.[246] A wife (or cohabitee) who has been induced to stand as surety for her husband's debts by his undue influence or misrepresentation has an equity as against him to set aside the transaction. This right is further enforceable against third parties if the husband was acting as the third-party's agent or the third party had actual or constructive notice of the facts giving rise to her equity.

A creditor is put on enquiry when a wife offers to stand as surety for her husband's debts by the fact that the transaction is not at face value to her financial advantage and there is a substantial risk of the husband committing a legal or equitable wrong that entitles the wife to set aside the transaction.

Unless the creditor then takes reasonable steps to satisfy himself that the wife's agreement has been properly obtained, he will have constructive notice of the wife's rights. This means that the wife should be advised to take independent advice (*ie*, independent of both the creditor and her husband) so that she understands the risk to herself and the matrimonial home.

On the facts of that case the bank knew that the parties were husband and wife and should have enquired as to the circumstances in which the wife had agreed to stand as surety for the debts of the husband. The failure by the bank to warn the wife of her full liability or to recommend that she take legal advice fixed the bank with constructive notice of the wrongful misrepresentation made by the husband to her and she was therefore entitled as against the bank to set aside the legal charge on the matrimonial home securing the husband's liability.

Application of the doctrine of notice

28.25 In *CIBC Mortgages v Pitt*[247] the spouses jointly owned the matrimonial home and jointly borrowed money to speculate on the stock market but the wife's agreement to it was very reluctant. The husband told the mortgagee that the loan was to pay off their existing mortgage and to buy a holiday home. The House of Lords held that a claimant who proved actual undue influence was not under the further burden of proving that the transaction was manifestly disadvantageous but was entitled as of right to have it set aside.

Actual undue influence is a type of fraud and a person who has been induced by undue influence to carry out a transaction is entitled to have it set aside as of

---

[245] [1993] 4 All ER 417 (HL).
[246] There does not seem to be any explanation as to how the doctrine of constructive notice as applied by the House of Lords in this case can be reconciled with the principles of registration of title, in particular the Land Registration Act (NI) 1970, Sch 5, Pt I, para 15.
[247] [1993] 4 All ER 433 (HL).

right. It cannot be argued that the transaction was beneficial to the person defrauded.

However, although the wife had established actual undue influence by the husband, the mortgagee was not affected by it because the husband had not acted as its agent in procuring her agreement and the mortgagee had no actual or constructive notice of the undue influence. So far as the mortgagee was aware, the loan was made to the spouses jointly and there was nothing to indicate that it was anything other than a normal advance to spouses for their joint benefit. The mere fact that there was a risk of there being undue influence because one of the borrowers was the wife was in itself not sufficient to put the mortgagee on enquiry.

The *Pitt* case was distinguished from *O'Brien*, not on the ground that one was a surety case and the other a joint loan, but on the grounds of notice. In *O'Brien*, the bank had notice of the wife's equitable right because it was aware of the existence of the relationship between the parties and the possibility of undue influence or misrepresentation. There was also a greater risk of wrongdoing because the loan was not for the wife's benefit. In *Pitt*, the bank had no actual knowledge of the acts constituting undue influence and no idea that the loan was not partly for the wife's benefit.

Obligation to take advice

28.26 The mortgagee was successful again in *Midland Bank plc v Massey*.[248] In that case a woman was persuaded by the misrepresentations of her lover, who did not live with her, to execute a legal charge on her house in favour of the bank to secure overdraft facilities for him. The bank required her to take independent legal advice. When her lover's business went into liquidation the bank claimed possession of the woman's house. The court asked whether the bank was put on inquiry as to the circumstances in which the woman agreed to provide the security and if so, whether the bank had taken reasonable steps to ensure that her agreement to the charge was properly obtained.

The fact that the transaction was not to the woman's advantage and was likely to have been brought about by some legal or equitable wrong on the part of the lover was sufficient to put the bank on inquiry as to the possible existence of rights for the woman to seek to set aside the transaction. However, the bank's requirement that she should seek independent advice in the circumstances amounted to reasonable steps to ensure that her consent had been properly obtained.[249]

Similar reasoning was applied in *Banco Exterior International v Mann and others*[250] when the bank took a second charge over the matrimonial home held in the sole name of the husband as security for a loan to the husband's company. It was held that the bank was entitled to rely on the company's solicitor to give independent advice when advising the wife of the effect of a declaration waiving her rights in the matrimonial home in favour of the bank.

---

[248] [1994] 2 FLR 342.
[249] *O'Brien* was followed.
[250] [1995] 1 All ER 936.

The test was how the transaction appeared to the bank, which was entitled to assume that the solicitor would regard it as his professional duty to explain not only the nature and effect of the documents to the wife but also that she could lose her rights in the house and that it was for her to decide whether she was willing to take that risk.[251]

On the same basis, in *Northern Bank Ltd* v *McCarron*,[252] Carswell LJ granted possession to the bank of the matrimonial home held in joint names, over which the bank had a second charge. Although the wife in that case may have been subject to the undue influence of her husband, she did question the transaction and knew quite well what she was being asked to do. Despite her misgivings, she signed the mortgage document and a guarantee.

The wife would have been entitled in equity to have the transaction set aside against her husband but her right to resist the claims of the bank, which had no actual notice of the undue influence, depended on the operation of the doctrine of notice. If the bank acted reasonably in the steps which it took to see that the borrower was not subjected to undue influence, it was not obliged to ensure that the advisers carried out their duties properly. Nor was it required to stipulate the nature and extent of the advice.

In that case the steps taken by the bank in having the wife advised by a solicitor were sufficient to avoid it being fixed with constructive notice of the undue influence exercised by the husband upon the wife. It was reasonable for the bank to suppose that the solicitor would advise her in a fashion and in circumstances which would allow a fair estimate of the reality of her consent.

A different conclusion was reached by the Court of Appeal in *Credit Lyonnais Bank Nederland NV* v *Burch*.[253] The respondent pledged her home, without limit, as security for her employer's company overdraft. The bank told her repeatedly that the loan was without limit and advised her to take independent legal advice. She failed to do so. When the company went into liquidation the bank applied for possession and the respondent sought to set aside the mortgage. The court found that there was a Class 2B relationship of trust and confidence between the respondent and her employer such as to raise a presumption of undue influence. Once this presumption is raised there is no need to prove that actual undue influence has been exerted. The bank had not taken reasonable steps to satisfy itself that the respondent's agreement to stand surety had been properly obtained and ordered that the transaction be set aside.

Nourse LJ went on to say that because the transaction was so manifestly disadvantageous to the respondent, the bank could not be said to have taken reasonable steps to avoid being fixed with constructive notice of her employer's undue influence. Neither the potential extent of her liability had been explained to her, nor had she received independent advice. It was not enough for the bank to advise her to take independent advice, it was at the least necessary that she should take such advice. Although the court considered this case to be an

---

[251] *O'Brien* was applied and *Massey* followed.
[252] [1995] NI 259 (Ch D).
[253] [1997] 1 All ER 144.

extreme one, manifestly to the disadvantage of the respondent, it may have departed from the guidance of the House of Lords in *O'Brien* without sufficient justification.

However in *Barclays Bank plc* v *Thomson*[254] solicitors acting for both the husband and the wife explained to the wife the full content of the legal charge and certified to the bank that they had done so. The solicitors' advice was held to be deficient because they did not explain that the charge was unlimited in effect both in respect of amount and period.

A different approach was taken in *Royal Bank of Scotland* v *Etridge (No 1)*[255] in which a wife signed a legal charge in favour of the bank by way of mortgage on her property as security for an overdraft facility granted to her husband for business purposes. The bank appointed a solicitor to act on its behalf and he saw both spouses together. When the bank subsequently sought possession the wife claimed that she had not seen the solicitor alone and that she viewed him as being employed by her husband to advance his own interests. She had not read the charge, although the charge was endorsed with a certificate signed by the solicitor stating that he had explained the contents and effect of the charge to the wife.

The Court of Appeal held that where the bank instructed a solicitor to ensure that a wife received independent advice the bank was responsible for the solicitor's discharge of his duty and would be fixed with constructive notice of any undue influence notwithstanding the terms of the endorsement on the charge to the effect that the advice had been given.

Thus there are two conflicting lines of authority relating to the role of legal advice. These different strands of authority were reviewed by the Court of Appeal in *Royal Bank of Scotland* v *Etridge (No 2) and Other Conjoined Appeals*.[256] It laid down general guidelines for future reference in an effort to provide a measure of clarity and consistency in the law.

In that case Stuart-Smith LJ noted that in case of actual (or express) undue influence it is necessary to prove that the transaction was entered into as a result of that undue influence and not of free will. In cases of presumed undue influence it is sufficient to establish the existence of a relationship of trust and confidence of such a nature that it is fair to presume that the wrongdoer abused the relationship. Once the relationship has been established the burden shifts to the wrongdoer to prove that the complainant entered into the transaction with full free and informed thought. Manifest disadvantage is a powerful evidential factor in establishing a claim against the wrongdoers and is relevant to the way the transaction is viewed by a third party.

A transaction is liable to be set aside if the third party has notice, actual constructive or imputed, that the consent was procured by improper means. Notice of wrongful action should affect the conscience of the third party and

---

[254] [1997] 4 All ER 816.
[255] [1997] 3 All ER 628.
[256] [1998] 4 All ER 705. At the time of writing, this case is the subject of an appeal to the House of Lords.

this forms the foundation of the *O'Brien* doctrine. The key question is to identify the circumstances in which a creditor is put on enquiry as to the existence of the surety's equity to set aside the transaction.

Where the relationship between the parties brings the case within Class 2(A) so as to raise a legal presumption of undue influence, notice of the relationship will automatically put the creditor on inquiry. Where the creditor has no notice of any such relationship, but knows that the surety is accustomed to place implicit trust in the wrongdoer, the position is the same. Where the transaction is so extravagantly improvident that it is difficult to explain in the absence of impropriety, then the creditor may likewise be put on inquiry. It would appear that *inquiry* is synonymous with *notice*. However in the ordinary case the transaction by which a wife is asked to provide a guarantee or collateral security for the debts of the business from which the family derives its income cannot be said to be extravagantly or even necessarily improvident.

So the question where a creditor can exercise its legal rights against a surety depends first on whether the surety has an equity to set aside the transaction because of undue influence and secondly on whether, at the time it made the loan, the creditor had notice of the surety's equity. The first question depends on what actually happened between the parties and the second on how the transaction appeared to the creditor.

In many cases the protection which ought to have been afforded by the provision of independent legal advice has proved illusory. It has not been adequate to explain to the surety the real extent of her liability not to ensure that she was entering into the transaction of her own free will. A bank is not normally required to question a solicitor's independence nor the sufficiency of his advice, but the bank is entitled to expect the solicitor to regard himself as owing a duty to the surety alone when giving advice, regardless of who has instructed him. The bank is not fixed with imputed notice of what comes to the solicitor's notice during that course of advising a surety.

While a bank is normally entitled to assume that a solicitor will discharge his duties fully and completely, it cannot make any such assumptions if it knows or ought to know that it is false. In such circumstances the availability of legal advice is insufficient to avoid the bank being fixed with constructive notice. Ultimately, the issue is whether in the light of all the information in the bank's possession, including its knowledge of the state of the account, the relationship of the parties and the availability of legal advice for the surety, there is still a risk that the surety has entered into the transaction as a result of the misrepresentation, undue influence or other legal wrong of the wrongdoer.

The Court of Appeal was clearly influenced by the fact that the transactions which become the subject of litigation are very common and that the efficient funding of small businesses is dependent on their validity. Lending institutions must be entitled to proceed in accordance with a settled practice which is effective to secure the validity of the transaction while at the same time affording the surety the protection of proper legal advice.

It is important to remember that the lending institutions do not take steps to ensure that the surety is properly advised in order to benefit the surety but for their own protection. Therefore when advising a surety a solicitor has to ensure that a proper explanation of the transaction is given. The surety must be given clear and comprehensive advice based on full knowledge of the material facts. The solicitor must be satisfied that the transaction is one which the client could sensibly enter into if free from improper influence. If the solicitor is not satisfied that his client can enter into the transaction free from improper influence then his duty is to advise the surety not to enter it and to refuse to act further if the surety so persists.

Possibility of restitution

28.27 There is also the possibility of the lender succeeding to an extent on a different principle. In *Dunbar Bank plc v Nadeem and another*[257] the husband used a bank loan to purchase a property in the joint names of himself and his wife and the property was also charged to secure his personal borrowings from the bank. This was a straightforward substitution of a joint debt for one in respect of which the husband was solely liable. *O'Brien* and *Pitt* were distinguished as being respectively for a pure surety and a joint borrowing for joint purposes.

The transaction as a whole was considered to be manifestly disadvantageous to the wife. The presumption of undue influence arose and there was nothing to rebut it. The circumstances as a whole were such as to put the bank on inquiry of the possible existence of undue influence and that as it had not taken any, let alone reasonable steps, to ascertain whether the wife fully appreciated what she was doing it had constructive notice of the undue influence.

It followed that but for an important consideration, the wife would be entitled to set aside the charge against the bank. Passages in the speech of Lord Blackburn in *Erlanger v New Sombrero Phosphate Co*[258] were relied on to the effect that a party seeking rescission had to be in a position to make *restitutio in integrum*.[259] There could be no setting aside unless the wife accounted to the bank for the benefit she had received from the use of its money. The amount she was required to repay was one half of that part of the loan used to acquire the property. If she was unable or unwilling to comply, the charge would not be set aside as against her.

Procedural precautions

28.28 Where a creditor is aware that security is being taken from a surety who is likely to be influenced by and to have some degree of reliance on the debtor, for the benefit of a debtor, the creditor should be seeking to ensure that unfair advantage is not taken of the surety. If however a creditor has taken reasonable steps, such as advising the surety to take independent advice or if the surety declines to do so, offering a fair explanation of the security document before the surety signs it, there is no reason why equity should intervene.[260]

---

[257] [1998] 3 All ER 876.
[258] (1878) 3 App Cas 1218.
[259] Restoration to the original position.
[260] *Per* Scott LJ in *Barclays Bank plc v O'Brien* in the Court of Appeal [1992] 3 WLR 593 (CA).

It is inadvisable to send the security document to the surety for signature unless it is accompanied by a recommendation to obtain independent legal advice. It is particularly inappropriate for the creditor to entrust the security document to the debtor with a view to him obtaining the surety's signature. If the surety is invited to sign the security document in the creditor's offices the creditor should, before the document is signed, explain its nature and effect to the surety.[261]

The fact is that no lender can ever be absolutely sure that a guarantor is not being subject to pressure from the principal debtor. Taking a pro-lender approach, it can be argued that to require it to do more than properly and fairly point out to the guarantor the desirability of obtaining independent advice and to require the documents to be executed in the presence of a solicitor is to impose an additional burden upon commercial lenders.[262] On the other hand it may be argued that unduly influenced wives need more protection from the law than lending institutions.

When giving advice, it is accepted that there are limits to the type of inquiry which can be made of a wife or other surety in an interview. If a competent solicitor properly performs his function he will explain the nature of the document and the effect of the transaction. It is not for him to advise the wife not to sign. Having had the matter explained to her the wife should be able to appreciate her position and make an informed decision.[263]

A solicitor in a case where undue influence exists should insist on the wife obtaining independent advice and otherwise refuse to act. The lender does not have to concern itself with the scope, nature, circumstances or adequacy of the advice given to the guarantor if the same lawyer advises both guarantor and creditor.[264] Where however, the bank requests that the wife guarantor be separately advised, the bank is not entitled to rely on the assurances of the husband's company that such advice would be given.[265] The lender must satisfy itself that the advice was given.

Elderly relatives

28.29 A transaction may be set aside for undue influence where it is of a fiduciary character other than between spouses. This may arise where an elderly person provides capital to finance the purchase of a house for a younger relative, as in *Cheese* v *Thomas*.[266]

---

[261] *Ibid*.
[262] *Per* Oliver LJ in *Coldunell Ltd* v *Gallon* [1986] 2 WLR 466 (CA).
[263] *Per* Carswell LJ in *Northern Bank Ltd* v *McCarron*.
[264] *Massey* v *Midland Bank* [1995] 1 All ER 929. See also *Halifax Mortgage Service* v *Stepsky* [1995] 4 All ER 656 where a solicitor who acted for both borrower and lender, although in breach of his duty to the lender, did not automatically fix the lender with imputed notice of undue influence or misrepresentation known to him.
[265] *Bank Melli Iran* v *Samadi - Rad* [1995] NPC 76.
[266] [1994] 1 All ER 35.

The Court of Appeal in that case took the view that the elderly relative was entitled to have the transaction set aside because a disadvantage arose from using all his capital to purchase a right to reside with his great-nephew, which was not a beneficial interest of any kind. This right was insecure and tied him to a particular house. Further, he was not in a position to compel a sale and the return of his money and would be in danger if his great-nephew failed to repay the mortgage.

Although on sale the property did not realise the original purchase price, the objective of equity was to restore the parties as closely as possible to their original positions, even if a precise restitution was not possible. The great-nephew had not acted with any impropriety and accordingly should not bear the whole loss resulting from the fall in value. The elderly relative was entitled to a proportionate share of the proceeds rather than the sum advanced.

In the case of *Baker* v *Baker* [267] in which the facts are similar, the plaintiff's claim to an interest under a resulting trust failed, presumably on the ground that he intended the house to belong to the defendants but his claim for compensation on the basis of proprietary estoppel succeeded. The extent of the equity was the value of his expectation, which was a much smaller sum than his original contribution plus interest, and the minimum amount to do justice to him.

The justification for awarding the plaintiff less than his outlay was explained on the basis that part of the money was to be the defendants' inheritance. A person who makes an absolute gift cannot complain later if subsequent events make him regret it. If however the gift was made on the understanding that the donor would acquire certain rights, then it could not be treated as an absolute gift.

In the *Baker* case there was no question of undue influence because the plaintiff was mentally sound and articulate, though elderly and frail.

These decisions reveal the pitfalls of making informal arrangements of this kind. The possibilities which should be considered at the time of the agreement include:

(1) Breakdown of the relationship;

(2) Claims by a spouse or ex-spouse;

(3) Bankruptcy of the legal owner;

(4) Repossession by a mortgagee;

(5) Deterioration in the health of the elderly person so that he has to move to a hospital, nursing home or sheltered accommodation.

For his own protection the elderly person should have a legal interest in the property. Such an interest provides greater security, although not necessarily against a mortgagee.[268] Without a legal interest the younger relative has the

---

[267] (1993) 25 HLR 408.
[268] See *Abbey National Building Society* v *Cann* above.

benefit of the capital contribution even if the relationship breaks down and there is no security against a mortgagee or a trustee in bankruptcy.

Although some remedy may be available, the elderly person may not be able to recover all his capital expenditure and this may have a detrimental effect on his quality of life. The cases underline the need to give proper thought to these considerations, to take independent advice and to have a written agreement.

CHARGING ORDERS AFFECTING INTERESTS IN LAND

28.30 The current system of enforcement of judgments was first introduced by the Judgments Enforcement Act (NI) 1969 and is now governed by the Judgments Enforcement (NI) Order 1981. The 1969 Act established a central Enforcement of Judgments Office through which most High Court and County Court judgments must be enforced. The EJO has a very wide jurisdiction to make an appropriate enforcement order for each judgment. It also keeps a register of judgments enforced.

Under the 1981 Order, article 45, a money judgment is enforceable against land. An order charging land may be imposed on the land or an estate in the land owned by the debtor to secure payment of the judgment debt. Such an order may be made absolutely or subject to specified conditions. An order charging land has no effect until it is registered in the Registry of Deeds or the Land Registry. After 12 years from the date of the judgment the order charging land ceases to have effect.

The court considered the nature and effect of an order charging land *In the matter of Folio 35420 Co Tyrone*[269] The husband and wife were the registered owners as tenants in common in equal shares of the lands comprised in the folio. On 15 June 1985 they executed a deed charging the lands in favour of the Britannia Building Society to secure an advance of £25,000. Registration was not effected until 16 April 1986. However, on 24 March 1986 the Bank of Ireland lodged for registration an order charging the interest of the husband on foot of a judgment obtained against him.

The issue between the bank and the building society was one of priority of registered burdens. The Land Registration Act (NI) 1970, section 40, provides that registered burdens which, if unregistered, would rank in priority according to the date of their creation shall rank according to the order in which they are entered on the register and not according to the order in which they are created or arise.

Prima facie, the bank's burden took priority over that of the building society because it was the first of the two to be registered. However, the order charging land was held not to be a transaction for valuable consideration and accordingly section 40 did not apply so as to give it priority.

Following general principles, the building society charge was for valuable consideration and until registered was an equitable charge which could not be defeated or postponed by the subsequent non-money transaction in favour of the bank. The ordinary rule of law that the priority of mortgages and charges is

---

[269] [1991] NI 273.

regulated by the dates on which they respectively are created or arise applied. Consequently, the building society charge took priority.

Charging order on joint interest

28.31 The question of the effect of a charging order on one co-owner's interest was subsequently considered in *Northern Bank Ltd* v *Haggerty*.[270] A husband and wife were joint owners of the matrimonial home. The bank obtained an order under the Judgments Enforcement (NI) Order 1981 charging the husband's interest in the house to secure payment of a debt and was granted leave to exercise the power of sale conferred by article 52 of that Order. Under the rule in *Tubman* v *Johnston*[271] a mortgagee or owner of a charge affecting only an undivided share in the land would not be able to pursue his normal remedy of possession against another co-owner in possession whose interest is free of the mortgage or charge. However, a mortgagee may be able to maintain a suit for possession.

The bank sought an order for a sale of the entire house in lieu of partition under the Partition Act 1868, section 4. The court concluded that an application under the Partition Act 1868 could be made only by a person having a legal or equitable estate in possession in the property. A creditor who registered a charging order did not thereby acquire any estate or interest but merely a charge to secure payment of a specific sum. Therefore, the only remedies available to such a person for enforcement of his security were those contained in the Judgments Enforcement Order itself.

Although the owner of the charge has in theory, for the purpose of enforcing it, the same powers of sale as a mortgagee under the Conveyancing Acts 1881-1911, it seemed to the court that when a charging order affected the individual interest of a joint tenant or a tenant in common the only method of enforcement actually available to the creditor was a sale of the debtor's interest under the Judgments Enforcement (NI) Order 1981, article 52. In reality such an interest might well prove unsaleable and the holder of an order charging land might be left without a satisfactory method of realising his security.

As a result of the problems highlighted by the *Haggerty* decision, an amendment to the law was included in the Property (NI) Order 1997 and now a creditor is more easily able to enforce his charge against jointly owned land. Article 48 of the 1997 Order made provision for the owner of a charge, including a charge under article 46 of the Judgments Enforcement (NI) Order 1981 on land held jointly or in undivided shares, to make a request under the Partition Acts 1868 and 1876 for an order for partition or for sale and distribution in lieu of partition. The owner of the charge is to be treated as a party interested for the purpose of the Partition Acts.[272]

---

[270] [1995] NI 211 (Ch D).
[271] [1981] NI 53.
[272] In *Ulster Bank Ltd* v *Carter* [1999] NI 93 High Ct (NI), Girvan J held that the bank was not entitled to an order for sale because art 48 does not apply to orders charging land created before 1 September 1997, the date on which art 48 became operative. He also hinted that it was hardly fair to the wife to grant an order for sale of the jointly owned property used as a

Article 49 of the 1997 Order confers power on a court making an order for partition or sale to impose such stay, suspension or conditions as it thinks fit in the circumstances of the case. Article 50 confirms that the creation of a charge on the estate of a joint tenant causes (and always has caused) a severance of the joint tenancy.

So far as registered land is concerned, the implications of *Haggerty* extend beyond the effect of orders charging land. The Land Registration Act (NI) 1970, Schedule 7, Part I, paragraph 1(2) makes it clear that all obligations to pay money which are secured on registered land are deemed to be charges. If, for any reason, the charge is effective only in respect of the interest of an individual co-owner the chargee will be unable to invoke the assistance of the Partition Acts 1868 and 1876.

There are other cases in which charges on registered land appearing to extend to the entire legal and beneficial estate in land may turn out to be enforceable only in respect of an undivided share or severable interest. For example, when one of two co-owners forges the signature of the other on the deed of charge.[273]

It may also occur where the execution of the deed of charge by one of the co-owners has been procured through the exercise of undue influence in circumstances entitling him to have the transaction set aside as against the chargee.[274]

More usually, when a charge is executed by a sole registered owner, it transpires that another person has a prior equitable interest in the property, the priority of which is protected under the Land Registration Act (NI) 1970, Schedule 5, Part I, paragraph 15. In all cases the chargee will face the same difficulties as the bank encountered in *Haggerty*.

The question of the possibility of enforcing a charge was considered in *Hughes* v *Hughes*[275] from a different perspective. In divorce proceedings the matrimonial home was subject to a property adjustment order and transferred to the wife, subject to a charge in the husband's favour of 20 per cent of the value thereof. The land was registered and therefore when the husband sought to enforce his charge he could seek possession only by agreement or by order of the court. It was held that the property adjustment order was intended to be realisable when the premises were sold by the wife, the intention being to provide her with a home and the husband could not be entitled to the relief sought.

MATRIMONIAL HOME RIGHTS

28.32 Where a husband and wife are co-owners of a matrimonial home either at law or in equity, each has a right to occupy the property. Problems may arise when the parties can no longer live in the property together and there is a dispute as to which one should occupy it. For a long time the position was even

---

family home even though only the husband owed money to the bank. Consequently the operation of art 48 is under review.

[273] *First National Securities Ltd* v *Hegerty* [1985] QB 850.
[274] See *Barclays Bank* v *O'Brien* above and subsequent cases.
[275] [1995] NI 119.

more difficult for a spouse who had no legal or equitable interest in the matrimonial home which was solely owned by the other spouse. Legislation was introduced to protect a spouse in this situation.

The Family Law (Miscellaneous Provisions) (NI) Order 1984 followed similar legislation in England.[276] It enabled a spouse in certain circumstances to register a matrimonial charge on the title in the Registry of Deeds or Land Registry, as appropriate. The provisions dealing with the occupation rights of spouses in the 1984 Order have now been replaced by the Family Homes and Domestic Violence (NI) Order 1998[277] which streamlines and consolidates the law on domestic violence and occupation of the family home.

The legislation relates to a right of occupation now known as a matrimonial home right which can be granted to a spouse who has no interest in a property owned by the other spouse. This matrimonial home right can be registered as a charge on the estate of the other spouse. As long as the property is or was their principal home the right to apply for occupation is available to a former spouse, co-habitee or former co-habitee.

To protect the matrimonial home right from a *bona fide* purchaser or mortgagee for value of a legal estate without notice it is important to obtain full protection by registration before the date of the contract or the deposit of title deeds in the case of an equitable mortgage. Otherwise the purchaser may not be affected by it. This will depend on the doctrines of notice and equitable priority. However if it is not registered, the non-owning spouse may still have priority over anyone later taking an equitable interest from the owning spouse or taking a legal interest for no valuable consideration.

The spouse entitled to a matrimonial home right may agree in writing that any mortgage or interest in the property shall rank in priority to the matrimonial home right.

The matrimonial home right of occupation is a charge on the estate of the owning spouse. It has the priority of an equitable interest created at the date of the marriage, the date of acquisition of the estate by the owning spouse, or 1 September 1989 the date the Family Law (Miscellaneous Provisions) (NI) Order 1984 became operative, whichever is the later. The right is determined on the death of the owning spouse or the dissolution of the marriage.

A charge for a particular person can only be registered against one property at a time because it is intended to represent a right of occupation. The spouse enjoying a registered matrimonial home right cannot be evicted or excluded from the property without a court order.

The spouse entitled to a matrimonial home right may release it by release in writing. On a sale, the matrimonial charge should be released prior to registration of the purchase deed. It may be deemed to be released on the delivery to the purchaser of the documents required to effect cancellation or the

---

[276] Matrimonial Homes Acts 1967 and 1983.
[277] Which came into operation on 1 January 1999.

lodging of such documents in the Land Registry or Registry of Deeds as the case may require.

Further, where both spouses have a legal interest in a matrimonial home as joint tenants or tenants in common, either may apply to the court during the subsistence of the marriage, for the right to occupy the property or to prohibit its use by the other, or otherwise to regulate the occupation.

Bankruptcy[278]

28.33 If the owning spouse is adjudged bankrupt, the matrimonial charge continues to subsist after the bankruptcy and binds the Official Assignee or a trustee in bankruptcy and his successors in title.[279]

However no rights of occupation may be acquired by the occupying spouse between the presentation of the petition and the vesting of the bankrupt's estate in the trustee.

Where the bankrupt and his spouse legally or in equity own the house jointly or as tenants in common it can only be sold by the trustee, in the absence of agreement between the parties, by an order for sale in lieu of partition under the Partition Act 1868. An application by the trustee for such an order must be made to the Bankruptcy Court which may make such order as it thinks fit and is not restricted by the narrow discretion given by the Partition Act.[280]

Enquiries before contract

28.34 The enquiries before contract should include a question as to the possibility of a matrimonial home right. If the reply shows that the vendor is aware of any existing, possible or contemplated registration of any rights, the purchaser should insert a clause in the contract to provide that any matrimonial home right registered under the Family Homes and Domestic Violence (NI) Order 1998 shall be vacated on or before completion at the expense of the vendor.

A spouse who has not registered a matrimonial home right may still have an interest protected by the rule in the *Boland* case which has not been registered. There may also be other persons with rights in the property to which the matrimonial legislation does not extend. It is therefore important for a purchaser or mortgagee to ensure that the vendor makes a full disclosure regarding the occupants of the property in the replies to the enquiries before contract.

---

[278] Cf paras 27.01-27.25.
[279] Insolvency (NI) Order 1989, art 309(2)(a) and Sch 10, repealing and replacing the Family Law (Misc Provs) (NI) Order 1984, art 5(7).
[280] Insolvency Order (NI) 1989, art 309.

CHAPTER TWENTY NINE
PROPERTY (NI) ORDER 1997

Introduction

29.01 Proposals for major reform of land law in Northern Ireland have been on the agenda since the late 1960s. Following publication of the Report on Registration of Title in Northern Ireland in 1967 ('the Lowry Report') a Land Law Working Party was set up at Queen's University by the Office of Law Reform with a very wide-ranging brief. It was required to examine all aspects of land law and the conveyancing system, with a view to producing a comprehensive and integrated package of measures along the lines of the Birkenhead 1925 property legislation for England and Wales. The Working Party produced the Survey of the Land Law of Northern Ireland in 1971 ('the Survey') containing amongst others, a scheme for the redemption of ground rents together with draft legislation to put the recommendations into effect.

Subsequently a Land Law Working Group was established by the Northern Ireland Office to review the proposals in the Survey. It produced a three-volume Report in 1990 ('the Final Report') with a more detailed consideration of the issues and extensive draft legislation. It was hoped that these measures would be taken as an integrated package and enacted as such, but that has not occurred. Aspects of the proposals in the Survey and the Final Report are being introduced gradually, as in the Property (NI) Order 1978 and the Wills and Administration Proceedings (NI) Order 1994, and parts of the Property (NI) Order 1997.

It has long been recognised that the pyramid interests which are so common in urban titles are unnecessarily complex and of diminishing commercial value. When the land was originally developed leases and sub-leases with ground rents were created so that the lessor could receive an annual income from the property and maintain a degree of control over it. In many cases now it is not viable to collect the rents, some of the covenants are obsolete or relate to matters which are really of no concern to the lessor, and since the introduction of planning controls the covenants which relate to user and development arguably can be controlled by other means.

In a more egalitarian society it is considered that an ordinary home-owner should be able to own his property outright and not be accountable to his ground landlord whose position is viewed as anachronistic. It is against this background and in this context that a comprehensive reform of the general law of property and the conveyancing system has been undertaken. It is generally accepted that an extension of the registration of title system is a necessary part of any comprehensive revision of the system because from a practical viewpoint it simplifies matters further, at least in theory, if a title is registered once it has been reduced to essentials.

Although the Land Registration Act (NI) 1970 was enacted following the Lowry Report the provisions in that Act for extension of compulsory registration to urban land have remain unused until quite recently when the

Comber area became the first area of compulsory registration. One of the reasons for this may be that there is little purpose in introducing compulsory registration of urban titles until the complexities of pyramid interests have been removed.

The Property (NI) Order 1997 ('the 1997 Order') is largely based on the proposals contained in the Final Report and begins to address the problems of the ground rent system. In addition the proposed draft Ground Rents Bill introduces proposals relating to the voluntary and compulsory redemption of ground rents which will be a further step towards a simpler system of tenure. These measures precede any further legislation designed to put into effect other provisions in the Final Report which are still outstanding, dealing not only with the general law of property and landlord and tenant law but also with important practical subjects like flat schemes and similar developments. In this sense the 1997 Order and the draft Ground Rents Bill are preliminary measures preparing the ground for a comprehensive reform of property law and the eventual extension of an efficient registration of title system to all land.

COMMENCEMENT

29.02 There have been two commencement orders introducing some of the provisions of the 1997 Order. The first became operative on 1 September 1997. It brought into operation Part I which is introductory, article 31 which provides that there shall be no future increase in ground rents and articles 48-50 relating to joint ownership. It also applied to article 39, thus no agreement can be made to avoid the provisions of the 1997 Order.

The second became operative on 10 January 2000 and brought in some important provisions which are dealt with in more detail in the paragraphs which follow. Briefly, these are the provisions which prohibit the future creation of any fee farm grant, any long lease of a dwelling house and also the provisions which apply to the running of freehold covenants in new conveyances.

The proposals relating to the redemption of ground rents contained in Part II of the 1997 Order were revised and are now contained in the draft Ground Rents Bill. Consequently, articles 5-27 of the 1997 Order (which related to the redemption of ground rents) will be repealed.

In the meantime the provisions of the 1997 Order which are in effect are considered below.

PROHIBITION OF CREATION OF GROUND RENTS

29.03 In order to assist the phasing out of pyramid titles and to prevent tiers of interests arising out of small pieces of property, particularly private dwelling houses, the 1997 Order prohibits the future creation of specified estates in land reserving a ground rent.

Fee farm grants

29.04 One of the major provisions in the 1997 Order is article 28 which provides that a fee farm grant shall be incapable of being made at law or in equity in respect of any type of property unless the obligation to do so was assumed before the appointed day (10 January 2000). This means that there can be no new fee farm grants of any description.

Rentcharges

29.05 Although the creation of rentcharges is not now very common, article 29 attempts to limit the classes of rentcharge that may be created. There is a general prohibition on the creation of a new rentcharge unless it is in pursuance of a obligation assumed before the appointed day (10 January 2000), is an annuity, is payable under an agreement of indemnity, is payable under any statutory provision or is paid under court order.

It may also be suggested that under article 29 it is no longer possible to create a rentcharge such as a charge of an apportioned rent on an assignment of part. However it may be arguable that such a situation might come within the exception in article 29(3) which relates to a rentcharge payable under an agreement of indemnity. It could also be argued that any such apportionment is contrary to the spirit of the legislation because it is in effect an attempt to create a new rent.[281]

Long leases of dwelling houses

29.06 Another far-reaching provision of the 1997 Order is article 30 which states that on or after the appointed day (10 January 2000) a lease of a dwelling house for a term of more than 50 years (a long lease) is incapable of being created at law or in equity. Any agreement to create a long lease made on or after the appointed day (10 January 2000) has effect as an agreement with the purchaser binding the vendor to acquire a fee simple estate in the land and to convey it to the purchaser at no additional expense to the purchaser.

Where the leasehold estate purported to be created is subject to a mortgage, the mortgage binds the fee simple as if it had been created in relation to the fee simple.

The general rule against the creation of long leases is subject to a number of exceptions:

(1) The grant of a long lease in pursuance of an obligation assumed before the appointed day (10 January 2000);

(2) The grant of a concurrent lease (which is thought to refer to a lease of the reversion on another lease);

(3) The grant of a long lease by way of mortgage;

(4) The grant of an equity-sharing lease;

(5) The grant of a long lease of a flat;

---

[281] At the time of writing (April 2000) it is too early to tell how the vexed question of apportionment should properly be interpreted. Already, since 10 January 2000, very different opinions have emerged.

(6) The grant of a long lease by the National Trust.

These exceptions are consistent with the exceptions to the proposed provisions for the voluntary and compulsory redemption of ground rents.

No increase in ground rent

29.07 Article 31 provides that any provision in a fee farm grant or long lease of a dwelling house made on or after the appointed day (1 September 1997) for the increase or review of a ground rent on more than one occasion is of no effect. This does not apply to a building lease or to a fee farm grant for purposes corresponding to those of a building lease merely because provision is made for increases in the ground rent which are related to periods or events in the progress of the building.

Perpetually renewable leases

29.08 Article 36 prevents the future creation of any perpetually renewable lease, such as a lease for lives renewable for ever or a lease for a term renewable for ever. It also provides for the automatic conversion on the appointed day (10 January 2000) of any such existing lease into a fee simple estate subject to a fee farm rent. This is one of the few instances where the 1997 Order brings about an automatic conversion to a fee simple as opposed to a conversion that requires action by any party. Detailed consequences of conversion are set out in Schedule 2 to the 1997 Order. The most significant is that the fee simple is for all purposes a graft on the estate created by the lease and is subject to any rights or equities arising from its being such a graft.

Lease for lives

29.09 Article 37 prevents the future creation (after 10 January 2000) of any lease at a rent or in consideration of a fine for a life or lives or until some other contingency, such as marriage. Any such existing lease is automatically converted into a term for a fixed period in accordance with Schedule 3 to the 1997 Order. For example, a lease for a life or lives is to be construed as a lease for a term of 90 years determinable by notice after the dropping of the only or last life. This is another area where the 1997 Order provides for automatic conversion rather than conversion by taking action.

FREEHOLD COVENANTS

29.10 With the abolition of the creation of intermediate interests in land it will be more important that there are practical rules for the enforcement of freehold covenants between relevant parties, notwithstanding that there is no privity of estate between them.[282] The introduction of the provisions which are set out in article 34 lays down a more viable statutory framework for the running of freehold covenants in deeds created after 10 January 2000 replacing the

---

[282] Cf Enforcement of Freehold Covenants paras 20.05-20.28. For freeholds created prior to 10 January 2000 see paras 20.26 - 20.29.

previous common law rules relating to enforceability between the owners of estates in fee simple.

However, because the new rules for enforceability do not apply to any covenant contained in a deed made before the appointed day or made pursuant to an obligation assumed before the appointed day (10 January 2000), the old rules will continue to apply to pre-existing deeds and the two systems will operate alongside each other. Other specified limitations are that article 34 does not apply to any covenant for title, or any covenant expressed to bind only the covenantor. Neither will the provision affect the enforceability of any covenant between the original parties to it; that is the original covenantee and the original covenantor.

Running of freehold covenants

29.11 Article 34 will only affect the running of the benefit and burden of the covenant to successors in title of the original parties.[283] Accordingly it is unlikely that the new provisions will completely remove the need for chains of indemnity between a covenantor and his successors, particularly when the person owning the land burdened by the covenant remains liable for any breach arising during the period of his ownership.

Article 34 will potentially enable a covenantee and his successors to enforce a covenant against a covenantor and his successors where it might not previously have been possible. Enforceability should be feasible between the following parties as owners for the time being of the lands respectively benefited and burdened by a covenant:

(1) Original covenantee and successor of covenantor;

(2) Successor of covenantee and original covenantor;

(3) Successor of covenantee and successor of covenantor.

It is important to remember that the covenants may still be released by a deed executed by the owners of the respective lands. Where there is a development the deed must be executed by *all* the parcel owners.

Enforceable covenants

29.12 The enforceable freehold covenants as set out in article 34(4) are as follows:

(1) covenants in respect of the maintenance, repair or renewal or party walls or fences or the preservation of boundaries;

(2) covenants to do, or to pay for or contribute to the costs of work on, or to permit works to be done on, or for access to be had to, or for any activity

---

[283] This article does not affect the enforceability of any covenant as between the original parties to the covenant. Arguably, this means that, contrary to Deasy's Act, s 16, liability may continue after the sale of the property.

to be pursued on, the land of the covenantor for the benefit of land of the covenantee or other land;

(3) covenants to do, or to pay for or contribute to the cost of, works on land of the covenantee or other land where the works benefit the land of the covenantor;

(4) covenants to reinstate in the event of damage or destruction;

(5) covenants for the protection of amenities or services or for compliance with a statutory provision, including -

  (a) covenants not to use the land of the covenantor for specified purposes or otherwise than for the purposes of a private dwelling,

  (b) covenants against causing nuisance, annoyance, damage or inconvenience,

  (c) covenants against interfering with facilities,

  (d) covenants prohibiting, regulating or restricting building works or the erection of any structure, or the planting, cutting or removal of vegetation (including grass, trees and shrubs) or requiring the tending of such vegetation;

  (e) covenants in relation to a body corporate formed for the management of land.

It is conclusively presumed that the benefit and burden of an appropriately drafted covenant of the types specified attaches permanently to the whole and every part of the land of the covenantee and the covenantor.

Developments

29.13 It is provided in article 34(6) that where there is a development the covenants made by parcel owners with the developer are enforceable as if they had been made also with other parcel owners to the extent that those covenants are capable of reciprocally benefiting and burdening the parcels of the various parcel owners.

For the purposes of this provision a development is defined in article 34(7) as arising where -

(1) land is divided into two or more parcels for conveyance to parcel owners; and

(2) there is an intention between the developer and parcel owners to create reciprocity of covenants; and

(3) that intention is shown expressly in conveyances to parcel owners or by implication from the parcels and covenants in question and the proximity of the relationship between parcel owners.

A developer means an owner who conveys parcels of land under a development and his successors in title. A parcel owner means a person who acquires or holds a parcel of land within a development, including a mortgagee in possession.

Remedies for breach of covenant

29.14 Under article 45(1) the following remedies for enforcement are available in the event of a breach of covenant to which article 34 (freehold) applies:

> (1) proceedings for an injunction (including a mandatory injunction) or other equitable relief;
>
> (2) an action for sums due under the covenant;
>
> (3) an action for damages (whether in respect of pecuniary or non-pecuniary kinds of damage).

Breaches which cause or which threaten or are anticipated to cause damage that is not damage to property or personal injury are placed in a restrictive category. No-one is entitled to equitable relief or damages except in respect of the extent to which he is or may be materially prejudiced by the real, anticipated or threatened breach. No definition is given as to what is meant by "materially prejudiced," but a court is directed to have particular regard to both the nature of the estate (if any) by virtue of which the plaintiff is entitled to enforce the covenant and the location of the land in which the plaintiff's estate subsists. The suggestion is that the less directly interested or physically further removed plaintiff may have difficulty in successful enforcement.

Special attention is also given to breaches that involve a failure to carry out any works. In such a case, where the works are actually carried out by a plaintiff entitled to enforce the covenant, the cost incurred by him in carrying out the works is to be included in the damages awarded. However, if the plaintiff would in the normal event have been bound to contribute to the cost of the works, the damages will be reduced by the amount that his contribution should have been. Where there has been a breach of covenant requiring the carrying out of works and the plaintiff has not carried out the works himself, this will not be used against him to reduce his damages on the ground that he has not mitigated his loss.

Supplementary

29.15 There are a number of supplementary provisions in articles 39-47 as follows:

(a) Avoidance of powers

Article 39 provides that the statutory provisions cannot be avoided by agreement, unless expressly authorised under the 1997 Order. Any unauthorised agreement to the effect that a provision will not apply or is to be modified in relation to a person or any land is void to that extent.

(b) Mental patients

Article 40 allows for representation of a person's interest under the 1997 Order where he is incapable of acting for himself by reason of mental disorder.

(c) Disputes

Article 42 sets out the jurisdiction of the Registrar of Titles and of the Lands Tribunal in the determination of disputes under the 1997 Order. The Lands Tribunal has appellate jurisdiction from the Registrar of Titles and original jurisdiction on a reference from him.

(d) Offences

Under article 43 a person who makes a statement which he knows to be false or recklessly makes a statement which is false is guilty of an offence and is liable on summary conviction to a fine.

(e) Civil remedy for misstatement

Where a person has suffered loss in consequence of any misstatement made in a document, article 44 provides that the person who made the misstatement is liable to damages notwithstanding that the misstatement was not made fraudulently, unless he proves that he had reasonable grounds to believe that the facts represented were true.

(f) Application to the Crown

The 1997 Order binds the Crown in accordance with article 47.

Miscellaneous

29.16 The most significant of the miscellaneous amendments to property law are those relating to land which is jointly owned which were added to the 1997 Order as a result of the problems highlighted by the case of *Northern Bank* v *Haggerty*.[284]

Enforcement of charge

29.17 Article 48 alters the common law position by providing that the owner of a charge under article 46 of the Judgments Enforcement (NI) Order 1981 on jointly owned land (that is, as joint tenants or tenants in common) is entitled to make a request under the Partition Acts 1868 and 1876 for an order for partition, or for sale and distribution. The owner of a charge shall now be treated as an interested party under the Partition Acts which he was not previously.[285]

---

[284] [1995] NI 211.
[285] In *Ulster Bank Ltd* v *Carter* [1999] NI 93 Girvan J hinted that, although a creditor bank could obtain an order for the sale of property owned by a husband and wife and used by them as their family home along with their children even though only the husband had owed money to the bank, this result could hardly be seen as fair to the wife. He suggested that a balance needs to be struck between the interests of creditors and innocent home-owners, especially spouses. Consequently the Office of Law Reform is reviewing art 48. The operation of art 48 is not retrospective and does not apply to orders charging land created before 1 September 1997.

Severance of joint tenancy by charge

29.18 Article 50 confirms that the creation of a charge on the estate or estates of one or more joint tenants causes and always has caused a severance of the joint tenancy.

Commencement Orders

29.19 The provisions of the 1997 Order which are operative at the time of writing came into effect as follows:

No 1: 1 September 1997

- Part I introductory
- Article 31 no increase or review of ground rents
- Article 39 no agreement to avoid provisions of 1997 Order
- Articles 48-50 relating to joint ownership.[286]

No 2: 10 January 2000

- Article 7(7) and 7(8) meaning of word "flat"
- Article 28 prohibition on creation of all fee farm grants and fee farm rents
- Article 29 prohibition on creation of rentcharges
- Article 30 prohibition on creation of long leases of dwelling-houses (subject to specified exceptions)
- Article 34 running of new freehold covenants
- Article 36 prohibition on creation of perpetually renewable leases and provision for conversion of any such existing lease
- Article 37 prohibition on creation of lease for lives and provision for conversion of any such existing lease
- Article 38 repeal of statutory provisions relating to agricultural tenancies
- Article 39 statutory provisions cannot be avoided by agreement
- Article 40 representation for mental patients
- Article 41 service of documents
- Article 42 disputes
- Article 43 offences
- Article 44 civil remedy for misstatements
- Article 45 enforcement of covenants

---

[286] Cf para 29.17. Operation of art 48 under review following *Ulster Bank Ltd* v *Carter* [1999] NI 93.

* Article 47 application to the Crown
* Schedule 2 consequences of conversion of perpetually renewable leases
* Schedule 3 conversion of leases for lives etc
* Article 53(1) and Schedule 4 (except para 2) amendments
* Article 52(2) and Schedule 5 (with exceptions) repeals

GROUND RENT REDEMPTION

29.20 At the time of writing the position in relation to the legislation providing for the redemption of ground rents remains uncertain. After extensive consultation, it became apparent that the provisions originally contained in the Property (NI) Order 1997 to redeem ground rents were extremely cumbersome. It was thought that the process would prove to be expensive and might cause unnecessary delays in conveyancing procedures. It was also suggested that it should not be a pre-condition of sale for the vendor to first redeem his ground rent.

Consequently, it is now proposed that the articles relating to ground rent redemption in the 1997 Order will not be introduced. A revised scheme has been drafted which is set out in the draft Ground Rents Bill.

The new proposals are for a procedure which is simpler and more straightforward than the original scheme envisaged by 1997 Order. The entire scheme will be administered by the Land Registry and it will become the responsibility of the purchaser, rather than the vendor, to redeem the ground rent when compulsory redemption comes into effect.

The draft Ground Rents Bill provides both for voluntary redemption and compulsory redemption of ground rents. It seems likely that these will be introduced in two stages. The voluntary redemption procedure may come into effect first and after a suitable period, when the necessary rules and regulations have been made, the second phase will extend to the compulsory procedure.

The provisions of the draft Ground Rents Bill are summarised below:

Clause 1 contains the power for a rent-payer voluntarily to redeem a ground rent to which his land is subject, unless the property is used for business purposes. Clause 2 provides for compulsory redemption of a ground rent of a dwelling house where the property is conveyed or transferred subject to a ground rent and the dwelling house is in a compulsory registration area.[287]

Compulsory redemption of ground rents is linked to compulsory registration of title in that where clause 2 applies, the Registrar of Titles shall refuse to accept the conveyance or transfer for registration unless he is satisfied that the ground rent has been redeemed. A point to note which has already been mentioned is that the responsibility for redeeming the ground rent is imposed on the purchaser of the property and that becomes a pre-condition of registration of the transaction.

---

[287] See para 7.07

The exceptions and restrictions on clauses 1 and 2 are set out in clause 3. The provisions for redemption do not apply where:

- the ground rent is payable under a lease extended under the Leasehold (Enlargement and Extension) Act (NI) 1971 or notice of a proposal to acquire the fee simple has been served under that Act;
- the lease has a short residuary term of 50 years or less;
- the lease is an equity-sharing lease (or on a conveyance/transfer upon termination of such a lease);
- the lease is of agricultural land (whether or not including farm houses and buildings);
- the lease is a National Trust lease;
- proceedings are pending in court for recovery of possession of the land;
- the property subject to the ground rent is a flat.

The redemption procedure is set out in clause 4. A rent-payer who wishes to redeem his ground rent applies to the Land Registry in the prescribed form. At the same time as making the application to the Land Registry, the rent-payer lodges:

- the redemption money;[288]
- the last receipt for payment of ground rent or the amount of arrears due;
- the sum required to discharge any apportionment;
- such evidence of title as may be prescribed;
- such sum as may be prescribed to defray expenses incurred in obtaining a certificate of redemption.

Then, immediately after making an application to the Land Registry, the rent-payer serves a notice on the rent-owner to the effect that he has applied to redeem his ground rent. He is not required to serve a notice if he does not know the name and address of the rent-owner or his agent, nor if a notice sent by post is returned undelivered.

In accordance with clause 5, the Registrar is required to keep a register of all monies lodged and such indexes as may be prescribed. All money lodged with the Land Registry for the purposes of ground rent redemption is to be paid into the Consolidated Fund. Where the Registrar receives a claim from any person (eg a rent-owner) to payment of the money so lodged and is satisfied that the person is so entitled, he shall certify accordingly. If he is not satisfied as to the person's entitlement, he shall refuse to certify.

---

[288] This is to be determined in accordance with Schedule 1 as a multiple of the ground rent and a number of years purchase. At the time of writing the multiplier has not been determined.

A person who makes a claim is not entitled to payment of the redemption money unless he is the rent-owner or a superior owner and, where there is a superior rent, has entered into appropriate arrangements to ensure that each relevant owner receives his appropriate share of the redemption money. There is a right of appeal to the Lands Tribunal from the Registrar's decision to issue or refuse a certificate.

Where a rent-payer has complied with the requirements the Registrar shall seal and issue a certificate of redemption in accordance with clause 7 which he will then send to the rent-payer. This certifies that the ground rent has been redeemed and operates as a full and final discharge of the land from the ground rent. Under clause 10 the certificate is conclusive evidence of the redemption of the ground rent to which it relates.

Clause 11 provides that when a ground rent is redeemed, all superior rents (if any) to which the land is subject are also redeemed. Where a superior rent is also charged on other land it is redeemed only to the extent that it is charged on the land on which the ground rent has been redeemed.

When a certificate of redemption is issued it operates to enlarge the rent-payer's estate into a fee simple and the estate of the rent-owner or any other superior owner is extinguished to the extent that those estates carry an entitlement to a ground rent. In the case of a registered leasehold estate, a certificate of redemption is sufficient authority for the Registrar, on receipt of an appropriate application, to cancel the entry relating to title to that estate and register the estate in fee simple vested in the rent-payer. If an unregistered leasehold estate is registered as a burden on a superior registered estate the fee simple can also similarly be vested in the rent-payer.

In relation to unregistered land, a certificate of redemption is a conveyance for the purposes of the Registration of Deeds Act (NI) 1970, as amended.

The fee simple estate into which a leasehold estate is enlarged is for all purposes a graft on the leasehold estate and is subject to any rights or equities arising from it being such a graft.

Any mortgage of the leasehold estate continues to have effect as if it were, and had originally been created as, a mortgage of the fee simple.

Where a certificate of redemption has been sealed in relation to unregistered land, or the Registrar has had the relevant entry in the register in relation to registered land, the types of covenants which continue to have effect are set out in clause 16.

These include:

- covenants for title
- covenants for indemnities (except in relation to a redeemed ground rent or superior rent)
- covenants listed in clause 16. This list is the same as that in article 34 of the 1997 Order in relation to the running of freehold covenants.[289]

---

[289] See para 29.12.

The provision for enforceability of such covenants included in clause 16 are set out in clause 17.

Any agreement that attempts to avoid the provisions is void.

APPENDIX A
HOME CHARTER SCHEME FORMS

HOME CHARTER CHECKLIST

You may find this Checklist helpful in assisting you to comply with the terms of the Home Charter Scheme. Please note, however, that it is not intended as an exhaustive list of all the steps which ought properly to be taken in a domestic conveyancing transaction and that it is necessary in all cases to comply with:

   (1) the Special and General Conditions of Sale;
   (2) any Practice Directions issued from time to time by the Law Society; and
   (3) the general law.

The various Forms referred to in the Checklist are those suggested by the Home Charter Committee. Practitioners are, however, free to develop and use their own forms, provided that such forms deal adequately with the matters set out in the Home Charter Rules.

Some general reminders may be helpful:

UNDERTAKINGS

1. Obtain client's instructions before giving any undertaking
2. Give any authorised undertaking in one of the forms approved by the Law Society [Forms 3 (a), (b), (c) and (d)]
3. If no Law Society approved form exists, ensure that the undertaking extends only to acts which can be performed by the firm itself
4. Undertakings over money should extend to money only **as and when** received by the firm
5. Furnish a copy of the undertaking to the client
6. Note **prominently** on file the fact that an undertaking has been given

REMEMBER IN ALL CASES:
- to respond to clients' requests for information within 3 working days;
- to respond to client's or colleague's telephone calls no later than the **next working day**;
- to take account of client's particular difficulties in arranging appointments
- to honour all appointments unless prevented by force majeure;
- to comply with any Law Society Practice Directions
- to obtain written authority for compliance inspection of client's file;

ACTING FOR VENDOR

1. **TAKING INSTRUCTIONS**
    1.1 Complete instructions form [Form 1]
    1.2 Bespeak title deeds and advance redemption figures from relevant financial institution
    1.3 Seek replies to Pre-Contract Enquiries
    1.4 Seek evidence of identity
    1.5 Seek details of all occupiers and obtain consent to sale if necessary
    1.6 Send terms of business letter [Form 2] and costs estimate
    1.7 Consider conflict of interest
    1.8 Send conflict of interest letter (if applicable) [Form 4 (a)]
    1.9 Report to client when draft contract furnished
    1.10 Obtain written authority for compliance inspection of client's file

2. **PROPERTY CERTIFICATES/SEARCHES**
    using prescribed forms:-
    2.1 requisition certificates from:
        2.1.1 Department of Environment
        2.1.2 Local Authority
        2.1.3 Northern Ireland Housing Executive

    2.2 requisition and furnish searches:-
        2.2.1 Registry of Deeds/Land Registry
        2.2.2 Statutory Charges
        2.2.3 Enforcement of Judgments
        2.2.4 Bankruptcy
        2.2.5 Companies Registry (if appropriate)

3. **POST-CONTRACT**
    3.1 Report to client on acceptance of contract/ receipt of deposit
    3.2 Diary completion date
    3.3 Diary request for, mortgage redemption figures (at least 2 weeks before completion)

4. **MORTGAGE REDEMPTION**
    4.1 Seek redemption figures
    4.2 Report to client with redemption figures
    4.3 Advise purchaser's solicitor of redemption figures *(if requested)*
    4.4 Send redemption cheque and mortgage deed to mortgagee
    4.5 Diary to follow-up in 10 days time
    4.6 Follow-up for vacated mortgage after 10 days
    4.7 (a) Register mortgage vacate
            OR
        (b) Send vacate and cheque to purchaser's solicitor
    4.8 (If 4.7 (a) applies, send registered vacate to purchaser's solicitor

5. **POST-COMPLETION MATTERS**
    5.1 Account to client
    5.2 Check Rates Collection Agency notified
    5.3 Check Ground Landlord notified
    5.4 If non-scheme members, close hand search (2 months max) and send to Purchasers' Solicitors

ACTING FOR BORROWER AND LENDER

1. **INTERVIEW WITH BORROWER**

    1.1 Seek interview to discuss mortgage instructions
    1.2 Discuss at interview:
        1.2.1 Lender's valuation (including rights, duties and liabilities attaching thereto)
        1.2.2 Collateral security requirements
        1.2.3 Lender's insurance requirements/proposal
        1.2.4 Effect of "all monies" provisions (if applicable)
        1.2.5 Building standards indemnity guarantee scheme or equivalent
        1.2.6 Payment/deduction from advance of:
            (a) mortgage guarantee premium) if
            (b) arrangement fee   ) applicable
    1.3 Check lender's requirements against title
    1.4 Register purchase deed and mortgage **immediately** after stamping of purchase deed
    1.5 [Land Registry cases] send copy of receipt card to lender on request
    1.6 [Land Registry cases] notify lender of return of deeds if not relodged within 7 days

ACTING FOR PURCHASER

1. **TAKING INSTRUCTIONS**

    1.1 Complete instructions form [Form 1]
    1.2 Seek evidence of identity
    1.3 Seek details of all occupiers and proposed occupiers
    1.4 Send terms of business letter [Form 2] and costs estimate
    1.5 Notify independent financial adviser (if applicable)
    1.6 Consider conflict of interest
    1.7 Send conflict of interest letter (if applicable) [Form 4(a)]
    1.8 Obtain authority for compliance inspection of client's file

2. **TITLE MATTERS**
   2.1 Bespeak title deeds and advance redemption figure from relevant financial institution
   2.2 Report to client when title received and obtain details of premises easements, extensions etc.
   2.3 Peruse title and provide client with copy of deed map
   2.4 Ask client to check boundaries
   2.5 Advise on potential challenges under insolvency law

3. **DEPOSIT**
   3.1 Obtain deposit from client
   3.2 Report to client when offer to purchase furnished to vendor's solicitors
   3.3 Report to client when offer to purchase is accepted
   3.4 Pay deposit within 5 days of acceptance of contract

4. **MORTGAGE**
   4.1 Report to client when mortgage instructions received
   4.2 Advise client in writing of consequences of mortgage [Form 5]
   4.3 Forward report on title in **good time**
   4.4 Report to client on financing of completion and completion arrangements

5. **COMPLETION**
   5.1 Send purchase deed for approval/ execution in **good time**
   5.2 Seek to obtain from client:
      (i) balance purchase money
      (ii) stamp duty
      (iii) Land Registry fees (if applicable)
      (iv) costs and outlay [Form 6]
   5.3 Lodge purchase deed in Stamp Office asap
   5.4 Pay stamp duty
   5.5 Lodge purchase and mortgage deeds for registration
   5.6 Report to client when deeds lodged for registration
   5.7 Close Registry of Deeds search
   5.8 Furnish cash statement to client

INDEX

FORM 1   INSTRUCTIONS

FORM 2   INFORMATION AND TERMS OF BUSINESS

FORM 3   FORMS OF UNDERTAKING

FORM 4   CONFLICTS OF INTEREST

FORM 5   MORTGAGE LETTER

FORM 6   FUNDS LETTER

SCHEDULE   DOMESTIC CONVEYANCING CHARGES

FORM 1A - INSTRUCTIONS SHEET
SALE

Client
Name:_____
Address:_____

Telephone (Business)_____ (Home) _____
Joint Client (if appropriate)
Name:_____
Address:_____

Telephone (Business) _____
Is the Client known to you or the firm? _____
If not has any evidence of identity been obtained _____
Selling
Premises (Address) _____

Sale Price _____
Additional Items to be sold/purchased and price _____

Purchaser (if known)
Name _____
Solicitors _____
Details _____
Any persons resident on premises? _____
Proposed Completion date (if known) _____
Reasons/requirements for Completion date _____
Estate Agents _____
Address: _____

Telephone No. _____
Situation of Deeds _____
Building Society Roll Number if known or Branch _____
Other Existing Mortgages or Charges _____
Any collateral security to be receipted discharged _____
Client's Bank_____
Any undertaking required? (if so NOTE ON FILE)_____
Name of ground landlord/agent collecting ground rent/any land purchase annuity? _____
Further information _____
(Standing Orders to be cancelled? Capital Gains Tax implications?). _____
Property Enquiries/Questionnaire completed? _____

FORM 1B - INSTRUCTIONS SHEET
PURCHASE

CLIENT
Name: _____
Address: _____
_____
Telephone (Business) _____ (Home) _____
JOINT CLIENT (if appropriate)
Name: _____
Address: _____
_____
Telephone (Business) _____
Is the Client known to you or the firm? _____
If not has any evidence of identity been obtained? _____
BUYING
Premises (Address) _____
_____
Sale Price _____
Additional Items to be sold/purchased and prices _____

VENDOR
Name _____
Solicitors _____
Details _____
Any persons resident on premises? _____
(Consider William & Glyn's Bank -v- Boland) _____
Proposed Completion date (if known) _____
Reasons/requirements for Completion date _____
Estate Agents _____
Address: _____
_____
Telephone No. _____
LOAN
Amount of Loan required _____
Lender involved _____
Collateral security (take details) _____
Bridging finance required? _____
Client's Bank _____
Any undertaking needed? (if so NOTE ON FILE) _____
Is a survey required? ☐   Name of Surveyor _____
Any Mortgage quotation needed? _____
Law Society (NI) Financial Advice Ltd - any help required? ____
Additional information _____
(Use to be made of property? Any permissions required? Any special insurance needs?)

FORM 2 - INFORMATION AND TERMS OF BUSINESS

The Law Society's Home Charter Scheme is designed to give assured standards of quality. This leaflet explains the basis on which your work will be carried out and what you should do, if at any time, you have any questions or difficulties.

THE SALE/PURCHASE

The work involved in selling or buying property has many aspects but the main areas which your solicitor will be dealing with on your behalf are as follows:-

1. Supplying information for your buyer/obtaining information from your seller.

2. Checking that the sellers are in position to sell the property to you/making arrangements to satisfy your lender that the property is suitable as security.

3. Agreeing the terms of the contract dates.

4. Final signing and agreeing completion dates.

5. Making pre-completion arrangements and checks.

6. Obtaining mortgage monies/redemption figures.

7. Supervising completion.

8. Arranging for the registration of the sale on the public record.

In the case of a sale your solicitor will receive the purchase monies and pay off any existing mortgages. They will also arrange to pay for your new property, if applicable, and forward any balance monies to you with a statement of account.

In the case of a purchase your solicitor will arrange to obtain the loan monies from your lender. There will be Additional money required to make payment in full. That will include expenses and taxes paid on your behalf, such as stamp duty, and registration fees. These are dealt with in the section on fees later in this leaflet.

MORTGAGES

There are many Mortgage Lenders, each one offering various Mortgage packages, often at different rates. There are Mortgages with rates which go up and down according to Bank rates and there are other Mortgages which have fixed rates of interest. If you choose a fixed rate than you will find that there is a penalty if you withdraw early from the Mortgage.

IN EVERY CASE WHEN YOU RECEIVE AN OFFER OF LOAN FROM A LENDER YOU SHOULD STUDY IT CAREFULLY AND SPEAK TO YOUR SOLICITOR TO ENSURE THAT YOU UNDERSTAND IT. IF THE LOAN IS NOT REPAID THE LENDER HAS A RIGHT TO TAKE THE PROPERTY FROM YOU AND SELL IT. THIS RIGHT MAY ONLY BE EXERCISED IN CERTAIN CIRCUMSTANCES AND IF YOU, AT ANY TIME IN THE FUTURE, HAVE DIFFICULTY REPAYING THE LENDER YOU SHOULD IMMEDIATELY CONSULT YOUR SOLICITOR.

Your Lender will require a surveyor to value the property. Please note that unless you ask for a full condition report the survey report which you normally receive will only indicate an approximate value of the property and you will not get a full examination Report.

If you borrow more than 75% of the value then the Lender usually requires a Mortgage Indemnity Policy. This is a one-off charge for an Insurance Policy to protect the lender in the event that they have to re-possess the property and sell it for less than the amount of Mortgage then outstanding. The Policy is intended to protect the lender, it will not protect you from losing your house.

It is easy to get confused about the total cost of your mortgage payment per month and you should always insist on a written quotation.

A Repayment Mortgage involves a single monthly payment to the lender. At the end of the term of years fixed by the mortgage the loan will be totally repaid. In the early years the amount outstanding will not reduce much, but this will change as the years progress.

An Endowment Mortgage involves a payment of interest only each month. In addition an endowment policy is taken out. This will repay the mortgage in the event of death and will provide a savings plan so that at the end of the Mortgage there should be sufficient to pay off the mortgage and provide some additional funds to you. However, this is not always guaranteed.

There are other types of savings plans available and you should in every case talk to your solicitor so that you know precisely all the consequences of each choice of mortgage.

FINANCIAL SERVICES
Your solicitor can obtain quotations and advice for you from Law Society (NI) Financial Advice Ltd/ (Independent Financial Adviser). (This is a company which was set up and financed by the Law Society acting on behalf of the solicitor's profession generally. The purpose of this company is to help to provide a wider service for the community and to make sure that independent financial advice is available). Independent financial advice is getting harder to find as many advisers sell only the financial products of particular investment companies.

There is an arrangement between the company and your solicitor whereby any commission which the company receives as a result of business written is shared with the solicitor who introduces the business. This, of course, only applies where business is actually written for the client after discussion and advice. If any business is written for you your solicitor will advise you of the precise amount he or she receives.

If you do use Law Society (NI) Financial Advice it is hoped that you will find them helpful. If they are in any way unsatisfactory please tell us so that we can report the matter to the Law Society so that improvements can be made for the future.

SERVICES
You should ensure that companies which supply services such as electricity and telephones are notified of the change of ownership of the property and the date on which the change of ownership will take place so that there will be no disruption of supply. You should ensure that the Rates Collection Agency knows the date of your moving into or out of the house.

FEES

A Form of estimate of the firm's account will be sent to you at the beginning of the case. This account is divided into two parts. First there are the fees due to the Solicitor. Secondly there are sums of money spent on your behalf. These are normally called "outlay". If you are obtaining a loan from a building society or other financial institution they will insist on these matters being dealt with and paid prior to completion. The main items of "outlay" are as follow:-

1. **Stamp Duty**
   This is a 1% tax on property purchases. It applies only to purchases of £60,000 or more but it is charged on the total sum and not the sum in excess of £60,000. Thus a purchase of £65,000 will attract stamp duty of £650.

2. **Search Fees**
   These are fees paid to check in the various registries that the person selling the house to you has no charges registered against the property and that he or she is registered as owner of the property. If you are selling a property then your solicitor will be required to bring the searches up to date.

3. **Property Certificates**
   These are required from various statutory authorities to ensure that the property complies with various regulations such as Planning and Building Control.

4. **Registration Fees**
   These are paid to the appropriate Registry each time a transaction is registered. For example a Land Registry transaction for the purchase of an average house could cost approximately £300. It should be remembered that these fees are increased by Government from time to time.

DIFFICULTIES

The Charter exists to ensure that you obtain a quality service. One of the ways in which the quality of our work is checked is by regular and random inspection by the Law Society of the files which members of the scheme are holding. It is possible that your file may be subject to inspection like this. If you have any objection to that being done you should tell your solicitor at once.

If you have cause for complaint you should initially contact the solicitor who has charge of your case. If he is unable to resolve the problem you should contact the senior partner of the firm. In some cases this may be the same person and in that case, or should the senior partner not be able to resolve the matter, then you can refer it to the Charter Committee of the Law Society of Northern Ireland at 98 Victoria Street, Belfast.

If you feel that the account for professional fees is unreasonable then you have a right to have this matter resolved through an Officer of the Court. Alternatively you have a right within three months of the bill being delivered to seek a certificate from the Law Society of Northern Ireland to state whether the fee is reasonable or what the proper fee should be. Your solicitor is obliged to provide you with full information on these processes should this arise.

This leaflet is designed to provide you with as much information as is possible on the purpose and value of the Home Charter Scheme. If you have any additional queries please do not hesitate to contact the Charter Committee of the Law Society. They will be only too pleased to help.

FORM 3A - FORM OF UNDERTAKING

Undertaking by Solicitor - Title Deeds/Land Certificate(s) lent to the Solicitor for purpose of inspection only and return.

....................20....

TO   BANK LIMITED

I/We hereby acknowledge to have received from you the Title Deeds/Land Certificate(s) and documents relating to .... in accordance with the schedule hereto.

I/We undertake to hold them on your behalf and to return them to you on demand in the same condition in which they now are and without the property to which they relate or any interest therein being, to my/our knowledge, in any way charged, conveyed, assigned, leased, encumbered, disposed of or dealt with.

Signature ....

Note:- This undertaking should be signed by the Solicitor in person or (in the case of a firm) by a partner.

SCHEDULE

FORM 3B - FORM OF UNDERTAKING

Undertaking by Solicitor - Title Deeds/Land Certificate(s) handed to the Solicitor re Sale or Mortgage of Property, or part of it, and to account to Bank for net proceeds.

.... 20....

TO: **BANK LIMITED**

I/We hereby acknowledge to have received from you the Title Deeds/Land Certificate(s) and documents relating to .... in accordance with the schedule hereto for the purpose of the sale/mortgage of this property or part thereof.

Pending completion of such transaction I/We undertake to hold them on your behalf and to return them to you on demand in the same condition in which they now are and without the property to which they relate or any interest therein being, to my/our knowledge, in any way charged, conveyed, assigned, leased, encumbered, disposed of or dealt with.

If the transaction is completed I/We undertake -

(a) to pay to you the amount of the proceeds of sale/mortgage as and when received, subject only to the deduction therefrom of the necessary legal costs and outlays relating to the particular transaction.

(b) If the Title Deeds/Land Certificate(s) and documents relate to property in addition to that which is the subject of the proposed sale or mortgage, to return them to you together with the appropriate instrument or instruments evidencing the transaction (if applicable).

Signature ....

NOTE:- This undertaking should be signed by the Solicitor in person or (in the case of a firm) by a partner.

FORM 3C - FORM OF UNDERTAKING

Undertaking by Solicitor - to deliver Title Deeds/Land Certificates(s) to bank on completion of a purchase, the purchase money in whole or in part being provided by the Bank.

.... 20..

TO: BANK LIMITED

If you provide facilities to my/our client.................. for or towards the purchase of the Freehold/leasehold property

....
(description of property)

I/We undertake

(a) that any sums received from you or your client for the purpose of this transaction will be applied solely for acquiring a good marketable title to such property and in paying any necessary legal costs and outlays in connection with such purchase.

(The purchase price contemplated is £....... and with apportionments and any necessary outlays, is not expected to exceed £..........).

(b) after the property has been acquired by .... and all necessary stamping and registration has been completed, to deliver the Title Deeds/Land Certificate(s) and documents to you and in the meantime to hold them to your order.

I/We deserve the right to discharge this undertaking by repaying to you all monies advanced by you to my/our client through me/us together with appropriate interest thereon.

                     Signature ....

                     Note: This undertaking should be signed by the Solicitor in person or (in the case of a firm) by a partner.

FORM 3D - FORM OF UNDERTAKING

Undertaking by Solicitor - for use in connection with bridging finance

Authority from Client(s)

DATE...........20....

TO...
(name and address of Solicitors)

I/We hereby irrevocably authorise and direct you to give an undertaking in the form set out below and to pay the net proceeds of the sale of my/our property at .... (the existing property) and the net proceeds of the loan being sought by me/us in respect of the purchase of property at .... (the new property) respectively therein mentioned to .... Bank Limited.

....
Signature(s) of Client(s)

UNDERTAKING

Date ......20......

TO   BANK LIMITED

If you provide facilities to my/our client ....for or towards the purchase of the new property ....

I/we undertake

1   That any sums received from you or your client will be applied only for the following purposes:-

(a) in acquiring a good marketable title to the new property and in paying any necessary legal costs and outlays in connection with such purchase.

(The purchase price contemplated is £ .... and with apportionments and any necessary legal costs and outlays is not expected to exceed £........).

(b) (if the existing property is subject to a mortgage/charge) in discharging the mortgage/charge now affecting the existing property in favour of .... and in paying any necessary legal costs and outlays in connection with such discharge.

(The amount required to discharge the said mortgage charge is approximately £.........)

2
(a) To pay you the net proceeds of a loan of £........ from ....(name of building society or other lending institution) to our client in respect of the new property if and when received (as evidenced by the copy letter of approval or instructions to solicitor annexed hereto).

(The net proceeds of such loan after deduction of the necessary legal costs and outlays in connection with the transaction should be not less than £.........)

(b) After completion of the purchase of the new property and pending completion of such loan transaction to hold the Title Deeds/Land Certificate(s) of the new property in trust for you and to your order.

3   (if clause 2 is not applicable)

After completion of the purchase of the new property to hold the Title Deeds/Land Certificate(s) thereof in trust for your and to your order.

4   (If the existing property is to be sold)

(a) to pay to you the net proceeds of the sale of the existing property as and when received.

(The sale price contemplated is £....... The net proceeds of such sale after deduction of the necessary legal costs and outlays in connection with the transaction should be not less than £.........)

(b) pending completion of such sale to hold the Title Deeds/ Land Certificate(s) relating to the existing property in trust for you and to your order, upon the discharge of such mortgage/charge (if any) as is specified hereunder, that is to say ....

Signature ....

Note:- This undertaking should be signed by the Solicitor in person or (in the case of a firm) by a partner.

FORM 4A - CONFLICTS OF INTEREST

Dear

RE

In this case we have also been instructed to act on behalf of the proposed Vendor/Purchasers. If there were any question of a conflict of interest between yourselves and them the Law Society's Regulations would prohibit us from acting for you and the proposed Vendor/Purchaser as well. Having considered the matter we can confirm that there does not appear to be any such conflict at the present time.

If, for any reason, such a conflict does develop we would be unable, under Law Society Regulations, to continue to act for either you or the proposed vendor/purchasers but would have to arrange for alternative representation.

If you have any queries about the matter please write to us forthwith.

Yours

FORM 4B - CONFLICTS OF INTEREST

Dear

RE

You will remember that at the beginning of this transaction, we advised you that we had been instructed to act for the proposed Vendor/Purchasers as well as yourself /yourselves. We said then that if any conflict of interest were to develop between you we would be unable to continue to act for either you or the Vendor/Purchaser.

As you know such a conflict has now developed. In these circumstances it is necessary that all parties should be separately represented. Can you please advise us which firm you would like to represent you for the remainder of the matter and we will arrange for your papers to be passed on to them as soon as possible?

Yours

FORM 5 - MORTGAGE LETTER

To help buy this property you are taking a loan from a Lender. It is important to understand that the arrangement between you and the Lender is a business transaction which imposes legal duties on you. The most important of these is that you are required to make regular monthly payments of the amount and at the time specified by the Bank/Building Society. If you do not make these payments then you risk losing your home. However, the courts do have the power to give relief in some cases if it seems likely that the borrower will be able to make satisfactory arrangements within a reasonable time. So if you do fall into arrears you should inform the Lender immediately and also consult us. We will try to protect your interests. Remember the Lender is in business to make a profit from lending money.

You will have received a letter of offer from the Lender and you should study this carefully. If you have any doubts or questions about anything in the letter we will be happy to explain it. In particular you should study what it says about the insurance of the structure of the property. You should also remember to take out separate insurance to cover the contents of the house. It may also be wise to take out some kind of life assurance so that in the event of your death the mortgage will be paid off. That is something we would be happy to discuss with you if you want. If this is to be done then all arrangements should be made well before completion. Remember the Lender will hold the deeds of your property until the sum is paid off. You should receive a statement of account from the Lender from time to time. Check it carefully.

Finally you should note that in some cases the Lender has the right to use your house as security for other money which it has lent to you for reasons other than the purchase. You would need to be particularly careful if this is the case and to consider your position before taking on the responsibility.

FORM 6 - FUNDS LETTER

Dear Client,

Sale of existing property
Purchase of new property

As you know we hope to complete the above transaction on [date] and to enable us to do so we shall require the following amount by [date at least three days prior to completion]. This amount is made up as follows:

NEW PROPERTY

Deposit already paid (and received)	(-)	-
Balance purchase price		-
Stamp Duty		-
Land Registry Fees (estimated)/ Registry of Deeds fees		-
Money spent on your behalf		-
Mortgage advance	-	

OLD PROPERTY

Deposit already received and paid	-	(-)
Balance sale price	-	
Amount to redeem mortgage		-
Money spent on your behalf		-
Our Costs *(if this has been agreed)*		-
BALANCE DUE BY YOU	___	___
	___	___

Estate Agents fees and outlay amounting to £........ will also be payable.

SCHEDULE
DOMESTIC CONVEYANCING CHARGES

Solicitors' Firm Name _____
Address _____
_____ Tel. No: _____

NOTE: This form, which has been produced by the Law Society of Northern Ireland, pursuant to Regulation 5(2) of the Solicitors (Advertising) Practice Regulations 1989, is an indication of charges on the basis of details presently known and on the assumption that the transaction will not prove to be substantially more complex or time-consuming then expected. If the matter does not proceed to completion, work done and payments made up to that point will remain chargeable.

Client's Name _____
Address _____
_____ Tel. No: _____

ADDRESS OF PROPERTY TO BE SOLD _____
_____

Freehold/Leasehold; Registered/Unregistered; Mortgaged/Unmortgaged.
Price £ _____
Name of Building Society or other lender _____
Amount of mortgage advance £ _____ Repayment/Endowment £ _____
ON THIS INFORMATION WE EXPECT OUR CHARGES WILL BE:
On your sale including discharge of your mortgage   £_____
On your purchase   £_____
On your mortgage   £_____
Our charges   £_____
IN ADDITION WE WILL HAVE TO MAKE A NUMBER OF PAYMENTS TO GOVERNMENT AND OTHERS INCLUDING (AT PRESENT RATES):

VAT on our charges	£_____	
Stamp duty	£_____	
Land Registry/Registry of Deed Fees	£_____	
Search Fees	£_____	SUMMARY:
Statutory Charges	£_____	
Other Search Fees	£_____	Our charges £_____
Property Enquiries	£_____	
Landlord Fees for Notices, Licenses etc	£_____	Payments to others £_____
Mapping Fees	£_____	
_____ Payments to others	£_____	TOTAL £_____

Please note that the total amount of VAT, Stamp Duty and other payments may be subject to alteration if the rates are changed after the date of this form. In addition to the above, you may have to provide for payments to other parties, eg, your Building Society or other lender, for their survey, legal and other fees, your surveyor, or your estate agent and you should check with them the amounts they will require inclusive of VAT where appropriate.

Signed _____ Date _____

APPENDIX B
HOME IMPROVEMENT GRANTS

Introduction

Current provisions relating to grants are contained in Part III of the Housing (NI) Order 1992.

The owner or tenant of a property in need of repair or work to bring it up to modern standards may be able to get a grant from the Northern Ireland Housing Executive (' NIHE') to meet all or part of the cost.

An owner is defined as being a person who has, either alone or jointly with others, a freehold interest in possession (whether legal or equitable) or a tenancy granted or extended for a term of years of which not less than five years remain unexpired at the date of the application.[1]

A tenant is not specifically defined for general purposes but NIHE may not entertain a tenant's application for a grant unless the tenant is required by the terms of his tenancy to carry out the relevant works and he signed an agreement in respect of the tenancy before 5 December 1991, or his application is for a disabled facilities grant.[2]

There are different kinds of grant to suit different needs, depending on the type of property involved and the scale and type of works proposed.

A home improvement grant is not available if:

(1) The property was built or converted less than ten years before the date of the grant application;

(2) The property is a second or holiday home;

(3) The proposed works are not considered essential by NIHE;

(4) The applicant is a tenant of NIHE or of a registered Housing Association;

(5) The work is eligible for assistance under the Defective Premises (NI) Order 1975 because it is defective.

If a grant has been paid previously for works on the property, it may not be possible to receive any further grant. For this reason it is advisable, when acting for a purchaser, to ascertain whether a grant has been paid and if so, for how much.

Grants may be mandatory or discretionary. In most cases, a test of financial resources is made to decide how much the applicant can afford to pay himself and how much of the costs can be covered by grant.

TYPES OF HOME IMPROVEMENT GRANT

Renovation grant

This grant is for the improvement or repair of houses, including maisonettes and flats, and for the conversion of houses and other buildings into flats for letting. It is the main grant for which owner-occupiers and landlords are likely to apply.

---

[1] Housing (NI) Order 1992, art 42(2).
[2] Art 42 (6).

A renovation grant is only available when a property is unfit for human habitation and NIHE is required to take action. The main purpose of the grant is to bring a property up to standard. If renovation is considered appropriate the grant is mandatory and all the work required should be eligible for the grant.

If the property is listed or in a conservation area, special considerations may be applied to design and to the type of building materials used.

Work such as rewiring, plumbing and the installation of a damp proof course can be covered by the grant but it is not usually available for internal decoration nor simply to enlarge a house to provide more bedrooms or living space.

(a) Owner-occupier
An owner-occupier can apply for a renovation grant provided that he has a freehold or leasehold interest in the property, with at least five years unexpired of any lease and the property is the only or main residence for himself or a member of his family

(b) Landlord
A landlord can apply for a renovation grant provided that he has a freehold or leasehold interest in the property, with at least five years unexpired of any lease, and the application relates to a property let on a residential basis (not, for example, as a holiday home).

(c) Tenant
A tenant can apply for a renovation grant if he is specifically liable, under the terms of the lease, for carrying out the work in question.

Disabled facilities grant

Disabled facilities grant is a grant for adapting or providing facilities for the home of a disabled person to make it more suitable for him to live in and to help him manage more independently in the home.

Anyone registered or registrable as a disabled person can apply for the grant as an owner-occupier or a tenant. A landlord can also apply on behalf of a disabled tenant.

On receipt of an application NIHE has to determine that the proposed work is necessary and appropriate to meet the needs of the disabled occupant. Also, that the work is reasonable and practicable given the age and condition of the property.

Provided that NIHE is satisfied on these grounds, a mandatory grant is available for such work as:

(1) Facilitating access to and from the property;

(2) Making access easier to the rooms in the property;

(3) Providing suitable bathroom and kitchen facilities that the disabled person can use independently;

(4) Adapting heating or lighting controls to facilitate use;

(5) Improving the heating system;

(6) Making provision to help a disabled person care for any dependants.

A discretionary grant is also available for other work to make a home suitable for a disabled person's accommodation, welfare or employment.

Repairs grant

A repairs grant is intended to assist owners of older houses to carry out essential repairs. The grant is available to help with the cost of repairs to property following the service of certain statutory notices. For example, certificates of disrepair or public health notices. Property less than ten years old is not eligible for a repairs grant.

A landlord, owner-occupier, agent or tenant who has a repairing obligation may apply for a repairs grant. This grant is not means tested.

A repairs grant is available for the repair of existing items. It is not intended to provide any element of improvement or amenity for the first time.

The grant may be paid for work outside the main structure within the curtilage of the main dwelling, but not for outhouses such as garages or garden sheds.

Once a notice has been served, grant aid is normally mandatory. However, if the property is within an area due for demolition within five years of service of the notice, grant aid becomes discretionary.

Replacement grant

Replacement grant is a grant available for the replacement of isolated rural dwellings where complete replacement is considered preferable to renovation. The grant is only available to owner-occupiers and landlords, not to tenants.

To be eligible the property must be in an isolated rural area and must be shown to be in such a state of disrepair that renovation would exceed permitted demolition guidelines or would not be cost effective. The property may be occupied or vacant but, if it is vacant, the applicant must be in urgent housing need.

The grant may be given for the complete demolition of an existing dwelling and its replacement with a new dwelling. The replacement is normally located on the site of the original but, exceptionally, may be located elsewhere on the applicant's land.

Minor works assistance

Minor works assistance is a grant which covers small but essential works to the property where large scale work is not required. The assistance covers the cost of the work, including labour, to employ a contractor or the cost of materials used. It is always discretionary.

Assistance can cover either the full cost of the work or the provision of materials or a mixture of both. It can also include the cost of advice relating to the work.

Assistance is only available to owner-occupiers and private sector tenants who receive an income related benefit. There are no limits on the age of the property.

Applicants who need assistance with work to help them stay in their home must generally be 60 years old or more.

The purpose of assistance is as noted below.

(a) Staying put
To repair, improve or adapt a property for elderly occupants over 60 years old. For example, basic safety and security measures.

(b) Elderly resident
To adapt a property to enable an elderly person aged over 60 to stay or move in with relatives. For example, an additional toilet, handbasin or bath/shower unit, or additional cooking or heating facility.

(c) Patch and mend

To carry out repairs to property in a clearance or redevelopment area to ensure that it is at least wind and weatherproof. For example, replacing loose or missing tiles or slates and repairs to doors, windows and drainage systems.

(d) Lead pipes

To replace lead piping for the mains water supply or for electrical earthing purposes. The applicant must be in financial hardship but need not be over 60 years of age. A tenant must have the landlord's consent.

(e) Disabled adaptations

To provide small scale adaptations for a handicapped person. The application must be supported by an occupational therapist recommendation. Owner-occupiers and tenants may apply. Applicants need not be elderly but must be in financial hardship.

Houses in multiple occupation grant

A house in multiple occupation ('HMO') grant is available to cover a wide range of work to houses in multiple occupation where the occupants do not form a single household.

Only a landlord can apply for the grant. He must provide a certificate stating that he has an owner's interest in the property and that he intends to let or license the HMO or part of it as a residence to people other than members of his family.

The grant is available for work required to make a HMO fit for human habitation and to make it fit for the number of people living there. This depends on the adequacy of cooking, food storage, washing, and toilet facilities and fire safety measures.

The grant is normally discretionary. However, if the work is required to comply with a statutory notice then it is mandatory. Where there is overcrowding, the NIHE may take steps to reduce the number of occupants in the house, rather than favouring improvements to make it fit for the existing occupants.

Common parts grant

A common parts grant is a grant which is available to help with the improvement or repair of the common parts of buildings containing one or more flats, such as the roof, communal halls and staircases. The grant is normally discretionary. However, a landlord served with a repair notice requiring works to be carried out in the common parts is eligible for a mandatory grant towards the costs of the work.

The building for which a grant is made must include self-contained flats. In a converted building, the conversion must have been completed more than ten years before the grant application. For all applications, at least three quarters of the flats in the building must be occupied by occupying tenants; that is, those who own flats including long leaseholders or are tenants and whose flats are their only residence.

Either a landlord or a tenant may apply for a common parts grant. For this purpose a landlord is a person, who has alone or jointly with others, a freehold estate in possession (whether legal or equitable) or an interest for a term of which not less than five years remain unexpired. A tenant can also be a person with an interest in a term of years, of which at least five remain unexpired, or a person with a protected tenancy, a statutory tenancy or a tenancy which satisfies such conditions as may be specified by order.[3]

---

[3] Housing (NI) Order 1992, art 43(4).

A landlord can apply for a grant on his own or with the occupying tenants as a participating landlord. The landlord has to pass the benefit of the grant on to the tenants and not charge them for any costs reimbursed by the grant.

Occupying tenants can apply for the grant together provided that they are all liable, under the terms of their leases, for carrying out or contributing to the costs of the works in question. At least three quarters of the occupying tenants must participate in the application.

The types of work which might qualify for the grant include re-roofing, structural repairs and improvements to areas such as communal halls and staircases.

Group repair

In addition to the grants for which an individual may apply, NIHE may include the property in a group repair scheme. This can only be done with the consent of the owner. Any work which is required to the external fabric of a block of houses is done at the same time by the same contractor. The work is organised and supervised by NIHE which meets at least 50 per cent of the cost.

OTHER GRANTS

Home insulation grants

Insulation grants are no longer available from NIHE. The administrative process has been transferred to the Department of Economic Development and applications are now made to the Energy Action Grants Agency. An insulation grant is only available to elderly people in receipt of certain benefits.

Environmental grants

Limited grant aid is available for external environmental work to any person having a legal estate in a building in a Housing Action Area. The grant is intended for items such as exterior decoration, new garden fencing and repairs to outside walls.

Historic buildings

Particular problems may arise in respect of buildings which are officially listed as of special historic or architectural interest or which are in conservation areas. Works of a special nature may be prescribed by NIHE to preserve the character of the building and additional grant aid may be payable to cover some or all of the extra cost. Buildings occupied as dwellings are eligible for all ordinary grants.

HOUSING ACTION AREAS

In a Housing Action Area NIHE has more extensive powers to encourage both owner-occupiers and landlords to rehabilitate their houses, if necessary to compel them to do so and ultimately to compulsorily purchase houses from those who do not co-operate.

The amount of grant aid payable in most cases is increased if the property is situate within such an area.

MAKING A GRANT APPLICATION

To qualify:

(1) The property must be at least ten years old, except for a disabled facilities grant or minor works assistance.

(2) The applicant must be an owner-occupier, landlord or tenant responsible for his own repairs.

Procedure

The procedure for making an application is as follows.

(1) The applicant completes a preliminary enquiry form.
(2) The applicant provides proof of ownership. NIHE requires a letter confirming ownership of the property and the landlord's consent for a tenant's application.
(3) The applicant completes a preliminary test of resources by providing details of income and family circumstances unless he is applying for minor works assistance or a repairs grant in which case the test is not required.
(4) NIHE advises the applicant of his contribution (if any) towards the cost of the work.
(5) The applicant decides whether or not to proceed.
(6) If he does proceed, NIHE inspects the property.
(7) NIHE provides a list of all works to be carried out for grant aid.
(8) The applicant provides NIHE with all necessary documentation, such as plans, estimates, building control, planning approval, discharge consent.
(9) The applicant completes a formal test of resources form.
(10) Details of his income, family circumstances etc are checked and his contribution confirmed.
(11) The application is formally approved by NIHE giving the applicant permission to proceed with the approved works; advising him of the amount of grant aid he will receive and the amount he has to pay.
(12) NIHE must give the applicant one year from the date of formal approval to complete the work, although extensions of time are possible. If the applicant has received a statutory notice, he may have less time in which to complete the work.
(13) Upon satisfactory completion of the work, the grant money is paid out. It may be necessary to inspect the property when the work is finished. NIHE requires invoices, receipts and certificates as appropriate.
(14) If an owner-occupier sells the property within three years or a landlord sells within five years, he may have to repay all or part of the grant.[4] Exceptional circumstances may prevail when repayment will not be required. If the property is sold before the grant work is completed final payment of the grant cannot be made.

A disabled facilities grant or a common parts grant does not have to be repaid on sale of the property.

---

[4] Housing (NI) Order 1992, arts 58 and 59.

INDEX

acquisition of interests
   easements and profits, of 21.18-21.25
action
   adverse possession, for 23.01, 23.04, 23.05
   beneficiaries of trust, for 25.28
   breach of contract, for 15.22
   damages for breach of covenant, for 20.15, 20.16, 20.30
   ejectment, for 19.25-19.28
   mortgagee, for 26.10, 26.16, 26.17
   mortgagor for 26.21
   pending 7.28, 7.65
   possession, for 7.41, 23.01
   Prescription Act (Ir) 1858, under 21.28
   proprietary estoppel, for 22.18
   re-entry, for 19.19
   relief against forfeiture, for 19.15
additions
   tenant to property, by 14.09
adjudication, Stamp Duty, of 16.04
administration
   bankrupt's estate, of 27.01-27.11
   deceased's estate, of 6.18
   trusts, of 25.18-25.25
advancement
   presumption of 25.06-25.10, 29.09
adverse possession 6.19, 7.18, 7.41, 7.53, 23.01-23.12
agistment 21.12, 22.17
agreement
   caretakers 22.09
   conveyance and building agreement, for 9.03
   create contract, to 3.10
   lease of flat, for 8.01, 8.02
   mistake, effect on 4.16
   obligation, to create 20.01
   private streets 5.14, 9.07
   rectification to effect 4.23
   specific performance to effect 15.25
   Stamp Duty on 16.22
      agreement to surrender 16.24
   take possession, to 15.42
   tenancy, to create 19.01
agricultural
   agreements 22.16-22.17
   buildings 11.19, 12.04
   occupancy 5.20, 11.35

alterations
  life tenant, power of...24.09
  planning permission for 11.02, 11.14, 11.36
  tenant, by..20.06
annexation, fixtures, of...14.01-14.04
apartments...8.01-8.15
assent..6.18, 7.49, 17.08
assignment
  chain of title, in 6.10, 6.12
  covenant against 20.06, 20.13
  covenants for title on..17.03, 17.04
  enforcement of covenants on 8.12, 20.21, 20.22
  leasehold of 19.03-19.04
  mortgage by..26.05
  premises, part of..20.23
  registration of..7.09
  root of title, as 2.18
  Vendor and Purchaser Act 1874, s 2...2.21
attestation 6.32
attorney
  execution by 7.69
  mortgagor, appointment by..26.05
  power of...25.35-25.39
  Trustee Act (NI) 1956, s 26 power of under...25.25
attornment clause 26.11, 26.05

bankruptcy *see also* **insolvency**
  bankruptcy proceedings
    bankrupt's home...27.11
    bankruptcy order...27.05
    conclusion of administration 27.09
    creditor's petition 27.04
    debtor's petition..27.03
    discharge from bankruptcy 27.10
    distribution of estate 27.08
    investigation of affairs 27.07
    protection of bankrupt's estate 27.06
  defeasance on bankruptcy...7.51
  gift on title..6.22, 27.23
  Insolvency (No 2) Act 1994..27.24
  matrimonial charge, effect of..28.33
  matrimonial home, effect on..28.03, 28.04
  orders to recover property on..27.22
  preferences 27.20
  purchaser, of..15.14, 27.17, 27.18
  search..5.09, 27.15
  severance of joint tenancy..18.41
  transactions at undervalue..27.19
  transactions defrauding creditors...27.21
  vendor, of...7.54, 15.07, 15.08, 27.12-27.14
  void dispositions...6.27, 27.23

voluntary conveyance by	6.22, 27.24

beneficiary
purchaser as, after contract	15.01
remedies for	25.28
trust, under	6.15, 25.01
variation of trust by	25.26
will, under	5.16, 5.17, 6.18

***bona fide* purchaser**
enforcement of covenant against	20.24, 20.28, 21.42
insolvency, effect on	27.22-27.24
licence, effect on	22.03
rights of occupation against	28.08, 28.15, 28.32
tracing against	25.29

breach
building control, of	12.19, 12.20
conditions, of	19.17
contract, of	4.02, 15.19-15.21, 15.38, 15.39
covenant, of	19.16, 20.14-20.18
planning permission, of	11.31, 11.35
statutory duty, of	12.23
trust, of	25.27-25.29

building control
appeal	12.16
building regulations	12.01, 12.11-12.12
comfort letters	12.19
completion certificates	12.18
contravention	12.17
dangerous places and structures	12.22
declarations of no effect	12.21
exemptions	12.03-12.10
negligent application	12.23
procedure for making application	12.13-12.14
property certificates	12.24
regularisation certificates	12.20
relaxation of regulations	12.15
work requiring approval	12.02

building schemes	20.29, 29.13

burden
covenant, of	19.04, 20.01, 20.21, 20.24
Land Registry	7.28-7.30, 7.39-7.45
business tenancy	19.06, 20.13

capacity
company, of	6.21
parties to contract, of	3.15
party to conveyance, of	17.03-17.09
caretaker	15.42, 22.09

caution
Land Registry in	7.14, 7.27, 7.57
caveat emptor	2.02-2.09, 2.11, 4.12

certificate
   appointment of trustee in bankruptcy, of...27.05
   building control
      completion certificate...12.18
      regularisation certificate...12.20
   certificate of value, Stamp Duty, for..16.16, 16.18
   charge, of...7.27, 7.63
   debt, of..27.04
   discharge from bankruptcy, of...27.10
   incorporation, of..6.21, 9.09
   insurance of...8.01
   Land Certificate.. 7.05, 7.35, 7.63-7.65
   marriage/death, of.. 6.17, 6.26, 7.49
   priority, of..15.16
   property 5.01, 5.12-5.29
   registration, of in Registry of Deeds...6.07, 6.34
   search, of..7.60, 7.61
   solicitors...7.10, 7.67
charge
   equitable 15.02, 26.02, 26.04
   Land Registry 7.27
   matrimonial 28.32
   mortgage of, distinction..26.03
   order charging land... 5.08, 28.30, 28.31
   road 5.15
   service 8.02, 8.09
   statutory... 5.07, 11.35, 11.37
chattels..14.01-14.06
commercial lease...18.14
   assignment of...19.04, 20.22
   covenants in..20.05
common law
   attestation..6.32
   covenants implied by 20.02, 20.07
   enforcement of covenants at 8.12
   incorporeal hereditaments at 21.01
   joint interests...18.38
   licences..22.02
   lien for unpaid purchase money..15.02
   local customary rights...21.42
   merger..23.14
   mortgages 26.01, 26.14, 26.21
   public rights...21.40
   remedies for enforcement of contract... 15.22, 15.23
   rule against perpetuities..18.28
   status of purchaser in possession..15.42
   tenant's fixtures...14.09
common parts.. 8.01-8.06
   grants ....Appendix B
commorientes..18.30

company
- authority to enter transaction 6.21, 9.09
- management company *see* **management company**
- purchaser in liquidation 15.15, 27.17
- searches 5.10
- vendor in liquidation 15.09, 27.16

conacre 22.16

completion 15.01-15.21
- notice to complete 15.21
- possession before completion 15.42
- post-completion remedies 4.22, 17.01-17.20

consent
- assignment, to 19.04, 20.22
- breach of covenant, to 20.18
- life tenant under trust, of 25.12
- occupants to sale or mortgage, of 28.07, 28.09, 28.15, 28.18
- specific covenants, to 20.13
- subletting, to 19.05
- unreasonably withheld 20.13
- user of easement, to 21.26-21.34
- wife, to transaction 28.18

contract
- bankruptcy, effect on 15.06-15.08, 15.14
- breach of 15.19-15.21, 20.30
- conacre and agistment, for 22.16, 22.17
- contents of 3.14-3.19
- contractual licence 22.07
- Deasy's Act, s 3 .... 18.09
- death, effect on 15.05, 15.13
- deposit payable 3.20
- description of title in, ... 2.18-2.26
- disclosure
  - physical defects 2.03
  - title, defects in 2.04
- formation of 3.02-3.08
- from, to completion 15.01-15.18
- merger of, in conveyance 17.02
- misdescription in 4.02-4.08
- misrepresentation prior to 4.09-4.12
- mistake 4.15-4.23
- part performance of 3.05-3.08
- privity of 20.20, 20.21, 20.27
- provision in for fixtures and fittings 14.10
- remedies for enforcement of breach of 15.22-15.41
- Stamp Duty on 16.37-16.40
- types of
  - conditional 3.11
  - formal 3.13
  - informal 3.10
  - options 3.12

when binding..15.01
contingent interest..18.24
controller..6.20
conversion
    church leases, of...18.07
    doctrine of..15.01
    flats, into...11.14, Appendix B
    fee farm conversion grants...18.06
    Renewable Leasehold Conversion Act 1849..18.08
conveyance
    chain of title in..6.11
    covenants for title implied in..17.03
    fee simple of..18.02-18.04
    fee tail of...18.10
    future interest of...18.20-18.28
    matters of..2.16
    merger of contract in..17.02
    registration
        Land Registry, in..7.08
        Registry of Deeds, in...6.34
    restrictive and positive covenants in..20.25-20.28
    root of title as...2.18
    Stamp Duty on...16.17-16.20
    voluntary...6.22, 27.24
court order
    appointing controller of estate..6.20
    discharge obligations under contract.......................15.07, 15.14, 27.12-27.14
    order to eliminate source of danger to public...12.22
    possession, for..26.14
    rectification by...4.23, 17.20
    re-entry, for...19.19
    sale, for...26.16
covenants
    benefit...................................17.11, 19.04, 20.01, 20.19-20.25, 20.28
    breach of.....................19.16, 19.18-19.21, 20.14-20.16, 20.18, 20.30-20.31
    burden..17.12, 20.28
    consent to...20.13
    disclosure of...2.06-2.07, 2.23, 2.24
    enforcement of...8.12-8.15, 20.19-20.22
    express...20.04-20.06
    freehold...20.25-20.29
    implied..20.07-20.12
    leasehold..8.10-8.11, 20.02-20.24
    modification and removal of..20.33
    restrictive............................2.06, 7.28, 7.39, 8.01-8.02, 8.10-8.11, 21.42
    title for..6.23, 7.48, 17.03-17.18
    waiver of breach..20.17
creditors
    distribution to..27.08
    meeting of...27.05, 27.09
    petition by..27.04

representation of 27.07
transactions defrauding... 27.21

damages
  breach
    contract, of 15.23, 15.38-15.40, 20.30
    covenant, of... 20.15, 20.30
  misdescription, for 4.05
  misrepresentation, for 4.10, 4.11
death 6.17, 6.18, 7 49, 15.05, 15.13
declaration
  statutory declaration.. 6.27, 7.69, 27.23
  trust, of 6.15
deed(s)
  appointment of trustees 6.15, 25.20
  assignment of lease 6.10, 19.04
  attestation of 6.32
  chain of title.. 6.09-6.29
  covenant.. 20.01
  deduction of title 2.10-2.26
  defects in title in 2.06, 2.08
  development property, for... 9.02
  doctrine of notice as it applies to matters in 2.09
  execution of 6.31, 7.68, 16.10
  fee simple estate, to create.. 18.02
  implied covenants for title in 17.04-17.09
  incorporeal hereditaments 21.01, 21.19, 21.36
  leasehold estate, to create... 18.13
  lost deeds 6.27, 7.64
  memorial of.. 6.06, 6.08, 6.34
  mortgage 6.13, 26.05
  partition 18.42
  physical description, in... 3.18, 6.30
  power of appointment... 25.31-25.34
  power of attorney 25.35-25.39
  rectification 4.23
  registration
    Land Registry, in 7.02-7.07
    Registry of Deeds 6.05-6.07
  restrictive covenants... 21.42
  rights of residence 22.13
  settlement 6.14, 24.01
  Stamp Duty on 16.01-16.40
  stamping of 6.33, 7.66
  surrender of lease 19.13
defects
  building construction, in.. 9.08, 12.23, 13.07-13.11
  physical 2.03-2.05
  title, in... 2.06-2.08, 2.11
demand
  possession, for.. 18.15, 19.25-19.27

rent, for 19.20, 19.28
statutory 27.04
deposit 3.03, 3.20, 3.15, 15.12, 15.21, 15.41
description
   legal 3.17, 4.03, 4.05-4.08
   physical 3.18, 4.04-4.08, 6.30, 7.04
determination
   lease of 19.06-19.31
development
   building control purposes, for 12.01-12.02
   building development 9.01-9.11, 20.29, 29.13
   flat 8.01-8.15
   planning purposes, for 11.01-11.03, 11.09-11.20
disclosure
   latent defects in title 2.06, 2.07-2.08, 2.23, 2.25
   latent physical defects 2.04-2.05, 2.07-2.08, 4.12
   occupants of property 28.34
   vendor's duty of, ... 4.03, 2.03-2.08
documents
   consequence of failure to request 15.18
   defects in title 2.06, 2.08
   documents registrable 6.03, 7.08-7.09
   furnished on deduction of title 2.11
   miscellaneous 6.26
   rectification of 4.23
   registration in Registry of Deeds 6.34
   Stamp Duty on 16.01-16.02
   written evidence of contract, sufficient 3.03-3.04
dominant tenement 21.03-21.04, 21.11, 21.40, 21.42
duress 15.30
duty of care
   mortgagee's duty on sale 26.15
   negligent misstatement, for 4.13
easements
   acquisition of 21.18-21.34
   burden on registered land, as 7.28, 7.30, 7.45
   common types of 21.07-21.10
   definition 21.01-21.02
   elements of 21.03-21.06
   extinguishment of 21.35-21.37
   necessity of 21.21
   required for flats/apartments 8.03-8.05
   rights
      light, of 21.08
      support, of 21.10
      water, of 21.09
      way, of 2.06, 21.07
   sale subject to 2.06, 2.24, 4.12
   septic tank, for 9.11
ejectment 19.25-19.27, 26.17

Index

electricity 9.10, 8.02
elderly relatives 28.29
enforcement
    building regulations, of 12.17-12.23
    contract, of 15.22-15.25
    covenants for title, of 17.10-17.12
    covenants/obligations, of 8.12-8.13, 20.19-20.22
    planning, of 11.03, 11.31, 11.35
    searches 5.08
    security by mortgagee 26.09-26.19
enlargement
    lease, of 19.30
    house, of 11.14
enquiries
    assent, as to 6.18
    contract, before 4.12, 15.17, 28.34
    prior title, as to 2.19
equitable interest
    implied trusts 25.06
    interest in occupation 28.11-28.17
    matrimonial charge 28.32
    mortgage 7.27
    trusts 25.01
    wife's interest 28.07-28.10
equitable relief
    damages 15.38-15.40
    enforcement of freehold covenants, for 20.28
    forfeiture and recovery of deposit 15.41
    injunction 20.31
    mistake, for 4.15-4.17, 4.20, 4.22-4.23, 17.20
    part performance 3.05-3.08
    rectification 17.20
    rescission 15.34, 17.19
    specific performance 15.25-15.33
    unpaid purchase money, for 15.02
equities
    registered land, on 7.26, 7.18, 7.37
equity
    binding contract, effect of 15.01
    creation of joint interests 18.38-18.40, 25.08
    estoppel licences 22.08
    failure by grantee to execute deed, effect of 6.31
    matrimonial interests, implied by 28.03
    merger of estates, in 23.15
    mortgages 26.01-26.02, 26.06-26.08
    mutual wills 25.09
    proprietary estoppel 22.18, 28.03, 28.29
    registered as owner of registered land, in 15.16
    remedy in for mistake as to identity 4.19
    rescission for misrepresentation 4.11
    time not of the essence in 15.23

tracing 25.29
equity of redemption..26.08
estate
    bankrupt, of..27.03-27.06, 27.08-27.09
    deceased, of..6.17-6.18, 7.49
    estate agents 4.14
    freehold 18.02-18.12
    future...18.20-18.28
    leasehold 18.13-18.19
    life 18.11, 22.14-22.15, 24.04
    privity of 19.03, 20.19-20.24
    scheme 20.29, 29.13
estoppel
    estoppel licences...22.08
    proprietary..22.18, 28.03, 28.29
    tenancy by...18.19
evidence
    insufficiently stamped instrument as 16.14-16.15
exceptions and reservations..7.04, 8.06
execution of documents..4.22, 6.31, 7.68, 16.10
extinguishment of lease...7.55

fee farm grant
    Church grants 18.07
    covenants in 20.02
    Deasy's Act grants 18.09
    deduction of, for contract 2.20-2.21
    definition of 18.05
    fee-farm conversion grants 18.06
    formalities for creation of 19.02
    Land Registry title, in 7.17, 7.21
    prohibition on future creation of 29.04
    Renewable Leasehold Conversion Act 1849 ....18.08
    Stamp Duty on 16.21
fee simple 7.16, 18.02-18.04
fee tail..18.10
feudal system..18.01, 18.13, 18.28
financing the purchase
    ancillary costs 10.02
    collateral security 10.08
    combination mortgage 10.18
    income of borrower 10.07
    interest only mortgage 10.10
    lenders 10.04
    mortgage indemnity 10.06
    mortgage schemes 10.09-10.19
    repayment mortgage 10.09
    second mortgage 10.19
    tax on mortgages 10.20-10.24
    valuation fees 10.03
    value of property 10.05

Index

fishing rights 21.15, 21.40, 22.06
fittings 14.01-14.06
fixtures 14.01-14.14, 16.19
flats/apartments .... 8.01-8.13, 11.14, Appendix B
folios
    Land Registry.. 7.04
foreclosure.. 26.19, 26.37
forfeiture 15.41, 19.14-19.18, 20.18, 23.04
formalities
    contract, for.. 3.03-3.04
    lack of 15.27
fraud
    breach of trust caused by 25.28
    constructive trust imposed to avoid 25.11
    defence to specific performance, as.. 15.30
    defrauding creditors 27.21
    exercise of power of appointment, in 25.31, 25.33
    fraudulent misdescription... 4.05
    fraudulent misrepresentation 4.10
    non-disclosure of latent defects in title............................... 2.06, 2.08
    rectification of mistake by 4.23
    registration of deeds to protect from 6.02
    remedy for.. 17.01-17.02, 17.19
    running of time discounted, for 23.10
    Statute of Frauds (Ir) 1695 .... 3.03-3.08
    trustee, by 7.32, 25.28
    undue influence as a type of 28.19-28.26
freehold estate
    covenants 20.25-20.29, 29.10-29.14
    fee farm grants 18.05-18.09
    fee simple 18.02-18.04
    fee tail 18.10
    interests in land 18.01
    life estate 18.11-18.12
    purchase of as superior interest.. 6.25
    registration of..7.08, 7.16, 7.21
    root of title... 2.17-2.19
    rules against remoteness 18.25-18.28
    title expressed in contract... 3.17
frustration 19.31
future interests
    contingent interests 18.24
    remainders 18.22
    reversions 18.21
    rule against inalienability 18.26
    rule against perpetuities 18.28
    rule against remoteness 18.25
    rule in *Whitby* v *Mitchell* 18.27
    vested interests 18.23
gains and losses 15.11

grants	11.36, Appendix B
ground rent redemption	6.24, 9.02, 20.01, 29.01, 29.02, 29.20
hardship	15.30
historic buildings	11.36, 11.38, Appendix B
incorporeal hereditaments	21.01-21.43
index	
memorials in Registry of Deeds	6.08
infants	24.03
inhibition	7.32, 7.48, 7.57, 7.65
injunction	20.31
insolvency	
bankrupt's home	27.11
bankruptcy	
jurisdiction	27.01
proceedings	27.02-27.10
purchaser, of	15.14, 27.17, 27.18
vendor, of	7.54, 15.07, 15.08, 27.12-27.14
bona fide purchaser, effect on	27.22-27.24
conveyancing transaction, effect on	6.22, 15.06-15.09, 15.14-15.15, 27.12-27.18
gift on title	27.23
Insolvency (No 2) Act 1994	27.24
orders	27.05
preferences	27.20
transactions	
defrauding creditors	27.21
setting aside	27.19-27.24
undervalue	27.19
insurance	8.07
joint ownership	6.16, 7.31, 18.29-18.44
creation of	18.38-18.40
determination of	18.41-18.44
joint tenancy	18.30-18.34
tenancy in common	18.35-18.37
Land Registry	
adverse possession	7.41, 7.53
alteration of documents	7.70
appurtenant rights	7.30
bankruptcy of registered owner	7.51, 7.54
cautions and inhibitions	7.57
certificates of charge	7.27, 7.63
changes of ownership	7.47-7.53
charges	7.27
classes of title	7.15-7.19
compulsory first registration	7.07
defeasance	7.50
equities note	7.37
execution of documents	7.68-7.69
first registration	7.06-7.14

folios	7.04
joint ownership	7.31
land certificate	7.05, 7.35, 7.63-7.65
limitations of system	7.34-7.46
lodgment of dealings	7.66
merger and extinguishment of leases	7.55
mineral rights	7.42
priorities	7.56
proof of title on registration	7.20-7.24
reclassification of title	7.25-7.26
registered burdens	7.28
registers	7.02-7.03
rights of residence/occupation	7.29, 7.40, 24.04, 28.06-28.07
sale by owner of charge	7.52
searches	5.08-5.09, 5.11, 7.58-7.62
settlements	7.33
solicitors' certificates	7.67
systems of registration	7.01
transfers	7.48
transmission on death	7.49
trust	7.32
unregistered burdens	7.39-7.45
unregistered dispositions	7.38, 15.16

lease

assignment and subletting	19.03-19.05
chain of title, in	6.12
contractual evidence required to create	3.03-3.04
covenants, in	20.02-20.24
description in contract of estate to be sold	3.17
determination	19.06-19.31
duty of vendor to disclose covenants	2.06
ejectment	19.25-19.26
enlargement	19.30
extinguishment	7.55, 19.29, 23.04
flat, of	8.03-8.15
formalities	19.02
frustration	19.31
good holding title, as	2.13
implied covenants for title in	17.05
intention to create	19.01
Land Registry	7.04-7.05, 7.09, 7.17, 7.16, 7.22, 7.28, 7.36, 7.43
leasehold estates	18.13-18.19
licence or lease	22.04
life tenant, power to	24.07
limitation of vendor's duty of disclosure of	2.07
lives, for	18.12, 29.09
merger	7.55, 19.29, 23.04
modification of statutory provisions by contract	2.24
mortgagor and mortgagee, power to	26.26
new house, for	9.02
periodic tenancy	18.15

    purchase of superior interest 6.25, 7.55
    re-entry... 19.18-19.23
    registration in Registry of Deeds 6.03, 6.34
    renewable 18.08
    root of title, as 2.18
    Stamp Duty on 16.21-16.22
    statutory provision for deduction of leasehold title.............................. 2.20-2.23
    statutory tenancy 18.18
    surrender of 16.24
    tenancy at sufferance 18.17
    tenancy at will 18.16
    tenancy by estoppel 18.19
    term certain 18.14

lessee
    covenants in lease.. 8.10-8.11, 20.06, 20.09, 20.12
    enforcement of obligations by.. 8.12-8.15, 20.19-20.22
    purchase of superior interest 6.25, 7.55
    right to request title to freehold 2.23-2.25
    rights of, granted as easement 8.04

lessor
    covenants
        lease, in 20.05, 20.08, 20.11
        title, for 17.09
    enforcement of obligations by.. 8.12-8.15, 20.19-20.22
    exceptions and reservations for 8.06

liability
    breach of trust, for 25.27
    breaches of covenant, for... 19.04, 20.19-20.24
    expenses for construction of road, for 5.13
    negligent application of building regulations 12.23
    replies to enquiries before contract, for 4.12-4.13
    restriction of by vendor under contract 2.26

licence
    definition.. 21.43, 22.02-22.04
    features of.. 22.03
    right of residence 22.13-22.15, 24.04
    tenancy, as distinct from 19.01, 22.04

lien.. 15.12

life estate
    fee tail 18.10
    lease for lives renewable for ever 18.12
    definition... 18.11
    right of residence 22.14, 24.04
    rule against inalienability.. 18.26

life tenant
    death of 6.17, 14.12
    definition... 18.11
    powers of life tenant 6.14, 24.06-24.09
    registration as limited owner... 7.33
    right of residence 22.14, 24.04
    rule against inalienability.. 18.26

settlement	24.02, 24.05
trust for sale	6.15, 25.13
variation of trusts	25.26

limitation periods
acquisition of easement by prescription, for	21.26-21.33
breach of trust, action for	25.28
extinguishment of interests, for	23.01, 23.09-23.11

liquidation	15.09, 15.15, 27.16, 27.17

loan
ancillary costs	10.02
collateral security	10.08
condition of contract, as	3.15
income of borrower	10.07
interest only mortgage	10.10-10.17
lenders	10.04
mortgage indemnity	10.06
mortgage schemes	10.09-10.19
offer of,	9.04
repayment mortgage	10.09
survey	2.05
valuation fees	10.03
value of property	10.05

lodgers and guests	22.11

maintenance
flat, of	8.02, 8.09, 8.10
landlord's responsibility for,	20.05

management company
enforcement of obligations against	8.12
responsibilities of	8.03, 8.05, 8.07
role of	8.02
running of	8.08-8.09

married couples	18.40, 28.02, 28.04-28.05, 28.32-28.34

matrimonial interests
charging orders affecting	28.30-28.31
consent to transaction	28.18
Married Women's Property Act 1882, s17	28.04
Matrimonial Causes (NI) Order 1978	28.05
matrimonial home rights	28.32-28.34
rights of occupation	28.06-28.17
title	
husband's sole name, in	28.03
joint names, in	28.02
undue influence	28.19-28.29

memorandum of association	6.21, 8.02, 8.08
memorandum of sale	3.15, 3.03-3.04, 3.20
memorial	5.06, 6.06, 6.27, 6.32, 6.34, 7.07, 7.13

merger
chattel with realty	14.02
contract with conveyance, of	17.02-17.03
equity of redemption, of	16.25

lease, of 7.55, 19.29, 23.04, 23.13-23.15
misdescription
   fraudulent 4.05
   innocent 4.06-4.08, 15.32
   legal description 3.17, 4.03
   physical description 4.04
   Property Misdescriptions Act 1991 .... 4.14
misrepresentation
   enquiries before contract, in 4.12
   fraudulent... 4.10
   innocent 4.11
   post-completion 17.01, 17.19
misstatement... 4.13
mistake
   adverse possession by 23.01
   common law 4.16
   equity 4.17
   post-completion 4.22-4.23, 7.70, 17.01-17.02, 17.19-17.20
   types of 4.18-4.21
   unilateral 4.15
mortgage
   adverse possession, effect of 23.06
   chain of title, in 6.13
   enforcement of security by mortgagee... 26.09-26.19
   features of.. 26.06-26.08
   finance... 10.01-10.15
   joint mortgage, implied trust 25.08
   legal and equitable.. 26.02
   mortgage and charge 26.03
   power of life tenant to 24.08
   priority of registration 6.04
   redemption 26.06-26.08, 26.25
   registered land, on 7.27, 26.04
   requirement for survey 2.05
   rights common to both parties 26.26-26.29
   rights of mortgagor... 26.20-26.25
   second mortgages... 26.30-26.32
   spouse
      consent, to 28.18
      occupation, effect on 28.06-28.17
   Stamp Duty on transfer of.. 16.20
   subsequent mortgages, disadvantages of... 26.33-26.37
   tacking of 26.33
   undue influence
      elderly relatives, on 28.29
      spouse, on 28.19-28.28
   unregistered land, on... 26.05
mortgagee
   adverse possession, by 23.06
   constructive trust on sale, by 25.11
   definition of.. 26.01

    effect of vendor's insolvency on 6.22
    enforcement of security by mortgagee 26.09
        appointment of receiver 26.18
        common law right to possession 26.10
        court order for sale 26.14, 26.16
        foreclosure 26.19
        order for possession and sale 26.14
        sale 26.15
        taking possession 26.17
    power to lease 26.26
    rights of occupier, as against 28.06-28.18
    second mortgagee, sale by 26.30
    transfer of rights 26.27, 26.29
mortgagor
    action taken by mortgagee against 26.09-26.19
    adverse possession on right to redeem, effect of 23.06
    constructive trust, sale by mortgagee 25.11
    creation of mortgage 26.02-26.05
    definition 26.01
    power to lease 26.26
    rights of 26.20-26.25
        actions 26.21
        possession 26.20
        sale 26.23
        sale of equity of redemption 26.24
        title documents 26.22
    transfer of equity of redemption 26.28

National House Building Council (NHBC) 13.01-13.16
natural rights 21.39
Northern Ireland Housing Executive (NIHE) .... 5.01, 5.29, 16.19, Appendix B
notice
    bankruptcy, of 7.54, 15.14, 27.14, 27.17-27.18, 27.24
    blight 11.33
    cautioners and inhibitioners, given to 7.57
    completion, of 15.21
    contravention (building regulations) 12.17
    doctrine of 2.06-2.09, 2.17, 2.23-2.25, 7.32, 15.17, 27.23
    enforcement (planning) 11.31
    judgment, of 5.08
    planning decision, of 11.29
    purchase 11.34
    repair, of 20.15
    requiring payment of mortgage 26.15
    right to light, of 21.33
    second mortgage, of 26.30
    specifying breach of covenant 19.21
    spouse's interest in occupation, of 28.07-28.09, 28.15-28.18
    to quit 19.07-19.12
    unregistered, burden 7.39

obligations
    as modified by contract 2.24-2.26
    flat owners, of 8.01, 8.05, 8.07, 8.09-8.11
    option agreement, under... 3.12
    specific performance to compel compliance with 15.25-15.33
    tenant to remove fixtures, of.. 14.08-14.09
    to complete contract if other party bankrupt.................... 15.06-15.08, 15.14, 27.27
    vendor
        deduce title to 2.10-2.26
        disclose defects to 2.03, 2.06
        provide search, of 16.28

occupation
    adverse possession, by 6.19, 7.18, 7.26, 7.41, 23.01, 23.12
    agistment agreement, under 22.17
    agricultural purposes, for 11.35
    bankrupt's home, of.. 27.11
    caretaker, as... 22.09
    conacre agreement, under.. 22.16
    land benefited or burdened by easement, of............................ 21.05, 21.26
    licence, under 21.43
    non-owning spouse, by... 28.03, 28.06-28.17
    planning purposes, for.. 11.06
    protected by matrimonial home rights 28.32
    purchaser going into before completion 15.10, 15.42
    unregistered rights of occupation... 7.40
    without title *see* **adverse possession**

Official Receiver 27.05, 27.07, 27.09, 27.21
options 3.12
orders
    Controller, to appoint.. 6.20
    bankruptcy,
        contract, effect on 15.06-15.08, 15.14
        discharge from 27.10
        procedure 27.02-27.05
        purchaser, against 15.14, 27.17-27.18
        searches 27.15
        vendor, against................................... 7.54, 15.06-15.08, 27.12-27.14
    charging land.. 5.08, 7.65, 28.30
    extinguish public right of way, to 21.40
    forfeiture of lease, for 19.19
    life tenant to prevent sale by trustees, by... 25.13
    Married Women's Property Act 1882, s 17..................................... 28.04
    Matrimonial Causes (NI) Order 1978, art 26 .... 28.05
    modification or extinguishment of restrictive covenant, for.......... 20.33
    order to eliminate source of danger to public.................................. 12.22
    possession and sale by mortgagee, for 26.14, 26.16
    recovery of bankrupt's property, for 27.19-27.25
    rectification, for 4.23, 17.20
    registrar's order 7.57
    sale on bankruptcy, for... 27.11

tree preservation	11.37
trustees, to appoint	25.20
vary trust, to	25.26
overholding	18.17, 19.27
overreaching	28.12
part performance	3.05-3.08, 19.02
partition	18.42-18.44, 28.30-28.31

penalties
Stamp Duty	16.10, 16.12
periodic tenancy	18.15
perpetuities, rule against	3.12, 18.28, 25.12, 25.15-25.16, 25.32

personal representative(s)
convenants for title by	17.07
purchaser, of	15.13
sale by	6.17-6.18
searches against	6.28
trustees for beneficiaries, as	25.02, 25.20
trustees of settlement, as	24.10
vendor, of	7.49, 15.05
personalty	18.13

planning permission
activities which are not development	11.09-11.11
agricultural buildings and operations	11.19
caravan sites	11.18
changes of use	11.16
development within curtilage of house	11.14
forestry buildings and operations	11.20
incidental use	11.12
minor operations	11.15
permitted development	11.13
temporary buildings	11.17
use classes	11.09-11.10
agricultural occupancy	11.35
blight notices	11.33
condition of contract, as	3.11
development	11.02-11.03
essential document, as	9.05
historic buildings	11.36
making an application for planning permission	11.21-11.30
advertisements	11.27
appeal	11.32
determination	11.29
enforcement of appeal	11.31
neighbour notification	11.28
time limits	11.30
material change of use	11.04-11.08
matters to check	11.38
planning replies on property certificate	5.20
purchase notices	11.34
tree preservation orders	11.37

possession
    agistment, agreement under 22.17
    as act of part performance 3.06
    bankrupt's home, of...27.11
    caretaker, by 22.09
    conacre agreement, under..22.16
    discretionary trust, interest in...25.14
    establish good holding title, to 2.13
    exclusive, importance of 18.13, 19.01
    extinguish title of original owner, to.............................7.23, 7.26
    for repairs etc..15.10
    freehold 18.01, 18.03, 18.28
    future...18.21-18.22
    guest by 22.12
    implied covenant to give up 20.09
    interest vested, in...18.23
    landlord
        ejectment, taking by 19.25-19.28
        re-entry, taking by..19.19
    life tenant, by...24.05
    lodger by..22.11
    mortgagee, right to 26.10-26.13, 26.31
    mortgagor, by..26.20-26.21
    proprietary estoppel 22.18
    recovery of, by vendor..15.35
    retention of, by vendor 15.02, 15.42
    servant or employee by..22.10
    tenancy in 18.14-18.19
    tenant in tail in 18.10
    unity of
        dominant and servient tenements 21.37
        joint tenants...18.31
        tenants in common..18.37
        two estates, of..23.14

powers
    appointment, of..2.18, 25.30-25.34
    attorney, of 6.26, 25.35-25.38
    convey, to 17.24
    enduring power of attorney..25.39
    life tenant, of...7.33, 24.05, 24.07-24.09
    management company, of..8.02, 8.08
    mortgagee, of..26.10-26.19, 26.26, 26.29
    sale, of..6.15, 7.50, 24.06, 25.30
    trustees, of...24.10, 25.23

preference 27.20, 27.22
prescription..7.45, 21.26-21.34
presumption
    abandonment of easement or profit, of..................................21.36
    advancement, of...25.10, 28.09
    dedication of public right of way, of......................................21.40
    favour of joint tenancy, in 18.38

favour of tenancy in common in 18.39
grant of easement, of 21.25
implied trust, of 25.06
power of attorney not revoked, that 7.69
resulting trust, of 25.10, 28.04
time not of the essence, that 15.20
undue influence, of 28.19-28.26

priority
    act over bankruptcy petition/order 27.15
    bankrupt's home, of interests in 27.11
    documents registered in Registry of Deeds, between 6.04, 6.34
    equitable interest
        matrimonial charge, protection by 28.32-28.34
        mortgage, over 28.08-28.18
    Land Registry, in 7.27-7.30, 7.56
    mortgages of 26.30, 26.33
    order charging land for rates of 26.15
    proprietary rights created by option, of 2.35
    registered burdens of 28.30-28.31
    search 2.80, 5.11, 7.54, 7.61, 15.16, 27.15

privity
    contract, of 8.12-8.13, 20.20, 20.27
    estate, of 8.12-8.13, 19.03, 20.21, 20.28

proceedings
    bankruptcy 27.02-27.10
    building control, for 12.19, 5.23
    enforcement, building control for 5.23, 12.19
    environmental health, for 5.25
    planning purposes, for 5.20, 11.31, 11.35
    recover possession, to 15.42

profit à prendre 21.03, 21.11-21.17, 21.18-21.25, 21.35-21.37

property certificates
    Dept of the Environment 5.12-5.21, 11.35-11.36, 11.39
    duty of vendor to obtain 5.01
    local district council 5.22-5.28, 12.24
    NIHE 5.29

proprietary estoppel 18.19, 22.18
public rights 21.40

purchaser
    bankruptcy of 15.14, 27.17-27.18
    breach of contract, effect on 15.20-15.21
    compulsory first registration, responsibility of 7.07
    conditions of sale, effect on 3.19
    covenants for title, effect on 17.03-17.18
    development property, of 9.01-9.11
    fixtures as between vendor and 14.10
    flat, of 8.01-8.15
    investigation of title, by 2.11
    merger of contract with conveyance, effect on 17.02
    misdescription, effect on 4.02-4.08

misrepresentation, effect on 4.09-4.14
mistake, effect on..4.15-4.23
NHBC cover for... 13.01-13.03, 13.05-13.15
onus on, *caveat emptor* 2.02-2.09, 2.11
party to contract, as..3.04
payment of deposit by..3.20
position between contract and completion 15.01, 15.10, 15.18
possession by before completion 15.42
possessory title 7.18, 7.26
priority search by..7.61
rectification for...17.20
registered burden, effect on..7.28
remedies for enforcement of contract...2.86-2.88
    damages for 15.38
    forfeiture and recovery of deposit 15.41
    rescission by 15.34
    specific performance 15.25
        defence of 15.26-15.33
searches obtained by 5.01
Stamp Duty to be paid by...16.01
taking possession as act of part performance 3.06
trusts, effect on 6.15, 7.32
unbroken chain of title, importance of...6.10-6.34
unregistered burdens, effect on..7.39-7.46
vendor's bankruptcy, effect on 27.12-27.16

quiet enjoyment 17.16, 20.05, 20.25

realty...18.13
    fixtures attached to 14.01-14.03
receiver..26.18
rectification..4.17, 4.23, 7.70, 17.20
redemption
    date for...26.06-26.07, 26.15, 26.25
    equity of 26.08, 26.15, 26.24-26.25, 26.28, 28.12
    ground rent, of..................................6.24, 9.02, 20.01, 29.01, 29.02, 29.20
    mortgagee, of..26.34
    mortgagor, of..26.25
    proviso for 26.05
re-entry, right of 19.19-19.21
registered land *see also* **Land Registry**
    adverse possession on 23.08
    equity of estoppel on..22.18
    interest under contract 15.16
    mortgages and charges of 26.02-26.04
    orders charging land, on..28.30-28.31
    owner of charge on 26.12, 26.17
    registers 7.02-7.04, 7.34
    right of residence on 22.14, 28.07, 28.10
    Stamp Duty on transactions 16.15
    system of registration 7.01

registration
  charges of 7.27
  Land Registry, in 7.02-7.12
    application for 7.66-7.67
    compulsory first registration 7.07-7.13
    first registration 7.06
    matrimonial home right 28.32
    priority of 7.56, 15.16
    rights of occupation 28.07, 28.32
    rights of squatter 23.08
    systems of 7.01-7.04
  Registry of Deeds, in 6.34
    certificate of 6.07
    deeds 6.34
    documents registrable 6.03
    indexes 6.08
    matrimonial home right, of 28.32
    memorials 6.06
    priorities 6.04, 26.33
    responsibility for 6.05
    searches 5.01-5.06, 6.28
    system of 6.01-6.02

release
  covenant, of 20.30
  easement, of 21.36
  joint tenancy, of 18.44
  life tenant's powers 24.05
  power of appointment, of 25.34
  trustee's powers, of 25.26

relief
  completion, after 17.01-17.20
  creditor, for 27.21
  defrauded creditor, for 27.21
  forfeiture, from 19.15, 19.22
  misrepresentation, for 4.09-4.14
  mistake, for 4.15-4.23
  mortgagor, for 26.11
  Stamp Duty, from 16.04, 16.19

remainder
  fee tail 18.10
  future interests 18.22, 18.28

remedies
  breach of contract, for 15.21-15.41
  breach of covenant, for 20.19, 20.30-20.31
  failure to exercise power of attorney, for 25.33
  misdescription, for 4.05-4.08
  misrepresentation, for 4.09-4.14
  mistake, for 4.15-4.23
  mortgagee against mortgaged land, for 26.09-26.19, 26.31
  non-disclosure, for 2.08
  post-completion 17.01-17.20

remoteness, rules against 18.25
rent
   fee farm rents 18.05-18.09
   leasehold rents
      covenant for title as to 17.05
      covenant to pay 8.10, 20.06
      creation as evidence of intention to create lease 19.01, 22.04
      ejectment for non-payment of 19.28
      essential for application of Deasy's Act 19.02
      implied covenant that all rent etc due will be paid 20.09
      lives renewable for ever, under 18.12, 29.08
      re-entry for non-payment of 19.19-19.20
      Stamp Duty on 16.21
      sub-rent under sub-lease 19.03
      waiver of breach of covenant to pay 20.17
repair
   breach of covenant, to 20.14-20.16, 20.18
   covenant by landlord 20.05
   purchaser in possession, by 15.42
   covenants by tenant 20.06
   dangerous places and structures 12.22
   grant for repair .... Appendix B
   NHBC structural guarantee period 13.08, 13.11, 13.15
   responsibility for, of flat 8.02, 8.05-8.06, 8.09
requisitions on title 2.09, 2.25, 15.17-15.18, 15.37
rescission
   after completion 17.02, 17.19
   breach of contract, for 15.34-15.37
   counterclaim to specific performance 15.30
   failure to complete, for 15.23
   innocent misrepresentation, for 4.11
   mistake for, ... 4.16-4.17
reservation(s)
   easements and profits à prendre, of 21.19-21.20
   exceptions and reservations 8.06
residence
   rights of 22.13-22.15, 24.04, 7.29
residential use
   planning purposes, for 11.10
   grant purposes, for .... Appendix B
restrictive covenants 20.01-20.33
      see also **covenants**
   burdens on registered land 7.28
   creation of 21.42
   enforcement of 8.13-8.15
   purchaser deemed to have knowledge of 2.07, 2.23
reversion
   Deasy's Act, s 3 .... 18.09
   fee tail 18.10
   future interest 18.21

    lease 18.13, 19.03
    merger of lease, on 19.29
    title to 2.22-2.23
rights
    estovers of.. 21.17
    mine to... 21.14
    natural 21.39
    local customary 21.41
    occupation *see* **occupation**
    public... 24.40
    support to...21.10, 21.39
    way of 21.07, 21.19-21.20, 21.34, 21.40
road bond 5.14, 9.07
roads
    access 8.01, 11.03, 11.15, 11.39
    bond 9.07
    property certificates, information on 5.13-5.16
    public right of way, as 21.40
    traffic safety 11.38
sale, power of
    life tenant by 24.06
    mortgagee by... 26.15
sale, trust for 25.13
searches
    bankruptcy 5.09
    company 5.10
    disclosure of matters by 5.01-5.02, 15.37
    enforcement 5.08
    Land Registry 5.11, 7.58-7.62
    lost title, to provide evidence of... 6.27
    priority...2.80, 5.11, 7.54, 7.61, 15.16, 27.15
    provided with title 6.28
    Registry of Deeds 5.03-5.06
    statutory charges 5.07
security of tenure 15.42, 18.13
seisin..18.01, 18.28
septic tank 5.17, 9.11, 11.39, 12.12,
service charge.. 8.02, 8.09
servient tenement
    definition of 21.03
    easements over... 21.20-21.33
    restrictive covenants.. 21.42
settlements
    covenants for title, in.. 17.04
    definition 24.01
    fee tail.. 18.10
    future interests 18.26
    infants... 24.03
    Land Registry title, on... 7.33, 7.49
    life tenant... 24.05

    powers of 24.07-24.09
    power of sale 24.06
    Registry of Deeds title, on 6.14
    rights of residence 24.04
    strict 24.02
    trust, as distinct from 25.13
    Trustee Act (NI) 1967, application of 25.26
    trustees of 24.10
severance of joint tenancy 18.41
sewers 9.11
specific performance
    bankruptcy, on 15.07, 15.09, 15.14, 27.13-27.14, 27.17
    completion notice, after 15.21
    contract, of 3.04-3.05, 15.25-15.33, 15.42
    covenants, of 20.15
    insubstantial misdescription, where 4.08
    lease, of 19.02
    mistake, where 4.17
    non-disclosure of defects, for 2.08, 2.11, 2.12, 2.19
    time in which to seek 15.23
squatter 7.18, 7.41, 7.53, 23.01-23.13
Stamp Duty
    ad valorem 16.16-16.17
    adjudication 16.04
    agreement for lease/conveyance/transfer, on 16.22
    appeal 16.05
    calculating consideration 16.19-16.24
    certificates of value 16.18
    conveyance subject to debt, on 16.20
    conveyancing 6.29, 16.15
    denoting stamps 16.08
    duplicate or counterpart 16.26
    evidence in court 16.14
    exchange, on 16.23
    execution of documents, for 16.10
    fast-track 16.07
    fines 16.13
    fixed duty 16.25-16.30
    leases, on 16.21
    method of 16.03
    new houses, on 16.37-16.40
    no duty 16.31-16.36
    penalties 16.12
    principles of 16.01-16.02
    produced (PD) stamp 16.06
    sanctions for non-payment of 16.11
    surrender, on 16.24, 16.27
    time for stamping 16.09
    voluntary dispositions 16.28
statutory charges 2.09, 5.01, 5.07, 11.35

Index

subletting 19.05, 20.06, 20.13, 20.17
succession 6.17, 18.26, 24.01, 25.01
successors in title
    assignment and subletting, on 19.03-19.05
    enforcement of obligations between 8.02, 17.10-17.12, 20.19-20.29
    fee simple 18.02
    incorporeal hereditaments, applicability of 21.01
    licence, applicability of 22.03, 22.15
    life estate, applicability of 22.14-22.15
    proprietary estoppel applicability of 22.18
    restrictive covenants, applicability of 21.42
    tenancy by estoppel 18.19
superior interest 6.25
surrender 7.55, 16.24, 16.27, 19.13, 23.04, 26.26
survey 2.05, 4.12, 10.03
survivorship 18.30, 18.36, 18.41, 6.16
systems of registration of land *see also* **registration**
    Registry of Deeds 6.01-6.03
    Land Registry 7.01-7.04

tenancy
    assignment and subletting 19.03-19.05
    creation of the relationship 19.01-19.02, 22.04
    determination of the relationship 19.06-19.31
    estoppel, by 18.19
    in common 6.16, 6.17, 7.49, 18.35-18.37, 18.39, 18.42
    joint 6.16, 6.17, 7.49, 18.29-18.34, 18.38, 18.41, 28.02
    life 18.11, 18.28, 22.14, 24.02, 24.05-24.09, 25.13
    periodic 18.15, 19.02, 19.07
    statutory 18.18
    sufferance, at 18.17, 19.07
    will, at 18.16, 19.02, 19.07
tenant
    covenants of 20.04-20.24
    distinction between assignment and sub-lease 19.03
    expenditure by 3.07
    fixtures, of 14.08-14.09
    grant purposes, for .... Appendix B
    life tenant *see* **life tenant**
    periodic tenancy under 18.15
    relationship of landlord and 18.09, 18.13
    statutory tenancy under 18.18
    tenancy at sufferance under 18.17
    tenancy at will under 18.16
    tenancy by estoppel under 18.19
tenure 4.03, 7.04, 15.42, 18.01
term
    certain 18.14
    lease of 3.04, 18.13, 19.01, 22.04, 24.07
    mortgage of 26.05
    term of contract 4.11

    term of years 2.20-2.23
third parties
    act of company, affecting 6.21
    burdens and equities held by 7.37
    mistake on, effect of 4.16
    guest on, effect of 22.12
    insolvency affecting 6.22, 27.23-27.24
    licence on, effect of 22.02
    possessory title on, effect of 23.02
    responsibility of trustees to 24.10
    right of mortgagor against 26.21
    rights of, to chattels 14.14
time
    acquisition of easement/profit for 21.28-21.33
    adverse possession, for 23.01
    complete contract on 15.20, 15.23
    comply with completion notice, to 15.21
    condition of planning permission 11.30
    immemorial 21.26
    limit for action against trustee 25.28
    limit for raising requisitions on title 15.17
    running of 23.10-23.11
    stamping document, for 16.09-16.10
title
    covenants for 6.23, 7.48, 17.03-17.18
    deduction of 2.10-2.26
    defects in 2.06-2.08, 15.33, 15.38, 15.42
    disclosure of 2.06-2.09, 3.17, 4.03, 4.07, 15.17
    gift on 27.24-27.25
    investigation of 2.09, 4.12
    lack of/bad 2.15, 15.33
    length of 2.17
    lost 6.27, 7.64
    new property, to 9.02
    possessory 6.19, 7.18, 7.23, 7.41
    registered property, to 7.01-7.04
    root of 2.18
    unregistered land, to 6.01-6.04
transfer
    joint interest, of 18.17
    Land Registry 7.48
    ownership of 7.48
    priority of 7.56, 15.16
    rights under mortgage, of 26.28
tree preservation orders 11.37
trustee(s)
    appointment, retirement and removal of 25.20-25.22
    covenants for title by 17.07
    delegation 25.25
    duties of 25.24
    mortgagee as trustee of sale proceeds 26.15

personal representative as	6.17
position of	25.19-25.25
powers of	25.23
sale by	29.12
settlement of	24.10, 25.01
vendor as	15.01, 15.03

trustee in bankruptcy
bankruptcy on	27.05, 27.17, 27.18
Insolvency (No 2) Act 1994	27.24
preferences	27.20
purchaser of	15.08, 15.14, 27.17-27.18
registration as owner	7.51
sale of bankrupt's home by	27.11
transactions at undervalue	27.19
vendor of	15.07, 27.12-27.14
void dispositions	25.12
voluntary conveyances	6.22, 27.23-27.24

trusts
administration of	25.18-25.25
breach of	25.27-25.29
charitable	25.15-25.16
constructive	25.11
definition	25.01
discretionary	25.14
express	25.03
imperfect obligation of	25.17
implied	25.06-25.09
resulting	25.10
sale for	25.13, 28.12
secret	25.05
statutory	25.02
title on	6.15, 7.32
variation of	25.26
void and voidable	25.12
wills	25.04

turbary	21.13

undervalue
transactions at	27.19, 27.24-27.25

undue influence
donee of property, on	27.25
elderly relatives, on	28.29
specific performance, defence to	15.30
voidable trusts	25.12
wife and others, on	28.19-28.29

unregistered burdens	7.39
unregistered dispositions	7.38

unregistered land
certificate of registration	6.07
chain of title	6.09-6.22
documents registrable	6.03-6.05

indexes of documents 6.08
memorials 6.06
mortgages of 26.05, 26.11
title to 6.01-6.02
use of land
application for planning permission for change of................................11.21
change of use 11.16, 12.02
planning purposes, for...11.02-11.12
temporary use 11.17
user
covenant 8.10, 20.13, 20.31
easement, as to 21.25-21.26, 21.28, 21.40

value, certificate of 16.18
valuation..2.05, 10.03, 10.05
variation
contract, of..3.04
Stamp Duty on deed, of..16.30
trusts, of 25.26
vendor
bankruptcy of...7.54, 15.07, 27.12-27.14
breach of contract, effect on 15.20-15.21, 15.22-15.35
covenants for title by...17.03-17.18
description of property by...3.16-3.18
duty of disclosure to purchaser 5.01
duty to disclose defects 2.02-2.09
execution of documents by 16.10
fixtures as between purchaser and 14.10
misdescription by..4.02-4.08
misrepresentation by..4.09-4.14
mistake..4.15-4.23
obligation to show good title 2.10-2.19, 6.09-6.10, 6.27
party to contract, as..3.04
payment of deposit to...3.20
personal representatives as...6.18
position of, between contract and completion 15.02-15.09, 15.12
possessory title, with..6.19
purchaser taking possession before completion, effect on.......................15.42
purchaser's bankruptcy, effect on 15.14, 27.17
remedies for breach of contract 15.22-15.41
damages..15.38
forfeiture of deposit 15.41
rescission..15.34-15.36
specific performance..15.25
defences to 15.26-15.33
searches provided by 5.02-5.11
trustee as 25.11
vested interest...18.23, 18.25
voluntary assurance
gift on title 27.23-27.25
orders 27.22

preferences 27.20
transactions at undervalue 27.19
transactions defrauding creditors 27.21
waiver 15.18, 15.42
   breach of covenant, of 20.17
   notice to quit, of 19.12
warranty
   collateral, independent of contract 17.02
   fitness of premises, as to 20.11A
   misrepresentation as 4.11
   NHBC warranty 13.01, 13.05, 13.08
   solicitor's certificate, by 7.67
   state of property, as to 2.03
   title, as to 17.12-17.13
water
   drainage, building regulation purposes, for 12.12
   property certificate, information on 5.17
   rights of 21.09, 21.39, 21.42
   supply for new developments 9.10, 11.39
   Water Act (NI) 1972 consents 5.18-5.19
wills
   chain of title, in 6.17-6.18
   mutual 25.09
   powers created by 25.30, 25.31, 25.32
   registration of ownership under 7.49
   right of residence created by 22.13-22.14
   root of title, as 2.18
   settlement created by 24.01-24.02
   trustees appointed by 24.10
words of limitation
   Deasy's Act fee farm grants, to create 18.09
   fee farm conversion grant, to create 18.06
   fee simple, to pass 18.02
   life estate, to create 18.11
   transfer, in 7.48